Major Figures in Spanish and
Latin American Literature and the Arts
Roberto González Echevarría,
Series Editor

K. David Jackson

Machado de Assis

A Literary Life

Yale UNIVERSITY PRESS/NEW HAVEN & LONDON

Title page photo: Machado de Assis in O Álbum (1893).
Reproduced by permission of the Instituto Moreira Salles.

Yale University Press books may be purchased in quantity for educational,
business, or promotional use. For information, please e-mail sales.press@yale.edu
(U.S. office) or sales@yaleup.co.uk (U.K. office).

Set in Bulmer type by Westchester Book Group, Danbury, Connecticut.
Printed in the United States of America.

Library of Congress Cataloging-in-Publication Data

Jackson, K. David (Kenneth David)
Machado de Assis : a literary life / K. David Jackson.
    pages   cm. — (Major figures in Spanish and Latin American literature and the arts)
Includes bibliographical references and index.
ISBN 978-0-300-18082-4 (cloth : alk. paper)   1. Machado de Assis, 1839–1908—
Criticism and interpretation.   I. Title.
PQ9697.M18Z6665 2015
869.3'3—dc23
2014036996

A catalogue record for this book is available from the British Library.

This paper meets the requirements of ANSI/NISO Z39.48-1992 (Permanence of Paper).

10 9 8 7 6 5 4 3 2 1

Major Figures in Spanish and Latin American Literature and the Arts will publish comprehensive books on canonical authors and artists from any period, adhering to a variety of approaches, but generally following the form of a literary biography. Grounded in thorough and original scholarship, and written in a jargon-free style, the books should be accessible to the educated nonspecialist.

To Helen Caldwell and Raymond Sayers,
American scholars of Machado de Assis

Contents

Preface

PERHAPS I DID BEGIN studying the Portuguese language after all so that I could read the works of Joaquim Maria Machado de Assis (1839–1908) in the original. When as a young student I first entered the office of the venerable Wisconsin professor Lloyd Kasten during a summer language program in 1965, his first comment was, "I hear that you like Machado de Assis." Like the fortune-teller's words in one of the novels, Kasten's comment turned out to be a prediction of "things of the future." After the enlightening seminars offered by Jorge de Sena at Wisconsin, study with the specialists Antônio Cândido and Alfredo Bosi in Brazil, and many readings and rereadings of major works by Machado de Assis, they retain a freshness, an allure, and a profundity that time has only sharpened. First-time readers and undergraduate students alike who are introduced to his works feel the same allure.

To write a comprehensive introduction and interpretation of Machado de Assis is a daunting task, in view of José Galante de Sousa's massive bibliography, new work appearing in e-journals such as *Espelho: revista machadiana* and *Machado de Assis em linha,* and the production of a new generation of Brazilian scholars. Stories and columns that Machado signed with pseudonyms are only now being located and authenticated, while missing segments of short stories published in ephemeral journals are still being discovered. The greatest challenges, no doubt, are the complexity of Machado de Assis's ideas, the great number and variety of his sources, his relationship with the world literature of his day, and his portrayal of the psychological and social world of the Brazilian empire, all of which have discouraged the widespread writing of comprehensive interpretations of his large literary production. I have at the same time benefited greatly from numerous classic works on Machado de Assis by Brazilian essayists who were closer to him and his time, especially José Barreto Filho's introductory book and Agrippino Grieco's study of his literary sources, as well as the works of many contemporary scholars. The examples

I have cited from Machado's works are generally limited to the major novels and short stories that are available to the reader in English translation, although I have included selections from his journalism, drama, correspondence, poetry, and selected short stories in my own translations.

The author Zulficar Ghose asks why a writer of the quality of Brazil's greatest literary figure, Joaquim Maria Machado de Assis, is not world famous or at least as well known as his contemporaries Anton Chekhov, Henry James, and Guy de Maupassant. His writings have been placed alongside those of Fyodor Dostoevsky, Nikolai Gogol, Thomas Hardy, Herman Melville, Stendhal, and Gustave Flaubert. He was a translator of Charles Dickens and Victor Hugo into Portuguese. His life and works dialogue with the supreme Portuguese realist, José Maria de Eça de Queirós, and parallel the renowned Spanish novelists Clarín (Leopoldo García-Alas y Ureña), the urban novel of Benito Pérez Galdós, and the challenge to realism in Emilia Pardo Bazán. As the narrator of a city-universe, his vision matches those of Constantine Cavafy's Alexandria, Dostoevsky's St. Petersburg, and the Paris of Marcel Proust. His unreliable narrators are conscious followers of Laurence Sterne, Xavier de Maistre, and Denis Diderot yet extend to Italo Svevo's irascible narrator Zeno and Lawrence Durrell's *Alexandria Quartet*.

An inventor of modernist narratives, Machado de Assis is said to anticipate features of Proust, James Joyce, T. S. Eliot, Albert Camus, Thomas Mann, and Jorge Luis Borges. One of few masters of the short story, the author of three novels that rank among the masterpieces of world fiction, his country's greatest writer with an unprecedented fifty years of literary life, and arguably the major literary figure of all time in Latin American literature, why should his name remain a mystery to world literature and his works still be comparatively unknown?

THIS BOOK is the result of more than forty years of reading the works of Machado de Assis. It is meant to help establish his place in the central corpus of comparative literature and to promote the reading of his works by highlighting his central role in transforming literary realism into modernist prose. Machado takes his place among the canonical figures of world literature for transforming the world of the Brazilian empire in nineteenth-century Rio de Janeiro into the human theater of a modern literary universe, a feat he accomplished by devouring and altering received tradition.

My goal in this book is to interpret Machado de Assis, the writer, and his fictional world. The central idea is that in his fiction Machado put before us the theater of the world of Rio de Janeiro during Brazil's nineteenth-century empire, in the tradition of the Jesuit Antônio Vieira's seventeenth-century cosmopolitan concept of the Portuguese maritime baroque world in his *History of the Future* (1718): "Today we place our History in the theater of the world." Its theory is that Machado constructed a hybrid literary world out of contradictions and tensions inherent in his experience, social world, and cosmopolitan life of letters and arts. From his humble beginnings—his parents were servants on an estate—he came to view society from both outside and inside, as reclusive observer and active participant. His writing exemplified hybridity and metaliterary play in a conceptual blending of diverse sources that emanated from his exceptionally wide reading. By his invention of character–narrators to replace himself as author, his selective quotation from a universal library, manipulation of retrospective narrative frames, and ample application of satire and comedy, Machado forged a deserved place as an inventor of the modernist novel and as a wry, wise observer of humanity.

Part One, "The Literary World of Machado de Assis," defines the main lines of interpretation of Machado and the principles with which he constructed his literary world. The concept of formative period is applied to his early literary life, which develops in close contact with Rio de Janeiro's operas and theaters, literary associations, and journalism. The theater was instrumental in the development of his future fiction; the young Machado wrote plays, translated libretti, and followed the great stars. His first four novels, written during the 1870s, revealed the themes, psychology, and narrative structures that he would refine throughout his fiction in the next three decades. His hybrid style produced creative qualities that the modernist novel of the twentieth century would continue to champion.

The second part, "Reading Machado de Assis," describes key principles of Machado's writing, centering on his wish to bypass chronological time by creating points of view through distanced or eternal perspectives. By taking the perspective of the universe, the author raises philosophical, ethical, and moral judgments about human action, while viewing the city-universe from afar, as a spectator would a theatrical or operatic production. By exploiting a rhetoric of substitution, Machado brings together opposites in a display of the unpredictable oscillation of events and circumstances in the contradictory and reversible symmetry of life. On this point in his fiction, Machado opens a space between form and meaning, exploited by the interjection of seemingly extraneous interruptions that break the narrative frame. The sources for his hybrid fiction are explored through a world library of reading and quotation in his works. His craftsmanship as a miniaturist is explored through readings of selected well-known stories.

Part Three follows three characteristic motifs in Machado's work identified by the philosopher and literary essayist Benedito Nunes in his study of the origin of Machado de Assis's ideas: the delirium in which Brás Cubas rides to the beginning of time on the back of a flying hippopotamus; the philosophy of *Humanitas* propounded by the mad Quincas Borba; and the metaphor or parable of the world as an opera in a joint effort by God and Satan, in *Dom Casmurro*.

The fourth part unites and describes for the first time together the three character-narrators—Brás Cubas, Bento Santiago, and Counselor Ayres—who write and narrate their retrospective memoirs, and in the cases of Cubas and Ayres after their death. When taken together, these narrators demonstrate the overriding unity in theme and narrative structure of Machado's writing.

The conclusion, "Machado and the Spectacle of the World," discusses Machado as contrary philosopher, analyst, and keen observer from afar of the customs and rituals of life in his city-universe. He is a rational moralist in pursuit of wisdom through his world theater, but he nevertheless doubts the existence of underlying truths and principles, which may be nothing more than a function of life's repeating scenarios. In view of the world's illogic, the repetitive patterns of experience and behavior, and the transitory nature of life, Machado ultimately uses an operatic metaphor to describe the roles being performed on his human and social stage as "a dance in rented coats."

MORE THAN FORTY YEARS AGO the American translator and classicist Helen Caldwell, a lecturer in Greek and Latin at UCLA, opened her second book on the Brazilian author by affirming, "Machado de Assis is no longer unknown to us" (1970, 3). At that time, 4 of his 9 novels and about 15 of his 226 short stories had appeared in English translation, and Caldwell had translated most of them herself. She had dedicated her research to Machado and was at the time one of few scholars who wrote about him in English. Her pioneering work remains a model for readers and students of the Brazilian author. Caldwell remarked almost half a century ago that enthusiastic new American readers were indignant not to have known about Machado's existence, so excited were they to discover his works, even if they could not yet pronounce his name. New readers were continually discovering the pleasure of reading Machado and delighting in his wit, humor, and self-conscious style.

Following Caldwell's translations and books, some fifty doctoral theses and nineteen books in English on Machado have been written in the ensuing sixty years. The novelist, historian, and social critic Waldo Frank, who traveled widely in South America, wrote a perceptive introduction to Caldwell's translation in 1953 of *Dom Casmurro,* in which he anticipated points of literary interpretation that would be taken up by others. Three public intellectuals in the United States promoted Machado's works in the press: Susan Sontag, Michael Wood, and Elizabeth Hardwick. The authors John Barth and John Updike cited him as a model, as did the film director and writer Woody Allen. In the 1990s the Oxford University Press Library of Latin America had four of the novels retranslated with new introductions by American, British, and Brazilian scholars. The Mexican author Carlos Fuentes ranked the Brazilian's achievements in the novel alongside those of Cervantes in his striking book *Machado de la Mancha* (2001), considering him the successor in world literature of

Cervantine wisdom and humor. Still, his name and works have remained largely outside mainstream parameters of continental American, Hispanic American, and European literary study and general readership, since, as a Brazilian writing in the Portuguese language, he did not belong to any of those categories. The isolation of his writings was also the isolation of Brazil, which was part of the worldwide Portuguese empire in America, featuring close ties to Africa and Asia that are reflected in the novels and stories.

Given the initial early attention to and sporadic reintroduction of Machado de Assis's work in English translation by prominent scholars and intellectuals, the fact that his writings remain little known represents above all a failure of criticism. In 1950, speaking in Washington, D.C., at the first International Colloquium on Luso-Brazilian Studies, one of Brazil's leading literary figures, Antônio Cândido, stated that Machado's "restlessness, rebellion, passion for form, and universality" are generally misunderstood because readers tend to appreciate what is superficial and easily communicated, in the style of an Anatole France, while ignoring his true greatness as a master of misleading prose, alongside Dostoevsky. Why would Caldwell, an American teacher of Catullus, Horace, Virgil, Plautus, Tacitus, Ovid, Roman comedies, and Greek tragedies, sustain a passion for Machado throughout her life? Notes to Caldwell's books demonstrate that she had pored over almost every page ever written about him. Could it be the connection between his allusions to the classical world and its literature that drew her passionate interest, as archetypes recast into situations in Brazil? Her curious book *Ancient Poets' Guide to UCLA Gardens* (1968) gathered two distant worlds in a contemporary garden setting. Did she likewise find Machado's narrative guides to the human gardens of Rio de Janeiro irresistible and insatiable sources of comparative study and unexpected juxtapositions as well as intriguing reading?

In a preface to Honoré de Balzac's *The Two Young Brides*, Henry James distinguishes the qualities of books and authors that have become important to generations of readers:

The authors and the books that have, as the phrase is, done something for us, formed a solid part of the answer to our curi-

osity when our curiosity had the freshness of youth, these particular agents exist for us, with the lapse of time, as the substance
itself of knowledge: they have been intellectually so swallowed, digested, and assimilated that we take their general use
and suggestion for granted, cease to be aware of them because
they have passed out of sight. But they have passed out of sight
simply by having passed into our lives. They have become a
part of our personal history, a part of ourselves, very often, so
far as we may have succeeded in best expressing ourselves.

For Machado de Assis, who was both tutored and self-educated, literature
was transforming and transformational. In literature he found an escape
into an alternate world that would give margin to his genius and social
position to his intellect. There he would make his profession while com-
muting his life into art. On his death as a distinguished author and beloved public figure in 1908, his most enduring characteristic was his
erudition after a long literary life. He was a founder of the Brazilian Academy of Letters, which in its first century has become the country's foremost
intellectual institution. The academy's Machado de Assis Prize, awarded
to Brazil's most distinguished writers, recognizes that they follow the precedent established by the figure and literary works of Machado de Assis.
To follow James's argument, Machado's works are here to become part of
our personal history, a meaningful part of our very selves, our lives, and
our literary memories.

Acknowledgments

I OWE VERY special thanks to Elizabeth A. Jackson, who made valuable comments on the manuscript at every stage with her usual sharp eye, as well as to the helpful suggestions of the readers and editors contacted by Yale University Press. I am grateful for the excellent introduction to the works of Machado de Assis I received in seminars with Jorge de Sena and lectures by Antônio Cândido at the University of Wisconsin, Madison. I also wish to recognize students and colleagues who contributed their insights into the reading and interpretation of Machado's works over the years in seminars at the University of Texas at Austin and Yale University and in conferences of professional associations. I especially thank Steve Wasserman, my editor at Yale University Press, who has provided professional guidance and wise advice at critical points. The greatest debt of all must be to Machado de Assis for his example of a life lived intensively in a world theater and library of arts and letters.

PART ONE

The Literary World of
Machado de Assis

Machado de Assis (seated, second from left) with members of the literary club A Panelinha during a luncheon at the Hotel Rio Branco in 1901. Reproduced by permission of the Instituto Moreira Salles.

The Wizard of Cosme Velho

É o que soube viver intensamente da arte.
[He is one who knew how to live intensely from art.]

—Rui Barbosa, "Adeus a Machado de Assis"

Em prosa é mais difícil de se outrar.
[In prose it is more difficult to become another.]

—Fernando Pessoa, "Ficções do interlúdio"

IN A PHOTOGRAPH from 1901 the stately, patrician Joaquim Maria Machado de Assis, peering through his pince-nez, sits in a chair among the premier figures of the former Brazilian empire: statesmen, writers, and nobility. He is the magnetic point of reference, a master of letters whose profundity, learning, and powers of observation were considered to such a degree unexplainable and superior to those of his coterie that he commanded a combination of awe and respect.[1] Could his companions have suspected the presence in their midst of an ironist, a skeptical destabilizer of systems, a dismantler of illusion? They called him the wizard of Cosme Velho ("o bruxo do Cosme Velho"), the district and street where he lived, and that year he was at the height of his powers. In 1897 he had cofounded the Brazilian Academy of Letters, of which he was elected president, published his most enduring and enigmatic novels, short stories, and chronicles during the previous three decades, and continued to reside in the two-story cottage in the Cosme Velho district with his wife, Carolina Augusta Xavier de Novaes (1835–1904), three years before her death after thirty-five years of marriage. Machado had entered his fifth decade of literary activity in Rio de Janeiro, having lived his entire life in the city that served as a microcosm of his expansive and imaginative literary world. He called it a universe. Machado would publish two final novels of his celebrated "Carioca quintet"

3

and a further collection of short stories before his death in 1908 at the age of sixty-nine. Today, his statue sits at the entrance to the Brazilian Academy of Letters in Rio de Janeiro, where his writing desk and much of his library are displayed. He is universally recognized as the greatest writer of Brazil and perhaps of the Americas, and the bibliography citing him and his works today is practically inexhaustible. His major works can be read online in hypertext, accompanied by lists that identify hundreds of citations and allusions found in his novels and short stories. His image appeared on a Brazilian banknote in 1988, and in 2008 he was the featured author at the International Literary Festival of Paraty. At the centenary exposition in 1939, he was presented by the poet and journalist Augusto Meyer as a disquieting shadow that cast a vast, empty, questioning space before his interpreters and readers with works that were smooth and polished on the surface yet pure profundity. On the centenary of his death in 2008 a new generation of readers and scholars intent on rethinking Machado is finding new meanings in the complexity of his craft of fiction on an international and comparative scale. His works echo in a range of modern writers across diverse national literatures, from James to Borges, Nabokov to Saramago.

Readers are especially drawn to Machado's fiction because of its conceptual challenges, self-conscious play, elusive narrative structure, dry humor, world of characters, and inventive imagination. He takes readers on a ride on the back of a flying hippopotamus to the beginning of time; invents the satirical philosophy of *Humanitas* that solves man's philosophical doubts once and for all; chronicles the depths of an imperial society in transition; proposes a mute parliament whose members communicate solely by gestures; and formulates a modest proposal for a literary coup d'état to promote national theater. He assigns sex to nouns and adjectives, accuses the reader of being the main problem in his novels, and suggests that readers need four stomachs, the better to ruminate on his deeper meanings. His imagination enlarges the world and the scope of fiction toward infinity: an idea hangs on a trapeze, waves its arms and legs in the shape of an X and warns, like the Great Sphinx, "Decipher me or I'll devour you." He counsels a character in one of the novels to read no further, even to burn the novel at hand to avoid the temptation to pick it up later. He offers to surrender pen and paper to readers who desire a different turn of events. Psychological analysis is a constant. Hallucinations, dreams, and obsessions that subvert rational exposition have been said to anticipate Sigmund Freud's oneiric theories. Hundreds of literary, philosophical, and historical references woven throughout his fiction draw the reader into a veritable world library of texts and ideas, creating a parallel reality of allusion and reference. Thus, every part of his fictional world fits into a larger totality, gaining an allegorical and aphoristic complexion. His natural qualities show through in his writing, which is a refined, reserved, modest, self-sufficient, serene yet insinuating way of telling, highly pertinent for unmasking appearances through subtlety, inference, dissimulation, and understatement. The novelist Haroldo Maranhão described the master in *Memorial do fim* (Memorial of the end) as punctual, organized ("whatever he had to do he did immediately"), and reserved: "a quiet man . . . his hands, for example, didn't move when he spoke about lively topics, animated stories, or opened to stronger emotions; they extended down to his long thighs, very quiet."

A conservative, moralistic skepticism underlies Machado's wry, ironic, satirical, and implacable analyses of the unchanging nature of the world and limits to the human condition. His profound skepticism applied to a comprehensive view of the human comedy forms the main guideline to his fictional thought. He succeeded both by defying and epitomizing his age, and he became the most learned figure of his generation. His fiction amounts to an inventory of life. From his subtle, critical observations of Rio de Janeiro during the empire, he creates a human comedy and theater of the world in his fiction, drawing his themes from notable works of music, literature, and philosophy. The fiction encompasses the city's social classes, professions, and even geography as an organic world theater, exhibited through a wide variety of sharply drawn characters and situations.

In view of his radical stylistic invention, prodigious writings, humanistic learning, and intellectual acumen, Machado was rightfully called a wizard in the Brazil of the Second Empire, yet he would have merited an equal sobriquet in any national literature of the day. Aside from Carolina, his only companion was literature, which substituted for an active public life after their marriage in 1869. To construct a philosophical and fictional world became his lifetime literary project, and he dedicated himself to the arts: "Long live the muses. Those ancient, beautiful young ladies neither grow old nor lose their beauty. After all, it's what's most solid under the sun" (March 11, 1894). In Brazil, where he was a singular presence, his pure exceptionality as a writer and learned man conferred on him an exalted status. In the view of the Brazilian poet and essayist Haroldo de Campos, Machado's presence could have been neither explained nor foreseen: a Ulysses, he became the mythological founder of modern Brazil, a devourer of tradition who led a constant dialogue between the national and the universal.[2] The literary historian and scholar Harold Bloom included Machado in his compilation of the world's one hundred most creative minds. A recent biography by Daniel Piza described Machado in only one word: Genius.

Machado de Assis's stature as an unexpected yet definitive figure in Brazilian letters of the nineteenth and early twentieth centuries and one of the greatest writers produced by the Americas is a challenge to any comprehensive critical understanding of his literary and cultural background, his writings, and his legacy to world literature. Machado was careful to keep details of his life private, such that for scholars and biographers at the centenary of his birth in 1939 he retained the charm of an old, faded photograph and the mystery of a writer who had made his life into a work of art. A new appreciation of Machado's works is all the more imperative because he is still not widely known outside of Brazil, where a dominant school of interpretation has focused primarily on his role as a social critic and nationalist, yet has not satisfactorily explained his modernity and creativity or how such an improbable writer succeeded in transforming the novel and short story. In her book on Brazil (1963, 104), Elizabeth Bishop attributed the inattention to his work to "lack of competition and serious criticism even more than from the relatively limited audience for Portuguese literature or from the deadening effects of facile journalism."

Machado's inventiveness and craft, developed in over thirty years of apprenticeship and practiced in another thirty as a professional, set him apart as a writer who was ahead of his time, one who was extremely well read and capable of drawing on an exceptionally wide repertoire of sources as well as of assembling them in surprising ways that challenged and altered the practices of literary realism of his day.[3] The craft of fiction dominates content throughout Machado's works, which are appreciated for their elegant and expressive use of the Portuguese language. This interpretation of his fiction departs from an investigation of principles and dynamics observed in his literary world, judging from the works themselves. Within selected parameters of analysis, my book seeks to contribute to the reinterpretation of Machado after the centenary of his death by reconfiguring the function and meaning of his special genius as a thinker and writer, redefining him as one of the fundamental authors of world literature.

Most notable in Machado are the many contradictions that provided him with an unusual perspective as an outside insider or an inside outsider.[4] He was an accepted member of Brazil's intellectual aristocracy and at the same time the grandson of freed slaves; his parents—Francisco José de Assis was said to be of mixed race, and Maria Leopoldina da Câmara Machado was a Portuguese from the Azores—were poor artisans, while his godmother, Maria José de Mendonça Barroso Perreira, was the widow of a distinguished senator of the Empire;[5] he joined erudite literary circles but was largely self-taught; his subject matter was taken from the Rio de Janeiro he knew so well yet was fictionalized by his recapitulating and rewriting of European literary sources and materials; in his fiction he distanced himself from surrounding reality yet recuperated it aesthetically in detail; he treated popular subjects in an elegant, refined style; as the modernist intellectual Alceu Amoroso Lima observed, he treated serious matters lightly and light things seriously for humorous effect; he published newspaper columns on society and politics, some written in rhymed quatrains, yet maintained a distance dictated by his penetrating intelligence; while almost never leaving the city, he became one of the century's most cosmopolitan writers; he adopted an eternal point of view to describe temporal events; he ridiculed philosophy, yet it is inseparable from his discourse; he moved within Brazil's ruling circle even while denouncing it with a subtle irony that most never grasped but found agreeably satirical; and by 1880 he had invented within the framework of literary realism a modern style in fiction featuring layered texts of mixed genres, unreliable narrators who manipulated retrospective memoirs, self-conscious literary play, and psychological portraits, all assembled from models and sources he had read. His singularity as a writer can be attributed in part to the way he selected, combined, and synthesized the myriad literary sources of a long literary apprenticeship, then folded them into an individual style that was at the same time very much part of his time and place, reflecting not only Brazil's language and society in the Americas but also its long dialogue with the classics, Europe, and the Portuguese maritime empire. Machado found sources for his writing by observing the contradictory nature of life: "Life's contrasts are works of the imagination right next to you" (August 23, 1896).

Contradictions and tensions were the building blocks of his literary world. He treated them with philosophical equanimity and even humor, recognizing in his words that contradiction is part of this world and that truth is incongruous. Machado's picaresque narrator Brás Cubas confesses that he was not made for complex situations: "That pushing and shoving of opposite things was getting me off balance" (chapter 109; hereafter in references to the novels the numbers will refer to chapters). Campos found that Machado assimilated his multiple sources and contrasting genres in a "complicated chemistry in which it was no longer possible to distinguish the assimilating organism from the stuff assimilated." In his book on Machado, however, the critic Agrippino Grieco identified multiple specific authors and works, particularly in eighteenth- and nineteenth-century European literatures, from whom Machado had borrowed, reshaped, and altered content in his stories and novels, yet never copying directly from any of the plethora of influential sources. Grieco cites his powerful originality coupled with his "diabolical" imitation; because of this unusual combination he was, continues Grieco, never completely himself but made all the materials that he assimilated his own. His original alteration of citations, the constant presence of aphorisms, the construction of subtle inference, and the persuasiveness of the unreliable narrator all contribute both to renovate literary form and to disguise and alter the authorial self.

Machado's later description of the making of fine furniture in Brazil parallels his own creative appropriation of European models: "Exquisite furniture . . . copied faithfully from French designs, some maintaining their original names, the *bijou de salon*, for example, others with hybrid names, like the porta-*bibelots*" (*Relato do restauro do mobiliário de Machado de Assis*, Academia Brasileira de Letras, 1998, 39). The expert shaping of national wood by means of European models describes a process that produced new modes of language and variable use of genre as well. In arguing that the tax on theatrical companies should be the same for national and international productions alike, Machado points out that the Teutonic-Brazilian from the South is neither German nor Brazilian but a mixture: "Franco-Brazilian art exists not because of the place of birth of the artists, but by a combination of Rio with Paris or Bordeaux. Neither the late Mme. Doche nor D. Estela would recognize that art because it no longer possesses the particular features of one or the other of the respective languages. It is legitimate in accordance with the fusion of elements from both its origins. It is a living thing, I don't ask for any other birth certificate. . . . It is a local fruit" (December 13, 1896). Examples of creative appropriation, rather than import of foreign goods, will contribute to the nation's progress, Machado writes in a commentary on an industrial exposition in 1861: "We do not lack capacity; perhaps some indolence and certainly the mania of preferring foreign things, that's what has been an obstacle to the development of our industrial genius. And, it must be said that it is not a simple lack, it is an impediment, to have such an opulent country and waste the gifts that it offers us, without preparing ourselves for the peaceful existence at work that the future offers to nations" (December 1, 1861).

The juxtaposition of European background with the world of Rio de Janeiro is highlighted in his first novel, when the character Lívia tells of her desire to go beyond the splendors of Paris and the elegance of European life: "I want to get to know Italy and Germany, to remember our Guanabara on the shores of the Arno or Rhine" (3). His vast world of reference, reflecting the geographical dimensions of the oceanic Portuguese world, creates inevitable tensions with local circumstances and characters that can be fully understood only when placed in the light of preceding models and archetypes, to which the author at times only obliquely alludes. When a Western literary form treats the diversity of Brazil over a long period of colony and empire, it can produce both an uncannily familiar and a strangely deceptive effect. Readers must become detectives to uncover clues that, in the language of Sherlock Holmes, Arthur Conan Doyle's character who was Machado's contemporary, they see but most often do not observe.

Machado's Brazilian literary world is both an image of its European predecessors seen through a distorting mirror and a lesson on the eternal human condition in a miscegenated, slaveholding, imperial society. Even his characters and narrators are often deceived about the true nature of situations and events in which they are involved. Machado, the devourer of antecedents, made sure that his writings and even his identity as a writer could be fully defined and comprehended only through other literatures, which he made relevant to his own purposes. He created his literary world through the lens of what he had read, resulting in a style of his own that could be called mannerist because of the lack of a dominant stylistic model. Charles Rosen in *Classical Style: Haydn, Mozart, Beethoven* comments on the general lack of direction in the period between the baroque and neoclassical, an absence he attributed to the contradiction between them and to composers' deficiencies of technique. As the literary composer of a proficient, synthetic style that borrowed qualities from authors and composers in each of those artistic periods and practices, Machado was able to marshal their differences and contradictions by juxtaposing them outside their normal contexts and incorporating them into what passed for realistic prose fiction of his day. But his deception went much deeper: He combined neobaroque drama of plot and theme with neoclassical symmetry in prose writing. To continue the parallel with Rosen's musical analysis of style, one may say that Machado was able to coordinate differences in the literary equivalents of phrase, rhythm, and harmony so as to command a style that could carry the weight of his entire literary production. Tensions between story and reference, author and narrator, source and originality, telling and meaning, sensuality and recusal, voluptuousness and abstinence were the basic chemistry of Machado's literary syntheses.

Machado fills his major novels with self-conscious play on writing, the book at hand, and problems of reality and representation developed in close dialogue and questioning with readers: "What dominates the narrative discourse of Machado is his doubting tone, the deceptive and equivocating way of telling, reticent and distrustful, if not deceitful and misleading, questioning his capacity to represent reality."[6] He describes his relationship with readers by invoking the metaphor of a chess game, in terms of the expert player seen in his character Iaiá Garcia: "Of the qualities necessary for playing chess Iaiá possessed the two essential ones: a quick eye and Benedictine patience—qualities precious in life itself, which is also a game of chess, with its problems and games, some won, some lost, others neither" (11). Like a chess master, Machado frequently misleads and even entraps inattentive readers by concealing deeper intentions through inferences, unreliable narrators and irony, characteristics intensified in Brás Cubas's posthumous memoirs. His intentions are satirical and not infrequently malicious. Machado works to throw readers off track, whether male readers of his day mainly interested in elucidating the symbolic universe that seems to lie just below what is being told or feminine readers thought to be more interested in the story at hand. Between the two, Machado plays the role of learned narrator-diplomat, an expert like his Counselor Ayres in the arts of discovering as well as covering his true meaning: "All diplomacy exists in these two related verbs" (*Esau and Jacob*, 98). He cynically excuses himself for restricting content ("restricted only so as not to tire the female reader"), deceiving impatient readers ("reasons that I withheld from the hurried reader"), and hiding his intended meaning ("If no one understands me, I can wait"). Machado dismisses the masculine reader who holds fixed ideas "on the other side of the page," whose interest is limited to literary precedents, and he further taunts the feminine reader who wishes to share the sentimental effusiveness of the plots: "Let my female reader guess, if she can: I'll give her twenty chapters to catch on." Machado obliges the reader to reread by referring to previous chapters lost from memory and to certain key chapters that produce the illusion of comprehending the allegorical or symbolic content, whereas the reader becomes lost as a result in the eternally recurring and self-referential structures of the text.

Entrapment is a narrative technique Machado could have learned from eighteenth-century novels and journals or from his reading of Henry Fielding. In a study of Fielding's *Journal of a Voyage to Lisbon* (1755), Melinda Rabb finds that the simplicity of the account is troubled by irony, self-representation, and fictionalization. The account is complicated by its multiple layers—as fact, metaphor, rhetoric, structure, and theme—and by the passage from ideal to real, from the narrator's mind to the reader's, and from linguistic signs and rhetorical devices to meaning. The narrator shifts between different subjects and styles, with countermovements, opposing ideas, and theories. Such advance and regress serve to encourage the reader to sympathize with the narrator's dilemmas. The reader is further entrapped by Fielding's claim to truth, whereas the journal was contrived in retrospect; by subject matter that does not fit the topic at hand; and by the existence of a subtext throughout, in this case a journey whose destination is not Lisbon but to reach the inevitability of death.[7] The theme of life as a narrative journey is central to all of Machado's major novels, and it ends with Counselor Ayres's return voyage to await death in Rio de Janeiro.

Metaliterary play begins in his first novel, when he corrects the "impatient reader" who wants the ending to come at the halfway point with the marriage of two couples, by pointing out that one of the couples was not in love, an impediment that could not be blamed on love itself and certainly not on the author (*Resurrection*, 12). The narrators often declare their independence and truthfulness while criticizing the habits of common readers who skip chapters and forget what has gone before. Brás Cubas rewards displeased readers with a snap of the fingers and a good-bye before blaming them for the tediousness of his memoirs: "The main defect of this book is you, reader. You're in a hurry to grow old and the book moves slowly. You love direct and continuous narration, a regular and fluid style, and this book and my style are like drunkards, they stagger left and right, they walk and stop, mumble, yell, cackle, shake their fists at the sky, stumble, and fall" (71). The narrator of *Esau and Jacob* eschews structure in announcing the novel's final two chapters with a theatrical flair reminiscent of commedia dell'arte: "All stories, if one cuts them into slices, end with a last chapter and a next-to-last chapter, but no author admits that. All prefer to give them their own titles. I adopt the opposite method. On top of each one of the next chapters, I write their precise names, their concluding role, and, without announcing their particular subject matter, I indicate the milepost at which we find ourselves"(119).

In *Dom Casmurro*, Bento Santiago addresses readers as a crafty law-yer would a jury in a criminal trial: "First, let us go over the motives which placed a pen in my hand" (2). He seeks to gain the reader's trust and soli-darity, especially at the most unbelievable junctures of his story: "Shake your head, reader. Make all the gestures of incredulity there are. Even throw away this book, if its tediousness has not already driven you to this long since; anything is possible. But if you have done so only now, rather than before, I trust you will pick it up again and open to the same page, without necessarily believing in the veracity of the author. And yet there is nothing more exact" (45). If *Quincas Borba* is a story told to a reader, *Esau and Jacob* is a dialogue and conversation: "I know there is an obscure point in the previous chapter. I write this one to clarify it" (21). The reader be-comes a confidant, which is also a form of entrapment: "I would not write this chapter if it were really about the shopping trip, but it is not"; "It is necessary to say one thing before I forget" (86). Addressing the reader di-rectly creates mutual sympathy: "I know, I know, I know, that there are many visions on those pages there" (103). Machado reaches the pinnacle of metaliterary play in his last novel, a found and edited manuscript in which Counselor Ayres acts as author, character, narrator, and self-conscious diarist. The reader is absorbed into his meditations and annotations as in an operatic performance, with its range of scenes, plots, motifs, and sub-plots. The work oscillates from immediate events to expansive symbolic planes and references, and the open structure of its written history expands the definition and possibility of the modern novel, as Ayres dissimulates, "If I were writing a novel I would strike the pages of the 12th and 22nd of this month. A work of fiction would not permit such an equivalence of events" (*Memorial*, September 30).

If one looks at the "advertencies" Machado wrote to draw the read-er's attention to his works, there is a progressive development of irony over time, evidence of an ever more sophisticated and complex relationship be-tween truth and fiction, reality and representation.[8] The introductions to the last two novels seem to cross the line and become part of the text, fol-lowing the tradition of *Lazarillo de Tormes* (1555) and Miguel de Cervantes's *Quixote* (1605 and 1615) or eighteenth-century prefaces that make claims of truth for fantastic scenarios, as in Daniel Defoe's *Robinson Crusoe* (1719) and Jonathan Swift's *Gulliver's Travels* (1726). Machado gives his characters progressively more independence to narrate, as Helen Caldwell observed: "With succeeding novels author and personage grew farther apart."[9] Machado remains, as it were, a polite observer, restricted in his own voice to the prefaces. By turning narration over to pseudo-omniscient author-narrators, the stories gain narrative power because the association of the narrator with the author makes readers more likely to believe what he says. The prefaces of Machado's last two novels further dissimulate with their litotic manner, as if to transmute Cervantes's references to the "desocupado lector" (idle reader) into a *desocupado autor* (idle author), whose works are of no particular importance, "fit to while away the time on the boat to Petrópolis."[10] The understatement is aimed at recovering some of the authenticity lost in the increasingly ironic distance between readable narratives that become ever more separated from the exterior reality they represent, and at demonstrating the sovereignty of the written word, which is faithful only to the principles of art. To paraphrase the opening line of a chapter in *Esau and Jacob*, "Machado would not have written his novels if they were really only about Brazil or social intercourse in Rio de Janeiro, but they are not" (57).

At the same time, Machado proclaims that he narrates not the happenings of the world or the century but only what happens in the city. Taken as a whole, Machado's fiction creates a thorough and profound portrait of the world of Carioca society during the Empire, which was the source of his themes. Grieco sees in Machado a Rio de Janeiro that ceased to exist at the end of the Empire: "Parliamentarianism, polished salon manners, drugstore parties, slow waltzes, newspapers with ponderous in-depth articles, classical culture with the obligation of citing Latin phrases, French comedy and Italian opera in abundance, the barons, the capes, the coaches, superfluous things" (*Machado de Assis*, 1960, 9). Eloy Pontes likewise sees the entire old world of the city reproduced in his novels: "All Rio de Janeiro . . . is there in his stories and novels . . . woven with reminiscences."[11] José Barreto Filho affirms in his perceptive introduction to Machado that the most elegant, refined writer in the literature expresses better than anyone the es-

sence of the people, not as a social class but as a group living under the pat-
rimony of a long tradition with its customs, symbols, beliefs, patterns of
morality and beauty, with the invisible genius of popular imagination. Pontes paints a picture of the old days: "In the salons people sang *lundus* between waltzes; they exchanged polished compliments on the street . . . at
carnival time, balls of wax filled with perfume appeared, which were broken over the frightened breasts of elegant young ladies. The more audacious
threw carbon, powder, or committed other violent acts. . . . Writers, poets, artists, and politicians met at the entrance to Paula Brito's bookstore"
(12–13). In a history and biography of Machado's characters, Francisco Pati
catalogues hundreds of names in the short stories and novels, representing
the breadth of the social world. Among the minor characters, readers of the
novels meet Pai João, the coach driver, Jean, the French cook, the rich
Baroness of Piauí, Bárbara, the Creole fortune-teller who sings folk quatrains, Gouveia, the single clerk looking for a girlfriend, the turbulent and
ill-fated Dona Plácida, the barber Lucien, the witty Padre Mendes, the
dedicated slave Raimundo, and the elegant youth D. Eulália, who died of
yellow fever.[12]

Machado fills his writings with interpretive clues, symbols, and allusions. He warns repeatedly in the novels of intentional gaps left between
narrator, story, and meaning that require a reader's quick eye and patience.
Brás Cubas cries out in frustration to a critic, "Good Lord! Do I have to
explain everything!" Chapter 17 in *Esau and Jacob*, titled "Everything
that I leave out," is indicative of a negative method challenging the reader to
discover all that is not being told or revealed yet may be accessible through
another dimension or through perceptive analyses of the game in progress.
Interruptions in the narrative and the many "useless chapters" or incon-
gruent episodes are signs of the open work of art, defined fifty years after
Machado by Umberto Eco and Campos; they clue the reader to pay closer
attention and to look beyond the narrative for other meanings. Machado
prefers to remove, withhold, or imply significant details, thereby creating
absences and opening inner spaces that he then fills externally with aphorisms, inferences, and allusions. Counselor Ayres reminds the reader in
Esau and Jacob that the only way to discover his subtle meaning is to read

carefully: "Explanations eat up time and paper; they hold up the action and end up in boredom. It's best to read with attention" (5). The inattentive reader can be caught up short by an unexpected reference to what happened in one of the more than one hundred previous chapters. Ayres calls on his readers to ponder: "For, the attentive, truly ruminative reader has four stomachs in his brain, and through these he passes and repasses the actions and events, until he declares the truth which was, or seemed to be, hidden" (55).

Readers must pay special attention because one of the tricks of Machado's narrators is to convince them to trust in their stories and accept their opinions and illusions, especially if narrator and reader belong to the same social class or background. The art historian Alois Riegl pointed out that understanding art depends on the involvement of viewers, whose perceptions and emotions are formed by their memory of comparable familiar scenes.[13] Machado challenged readers to question their acceptance of what they read or saw. He even questioned authorship, developing the conceit of a book written by someone else, even by a reader. In the opening chapter of *Dom Casmurro*, the aged Bento's annoyance with a young poet he meets on a suburban train who invents the sarcastic nickname "Dom Casmurro," meaning a grumpy and obstinate person, leads him to question all authorship as presumption and appropriation: "Since the title is his, he will be able to decide that the work is his" (1). Brás Cubas had interrupted his story to accuse the reader of damaging his novel by wanting a different kind of book. In *Esau and Jacob*, Counselor Ayres is ready to turn authorship over to an impatient reader: "If you want to write the book, I offer you the pen, paper, and an admiring reader" (27).

At the same time, Machado takes further steps to disguise his own hand as author, all but withdrawing from the major novels to appear only under his initials in the short prefaces, a much more radical distancing than he had used in a series of initials to sign columns in the early journalism: "Without even identifying himself, Machado set the tone in his first phase that would define those writings."[14] Erasing his presence as author, Machado invents a series of character-narrator-authors, all of whom are unreliable dissimulators who fail at life, whether or not they may be consciously aware of their hidden motives and rhetorical disguises. Their monologue-novels are essentially dramatic, theatrical, and rhetorical, and they must be read and judged by the reader for their credibility or dissimulation or a combination of the two. These narrator-protagonists are more like actors than other writers' first-person narrators both because of the clear difference in self-perception between the mature writers and their earlier selves and the critical objectification of their actions as characters, as if they were performing on stage for the observation of their authors. The writers as protagonists resemble theatrical characters, perhaps based on the many notable performances Machado attended in the theaters of Rio de Janeiro. In a review of the actress Adelaide Ristori, whom he saw in 1869, Machado praised this portrayer of "a hundred characters and a hundred masks" for her sudden change from tragedy and drama to comedy and farce and for the natural development of her characters.[15] After years of intensive experience with theatrical persona, Machado abandoned explicit authorship in favor of author-narrators who provided multiple possibilities of reading in the distance that the theater makes possible between fiction, reality, and authorial or dramatic voice. Citations from Shakespeare's plays are prominent in giving shape to Machado's novels, his themes, and the psychology of his characters.

Machado opens a space between the ostensible real world and the narrator's, and between the social world, occupied by the characters, and the atmospheres or dramatic interior spaces, imagined or conjured up by the characters or the character-narrators. Unlike the playwright Luigi Pirandello, who created characters in search of an author, Machado creates characters who are authors. Narrator, character, reader, and external author occupy competing yet superimposed spheres. Machado anticipates the contemporary novels of José Saramago in which readers are forced to participate because there is no clear distinction between the narrator and the story or subject, no punctuation or separation between the narrator and the characters' voices.[16] In crossing the same boundaries, Machado conflates the stratified worlds of society, the narrator, the story with its characters, and their dreams and imagination. The substitute character-narrators split his fiction into four different perspectives or levels of reading: narrator, character, reader, and omniscient author. They could be described as Machado's heteronyms, fictitious authors whose personalities and voices replace those of their writers. The role of heteronyms in modernist literature gained special prominence a few years after Machado in the case of the multiple, independent author-personalities created by the Portuguese poet Fernando Pessoa. The term is equally fitting for Machado's character-narrators, who charm and manipulate readers in retrospective memoirs through their personalities, biographies, styles, hidden agendas, and evasions. Machado's narrators become heteronyms because they are acutely aware of the difference between themselves as writers and as characters; each comments on his action as a character in the narrative with the wisdom of retrospection and the skill of authorship, and none is aware that he is not the author of the novel. Although not made aware of each other's existence, as Pessoa's heteronyms were, they share many of the same characteristics and philosophical outlook among "themselves," and although they do not comment on each other's writings, each writes in retrospect through a guiding genre: theater for Brás Cubas, the autobiography-confession for Bento Santiago, and the diary-memoir for Counselor Ayres.[17] Quincas Borba is equally an author of letters and of the four-hundred-page manuscript on the philosophy of *Humanitas* that he later destroys in his demented quest for perfection.

From the outset there is a notable consistency and stability in the themes and motifs found throughout Machado's fictional world. The reign of imagination in his fiction operates within a strictly limited stylistic and thematic repertoire, comparable to the range of expressive performances of a musical score. The variable baroque world of action is performed within a rational, classical language and setting that defines the limits Machado sets for himself. He tends to develop a fixed, unchanging set of concepts, motifs, techniques, and rhetorical strategies, which recur in variations and in different circumstances throughout his prose fiction. Repetition of key motifs was obvious to Pontes in 1939: "The return to the same ideas and to the same scenes in Machado de Assis . . . is not a verbal deficiency or lack of inventive spirit. It is a stigma, a diathesis, an obsession. At times, small facts, trivial episodes, common situations that arise suddenly, seen in a flash, remain eternally displayed in the dark chambers of memory" (288). His themes obey the aphorism from *Quincas Borba:* "Life is made up strictly of four or five situations, which circumstances vary and multiply" (187). The last novel, of 1908, continues a similar argument in the aphorism "Life has its imprescriptive laws" (February 22). The aged diplomat Ayres comments on the symmetries one finds in life, such that widely separated events are often identified and united by their underlying commonalities: "Life is a repetition of acts and gestures. . . . Events, no matter how much chance may weave and develop them, often occur at the same time and under the same circumstances, so it is with history, and the rest" (September 30).

Machado's first short story, "Três tesouros perdidos" (Three lost treasures, 1858), although limited by the conventions of a contrived bourgeois drawing room, concerns a betrayed husband who brings about his own downfall through failure to identify his wife's real lover. His mistake causes him to lose not only his wife and his best friend but also a large amount of money he has paid to send away the wrong person. The central role of irony continues throughout the later fiction. Machado's first dramatic attempt, the *Odisseia dos vinte anos* (A twenty-year-old's Odyssey), a "fantasy in one act," concerns a poet and painter named Luís, who laments his failures and disillusions, lapsing into an illness of soul beyond salvation that he compares to that of Lord Byron's *Manfred.* Deceit, self-deception, mistaken judgment, abandonment, and descent into madness and solitude make their debut as the dramatic and psychological motifs that are revisited and reworked from a variety of angles and with more profound humanity throughout Machado's writings. Legitimacy, chastity, and honesty are placed in doubt by hypocrisy, adultery, and cruelty. These common nineteenth-century themes receive a modernist rhetorical treatment.

Theme and variation are the structural form and pattern of this oeuvre, as Barreto Filho observed in his introduction to Machado: "The years of his passing life were a continuous reflection on some of his favorite themes, which were submitted to many variations" (29). To embody his themes in fiction, Machado relied on a rhetoric of substitution, employed through the figures of metonymy, synecdoche, metalypsis, and syllepsis to formalize dissimulation, substitution, deception, and displacement. In his essay on philosophy in Machado, Benedito Nunes finds three exemplary moments repeated in the works that express his skepticism and sense of Pascalian tragedy: the expansive "Delirium" in the *Posthumous Memoirs of Brás Cubas*, the ridicule of philosophy in Quincas Borba's Humanitism, and the allegory of life as opera, developed in chapter 9 of *Dom Casmurro*. In the delirium mode, Machado passes outside of time by adopting an eternal perspective, a point of view that encompasses the panorama of human history and humanity in a single look, whose classical referent is Tethys's revelation of the future to Vasco da Gama in *The Lusiads* (1572), the epic by the poet and voyager Luís de Camões.[18] In the ridicule of philosophy in *Humanitas*, he applied Voltairean parody to reach the limits of reason, or reason turned against itself and against the thinker.

Learning from the European operas and plays produced in the theaters of Rio de Janeiro, Machado dramatized the human comedy through its classical allegories and archetypes as well as through imitation and mimicry of its languages and rhythms. Barreto Filho found strong influence of the theater in Machado's characters on and off stage, in the montage of entrances and exits, in attitudes and gestures, in concentration on the interplay between characters and their passions, and in structures of successive short scenes. The series of brief, concentrated scenes, with a minimum of background, allowed Machado to explore human nature and character to profound depths as a theater, a theme explored by Barreto Filho in his introduction. In subsequent chapters my analysis of the dynamics of Machado's thought and writing will develop Nunes's outline of the allegorical, satirical, and dramatic modes that make up the hybrid prose style and modern skeptical point of view in Machado de Assis.

HYBRIDITY AND INTERTEXTUALITY are twin pillars of Machado's composite fictional constructions, synthesizing his observations of Rio de Janeiro with his broad knowledge of Western literature, philosophy, and the arts. In 1940 the Austrian writer Stefan Zweig encountered the beauty of Rio de Janeiro as a city not in the "useful or historical, but in the incomparable art of blending all contrasts harmoniously together."[19] Hybridity contributes to the tension and incongruity produced by the encounter of very diverse sources and references; it can be considered the-atrical because of its panoramic representation of diverse characters and sources. The classical scholar Karl Galinsky points out that Greco-Roman civilization set a precedent for involving many different races and cultures within a consciousness of their commonality. The encounter of cultures in the European expansion, by comparison, promotes a comparable hybrid-ity: "The ability to meld cultural contributions from variegated groups and heritages into ideas and customs that could be shared by all."[20] In the pro-logue to the *Posthumous Memoirs of Brás Cubas*, Machado raised related questions of genre and provenance: his novel had reminded Antônio Joaquim de Macedo Soares of Almeida Garrett's *Viagens na minha terra* (*Travels in My Land*, 1846), considered a novel by some but not by others, and his own narrator Brás Cubas compared his newfound "free form" to Laurence Sterne and to Xavier de Maistre's parody of travel writing in *Voy-age autour de ma chambre* (*Voyage Around My Room*, 1794). Machado made joking reference to the metaphorical application of travel literature to the novel in a questioning of fiction's generic identity. If Sterne in *Tris-tram Shandy*, for example, himself borrowed and mixed content from innumerable authors with the goal of making his work inimitable, then Machado could be considered to have followed his example by importing a comparable parallel world library of sources to depict his Brazilian city-universe of Rio de Janeiro. The incorporation of a Western canon into his works became an important part of his modernity and even of his originality.

In her study of Nabokov, to whose writings Machado's style is fre-quently compared, Marina Grishakova writes, "For Nabokov, mimicry is also a creative model. The act of false or incomplete imitation, an illusory resemblance is the conceptual kernel in a number of his novels."[21] The il-lusion of resemblance is one of Machado's most original ideas and may be relevant to his own contradictory double status and double perspectives as inside outsider and outside insider. The literary scholar Jean Bessière argues that miscegenated texts inevitably reflect a double condition, caught between historial context and universal meaning.[22] Machado's composite sources are transported to an "ex-centric"—Campos's term for being out of center or decentered—space, distinct from their origins as semantic and structural maps of reading and interpretation. Resemblance in the world of Rio de Janeiro produces the illusion of localist familiarity, whereas the actual diverse components of the city's cultural, geographical, and social worlds subtly subordinate local expressions to their universal archetypes and referents, indicating cultures and languages of origin in a city populated through immigration. In the opening pages of *Esau and Jacob*, for example, the old Indian *cabocla* of the Morro do Castelo (Castle Hill), known for her powers as a fortune-teller, attracts the visit of a wealthy patron, Natividade. Their meeting is one of class, ethnic, and linguistic extremes, since Natividade strays from her protected environment only because she is anxious to know the future of her unborn sons.

Machado's approach created open or hybrid works that illustrate a form of conceptual blending.[23] Blending is based on a set of separate metaphoric and metonymical compounds that produce creativity through structural correspondences, differences, and unpredictability when they are unexpectedly brought together. The reader is obliged to judge what is familiar on the basis of unexpected juxtapositions, nonstandard usage, or nonfamiliar or displaced concepts.[24] Such diverse compounds combine previously unrelated ideas to form a single synthetic concept involving a change in the reader's underlying cognitive processes of reception. Novel compounds oblige the hearer or reader to discover a link necessary to process the new relationship. Meaning is transposed from the original material and relocated both in the compositional blend and in the structural integration or confrontation of different meanings and domains.[25]

Blending of constituent parts may be based on association by concept, by relationship, or by relevance; it is the author who selects the content, which may repeat or be constantly changeable. Chapter 101 of the *Posthumous Memoirs*, for example, "The Dalmatian Revolution," is a model of shifting semantic and ethical sands: a sudden bloody, painful, and tragic revolution in Dalmatia calls home the Count, who, to Brás's annoyance, had been courting Virgília for three months and had succeeded in turning her head. Thus "The Dalmatian Revolution" stands for the sudden, chaotic introduction of apparently irrelevant material that alters meaning through the presence of an apparently extraneous event. In the short story "Dona Paula," rustling leaves seem to whisper secrets of yesteryear to a stunned Dona Paula because they have become the repositories of memory, secrets of stories repeated late at night in the kitchen by the slave women. The linguist Hans-Jörg Schmid suggests that a high degree of relevance is a trigger for blending and determines its pathways and structures, which are controlled by principles of maximization and intensification of vital relationships, such as space, time, category, similarity, and uniqueness (231). Sources to be blended are subject to diverse principles of compression, pattern, and integration; the hearer's familiarity with the sources is tested by new semantic patterns that disrupt templates stored in long-term memory, requiring a new kind of metaphoric thinking to understand them (Schmid, 241; Benczes, 249). The presence of so many unexpected forms in itself may produce comic effects or reactions through incongruity or surprise.

In an essay on hybrid texts, Wladimir Krysinski posits that hybridity is a law of the novelesque that has always existed as one of the most defining features of literature.[26] Giambattista Vico, in remarks on the works of Homer, so he recalls, finds the precise function of hybridity in a change of registers, stylistic inelegance, and a mixture of dialects or speech registers. Krysinski traces this function to Menippean satire, a form of hybridity to which Machado de Assis subscribed that puts into play a heterogeneity of forms and discourses, for which a primary narrative matrix is the ironic perspectivism of Cervantes's *Quixote*, followed systematically by Richard Burton's *Anatomy of Melancholy* (1621), Sterne's *Tristram Shandy* (published 1759–67), Thomas Carlyle's *Sartor Resartus* (1833–34), and Comte de Lautréamont's *Chants de Maldoror* (1868–69). Krysinski further traces the "polydiscursive hybridity" of this current to a series of twentieth-century writers who work with hybrid forms.[27] The Swiss literary critic Jean Starobinski sees in Burton's *Anatomy* a certain baroque style, an inclusive inventiveness inseparable from the thesaurus, and a melancholy, burlesque, or grotesque theater of the self, all qualities found in Machado.[28] The melancholy Brás Cubas pretends to cure with his plaster is taken from a concept in the lyrics of Camões, where sadness and melancholic suffering indicate a sharpened consciousness of human fragility, of an uncertain and fractured world, and of an anguished vision of the absurd, which may even turn on itself in the guise of pleasure in life as suffering.[29] Baroque universality and theatricality are central to expressing melancholy within a satirical tradition. For Machado, comic fantasy has a theatrical dimension in opera buffa, Italian commedia dell'arte, and the Spanish zarzuelas that he translated to be performed in the theaters of Rio de Janeiro. That he employed the language and rhythm of neoclassical symmetry to frame his comic and satirical materials, as Grieco observed, only made his prose even more modern.

Machado's selective critical reading of the universal literary code and his singular approach are what distinguish him as Brazil's representative writer. Local difference within a universal code originates in the baroque world and, following Haroldo de Campos, signifies "hybridism," "transgressive appropriation," and "telling oneself through the other, under the sign of difference." Jean-Claude Laborie defines contact with the baroque as a "systematic reconfiguration" of European models in a new context.[30] Although the baroque period came to an end in the late eighteenth or early nineteenth century in Brazil, its long-lasting legacy continued in the work of its artists and writers. Leopoldo Castedo speaks of a "Baroque prevalence in Brazilian art" continued in the exuberant visual legacy of the period that was necessarily part of a modernizing national portrait.[31] Characteristics of the baroque tradition in Brazil, as described by the historian A. J. R. Russell-Wood, carry over to Machado's work, including dramatic theatricality, complexity, an appeal to the intellect, and the engaging of the reader's participation in the sophisticated literary game. Duality, contrast, and contradiction form its ideological and structural centers. The critic Mário Faustino considered the free movement of the baroque to be a natural Brazilian style that Machado knew how to equilibrate. By way of this tradition, Machado de Assis joins a list of writers who occupy the position of ex-centrics writing at the edges of the colonial maritime world, theorized as figures leading "a dialogic movement of difference against the background of the universal" (Campos, 2005, 4). Machado participates in the neobaroque revivals of the late nineteenth century, exemplified architecturally by the scenic and decorative exuberance of the Ópera Garnier in Paris (1854–74), and his fiction anticipates neobaroque qualities in modernist literature, qualities especially relevant to works by the Spanish American writers José Lezama Lima, Severo Sarduy, Alejo Carpentier, and Borges.

As a continuation of transatlantic dialogue, Machado's extraordinary literary life could be said to parallel or even recapitulate in literature the art and accomplishments of the musician and chapel master José Maurício Nunes Garcia (1770–1830), the son of freed slaves, who showed precocious musical talent as a child.[32] His masses, motets, Te Deums, and many other religious and secular works re-created the neoclassical musical conventions of Joseph Haydn, Gioacchino Rossini, and Wolfgang Amadeus Mozart for the religious and courtly life of Rio de Janeiro. Emperor D. Pedro II's decoration of Machado in 1869 with the Imperial Ordem da Rosa mirrors the act of the emperor's grandfather D. João VI in naming José Maurício master of the Royal Chapel in 1808, placing the Afro-Brazilian composer above all Portuguese musicians. Writing during the Second Reign (1840–89) of the Brazilian Empire, while absorbing the dominant romantic mode of the mid-nineteenth century, particularly in French theater and prose, Machado continued the universal baroque dialogue exemplified by José Maurício by referencing classic works of European literature and history in a kind of personal encyclopedia, alongside major works of Portuguese historiography and literature of the seaborne empire, integrating them into his probing observation of Brazilian life and customs. He achieved fame in literature, as did José Maurício in music, by applying European genres to a Brazilian setting, although Machado cultivated an extraordinary talent for assimilating received tradition until it was thought to be indistinguishable from its new Brazilian setting. Grieco considers this mixture to be his secret literary formula: "To know how to guide his pen along the paper and transmit the sensation of something absolutely personal in writings that prolong the classical sobriety of overseas narrators" (10). His literary education took place in libraries and reading rooms brought to Rio de Janeiro by the Portuguese, and his life was changed by contact with Portuguese publishers and poets in Brazil, such as Faustino Xavier de Novaes, Carolina's brother. From a Portuguese perspective, his world library, like the Brazilian court and its massive library transferred from Lisbon in 1808, was an inheritance and perhaps a final expression of the baroque aesthetic in Brazil.

The Portuguese maritime baroque was a perspective and aesthetic outlook formed during overseas voyages that had extended stylistically from Manueline architecture of the early sixteenth century to colonial Minas Gerais in the late eighteenth century and even the early nineteenth, where Sacheverell Sitwell found its greatest originality in the painted wooden ceilings of the church at Tiradentes, to the arrival of the Portuguese court in 1808 (*Baroque and Rococo*, 198–223). The aesthetic possessed a mature linguistic code passed on by the highly structured sermons of Antônio Vieira, SJ, and the satirical poetry of Gregório de Matos and embodied an intellectual tradition dominated by literature and historiography, epitomized by Pero Vaz Caminha's founding letter of discovery in May 1500. Given its location at the western limit of Portugal's seaborne empire, Brazil found in Machado, as it had in the music of Nunes Garcia, an alternating current, a hybrid and dialogic transformation of metropolitan discourse into a national code of difference. Machado initiated what Campos would call a "transgressive translation" of an ex-centric rhetorical code, while drawing on an omnipresent baroque inheritance. Machado the outside insider and inside outsider is also an ex-centric eccentric in the two meanings, both for his reenactment of a baroque literary code at a court linked to the Portuguese colonial empire and for his clever and sometimes obscure assimilation, transformation, and rewriting of universal models.

Key to the presence of the baroque inheritance in Machado are its twin concepts of disconcert of the world, on the one hand, and of awakening from deception, or *desengano*, on the other. Disconcert is expressed through tensions in a world that changes in unforeseeable ways, always contrary to one's hopes or purposes, where classical gods and goddesses may be invoked to advance or hinder humans' quests. To be aware of the inexorable nature of fate is to be undeceived or disillusioned about the ways of the world: "What a multitude of factors in life, reader! Some things are born from others, bump into each other, repel each other, are confused with one another, and lose each other, and time marches on without losing itself" (*Esau and Jacob*, 48). Machado frequently cites or alludes to the work of Camões. In the novel *Quincas Borba*, Rubião is removed from his house in Botafogo because of his deliriums, and the crowd of guests that habitually dined there was given "a decree of exile." To describe their fate, Machado paraphrased a famous roundel by Camões, itself a paraphrase of Psalm 137, in which a poet held captive in Babylonia ponders whether he can sing a song of Zion in a strange land: "They would now go to Babylon like the exiles from Zion. Wherever the Euphrates might be, they would find the willows on which to hang their nostalgic harps—or, more exactly, hooks on which to put their hats. The difference between them and the prophets was that at the end of a week they would pick up their instruments again and pluck them with the same charm and strength. They would sing the old hymns, as fresh as on the first day, and Babel would end up being Zion itself, lost and recovered" (165). When Counselor Ayres is pondering whether Tristão has fallen in love with Fidélia, he alludes to the episode of the Twelve of England recounted in canto 6 of *The Lusiads*, concerning Portuguese knights in the reign of João I who traveled to England to defend the honor of certain English ladies at the request of the Duke of Lancaster. Ayres ironically contrasts their valor to his own weak efforts to court Fidélia: "'Battalion of the fallen in love,' that troop of Portuguese knights who fought for the love of their ladies" (November 12).

What distinguishes Camonian mannerism, described in a definitive essay by Jorge de Sena, is the writer's consciousness, captured in an aesthetic vision that distinguishes both actual and ideal forms, while living the tension between reality and the intellectual lessons to be gained from it.[33] To confront the inescapable reality of life is to dramatize a great cosmic "theater of the world," which is the baroque world of a Cervantes, Michel de Montaigne, John Donne, John Milton, Giordano Bruno, or Shakespeare. For Sena, the spectacle of this expressive world embraces the entire span of society and its contrasts, from economics to religion and the arts, in an anxious matrix of universal humanism. In his oeuvre Machado constructed a human and social theater of the second empire, one influenced by his own early works as a dramatist; the long sequence of theatrical scenes in the novels and stories, worthy of stage or opera, is a modern reconstruction reflecting Pedro Calderón de la Barca's theater of the world (*El gran teatro del mundo*, 1655) and operatic zarzuelas (*La púrpura de la rosa*, 1659), well known in nineteenth-century Carioca theater, combined with the allusive, allegorical episodes of Cervantes.[34] Machado linked these two writers in his story "Capitão de voluntários" ("Captain of Volunteers," 1906), in which an anonymous narrator relates a confession by the deceased Simão de Castro about his passion for a certain Maria, who at the time lived with Simão's dominating older friend X, whom Simão describes thus: "Finally—and this bit is capital—he had Castilian fiber, a drop of blood that circulates in the pages of Calderón, a moral attitude that I can compare, without depression or laughter, to that of Cervantes's hero." An echo of Calderón colors the early novel *Helena:* "Is this a dream?" asks Mendonça rhetorically at the prospect of marrying with Helena. "Life is nothing else," answers Melchior, "An old thought, an old truth" (16).

If Machado's acceptance of disconcert of the world endorsed his Camonian sense of fate and adversity, his intellectual foundations were solidly formed through readings in seventeenth- and eighteenth-century French rationalism and the Enlightenment. The coexistence of baroque disconcert with the provocative wit, extravagance, and ridicule of French enlightenment texts is another of the most distinctive contradictions lying at the heart of Machado's compositional method and literary world. He combined the brilliant theatrical wit and satire of Molière and Jean-Baptiste Racine with the philosophy of Montaigne, René Descartes, Voltaire, Jean-Jacques Rousseau, and Denis Diderot. Diderot's literary salons describe his critical method in fiction and speak to his orderly, encyclopedic collection of references: "Diderot's *Salons* are the beginning of all shifting, capricious, impatient, and unstable criticism . . . [in a] sequence of images in orderly rows that represent the most disparate moments of life."[35] Skepticism and the freethinking that attacked limits to ethics, morality, and knowledge became Machado's method, coming out of "that turbulent and perennially active workshop that resided in his head." Figuring prominently in Machado's references are Blaise Pascal's *Penseés* (1669), Molière's theater, Voltaire's *Zadig, ou la Destinée* (1747) and *Candide, ou l'Optimisme* (1759), and Diderot's *Le Neveu de Rameau, ou La Satire seconde* (1805). The mad philosopher Quincas Borba, on concluding that pain is an illusion, cited Voltaire's Pangloss as a positive example: "Pangloss wasn't so foolish as Voltaire imparted" (*Posthumous Memoirs*, 159). Before describing his celebrated delirium, Brás Cubas noted, "Science will thank me for it" (7). Machado joined in the tradition of Menippean, indirect satire developed through Lucian and followed in works of François Rabelais, Swift, Burton, Voltaire, Sterne, Lewis Carroll, and Carlyle. In "The Ships of the Piraeus" in the *Posthumous Memoirs* (154), the alienist who examined Quincas Borba recalls "that famous Athenian maniac who imagined that all ships entering the Piraeus were his property."

Machado returns to the trope of imaginary universal possession throughout his novels as a comic mode of deception and illusion. Rubião took possession of Sofia when he stepped into her carriage already fully assuming the identity of Napoleon III. In the novel *Helena*, when Dr. Camargo finally obtained Estácio's acceptance of his offers of politics and a bride, his victory augmented his sense of possession: "He . . . felt himself multiplied in size and importance; savored beforehand the sweets of notoriety and saw himself, as it were, the father-in-law of his country and the father of its institutions" (14). In *Esau and Jacob*, when Santos was made a baron, he presented his wife, Natividade, with a jewel: "Santos felt himself the designer of the jewel, inventor of shape and stones" (20). Flora, unable to choose, symbolically possessed the twins Pedro and Paulo by melding them in her mind into one individual. After admitting a new taste or fondness for children, an unconscious preparation for a proposal to the widow Fidélia, Ayres dreamed that "all the children of the world—with burden or without them—made a great circle around me and danced a dance that was so joyous I almost burst with laughter" (September 9, afternoon).

Machado's literary world follows a moral, although unpredictable, nature through the abundance of aphorisms, apologues, and fables imbedded in his fiction in the tradition of Jean La Fontaine or collections of wit, paradox, and rhetoric in the style of the 504 maxims (*Réflexions ou sentences et maximes morales*, 1665) of La Rochefoucauld. Rather than depict human behavior directly, he prefers to show its inner workings and consequences: "To show the consequences of evil seems to me the best way to make it mean and repugnant" (October 18, 1861). He is not beyond parodying these sources of his moral world: "On the table near the window the last book the counselor had read still lay open: it was the *Maxims* of the Marquis de Maricá."[36] This material in the style of seventeenth-century collections was reinforced by the neoclassical tragedies Machado saw performed in João Caetano's Theatro São Pedro de Alcântara. Almost any chapter or story is laced with pithy maxims, whether common sayings ("The opposite always seems a thing of the day before"), truisms ("Life, more especially for the old, is a tiresome business"; "Old age asks for rest"), qualities ("There is nothing more tenacious than a good hatred"), etiquette ("Ladies should not write letters"), wit ("God, when he wants to be Dante, is greater than Dante"), or original coinings ("Discord is not as ugly as they say"; "Death is a hypothesis").

Machado's foundation in the theater in the 1850s and 1860s was in comedy. In his voluminous criticism he found comedy to be the ideal form for developing the Brazilian theater, and he expressed the ambition in a letter to Quintino Bocaiúva urging him to compose more wide-reaching comedies by sharply delineating characters and social circumstances: comedy with a greater reach. In theater he saw reflected all sides of society— "frivolous, philosophic, rough, avaricious, self-interested, exalted, full of flowers and thorns, pains and pleasures, smiles and tears"—and thus the opportunity for drawing a moral lesson or conclusion, as in vice against virtue in Théodore Barrière's *Les Filles de marbre* (1853) or the love of a lost woman in *La Dame aux camélias* (1852), by Alexandre Dumas fils, one of his favorites.[37] Theater uncovered the underside of bourgeois virtues that motivated Machado's short stories, including marriage of convenience, adultery, prostitution, usury, illicit enrichment. The opera buffa, zarzuela, and opéra comique, much performed in the theaters of Rio de Janeiro, guided Machado's settings for dialogues and comic situations. He may well have attended performances of Gaetano Donizetti's *L'elisir d'amore* (1832) and *Don Pasquale* (1842) as well as Mozart's *Le nozze di Figaro, ossia la folle giornata* (1786) and Georges Bizet's *Carmen* (1875). In his short story "O Enfermeiro" ("The Nurse," 1896) Machado cites the opera buffa *Grand Mogol* (1877) by Henri Charles Chivot and Henri Alfred Duru.

Opera buffa was light opera on comic themes that developed in the early 1700s as a popular alternative to the opera seria of the high baroque.

Often presented as brief one-act interludes or intermezzi performed between acts to alleviate the weight of serious opera, it was a model for Machado's short chapters and comic characters. In *Iaiá Garcia*, the character Jorge mixed genres when he went straight to a theater to benumb himself and forget Estela's image: "He saw the end of a serious drama, which to him seemed light, and all of a comedy, which seemed doleful" (8). In parallel fashion, certain troublesome characteristics of hybridity of interest to Machado—identified as transgression, subversion of norms, uncertainty, contradiction, digression, ellipsis, and fragmentation—could be subsumed into and disguised by his comic theatrical adaptations.[38] The episodes in which Bento describes the death of Manduca in *Dom Casmurro* capture the digression into subversion and contradiction that casts the novel's epistemology into doubt. Manduca dies of leprosy, and Bento considers it an inconvenient interruption of his plans to visit Capitu: "To see a dead boy on the way home from a love tryst. . . The trouble was that the two things came together on the same afternoon, and that the death of one came and stuck its nose into the life of the other. That is the whole trouble" (84). Bento contrasts the joys of romance to his bothersome proximity to disease and suffering: "What intimacy could there be between his sickness and my health?" (90). The two boys had been joined as adversaries by a political polemic surrounding the Crimean War, with Manduca loudly and repeatedly proclaiming his motto, "The Russians will not enter Constantinople!" Bento wonders if the prediction is eternal or if, after all, everything must eventually yield to time, "if the Russians will one day enter Constantinople," just as his "leprous neighbor beneath his sad, torn, and filthy patchwork quilt" finally yielded to death? Foreshadowing dark turns to come in the novel, Machado frames Bento's incomprehension of the fatal dynamic governing love and illness as an allegory in the guise of a diversion or intermezzo.

Popular and comic episodes support the brilliance and wit of his formal style: "The brusque contrasts, the shock of opposites, the attack against common sense, the ironical inversion of common moral concepts, the mockery that leads to caricature, the melancholy treatment of the grotesque or the absurd that leads to shading and nuance, to the deadly humor of Mikhail Bakhtin, without the regenerative force of laughter" (Nunes, 14). His wry humor and vivacity was thought to come from his reading of Sterne and Burton. Barreto Filho, however, found its sources in the conversational conventions of Carioca society: "Its sources are the wisecracks, the defamations, the anecdotes of the Carioca . . . a type of play, less heavy than farce, less intelligent than irony, less gross than a jeer. . . . In intimate company he was a jester, a spirited jokester notwithstanding his pince-nez, and the rusty physiognomy of the portraits of his maturity and old age" (62). As if to agree, in a satirical column from 1893 Machado imagined translating *Hamlet* into city gossip: "If I had to give *Hamlet* using the speech of Rio, I would translate the celebrated reply of the Prince of Denmark: 'Words, words, words' this way: 'Rumors, rumors, rumors.' Really, there is no other that better translates the meaning of the great melancholic. Words, rumors, dust, nothing, nothing at all" (April 23, 1893).

A fusion of popular comic opera of the early 1700s with the satire of neoclassicism both explains and underpins the encounter in Machado's literary world of allegorical and existential themes of baroque origin with the rational analysis and wit of the classical Enlightenment. Machado combines baroque decoration and drama, with its low, prolonged level of tension, repeating rhythms, and balanced phrases, with classical style that valued symmetry, rhythmic variety, and harmonic resolution above all (see Rosen, 58–60, in sources, below). His classical, measured composition, with its profound and even tragic depths in which the individual confronts the vicissitudes of existence, is enlivened and energized by comedy and satire in the guise of rationalist challenges to its philosophical, moral, and religious foundations. Machado followed no orthodox beliefs, and his skepticism was but an indication of his philosophical nihilism and religious agnosticism. Carlos Fuentes's incisive and ingenious comparative study *Machado de la Mancha* found numerous references to *Don Quixote* in Machado's works. Quincas Borba cites it to support his philosophy of *Humanitas:* "Do you see this book? It's *Don Quixote.* If I were to destroy my copy, I wouldn't eliminate the work, which goes on eternally in surviving copies and editions yet to come" (6).

Rosen's evaluation of the nature of humor as an essential function of the classical style seems very close to a description of Machado's compositional method: "The style was, in its origins, basically a comic one. I do not mean that sentiments of the deepest and most tragic emotion could not be expressed by it, but the pacing of classical rhythm is the pacing of comic opera, its phrasing is the phrasing of dance music, and its large structures are these phrases dramatized" (96). The contrast in meaning between melody and accompaniment (action and background), for example, the play with voicing by using different instruments (characters and voices), unexpected meanings produced by strange modulations and surprising materials (empty or incongruous chapters) all comprise comic wit and what Rosen calls the buffoonery and civilized gaiety of neoclassicism, certainly visible to Machado in the atmosphere of Rio's imperial salons. These same qualities permeate the writings of Machado de Assis, complicated and darkened by a comprehensive moral and ethical critique.

The consciousness of time, eternity, and mortality forms a constant undercurrent to a comic exterior in Machado's works that establishes their moral, ethical, and philosophical depths. Brás Cubas, for example, writes from the grave, and his memoirs are punctuated by death at every turn: the ship captain's wife, Leocádia, died a cruel death, as did Brás's mother; Cotrim's son, Dr. Vilaça, Brás's father, D. Plácida's father, husband, and mother; Dr. Viegas; Brás's son in embryo; Brás's uncle the canon and two cousins; Cotrim's daughter Sara; Brás's future bride Nhã-loló; D. Plácida herself; Virgília's husband, Lobo Neves; Brás's Spanish lover Marcela; Quincas Borba, who will die once more in the next novel; Brás's own death; even the book Brás is writing dies in chapter 71. In *Quincas Borba*, the doctor who foresees Quincas Borba's second death dismisses Rubião's consolation that Quincas held "some kind of philosophy" that allowed him to accept death easily with the retort, "Philosophy is one thing, but actually dying is another" (4). Before Quincas Borba dies a second time, his uncle dies, leaving him his wealth, and Rubião's sister Piedade dies before her marriage to Quincas, thus making possible Rubião's inheritance. Quincas's grandmother dies under carriage wheels as an illustration of *Humanitas;* the Marquis of Paraná, Freitas, and D. Maria Augusta die naturally, but D. Tonica's fiancé dashes all her hopes by dying three days before the wedding; and finally, coming full circle, Quincas Borba, the dog, is found dead on the street. In *Dom Casmurro*, all the principal characters except Tio Cosme are dead by the time Bento Santiago feels the need to compose his memoirs. The heroine Flora dies in *Esau and Jacob* from her inability to break an impasse between the twins Paulo and Pedro, and *Counselor Ayres' Memorial* begins in the cemetery at the tomb of the widow Noronha's husband. The counselor meditates morbidly in his diary on "these eyes that one day the cold earth will devour" (December 22).

Death, disease, disfiguration, and suffering permeate the novels, as if they were strange and inexplicable backdrops, interludes, or punctuations to a comic human theater: "Time is a gnawing rat that diminishes or alters things by giving them another appearance" (*Esau and Jacob*, 21). For Barreto Filho, time is a devourer of forms in Machado. Counselor Ayres carries on a struggle between Eros and Thanatos, while old Aguiar meditates on the irremediable sovereignty of time: "Time will go fast till his [Tristão's] departure, and it will not stay in our command for us to remain in this life forever" (September 18). Time and the physical world form a passive and neutral accompaniment to the eternal human drama: "The clock in the dining room registered them dryly and systematically, as if reminding our two dear friends that man's passions neither accelerate nor moderate the rhythm of time" (*The Hand and the Glove*, 1).

In his essay on philosophy in Machado, Benedito Nunes summarizes his philosophical outlook as a conjunction of Montaigne's lessons on human nature; Pascal's tragic vision of the disquiet, disconsolate, and contradictory human condition, yet without the consolation of religion; skepticism tending toward nihilism; a rationality nevertheless disturbed by reason; and a Schopenhauerian pessimism. Nunes notes that Machado's literary works constitute yet another philosophic outlook in fictional guise, distinct from and not directly tied to beliefs of the author. Barreto Filho thinks Machado's anguished consciousness of the absurdity and inexorable nature of fate led him to face illusion and denounce all false states and sensations of permanence. His artistic character charted the inflexible destiny of man's contradictory condition with moral nobility and a concentrated aesthetic dedication. In *Iaiá Garcia*, the character Jorge defines a new, intense, and existential form of love in a letter to Luís Garcia: "I myself don't know how to explain what I feel, but I feel something new, a longing without hope but also without despair" (5). Machado's impassive analyses of the human and social world that he understood as an outside insider, skeptical to a point of despair redeemable only through literature or wisdom, make him our contemporary.

The Formative Period

MACHADO DE ASSIS constructed his literary world over a long formative period, one which set the stage for a life dedicated to writing and within writing that began in 1854 with a single poem. The term may be rightfully applied to Machado because he reached his definitive, successful style only at the age of forty, after twenty-five years of literary activity. The term has not been applied previously to Machado, even though his novels are often divided between four early so-called romantic novels—*Resurrection*, 1872; *The Hand and the Glove*, 1874; *Helena*, 1876; *Iaiá Garcia*, 1878—and the later five novels that compose what Jorge de Sena called his "Carioca quintet"—*Posthumous Memoirs of Brás Cubas*, 1880; *Quincas Borba*, 1890; *Dom Casmurro*, 1899; *Esau and Jacob*, 1904; *Counselor Ayres' Memorial*, 1908.[1] Caldwell supported the distinction, finding that social and class distinctions play a major role in the first four novels, giving way in the quintet to delving into the abyss of the human heart and its cruelty, greed, indifference, and self-love.[2]

During the 1850s and 1860s, "Machadinho" (Young Machado), as he was called, became Machado de Assis, according to an introduction to his correspondence by Sérgio Paulo Rouanet: he wrote promising comedies, published a first book of poetry (*Chrysalidas*, 1864), and, after gaining wide respect as a journalist for the *Diário do Rio de Janeiro*, he was invited by Quintino Bocaiúva to write for the *Jornal das Famílias* (1864). The articles he published in local journals in this period influenced the form of short chapters, short stories, and prose sketches that would continue to characterize his most celebrated writings; by the same token, reliance on abbreviated scenes and dialogues suggests the proximity of his fiction to theatrical plays. Jean-Michel Massa finds his youthful originality in the transposition of satirical prose into scenic prose.[3] Machado contributed as a translator to Charles Ribeyrolles's *Le Brésil pittoresque* (1861) and translated into Portuguese novels by Hugo (*Les travailleurs de la mer*, 1866) and Dickens (*Oliver Twist*, 1870). He translated Edgar Allan Poe's "The Raven," based on Baudelaire's French translation, and Hamlet's well-known monologue. Of his correspondence, half dates from the 1860s; the first of two volumes of the complete correspondence concludes with two surviving letters to his fiancée, Carolina Novaes, in March 1869. In his columns of the sixties and seventies Machado began to disguise his authorship by using more than twenty-five pseudonyms, initials, and abbreviations, among them M., M.A., Eleazar, Job, Manassés, Marco Aurélio, Max, Máximo, Otto, Próspero, Victor de Paula, Lara, Lélio, A., B.B., F., J., J.B., J.J., O.O., S., X., and Z.Z.Z. These and other disguises prefigure the invention of semi-independent personalities who assume authorship and replace Machado as principal character-narrator-authors in the major novels. The 1860s constitute a formative period of continuous and involved literary activities that shaped the writer in his twenties through theater, poetry, criticism, and journalism.

His first fifteen years in literature and the arts is a period of intensive practice and training by an active youth who courted actresses and opera divas: he wrote poems of effusive praise for Augusta Candiani, who sang in the first performance of Vincenzo Bellini's *Norma* at the Theatro São Pedro de Alcântara in 1859, while Anne Charton-Demeur, Annetta Casaloni, and Emmi La Grua, each supported by a group of young fans, performed in three other lyric theaters of Rio: the Gymnasio, the São Januário, and the Lyrico Fluminense. Chapter 2 of *The Hand and the Glove* describes the competition among rivalries: "Who doesn't recall or hasn't heard tell of the battles waged on that classical stage of Campo da Aclamação between the Casalonic legion and the Chartonic phalanx or, better yet, between the latter and the Lagruist regiment?" The character Estévão goes to the theater for the chance to catch a glimpse of Guiomar, "once at the Lyrico where *Sonâmbula* was being presented; the other at the Gymnasio where the *Parizienses* was showing." His correspondence from this period, as

Rouanet notes, shows a flirtatious young bohemian completing his literary apprenticeship by reading the poetry of Alfred de Musset and Álvares de Azevedo. His literary initiation was in reading and translating French literature, popular comic theater, and poetry by numerous authors, some no longer read or recognized today.[4]

Between the ages of fifteen and thirty, Machado published 6,000 verses of poetry in local journals, collected in the volumes *Chrysalidas* and *Phalenas* (1869), 6 plays, opera librettos, translations from French, 24 short stories, 182 columns, and some 20 critical essays. Theater, opera, poetry declamation, and literary circles constituted his main activities before he began to concentrate his writing on the short story and chronicle. João Roberto Faria describes his first occupations as pamphleteer, theater critic, literary critic, comedy writer, poet; as translator of poems, theatrical plays, and novels; and even as censor for the Dramatic Conservatory. With this beginning, he would write 226 short stories, most printed in magazines or newspapers starting in 1858; he selected among them for the volumes published throughout his career, titles interspersed with his novels, including *Contos fluminenses*, 1869; *Histórias da meia noite*, 1873; *Papéis avulsos*, 1882; *Histórias sem data*, 1884; *Várias histórias*, 1896; *Páginas recolhidas*, 1899; and *Relíquias da casa velha*, 1906. Machado published only 8 stories directly in books, and thus since 1937 editors have been assembling numerous collections taken from the magazines in which he was known to have published stories. The scholar Mauro Rosso finds it questionable and even paradoxical that Machado's fame rests mainly on his novels rather than on the stories, of which he was an undisputed master; fifty years earlier Grieco risked the opinion that even the major novels would be improved as short stories. The chronicles began to appear in 1859 in the periodicals *O Parahyba*, followed by *Correio Mercantil* (1859–64), *O Espelho* (1859–60), *Diário do Rio de Janeiro* (1860–63), *O Futuro* (1862–63), *Imprensa Acadêmica* (São Paulo, 1864–68), *A Semana Ilustrada* (1865–75), *Ilustração Brasileira* (1876–78), *O Cruzeiro* (1878), *Revista Brasileira* (1879), and *Gazeta de Notícias* (1881–1900). His final column appeared on November 4, 1900, marking four decades during which he became a master of the genre.

Rosso, who has located 51 titles with contributions by Machado, sees in his journalism many of the same qualities that marked his developing fiction, for which the chronicle functioned as a school for writing and a laboratory. There, Machado rehearsed satirical humor, simulation, subterfuge, hidden meanings, criticism, and the art of tying together apparently different meanings and mastered the relationship linking the art of narration to his readers.[5]

Massa further demarcates the writer's passage from fifteen years of youthful apprenticeship, meticulously documented, to the subsequent career in prose that produced the short stories and novels to which Machado owes his fame and international reputation as a literary master. His long apprenticeship was based on extensive reading in Portuguese and French literatures, particularly at the Biblioteca Nacional and the Real Gabinete Português de Leitura, including translations into French and debate in several literary circles to which he belonged on topics of classical literature and civilization as well as modern European literature and philosophy. He read especially Prosper Mérimée, Gustave Flaubert, Stendhal, Honoré de Balzac, Guy de Maupassant, and the Portuguese Almeida Garrett, Camilo Castelo-Branco, and Eça de Queirós. Grounding in European literature was the standard in a city that had been capital of the Portuguese Empire and maintained close ties to Portugal and to Europe after independence through the royal family, travel, education, and institutions. Exchanges with Europe depended on transatlantic ships, two English lines, one Portuguese, and one German, inaugurated in 1856, with two monthly departures each. Brazilian youths traveled to Europe for their higher education, and travel to Europe continued to be highly prized in Brazilian society.

The creative application of European literary models to the American context became Machado's method, refined through literary discussions led by the most distinguished intellectuals and authors of his day, many of whom had traveled to Brazil from Portugal. The first, led by Paula Brito, the publisher of the *Marmota Fluminense*, was the "Petalógica," where the young author could hear the names of the latest Italian operas, new books, dance steps, plays by Joaquim Manuel de Macedo and José de Alencar, and rumors of any kind. Through the *Marmota* he met many influential contributors and joined the Group of Five that met in the law office of Caetano Filgueiras.[6] At the Tipografia Nacional, from 1856–58, Machado received the support of its distinguished director, the novelist Manuel Antônio de Almeida.

During this time Machado was reading Portuguese and other European literatures, from the romantic Garrett to Camões, while composing poetry at a rapid pace. His own verses speak to a form of imitation as a technique of composition: a poem in 1855 dedicated to the memory of his mother is based on a French translation of William Cowper's "On the Receipt of My Mother's Picture" (1790), popularized in Brazil by Charles Augustin Sainte-Beuve. The early poetry evidences a taste for parody, rhetorical forms, mythological references, and philosophical themes. Adaptation is Machado's technique in the short story "Virginius" (Virginius, narrative of a lawyer, 1864), published in the *Jornal das Famílias*. The dramatic confrontation of slavery and ethics portrayed in the story is based on the play *Virginius* (1824) by the Irish dramatist James Sheridan Knowles, known to Machado either through contacts in the United States or through Charles Lamb's reviews. Machado's wide readings included the poet-philosophers Homer, Torquato Tasso, Jean-Antoine Roucher, Nicolas Gilbert, and André Chénier, along with four fundamental authors of Machado's generation, named by Joaquim Nabuco in his memoirs.[7] In the context of his comparative interests, the center of Machado's literary development remained French poetry, theater, and philosophical prose. Even without direct imitation, Massa confirms the influence of the proverbs of Octave Feuillet and the last novels of George Sand in the stories Machado published in the *Jornal das Famílias*.

From his earliest experiences as a writer, Machado showed interest in simultaneous multiple genres, and he dedicated equal youthful efforts to poetry, the theater, critical essays, literary translation, and the journalistic chronicle. These are the early forms in which he first expressed the themes that would remain identifying characteristics and gained the versatility to be able to write some of his later chronicles in the press in the form of satirical dialogues and poetry. Massa identifies the jealousy theme in his poetry as early as 1869. He would follow this pattern throughout his career by appropriating and altering the works he referenced. Massa further notes that some early translations have been confused with Machado's own plays.[8] *Desencantos* (Disillusions), his first original play, never produced, debates opposing rationales for marriage, while *O caminho da porta* (Show to the door, premiered September 12, 1862) introduces the theme of three men wooing the same woman, reminiscent of *The Hand and the Glove* and *Esau and Jacob*. A companion piece, *O protocolo* (Protocol, premiered December 4, 1862), is a drawing room comedy of bourgeois romance and jealousy. The successful comedy *Quase ministro* (Almost a minister, premiered November 22, 1863) modifies a motif from Gil Vicente's *Farsa de Inês Pereira* ("Farce of Inês Pereira," 1523), "Better an ass that carries me than a horse that throws me" in his concluding motto, "A sorrel doesn't carry anyone to power, or to disillusion." *Os deuses de casaca* (Gods in dress coats), produced on December 28, 1865, for the meeting of a poetry club, highlights Machado's allegorical dramatization of Greek mythology, with social criticism embedded in the wrath of Jupiter toward human worth. Machado continues in the following decade with two plays from 1878 written in alexandrines, *O bote do rapé* (The tin of snuff, 1878), a fantasy and comedy of manners, and *Antes da Missa* (Before Mass, 1878), a dialogue of the malicious gossip of two society ladies on their way to Mass. Machado would return to the theater in his mature phase with two plays dramatizing ironic reversals of fate: *Não consultes médico* (Don't go to the doctor, 1896) and *Lição de botânica* (Botanical lesson, 1906). The breadth of Machado's international literary interests during his first decades as a writer is documented by his translation in 1858 of "Ofélia," based on Shakespeare, in 1861 of a zarzuela by the Spanish dramaturg Luis de Olona Gaeta, in 1862 of the poem "Alpujarra" by Adam Michiewicz from a French translation by Christiano Ostrowski, in 1869 of an ode of Anacreon, Chinese poetry through French translations, poems of Alphonse Lamartine and Alfred de Musset, and a romantic poem, "O primeiro beijo," by the Chilean writer Guillermo Blest-Gana.

Machado's reputation and standing sprang not from his early plays or poetry but from his critical essays. The author and senator José de Alencar lauded his critical acumen and praised his work in correspondence. His cultural development, in the view of João Roberto Faria, resulted largely from his extraordinary critical capacity, a talent that would dominate his fiction as well as his journalism. Both his international vision and his interest in defining American writing come to the fore in one of his most important and influential essays, "Instinct of Nationality," which appeared in New York City in March 1873 in the Brazilian journal *O Novo Mundo*, published in Portuguese from 1870 to 1879 by José Carlos Rodrigues. The article brought news of current Brazilian literature to travelers and citizens residing abroad and examined its path to aesthetic independence, largely through emphasizing the "magnificence and splendor" of nature and history reflected in the theme of the Brazilian Indian. Machado observes that Shakespeare, to the contrary, is a universal genius while undoubtedly an English writer whose plays often bear little relationship to his homeland. With this example in mind, he affirms that what the writer should seek above all is a certain intimate feeling that is itself a confirmation of time and country, even when the subject matter is distant in time and space. Presented to an expatriate audience, this crucial point, radical for its literary and aesthetic independence from identifiably nationalistic concerns, is then applied as an ideal for a school of criticism that Machado finds lacking in Brazil. In an earlier essay, "The Ideal of the Critic" (October 1865), Machado had outlined the qualities of a literary science based on conscientious analysis, moderation, tolerance, and urbanity, where the search for truth lies in questioning aesthetic principles and persevering to find the soul or depth of meaning of a book. Were such a criticism in place, he asserts, although he could not imagine it would happen any time soon, Machado could then foresee a flowering of new talent and writing. Through these and other essays he affirmed the union of freely creative composition and impartial analysis to be an important key to his literary world in formation.

While Machado's life is inextricably involved with his writing, as demonstrated by Massa's research, no biography can come close to explaining the nature and functions of such complex literary works or their aesthetic principles. It became a commonplace nonetheless to use themes in the novels and stories as keys to explain Machado's biography and psychology, and

Raimundo Magalhães Jr. compiled a four-volume biography of his life and works. Modern readers, including Massa, agree that the works must speak for themselves; however, it is not commonly thought that they should be taken in their totality over Machado's long career, covering the many literary genres he practiced. A crucial turn in his career was his marriage to Carolina Novaes on November 12, 1869, a date that divides his published correspondence in half and, according to Massa, marks a moment when Machado's life takes on a new and definitive form. In his private, almost reclusive, existence with Carolina during the next thirty-five years Machado refines the concepts and practice of distance, dissimulation, and deception that will dominate the structure of narrative and the portrayal of character in his most significant prose writings. In one of two surviving letters to Carolina, Machado exhorts her to join him in rising above the world's "foolish glories and sterile ambitions." He establishes the point of view of an observer removed from the direct sphere of worldly action through apparent thematic and moral indifference to its eternal vicissitudes, including suspension of any form of judgment.

His subtle, indirect form of narration led critics to debate whether Machado ever took any moral stance or endorsed a tragic view of life, yet even in his early novels one finds strong political and ethical positions, as in a defense of the poor in *Helena*: "It is impossible for those in easy circumstances to comprehend the struggles of the poor; and the maxim that every man can with effort arrive at the same brilliant result will always appear as a great truth to the person carving a turkey. . . . Well, this is not the way it is" (21). One could not imagine a stronger condemnation of slavery than the conclusion of the short story "Father versus Mother." Massa documents his "courageous, active, engaged, and idealistic" social and political activity in the early 1860s, even if he would later abandon the journalistic satires of the series "Comentários da semana" (1861–62) to devote himself to more purely literary activities. In a chronicle in the "Gazeta de Holanda," written in verse, Machado allows a slave to speak for himself concerning the lack of appreciation among lawyers of the practical distinction between abolition and slavery:

My lord, year come
year go I work at this
There are a lot of kind masters
But mine is never seen.
Slaps when I'm not looking
Slaps that hurt and burn
If I look at what I'm selling
Slaps for arriving late. No time off
Saints' days or Sundays
Little food: a saucer of beans, a drop of coffee that wets my
    mouth.
Thus, I say to the mayor
of a grand and brave Institution:
You say it right
You free, I remain a slave. (September 27, 1887)

At this turning point in his life and career, as Massa observes, none of the works for which Machado came to be known had yet been written. Grieco adds that if Machado had disappeared at that time, he would scarcely be remembered as a writer today, yet the nucleus of his literary world had been firmly established.

THREE

Novels of the 1870s

AFTER A LONG APPRENTICESHIP writing in many genres, Machado created a prose style, consistent from his first to last novels, characterized by an interactive relationship with technique and substance. His early fiction is an inherent part of this development. The four novels of the 1870s both advance his work of the previous decade and continue to develop core ideas, themes, and techniques that would be perfected in his novels and short stories.[1] Almost all of Machado's main literary ideas are introduced in the early novels. While the plots of these novels involve romantic situations, the elements of composition reflect psychological, philosophical, and referential modes that increasingly dominate, subvert, and substitute romantic scenarios. All of his novels have literary referents, and many are based on quotes from Shakespeare, Dante, and others. *Resurrection*, his first novel and the last to be translated into English, is a fictional dramatization and trope taken from a verse from Shakespeare's *Measure for Measure* (1.5), as Machado explains in the preface: "Our doubts are traitors, / And make us lose the good we oft might win, / By fearing to attempt." In the novel, Félix loses the love of the good Lívia because of an existential, recurring, and uncontrollable, yet unfounded, doubt about her loyalty and faithfulness. Again borrowing from Shakespeare, Machado's obsession with *Othello* appears in *The Hand and the Glove*. Estévão attends a performance of the play and immediately afterward flirts with a married woman passing by. Luís Alves taps him on the shoulder and whispers, "Leave her be; she's not for you," giving Estévão the chance to retort that Luís Alves had attended the play "to cleanse your soul from the dust of the road" (2). *Othello* returns in the novel *Helena* in the scene in which Salvador, revealed to be Helena's true father, explains how he was deceived by Angela, Helena's mother, who abandoned him when she left with her young daughter to live with the wealthy Counselor Valle. Salvador had felt a desire "to go and strangle her" when a friend loaned him a dog-eared volume of Shakespeare; he felt a chill when he read as best he could a verse from *Othello*: " 'She has deceived her father,' Brabantio said to Othello, 'and may do thee' " (25).

Themes of doubt and obsessive jealousy pervade Machado's fiction. The desire to strangle provoked by jealousy and doubt returns in the case of Bento Santiago in *Dom Casmurro*, in which there is what could be called a double performance of *Othello*, both in attending the play and in Bento's self-conscious reenactment of it. Paulo in *Esau and Jacob* feels the urge to strangle Flora because she will not choose him over his brother, and Brás Cubas considers strangling his lover Virgília. Shakespeare is cited three times more than any of the hundreds of other authors referenced in Machado's works. His last two novels repeat the example of *Resurrection*, being likewise expansions on literary citations: *Esau and Jacob* on a verse from Dante and *Counselor Ayres' Memorial* on thirteenth-century Galician-Portuguese poems by the Portuguese king Dom Dinis and Joham Zorro.

Machado's habit of invoking world literature, overlaying the European and classical literary and philosophical background onto American reality, is established in his early novels, alongside Shakespeare. In this characteristic, Campos detects the presence of the legacy of the expansive baroque world. In *Resurrection* and *The Hand and the Glove* one finds references to the Bible, Homer, Aesop, Plutarch, Plato, Virgil, Dante, François Villon, Milton, Camões, Sá de Miranda, António Ferreira, Torquato Tasso, António José da Silva, Malthus, La Fontaine, Molière, Pascal, Defoe, Byron, Friedrich Klopstock, Vincenzo Bellini, Émile Augier, and Johann Wolfgang von Goethe's *Werther*. The novel *Helena* contains references to Moses, Homer, Dante, *Manon Lescault*—an opera by Giacomo Puccini performed in 1884 that was based on the novel *L'histoire du chevalier des Grieux et de Manon Lescault* (1731) by Abbé Provost—and Jacques-Henri Bernardin de Saint-Pierre's novel of colonial romance, *Paul et Virginie* (1787). As a counterpoint, Machado's growing taste for aphoristic wit from Enlightenment authors comes out in *Helena:* Estácio has lectured his intended fiancée, Eugênia, for allowing herself to be influenced by appearances, for her "frivolous superficialities," and in response she is pouting unapproachably. Carlos Barreto comes unexpectedly on the scene and invents the prospect of a ball; its effect on Eugênia is conveyed through an elucidative quote from Alex Prion's comedy *La Metromanie* (1738): "I laughed; suddenly I was disarmed" (5).

The witty aphorism in the style of Prion makes its presence felt in the early novels. Machado appropriates or adopts for the purposes of sarcasm, satire, superior wit, irony, and paradox the sayings he has culled from the maxims and sayings of La Rochefoucauld and other aphorists. Machado uses the aphorism to address such themes as hypocrisy: "The appearance of a sacrifice is oft-times worth more than the sacrifice itself"; optimism: "It's better to dream of the happiness we might have had than to mourn what we've lost"; habit: "Regularity was the common rule, and if the man molded things to suit his manner, it is no surprise *that his manner also molded the man himself*"; rhetoric: "Proclamations are like lotteries: fortune makes them sublime or vain"; frailty: "Not all souls are able to confront great crises"; nature: "Nature has its demanding laws; and man, a complex being, lives not only on love (it must be admitted) but also on food"; misanthropy: "Luís Garcia loved the species but spurned the individual"; fate: "Unbearable is the pain which denies one the right to question fortune"; love: "Love is a letter, a rather long one, written on vellum, gilt-edged, perfumed and elegant; a letter of good wishes when it is being read, and one of regrets when it is finished"; and the human heart: "The human heart is the region of the unexpected." The motif of devouring, a metonymy for the passing of time and the way of the world that comes to play a prominent role in the school of *Humanitas* and the gnawing bookworms of Brás Cubas, is introduced through an axiom of Lord Macaulay, the British poet and politician: "Macaulay's axiom that it is more profitable to digest one page of a book than to devour a volume" (*The Hand and the Glove*, 2).

Machado's increasing practice of addressing and challenging the reader directly or calling into question the nature of the very genre at hand parallels his use of literary references. In *Helena*, while telling a story within a story, the narrator declares, "I am not writing a novel," a rhetorical arti-fice repeated in Machado's last novel, *Counselor Ayres' Memorial*. The nar-rators affirm their "duty as storytellers [in *The Hand and the Glove*], while reminding the reader of what had gone before ("introduced in the previous chapter"), chastising impatience (in *Resurrection*, "impatient reader"), or adding exhortations to continue reading (in *The Hand and the Glove*, "Let us await the next chapter"; in *Iaiá Garcia*, "Let us see through what turn of destiny"). Brás Cubas dialogues intensely and play-fully with readers from the opening to his posthumous memoirs: "If it doesn't please you, I'll pay you with a snap of the finger and goodbye." All the novels invoke the conceit of the detached narrator (in *The Hand and the Glove*, "It is not I speaking, reader; I am simply and faithfully tran-scribing the lover's thoughts"), leading to assumptions of narrative omni-science or control (in *Resurrection*, "Reader, let us understand each other; I'm the one telling this story, and can assure you the letter was indeed from Luís Batista").

Comments on the nature of the novel and on writing itself, along with comments on the very nature and craft of writing, fill a constant stream of exterior consciousness and philosophical awareness in the novels, set apart from events and characters. Iaiá Garcia's sagacity, for example, had taught her "the syntax of life, while others never get beyond the alphabet" (6). Let-ters and papers are "an inventory of life" (4), and a novel is meant to last for centuries. Addressing the "benevolent reader" in chapter 9 of *The Hand and the Glove*, the narrator develops the disingenuous conceit of an "au-thor who is more concerned with painting one or two characters and ex-posing a few human feelings than he is with doing anything else," for the ostensible reason that he would be incapable of going beyond elemental char-acter sketches. Immediately, however, the reader learns of the "dagger pierc-ing our Estévão's bosom" in reaction to his beloved Guiomar's indifference when she learns of his impending absence. The world of sentiment is sub-ject to its own internal risks: as Guiomar gazes tranquilly at the moon over the waters, an eternal world remains passive and mute to the desires and pains of human sentiments, "our agitations, battles, anxieties, insatiable pas-sions, daily pains, and fleeting pleasures, which follow along and end with us" (9). In *Helena*, Salvador looks beyond the twelve feet of his backyard to see "the infinity of human indifference" (21). Throughout Machado's fiction the eternal is the "saddening lesson" that joins dissimulations of rhetoric to philosophy and of writing to the uncompromising lessons of existence that teach "the insoluble conflict of human affairs" (*Iaiá Garcia*, 7). Character sketches are the embryos of cyclical dramas of psychology and of destiny.

Psychological analysis and the dramatization of psychological states are the principal focuses of narrative in the first four novels. Delirium, depression, madness, jealousy, resentment, doubt, suspicion, illusion, remorse, cruelty, hatred, vanity, terror, malice, desperation, and anguish all contribute to scenarios that lead characters lost in darkness toward an abyss of fear and trembling: "Iaiá found herself thrown again into the vast and dark space of her old cogitations, abandoned, destitute of all human protection. All that remained for her was to doubt and tremble" (15). Human society is unfailingly avaricious and petty, and the depths of the human soul are inaccessible and unfathomable except to Providence. The early novels investigate the depths of the heart in its veiled intentions and passions. In *Resurrection*, Félix grounds a type of character who will reappear throughout the novels and stories, one aware that he is flawed, if not condemned, because of an obsessive, inherent trait determined by instinct, psychology, or social circumstances. Félix is responsible for bringing about his own profound unhappiness, yet even in his final isolation he once again entertains and accepts the suspicions and doubts cast over the pure and loving Lívia. His psychology shows a restless nature, ever seeking to obtain some other intimate affection while distrusting and rejecting the happiness surrounding him. The heart is "a great unconscious offender; it is restless, it mutters, it rebels, it goes astray in the guise of an ill-expressed, ill understood instinct" (*Helena*, 23). Even considering its mysterious vicissitudes, an overriding question arises as to why the human heart can take gratuitous pleasure in others' misfortunes and pain, a recurring trait questioned throughout Machado's fiction.

Revenge and compensation, sentiments common to all four novels, often present motives for attacking others: Iaiá Garcia "said nothing in order to better be able to enjoy the blow she had just dealt Estela; it was the interest accruing from her sacrifice" (16). Estela's soul "plunged into the vague and perfidious darkness of the future" (9). For the character Estévão, cruelty is a need, indeed a satisfaction that is described with a baroque metaphor of seeming contradiction, "the voluptuousness of pain, for the lack of a better word" (19). Desire and eroticism are ultimately a function of pain and death, which is their end. Helena cannot accept forgiveness for having assumed the role of Estácio's sister, which she knew to be false. The priest Merquior explains her psychology to Estácio: "She prefers poverty to shame, and the idea that you privately do not absolve her is the worm that gnaws at her heart" (27). In *Resurrection*, Félix is aware of the damage caused by his obsessive doubt, and "even if he wasn't certain of the widow's innocence, he was very certain of the brutality of his explosion, and this recognition was a new pain, almost as profound as the other" (14). In *Iaiá Garcia*, Estela represses her passion for Jorge and marries another without love but also without illusions: "Thus we lived some years in isolation without knowing any bitterness, which is what there is at the bottom of life" (16). Passion and doubt lead to states of madness: the priest Merquior chides Estácio and Mendonça for their conflict over Helena, "You are two madmen" (19), while in her confusion Iaiá's "absentminded look seemed [to Estela] more like one of madness than of indignation" (15).

Throughout the early novels Machado reaches the depths of what will come to be known as his nihilism through the depiction of cases of psychological and existential anguish and despair. His alienated narrators reveal themselves through "paranoid projection and schizophrenic response," including perversity, seduction, and violation connected with the margins of the city, in a counterpoint to Gogol's *Petersburg Tales* or Dostoevsky's *Notes from Underground*.[2] He is prepared to write from beyond the grave and as author to assume an eternal point of view, comparable to the strange detachment felt by the Swiss theologian and philosopher Henri-Frédéric Amiel, expressed in his widely read *Journal intime*: "And now I find myself regarding existence as though from beyond the tomb, from another world; all is strange to me; I am, as it were, outside my own body and individuality; I am *depersonalized*, detached, cut adrift. Is this madness?"[3] The 1870s represent a pivotal and distinct period of change and development in Machado's compositional ideas, founded on the accomplishments of the previous two decades, when his wit, satire, and narrative strategies gain the depth and dimensions that will characterize his future writing and create the titles responsible for his international reputation.

FOUR

The Literary Modernism
of Machado de Assis

BY 1880 MACHADO had chosen the compositional features that both altered and refined his fiction to constitute what is known as his mature style in short stories and in his "Carioca quintet," so named by Jorge de Sena. Sena's term recognizes the common links in theme and composition that unite the last five novels. In the first novel of the quintet, the *Posthumous Memoirs of Brás Cubas*, Machado's narrator refers to the Pentateuch, the first five novels of the Old Testament, from Genesis to Deuteronomy, to which he immodestly compares his book because it too is concerned with questions of genesis and legacy applied in a retrospective, reflective although deceptive autobiography, written by an outside author. Machado takes up the themes of genesis, testament, and legacy in all five novels. They dialogue like the instruments in a quintet because they share comparable literary and thematic material, and their composition is literary and aesthetic: books and men interchangeably follow the plots of their unseen authors.

The first three novels in the quintet are each separated by a decade, leading Barreto Filho to characterize Machado's literary development even in his mature phase as "a laborious and long incubator." The final two novels, composed between 1900 and 1908, are almost interchangeable. Even if separated over twenty-eight years, the five novels, like the chapters that make them up, are not independent of each other except in the act of reading. They should be thought of as a unified group, one in which the triviality of the action and the irrelevance of the learned citations are supported and coordinated by the author's repetition and concentration in variations of a half dozen literary themes that constitute the main content of life and the subtle element of chance seen in *Dom Casmurro*: "After all, there are no more than a half dozen expressions in the world, thus many similarities happen naturally" (131). In each novel of the quintet a male protagonist is writing near, or even after, the end of his life. They find themselves childless, single, and alone, facing the recurring issues of their genesis, the social isolation of their testaments, and the existential oblivion of their legacies. Each has been reluctant to accept the role of traditional fatherhood, yet at the moment of writing each faces mortality without a biological heir. All their legacies remain purely textual: Brás leafs through his memoirs from beyond the tomb; Counselor Ayres passes his own desire vicariously to Tristão and Fidélia; Quincas Borba burns the manuscript of his mad *Humanitas*; while Dom Casmurro disguises his bitterness and remorse in a text whose impossible purpose is to recover the legacy that the protagonist himself destroyed.

The most important advances in Machado's so-called mature phase, which convey directly into the twentieth-century modernist novel, are the predominance of irony and humor, textual self-consciousness and play with the reader, intensive use of references and symbols, probing of hidden psychological states and conditions, and mastery of the art of narration through techniques of distancing from immediate reality. The author's incontrovertible, if at times invisible, control of his subject matter is applied to the act of reading as a self-conscious theme. Machado feigns substituting his own authorship with character-narrators who are themselves masters of deceptive rhetorical strategies. Brás Cubas, Bento Santiago, and Counselor Ayres each pen retrospective memoirs in their attempts to reconstitute and justify their lives. From the outset each account conceals ulterior motives and psychological problems, whether to excuse the narrator's own deficiencies or to control the reader's interpretation, or both. Machado, the dramatist, is the creator and director of their staged memoirs. By abandoning explicit authorship, Machado creates multiple possibilities of reading; space opens between the ostensible real world and the narrator's world, between the social world occupied by the characters and their interior dramas, and between the narration and the external author's interventions. Parallel to his fiction, a certain sign of modernity can be perceived even in the way

Machado brought the outside world into his carefully furnished study on Rua Cosme Velho: "Machado is exemplarily modern because of the way he dwells and fashions his subjectivity in an invented space that is able to bring the world inside, while at the same time keeping other forces out."[1] More centrally, Machado sought the greatest distance from his text, a point of view of the eternal from which he could impassively overlook all of human existence and drama, as if he were reading a world encyclopedia or observing the human species from the Southern Cross constellation. The eternal was an abstraction, a spatial point of view, such as Brás's flight over the centuries in the Delirium and the clock without hands in *Dom Casmurro*; a timeless allegory, like that of the world as an opera divided between God and Satan in *Dom Casmurro*; and an omniscient revelation, exemplified by the mechanical model of the universe that the goddess Tethys revealed to Vasco da Gama in *The Lusiads*.

A third addition to Machado's evolving approach to composition was the coexistence of multiple literary genres in a hybrid structure resembling a collage. His keen observation of the social world was matched by his literary bricolage, replete with references to classical literatures and history employed to throw the reader off guard with unexpected descriptions and juxtapositions, full of ironic content. Machado enlarged his repertoire by recourse to multiple genres, displayed in a series of miniature chapters with witty titles. As a result, his prose features composite or hybrid structures that incorporate or digest diverse genres and forms of representation, arranged in a layered or sequential series, usually in short, numbered or titled chapters. Within this malleable structure Machado further broke the narrative frame with bizarre interruptions, graphics, and dreams and hallucinations as well as the introduction of apparently irrelevant or extraneous materials. His character-narrators became self-conscious, aware of their roles as writers through ad hoc comments, questionings, and challenges to the reader and at times by addressing the very paper on which they wrote, a convention Camões had used in his *Canção X*: "Come, my trusty writing desk / always at hand for scribbling protests / and paper for my pen to unburden its heart."[2] Finally, Machado greatly increased his use of aphorisms, maxims, allegories, and episodes meant to lend symbolic meanings and transcendent views of the human condition to his writings. After 1880 he enlarged his world of reference, alongside the expansive use of humor and irony with a satirical tone.

Machado found the basic themes for his novels in literary sources: lines from Shakespeare, Dante, and Goethe; Sterne to Flaubert; the *cantigas* of the early modern Iberian lyric, Camões, Bernardim Ribeiro to Almeida Garrett, and a world library. He incorporated numerous historical literary genres and forms into his novels, including the oral tale, biblical and moral texts, aphorisms and proverbs, satire and irony, dramatic comedy, the memoir, novel of education, and the philosophical essay. He relied increasingly on an external, allegorical, or referential point of view that subsumed the universal in the particular, along with pointed reciprocal interplay between comedy and tragedy, reason and madness, inclusion and alienation, thereby creating tensions that both question and dramatize his expositions. The presence of different genres in his prose is a reflection of the universal library or encyclopedia that constituted his field of information. He maintained a poetic sensibility throughout his prose career that proved essential in tying together such diverse contents. Signs of his radical modernization are communicated through characters' loss of existential unity; the inviability of systems and institutions; open, discontinuous, and nonfinite narrative; and a narrative strategy of classical elegance, distance, and openness that will typify the twentieth-century novel. Machado became an expert at telling what cannot be said and saying what cannot be told; he opened deep implications and thematic perspectives without mentioning them directly, yet embedding the concepts and suggestions subtly into the fabric of stories, situations, and characters.

As a result of these refinements and modifications in the recipe of his hybrid, synthetic compositional method, Machado de Assis takes his place as one of the creators of literary modernism in fiction, a reputation based on his last five novels and his notable production of short stories and novellas, which include such classics of the genre as "Missa do galo" ("Midnight Mass," 1894), "O espelho" ("The Mirror," 1882), and "O alienista" ("The Psychiatrist," 1881). He invented his literary modernity through intensive reading, hybridity, and creative appropriation.

Machado's stylistic and narrative innovations are evidence that the novel as later refined by renowned twentieth-century modernist authors owes its existence to inventive writers of the nineteenth. Reminding us of Emily Dickinson's maxim, "The Truth must dazzle gradually," the literary scholar Noël Valis returns to a neglected interior side of nineteenth-century realist prose, one whose creative variety has escaped attention perhaps because readers have become overly familiar with its stylistic conventions and thus insensitive to its inner forms and "invisible worlds." Machado's position as an outside insider, an ex-centric writing at the fringes of empire, expanded his freedom to mix and match from his world library of readings, to make a journey around literature. The breadth of his syntheses is demonstrated by the extended list of European writers of his century writing in French, English, Italian, Russian, and Portuguese to whom he has been compared.[3] His universe is tragic and indifferent like Hardy's; he brought out the dark underside of reality as did Melville, Gogol, and Dostoevsky; his stories unmask the social façades of a Maupassant; his laconic, compressed narratives have the poetic quality of Dickinson; the unconscious conflicts and deceptions of his characters mimic Chekhov's disintegrating society; and his psychological depth combines the perversity of Poe with the poised portraiture of James's novels.[4]

Machado's hybrid style endowed his fiction with characteristics that the modernist novel of the early twentieth century inherited, embraced, and advanced. In his short stories and novels, dating from the 1860s, he constructed original, cohesive, complex works of prose fiction that distinguished him as a writer from other masters of the realist novel because through art and imagination he drew from a much wider compositional frame. He used a bigger dictionary and read in a larger library. He wrote in opposition to the mechanical determinism of his age and the positivism that had taken hold in Brazil. The human depth of his encompassing vision was said to surpass the limits of the observable social world. To call Machado a precursor of the modernist novel would be to invert logic and discredit his inventiveness; he set the creative precedents, rather, for several generations of modernist writers who are his heirs and descendants. Brás Cubas, Quincas Borba, and Bento Santiago face major psychological and existential problems comparable to those found in Dostoevsky, Gogol, Chekhov, Hardy, and James, while for the interests of contemporary fiction Machado has as much in common with Fernando Pessoa as he does with the psychological and realist masters of his day. He cultivated a taste for the aphoristic paradox, reserved his personal life for literature, assigned his major novels to substitute authors, and found the nature of things to be ultimately mysterious, fatal, and unknowable by design.

As James wrote of Flaubert, "He was born and lived literary, and that to be literary constituted for him an almost overwhelming accident."[5] Machado was equally a somewhat unlikely reclusive painter of life in pursuit of a style. He assembled his nihilistic universe in elegant, rational prose, while continuing to write and think in poetry. His "Gazeta de Holanda," forty-eight chronicles on current affairs published in the *Gazeta de Notícias* in 1886–88, were all written in rhymed quatrains. Inspired by theater and opera, he invented heteronyms, the character-narrators who penned his major novels so convincingly along with their heroines. Counselor Ayres's variegated story of a city constructed through the narrator's involvement with a web of characters predates Lawrence Durrell's quartet of novels on Alexandria (1957–60), each told from the point of view of a different character. Ayres's self-deprecating introspection in *Counselor Ayres' Memorial*, with its airs of Proust, further anticipates Bernardo Soares's celebrated diary, *O Livro do desassossego* (*The Book of Disquietude*), composed over Pessoa's lifetime.[6] Just as Pessoa was plural, many Machados existed in his chronicles, plays, stories, and poetry through their mutual desire to be universal. Both writers were tempered by a sense of inexorable fate and philosophical disbelief. While Lisbon was a backdrop for Pessoa's expansive poetic imagination, Machado's city-universe of Rio de Janeiro was his subject of analysis and served as his stage. Machado's manipulation of fantasy and imagination has been connected to the writings of Borges, and his use of intertextuality and referentiality relates his writings to Nabokov. The Russian writer also narrated from beyond the tomb, evoked deliriums that lasted weeks, and filled his prose with rapid comic asides to readers. Through their metaphysical and artistic imaginations, both portrayed the deficiencies of their societies, the brevity of life, and the miserliness of the human condition. Machado's in-different universe and vulnerable characters resonate in Joyce's *Dublin-ers*, Eliot's myth and irony, Albert Camus's absurdity, and Thomas Mann's restless world; Counselor Ayres's fragile reconstitution of mem-ory links his memoirs to Proust's recollections in *À la recherche du temps perdu* (1913–27). José Guilherme Merquior found that Machado was not a realist at all, but an author of comic fantasies in the tradition of Mennipean satire, the form of parody and burlesque found in Aristophanes, Lucian, Petronius, and Apuleius and related to Bakhtin's theories of carnival inver-sion and alienation.[7] Taken as a whole, Machado de Assis's works are both a literary encyclopedia and compelling critical reenactments of his times. In his analysis and depiction of the human comedy and theater of Rio de Janeiro, he synthesized baroque drama with the satire of the age of reason. He disguised a diverse, hybrid compositional method within the realist con-ventions of his day, to which he belonged on the surface, while adding to its hidden repertoire of inventiveness, fantasy, and imagination where the modernist novel began.

PART TWO

Reading Machado de Assis

FIVE

Machado's Pendulum

A eternidade tem as suas pêndulas; nem por não acabar nunca deixa
de querer saber a duração das felicidades e dos suplícios.
[Eternity has its pendulums; even being eternal it does not cease
wishing to know how long joys and sufferings last.]

—*Dom Casmurro*, chapter 32

O mundo é extremamente recíproco.
[The world is utterly reciprocal.]

—Clarice Lispector, *The Passion According to G. H.*

IN 1851 LÉON FOUCAULT mounted tall pendulums that swung
freely in space in the Paris Observatory and in the Pantheon; because of
the earth's rotation the pendulums appeared to complete a full circle in a
time period related to latitude. The precession of Foucault's pendulums was
considered the first proof of the earth's rotation, in which a visible physical action was demonstrably subject to an invisible greater force.[1] In 1602
Galileo had discovered that the period of the pendulum is independent both
of the amplitude of its swing and of its mass, thereby opening its intimate
associate with time and timekeeping in pendulum clocks, which date from
Christiaan Huygens in 1656.

In the novel that is the centerpiece of his writing, *Dom Casmurro*,
Machado de Assis abolished chronological time with a pendulum by asking the reader to imagine a clock that had only a free pendulum and no hands:
"Imagine a clock that only had a pendulum and no face, so that you could
not see the figures for the hours. The pendulum would swing from side to
side, but no external indicator would show the march of time" (102). The
invitation to his readers is to imagine a paradox, a radical contradiction between form and function in the timeless and apparently meaningless swinging of a pendulum in a strange clock that denies its practical purpose for

existing, since it is incapable of showing readable time. Lacking numbers or measurements, however, the faceless clock would actually depict the greater fundamental unseen force that makes time possible, revealed by Foucault's swinging pendulum. Here, as a writer, Machado invokes the underlying unseen forces that act beyond plot, setting, and character, as represented metonymically by his unusual clock. Movement is time beyond our conventional manner of thinking or representation, and the disabled clock is only time's visible surface.[2] The idea of time as measurement of a linear temporal present has become entrenched in human thinking, whereas its fundamental function is to divide seemingly eternal duration on the basis of the earth's rotation. The pendulums in motion visualize that eternal force. Machado followed Baruch Spinoza's concept of eternity as the reality of duration and reconfirmed the idea in a chronicle: "There is no time or space, there is only eternity and the infinite, which carry us along with them" (September 16, 1894). In *Esau and Jacob*, when Paulo was judging whether Flora's eyes were trying to discover if he were the person she had dreamed and thought about, and he looked deeply into them searching for that critical and inquiring spirit, neither time nor memory nor watches existed (57).

Several key principles governing Machado's writing and ideas are put into play in his hypothetical and imaginative clock, principles which suggest metonymically how his refined approach to fiction operates. The philosopher Benedito Nunes describes how the disconnection between form and meaning creates humor, paradox, and absurdity in moments of abnormal yet telling imagination: "The dramatic contrast between opposing and irreducible forces becomes a quid pro quo, an imbroglio worthy of comic opera that mixes what should remain separate" (1989, 21). The confusion or neutralization of opposites dramatizes the interplay between psychological fantasy, projection, and narrative reality, as in a theatrical or operatic production: Brás Cubas had comically complained that he was not born for complex situations that threw him off balance. Because of its apparently meaningless swinging, the pendulum in motion satirizes and subverts a system of timekeeping, deconstructing a universal form of measuring existence that in fact it has made possible. Machado notes its changeable meanings in the short story "Linha reta e linha curva" (Straight line and curved line,

1865–66): "Time exists in our impressions. It lasts months for the unhappy and minutes for the venturous!" The confrontation of author and reader, which is standard throughout his writings, is illustrated humorously when Brás Cubas accuses his readers of being the greatest defect in his book: narrative tension is put in play between the dead narrator and slow book, with its omissions and strange jumps, and the live readers, who prefer a fluid narration with organic action and conclusion. Discontinuity serves to reveal fundamental unities that exist in different dimensions.

By seeming to abolish the march of time, the clock without hands further defines an eternal moment through oxymoron, where time is visibly unseen or absent. The clock is blank, the exterior setting is inconsequential, and the underlying principles are hidden: "There were no hours; time passed without the divisions given it by a clock, like a book without chapters" (January 6, 1885). One of the main characteristics of Machado's works, whether in his philosophic concerns, in his stylistic and formal innovations, or in the reception of his works by readers, is the consciousness of a temporal eternity and the adoption of an eternal point of view, located in the constellations of the sky, on mountain peaks, and in parables of eternal philosophical truths.

In his poetry Machado painted a theatrical and allegorical stage backdrop for earthly eternity:

> The creative hand of the universe
> hung the blue canvas in the large tent,
> where we sit for only a day
> we who came from nothing,
> we who hurriedly go in search of the covered land of eternity.
> ("O Almada," canto 8)

Taking the point of view of eternity additionally affects an author's judgment of moral, ethical, and philosophical questions, as seen in Counselor Ayres's résumé of Ecclesiastes: "All is fleeting in this world. If my eyes were not ailing, I would devote myself to composing another *Ecclesiastes*, *à la moderne*, although there must not be anything modern in that book. He was already saying that there was nothing new under the sun, and if there was nothing new in those days there has been nothing new since, or ever will be" (*Memorial*, August 24). The influential contemporary journal of the theologian Amiel described the sense of removal from earthly matters that accompanies eternal and absolute viewpoints: "When once a man has touched the absolute, all that might be other than what it is seems to him indifferent. All these ants pursuing their private ends excite his mirth. He looks down from the moon upon his hovel; he beholds the earth from the heights of the sun; he considers his life from the point of view of the Hindoo pondering the days of Brahma; he sees the finite from the distance of the infinite, and thenceforward the insignificance of all those things which men hold to be important makes effort ridiculous, passion burlesque, and prejudice absurd" (July 3, 1874).

Guiomar's heart, said Mrs. Oswald in *The Hand and the Glove*, is "the timepiece of life. Those who don't consult it naturally remain outside of time" (10). From that face of unlimited and pure atemporal duration, Machado forms the point of view of eternity that, while metaphorical and abstract, allows him to observe time and humanity from the outside in a much-enlarged frame of reference. Like a Brazilian Vasco da Gama surveying the known universe in a crystalline globe, as revealed by the goddess Tethys in *The Lusiads*, he can comprehend from a superior strategic overview all of its paradoxes and contradictions and project them into the future. He can satirize fixed ideas, just as in actuality Galileo is said to have whispered, "It still moves" ("Eppur si muove") to his inquisitors. Machado's eternal, comprehensive, and remote point of view remains far above the contradictions and oppositions represented by the opposite sides of the pendulum's swing, comprehending the underlying principles that unite them, both touched by the same motion, both viewed from the same eternal viewpoint. In a mock defense of discord, the narrator of *Esau and Jacob* notes how many books it has produced since Homer, "the great epics and tragedies that Discord gave life to" (36). The eternal point of view is also far removed and seemingly neutral to the human drama, which is limited and circumscribed by time, although such a conceit may serve to conceal the author's implicit moral, social, and psychological critiques.

Such is the final thought in the novel *Quincas Borba*: "The Southern Cross that the beautiful Sofia refused to behold as Rubião had asked her is so high up that it can't discern the laughter or the tears of men" (250).

References to eternity resound throughout Machado's writings, contrasting the idea of timelessness ("this dry and arid philosophy") with the transitory and unpredictable events of present time ("belonging entirely to life and the world"). In a column published on June 20, 1855, "Diálogo dos Astros" (Dialogue of the stars), the Sun and his subject Mercury, who addresses him as Your Clarity, are speaking. Dom Sol asks for all the newspapers so that he can keep up with what is happening in the Universe. The *Via-Láctea* has a circulation of three hundred billion copies. Mercury asks if he is acquainted with the *Diário do Brasil*, in spite of the barbarous name. Dom Sol sees that the letters in the *Diário do Brasil* treat him grumpily, giving him advice about essential obligations. Dom Sol observes how the Brazilians follow fashions of the day in their repetition of vocabulary: "Probably the word is in fashion; they find it pretty. Unforgettable! I've been told that in that country certain words are like the fitting of a morning coat; when one with a new cut arrives, everyone copies it to exhaustion, then comes another one. There was *immaculate*, then the style changed to *incomparable*, then the style *distinct*, now it's *unforgettable*. (Pause) It gets boring" (June 20, 1855).

In *The Hand and the Glove*, Guiomar confronts a similar contrast which sums up her lack of response to Estévão's strong passion: "Guiomar crossed from the armchair to the window, which she opened all the way in order to gaze out at the night—at the moon which reflected the serene and eternal skies upon the waters. Eternal, yes, eternal, my dear reader, which is the most saddening lesson God could give us in the midst of our agitations, battles, anxieties, insatiable passions, daily pains, and fleeting pleasures, which follow along and end with us underneath that blue eternity, impassive and mute like death" (9). In *Iaiá Garcia*, the suitor Jorge ponders Iaiá's coldness to him after the death of her father, Luís Garcia: "Jorge attributed the new attitude on the part of the girl to the deep blow her loss had dealt her. He knew all about Iaiá's filial devotion; he was a witness to her constant adoration, which seemed to look at life as though it were eternal." Estela, her stepmother, explained to Iaiá why Jorge, who once loved Estela, had changed after his passion had run its natural course: "He went to war, fought, and suffered, true to the sentiment that had taken him there, to the point of believing it to be eternal. Eternal! You know how long that eternity of a few years lasted. It is a cruel thing to hear, my dear, but there is nothing in this world that is eternal—nothing, nothing. The deepest of passions dies in time. A man sacrifices his leisure, risks his life, incurs the displeasure of his mother, rebels and seeks out death, and this violent and extraordinary passion ends up at the doors of a simple love affair, between two cups of tea" (16). In the story "The Mirror," the ticking of the grandfather clock communicates the horrifying eternity of time to the lieutenant, who had traded his soul for the outer symbols of rank: "The hours struck century to century on the old clock in the salon, whose pendulum tick-tack, tick-tack, wounded my interior soul like a continuous pinch from eternity."

In *Dom Casmurro*, Bento was looking into Capitu's eyes, which he compared to the tide that was drawing him in as if by some mysterious force. He saw her pupils as cavernous, dark, engulfing, and threatening to the point that they suspended time: "How many minutes did we pass in that game? Only the clocks of heaven will have noted this space of time that was infinite yet brief. Eternity has its clocks: even though it is endless, it wants to know how long joys and sufferings last." Bento goes on to temporalize eternity and to subject it to the human psychology of revenge that was consuming him: "It must double the pleasure of the blest in heaven to know the sum of torments that their enemies in hell suffer. And the amount of pleasure that their hated adversaries in heaven enjoy increases the agony of the damned in hell. This is a torment that escaped the divine Dante, but I do not care to emend poets at the moment" (32). In the story "Um quarto de século" (A quarter of a century, 1893) Tomás and Raquel marry after a twenty-five-year separation. Their excitement and enthusiasm for one another return as strong as ever, and Tomás is ready to extend their honeymoon in Petrópolis indefinitely, when his friend Oliveira inquires by letter if he would not like to return to Rio de Janeiro. Raquel immediately agrees, and her assent foreshadows the loss of passion and even enthusiasm on her part that comes with time and routine. Her passivity stifles Tomás's expectations, as normalcy eventually eliminates any expression of desire in the marriage on her part: "Eternity was reduced to a few centuries of centuries; but being like all eternities in this world the issue is to know in what proportion they were reduced. Well, they had two weeks of honeymoon; there have been many shorter ones."

By taking the point of view of eternity, outside of time and against time, Machado consolidates his narrative around a paradox, one described by the philosopher Peter Singer: "After surveying the evolution of philosophical thought from Socrates to Betty Friedan, Dr. Singer concludes that people ought to 'take the point of view of the universe' when making moral judgments about how to live their lives. . . . Even Dr. Singer conceded: 'This is not a phrase to be taken literally, for unless we are pantheists, the universe itself cannot have a point of view at all.'"[3] From such an impossible, abstract, and imagined position, Machado expands his frame of reference and at the same time contemplates the mystery of existence seemingly from the outside. Brás Cubas, as he lay dying, had a reverie in which he saw Virgília and himself as they once were, because "some mysterious Hezekiah had made the sun turn back to the days of our youth." For a moment his body magically defied time by turning the clock back to allow Brás a rapturous, nostalgic vision of his youthful passion. Eternity, however, to use one of Machado's words, is the incommensurable space into which death would soon scatter his ashes: "I shook off all my miseries, and this handful of dust that death was about to scatter into the eternity of nothingness was stronger than time, who is the minister of death" (6).

"If they should start making love . . ." is the warning José Dias gives to D. Glória about Bentinho and Capitu in *Dom Casmurro*, and while turning the phrase over in his mind the dizzy Bento's knees wobble. Although he hears messages from a coconut palm, birds, butterflies, and grasshoppers, all of which support the naturalness of his feelings, Bento is fearful. He is incapable of giving pleasure. In his meetings with Capitu, he describes her as expansive and infinite while he is prosaic and guilty: "She told how she had dreamed of me, extraordinary adventures, how we went to the top of Corcovado through the air, danced on the moon, and then angels came

to ask us our names to give them to other angels that had just been born"
(12). Corcovado is Rio de Janeiro's then-unoccupied peak from which the
imaginative Capitu dreams of observing life and eternity in a state of ethereal pleasure after a magical flight to the top.[4] After a few years have passed,
when Bento is sent off to the seminary of São José, he reports weeping
more tears than have been shed since Adam and Eve. His exaggeration
threatens to collapse time into a constant eternal weeping, and he both
excuses and undercuts his reaction by noting in his memory of the event
that "at the age of fifteen, everything is infinite" (50).

Flora, in *Esau and Jacob*, plays some of her favorite pieces on the
piano as a way of escaping the present moment by taking refuge in a dimension of eternity. On the eve of the revolution that overthrew the Empire, in the midst of her parents' consternation and the political maneuvering
of Pedro and Paulo, her suitors, Flora took refuge in music. Counselor
Ayres could not identify the sonata, but he noticed that her playing removed her from present time: "Music had for her the advantage of not being present, past, or future. It was something outside of time and of space,
a pure idea" (69). We may conjecture that Flora was playing a rhapsody or
impromptu rather than a sonata, since Ayres associates its formlessness
with the chaotic disharmony of the present political moment, there being
no definitive government. Her notes from the beyond, the "la, la, do, re,
sol, re, re, la" of the piano, were to Ayres's ears the perfect expressions of a
present absence. He compares it to the "anarchy of primitive innocence in
that corner of paradise which man lost because of his disobedience and
one day will regain, when perfection brings the eternal and only order . . . and life will be a clear sky." Flora's music is, for the unmusical
Ayres, eternal formlessness that can be understood only when its unbridled
primitivism—which he compares to the cycle of political revolutions—is
resolved in a perfect, stable, and permanent general order.

Ayres leaves the novel on the last page while patting an "eternal flower"
in his buttonhole. The twins, Paulo the republican and Pedro the monarchist, had fought even in the womb; they swore to obey their mother's
dying wish, however, which was that they would be friends. In the Chamber of Deputies their new union raised eyebrows, as they then did every-

thing together, scandalizing their diametrically opposed parties. Their unexpected accord was nourished by their mother's recent death, yet gradually they again agreed to disagree on political issues. Ayres knew that their posture of friendship could not last: "The eyes of their friends quickly noticed that they did not get along, and soon that they detested each other" (121). The president of the chamber was convinced that they were completely reformed and told Ayres as much. Diplomat to the end, Ayres does not contradict him, even nods to a hypothesis that their disagreements had to do with questions of inheritance. Yet he knows that the twins had been fated from the beginning and could no more change than the "eternal flower" forever seen in his lapel.

In his memoirs the counselor meets with Fidélia while both are still widower and widow, but after the announcement of her engagement to Tristão. Ayres is puzzled about her and still unprepared to relinquish his pretensions as the new husband who would substitute the one she buried; he has found out that she still takes flowers to the grave and wonders if she has not made a single being out of the deceased and future person. In the midst of his voluble and insincere praises of Tristão and the reading of an affectionate letter from her future mother-in-law, Fidélia spontaneously goes to the piano and plays with notable expression. Ayres jokes that Tristão should be able to hear it from Petrópolis, where he has gone to search for a honeymoon cottage, yet his deeper interest is in the nature of Fidélia's emotions. He was wondering if this music were perhaps an homage to a dear reality that was lost with time and the grave, which is more his world than Tristão's. Just as Rubião hoped to meet his Sofia by their both looking at the Southern Cross, Ayres senses his union with Fidélia to belong to a fragment of eternity occupied only by souls, the dead, and the absent: "Eternity is farther away, yet she has already sent fragments of her soul to that place. Music's great advantage is it speaks to the dead and the absent" ("Undated").

As author, Machado reads reality through the lens of his swinging pendulum, first from the point of view of the universe and eternity, such that the times of human actions—past, present, and future—are viewed from an atemporal perspective and at the same time from observations close to this earth, its inhabitants, and social reality. Such a dialectical perspective forges a link between the Brazilian world he observes, the microcosm of empire on the one hand, and the great eternal forces responsible for time and the universe on the other. The latter remain out of reach and, at times, distant from humans' understanding. Machado's intention is to investigate, reveal, and evoke not only truths of his time but also those of universal time. Writing beyond one's own time, according to the critic Wilson Martins, expresses a natural quest for eternal themes and values in works of art: "In the history of the arts, the lasting monuments were those not overly absorbed with their own time, but those which, although tied to circumstances to a greater or lesser degree, responded to the quest for the eternal that only man possesses among all the species. Reflecting the eternal and permanent, the work of art can respond to the passing demands of each epoch; if it reflected only the passing demands of each epoch, the work of art could not respond to the permanent and the eternal."[5] The point of view of the eternal, Ludwig Wittgenstein noted, is the defining characteristic of works of art: "The work of art is the object seen *sub specie aeternitatis*; and the good life is the world seen *sub specie aeternitatis*. This is the connection between art and ethics."[6] In Machado's fiction the characters inhabit a world-universe of epic meaning, lasting as long as the pendulums and governed by fatal gods or by occult forces that can be glimpsed by the reader only between the lines, in breaks in narrative coherence, and through Machado's wry, ironic, penetrating humor.

A third principle applicable to Machado's writing is to be found in the swinging of the pendulum in simple harmonic oscillation, continually touching the opposite limits of its motion, a reciprocal swinging motion governed by rules of displacement, amplitude, and frequency unaffected by human actions or emotions, as stated in chapter I of *The Hand and the Glove*: "Our passions neither accelerate nor moderate the passing of time." These rules are inherent in the chance distribution of fate, outlined in Machado's first novel: "Ten years have passed since the events recounted in this book, long and dull for some, light and gladsome for others, which is the general law of our miserable human society." What is oftentimes taken for ambiguity in Machado's novels can be explained by this reciprocal swinging

between contraries, meant to exemplify the contradictory yet simultaneous presence of opposites, conflicting emotions, tendencies, motives, and
changes brought about by time. Doubt in Machado's works, whether in cases
of inconclusive evidence or multiple possible meanings, is usually an attempt
by a narrator to cajole, persuade, or deceive readers by presenting limited,
conflicting, symbolic, or prejudicial evidence; whereas, to complete the picture the reader must search for the missing information from other clues in
the texts by reading more attentively, as Counselor Ayres advised, and on
a broader scale of interpretation. The counselor is aware that reciprocity
involves repetition that may be inimical to good fiction:

> A number of pages back I spoke of the symmetries one finds in
> life. I cited the example of Osório and Fidélia, both with sick
> fathers away from here, and both leaving here to go to them, each
> to his own. All this is repugnant to imaginary compositions,
> which demand variety, and even contradictions, in behavior.
> Life, on the other hand, is like that, a repetition of acts and ges-
> tures, as in receptions, meals, visits, and other amusements: in
> the matter of work it is the same thing. Events, no matter how
> much chance may weave and develop them, often occur at the
> same time and under the same circumstances, so it is with his-
> tory and the rest. (September 30)

Machado, the rational moralist, is suggestive rather than inconclusive about
the rhythm of life: the extreme points of the arc are always related through
the pendulum's motion and thus belong to a universe of reciprocal relationships and movement, described in the very arc by which opposite points
are related, if not conjoined. Brás Cubas defined it as "a certain reciprocal, regular, and perhaps periodic action—or, to use an image, something
similar to the tides on a beach in Flamengo, and of others equally marvelous" (100). In *Dom Casmurro*, Bento Santiago used his watch to mark his
good and evil intentions: "The Devil's seconds had got intercalated into
the minutes of God, and the watch was thus alternately marking my per-
dition and my salvation" (118). In the story "Um quarto de século," the

lawyer Tomás thought of becoming a minister of state, although he had no political convictions: "In Law School he had written and spoken about public liberties, the future of peoples, of democratic institutions, all of that, however without either profound or superficial convictions, from simple practice, a kind of obligatory prayer. Once the course was over, he had no thought either of liberating or of enslaving people." The Devil is enraged and mystified in the story "A Igreja do Diabo ("The Devil's Church," 1883) when some of the dishonest defrauders of the counterchurch he established begin to practice gratuitous good deeds without any personal interest or reward. Trembling, he complained to God, who replies, "What did you expect, my poor Devil? The cotton cloaks now have silken fringes, just as those of velvet had cotton fringes. What did you expect? It's the eternal human contradiction."

The reader's task, then, is not to decide between two alternatives or to create ambiguities but to discern velleities, to place them within the limits and rules of displacement, and to observe their fulfillment over time in patterns and rhythms of life and in examples of repetitive human psychology. Machado resolves contradictions, for example, by showing that one side or extreme is capable of being substituted by its inverse or opposite, to which it intuitively bears some degree of relation. Virgília's husband, Lobo Neves, rejects appointment as the governor of a province because the decree is dated the thirteenth but later accepts a second appointment because the date is the thirty-first. Reciprocal relationships invert the order of action and reaction, or of chronology, in the same way one literature depends on another. Machado uses William Wordsworth's line "The child is father of the man" ("O menino é pai do homem"), parodies Auguste Compte's axiom "Les morts gouvernent les vivants" (The dead govern the living), and coins the idea taken up by Miguel de Unamuno and Pirandello that books operate independently of their authors: "There are books which owe no more to their authors; some, not so much" (Dom Casmurro, 1).

The dual nature of life is also found in the physical realm. The Nobel chemist William Knowles's research into the drug L-dopa found two mirrored forms of molecules that were identical in composition yet had completely different properties and effects, one medicinal and the other toxic.[7] Machado's pendulum illustrates this mirrored reciprocity, with surface resemblances that are likewise purely formal yet whose effects may be diametrically opposite. In *Counselor Ayres' Memorial*, Fidélia has a dream in which her father and father-in-law, always diametrically opposed in life, appear over the bay of Rio de Janeiro hand in hand, finally reconciled by death, and accepting that all the hostilities of this world are pointless. Ayres immediately recognized that her dream contradicted reciprocity and the work of the pendulum, and he spoke up against this ideal union of opposites: "Eternal reconciliation between political enemies would, on the contrary, be an everlasting torment. I do not know any to equal it in the *Divine Comedy*. God, when he wants to be Dante, is greater than Dante" (August 1).

The eternal point of view assumed by author and narrators contrasts with the temporal and linear dimension of the readers; this tension is one of the building blocks of Machado's fiction. It recapitulates one of the aesthetic principles that the playwright and essayist Maurice Maeterlinck expressed in an aphorism: "It is only by the communications that we have with the infinite that we are to be distinguished from each other."[8] The swing of the pendulum joins eternal and temporal dimensions and perspectives of life, and in this way it plays both structural and thematic roles throughout the fiction. Brás Cubas thinks that each tick of his grandfather clock in the chapter "The Pendulum" is a countdown: "Every note of the mournful ticktock, slow and dry, seemed to say that I had one tick less of life . . . one less . . . one less . . . one less . . . one less." When the clock runs down he winds it immediately so as not to lose count of his lost instants of life. Permanence is attributed to the physical clock—"A clock is definitive and perpetual"—whereas mortal time continues to follow the illusion of its sequential ticks, as Brás ironized with devastating fatality: "The last man, as he says farewell to the cold and used-up sun, will have a watch in his pocket in order to know the exact time of his death" (54).

Having only pendulum motion, Machado's clock oscillates between hope for more ticks and despair over their absence, and throughout his fiction extremes meet, balance, and neutralize each other's one-sided radicalness.

Helena provides an example when she is approached by Camargo, the father of Eugênia, to ask her assistance in furthering his daughter's courtship with Estácio, Helena's presumed brother. Camargo resorts to intimidation bordering on extortion when he mentions having seen Helena enter a poorhouse with a blue flag at six o'clock in the morning. He insinuates that Helena's sexuality might disturb the intended engagement. This low blow brings Helena to tears of anguish and despair. She lies prostrate and as if dead for an immeasurable time "such as only clocks of despair and hope tell." In her prayers she takes advantage of Jacob's "mysterious stairway. . . . On it thoughts ascend to heaven; on it divine consolations descend to earth" (13). Camargo was said to be capable of going to any lengths to protect his daughter, who was his religion, yet this exclusive passion was also subject to the action of a pendulum: "But his love for his daughter, though violent, slavish, and blind, was a way this father had of loving himself" (14). In *Iaiá Garcia*, Estela's father, Mr. Antunes, foresaw the world in moral terms as a necessary balance of good and evil and concluded, that "not all is vanity under the sun, as *Ecclesiastes* suggests, nor all perfection, as Dr. Pangloss opines. He felt that there is a loose balance of good and evil, and that the art of living consists in getting the greatest good out of the greatest evil" (3).

A further philosophical inference to be made from the faceless clock is that of an underlying truth or unseen deeper principle, which is the fateful measurement of a finite world of undetermined yet uncertain duration. The invention of the clock began a countdown of the time of life left for each person. One of the shocks of a faceless clock is the consequent inability to hear or see the hands of fate, resulting in an enhancement of the indeterminacy and unpredictability of life. For the distraught Helena, clocks told of despair and hope simultaneously. The forces of motion that make it possible for a clock to measure time, as it were, are completely unconnected to one's reading of the hands, a process that involves human desires, emotions, and ideas. In a spooky grandfather clock, Brás Cubas hears only the fatal counting away not only of the instants of his life but of the very psychology of human existence; at the same time, Brás observes the fatal attraction of the mechanism, which both disguises and conveys a perverse desire and even a need to count each equal and lost instant, seeming to Brás to be like coins that a devil takes out of the sack of life and gives to death, one by one.

His Faustian metaphor describes a will to knowledge that is precise and scientific yet fatal and useless, leading steadily and inevitably to death in the bargain, like the last man who consults his watch to know the exact time his species becomes extinct. If, as Brás learns, all institutions are either transformed or die, it is only the illusory clock with its steady tick-tock that he calls definitive and perpetual. The faceless clock is scary, then, because it is a reminder of the distance and indifference of the fundamental forces from human perceptions and sentiments and likewise of the existential void left by the empty face, as if the missing hands and ticking, if restored, could confirm a few more moments of life left to be counted. The swinging pendulums are the silent predictors of the end and comic indicators of our dependence and vulnerability: "Take a look now at the neutrality of this globe that carries us through space like a lifeboat heading for shore: today a virtuous couple sleeps on the same plot of ground that once held a sinning couple. Tomorrow a churchman may sleep there, then a murderer, then a blacksmith, then a poet, and they will all bless that corner of earth that gave them a few illusions" (*Posthumous Memoirs*, 70).

Machado deals symbolically throughout his works in unanswered questions and unexplained actions. If time as measurement of life's duration were actually to stop with the absence of hands on the clock, for example, the resulting perception of nothingness would create an abyss of unknown proportions. Machado's major characters constantly face this abyss, which could be expressed metonymically by unmeasured, mysterious, and continuous swinging of pendulums in Rio de Janeiro's clocks. Salvador Dalí's paintings depict melted watches, signaling the collapse of time and the unconscious, employing precise plastic techniques to depict their surrealistic theme. Machado's clocks also convey the uncanny: they maintain their influence, position, shape, and function yet are estranged and emptied by the loss of their hands and thus of their meaning and purpose in their consequent inability to be read. The narrator of the short story "O espelho" ("The Mirror," 1882) remembers reading Henry Wadsworth Longfellow's poem "The Old Clock on the Stairs" (1845):

My solitude took on enormous proportions. Never had days
been so long, never had the sun burned into the earth with such
tiresome obstinacy. The hours were sounded from century to
century by the old clock in the parlor, and the ticktock, ticktock
of its pendulum flicked my inner soul, like a constant fillip of
eternity. Many years later, when I read an American poem—I
think it was one of Longfellow's—and came across the famous
refrain *Never, forever! Forever, never!* I tell you, it made me shiver,
and I thought back to those dreadful days. It was just so with
Aunt Marcolina's clock, *Never, forever!—Forever, never!* They
were not strokes of a pendulum: they were a dialogue from the
pit, a whisper from the void. And then at night! Not that the night
was more silent. Its silence was the same as the day's. But the
night was shadow, it was solitude still more close than the solitude of the day, or more vast. Ticktock, ticktock. No one in the
great rooms, or on the veranda, no one in the halls, no one on
the terrace, no one anywhere. (from *The Psychiatrist and Other
Stories*)

Machado returned to the same image in a chronicle eleven years later, with
an even more sinister hearing of the pendulum beats in what had become
a multiplication of clocks: "To the pre-historic scene, in which the sound
of a shot heard at night was a signal to consult and set the clocks, one
cannot compare these terrible days, in which the strokes seem like bangs
of an enormous clock, of a clock that stops at times, but whose cord is
easily wound: 'Never—forever / Forever—never.' Exactly like the ballad
by Longfellow. Poetry, my friends, is in everything, in war just as in love"
(November 12, 1893).

The ticking pendulum opens the space of an absence, visualizing the
abyss between form and meaning, introducing a gap or missing link, as if
the clock's missing hands pointed to an incoherent, unfinished, or useless
component of descriptive reality, a kind of junk DNA, an oneiric, fantastic
episode whose uncharted and eerie meanings also play a decisive role in
cognition, perception, and behavior. Machado's abysses are thresholds of

madness, estrangement, and surreal dimensions that loom like black holes in human experience and psychology. Here, Machado forms an image of time consonant with Dalí and René Magritte. His strange clock could be a possible subject for a canvas by Magritte, who could have painted the surprisingly surrealistic disconnect between object and concept in a sequence of long pendulums swinging without purpose, floating in seemingly timeless and estranged air, while stores nearby would be filled with elegant handless clocks. Machado's timeless and apparently futile pendulum clock is an imaginative representation of his open concept of narration, in which a far-reaching yet sudden discontinuity or paradox alters or challenges the organization or working of the world. The author breaks the logic of narration in an apparently comic or absurd manner with the intention of challenging the reader to think differently; one form of thinking and representation has been substituted by another, which implies a fault, deficiency, or limitation in the previously primary form.

In Machado's literary world, the characters are aware of the presence of an abyss, a threshold or limit representing the border of civilization with primitivism in its most atavistic psychological and social depths and nothingness in the realms of philosophy and religion. Throughout, Machado's characters face abysses, which correspond to the eerie, haunting, strange dimensions of the world we think we know. The mutual passion felt by Estácio and Helena, for example, when each thinks they are brother and sister, is the subject of a plea by Estácio that expresses a hidden truth that he could only suspect: "Are you sure this mysterious love is really without hope? Nothing in the world is absolutely fixed or unchangeable—neither misfortune nor prosperity. What you imagine lost may only be strayed or hidden from sight" (18). Change in its unexpected comic dimension shocks Brás Cubas when he meets his former schoolmate Quincas Borba, who is now poor and in rags. Before they met in the Passeio Público, Brás had felt "the attraction of the abyss," and on their separation he attempts to turn his thoughts into an adage, "I faced the chasm that separates the hopes of one time from the reality of another" (60). But his superior philosophy is undercut by the discovery that Quincas has stolen his watch. Brás's niece Sabina has promoted a new young bride for Brás, Nhã-loló, after Virgília sailed to the provinces. Sabrina's husband, Cotrim, however, has unstated moral objections, perhaps because of Brás's long affair with Virgília, which Brás attenuates in the telling: "It wasn't brought about by any hate, he appreciated my good qualities—they couldn't be more praiseworthy; it was true, and as for Nhã-loló, he could never deny that she was an excellent bride, but from there to advise marriage there was a wide abyss" (123). In *Esau and Jacob*, the owner of the "Teashop of the Empire," Custódio, is distraught when the republic is declared, since he thinks he will lose his customers because of the name; in a scene worthy of opera buffa, he laments his fate to Ayres and begs for help: "Having recounted what had just transpired, Custódio confessed everything he was losing with the name and the expense, the damage that keeping the name of the house would do, the impossibility of finding another, an abyss, in sum" (63).

The human heart with its unfathomable psychology is another of Machado's abysses. When Luís Alves first inspires curiosity and gratitude in Guiomar, in *The Hand and the Glove*, she delivers up her soul to him, "or into an abyss, which is sometimes the same thing" (13). In *Esau and Jacob*, Natividade had been inexplicably opposed to her husband Santos's idea of marrying Ayres, who long ago had showed interest in her, to his sister-in-law, which leads to another abyss of the heart: "Natividade was opposed; no one ever knew why. It was not jealousy; I don't think it was envy. . . . The displeasure of ceding him to another, or having them happy at her feet, it could not be, although the heart is the abyss of abysses. Let us suppose that it was to punish him for loving her" (12). In *Dom Casmurro*, Bento Santiago shows his readers that he is well aware of the disastrous course in his affairs that is reeling out of control after his reading of Sancha's eyes and his seductive intentions toward her, even if he does not understand the motivation: "The lady reader, who is my friend and has opened this book with the idea of relaxing between yesterday's cavatina and today's waltz, would like to close it in a hurry now that she sees we are skirting an abyss. . . . Don't do it, my dear. I'll wheel about" (119). If Bento had recalled his jealousy of the sea and of Capitu's eyes from chapter 107, he might have found a clue to explain his ulterior motives: "The simple recollection of a pair of eyes is enough to fix other eyes that remember them and delight in imagining them. There is no need of an actual, mortal sin" (107). His promise of restraint to the feminine readers is fortified by his long look at Escobar's photograph on his desk but abrogated for good by the shocking news of Escobar's death by drowning that immediately follows. In *Esau and Jacob*, one of the twins vying for Flora's affections resolves to give up the governorship of Rio if he could be with her in the most remote land possible; however, his romantic sacrifice originates in a malignant wish to exclude and vanquish his brother. Ayres, who is listening to the monologue, excuses it philosophically: "To whomever this monologue might seem egotistical, I ask on behalf of the souls of his parents and friends, who are in heaven, and ask that you consider the causes as well. Consider the state of mind of the young man, the closeness of the young woman, the roots and flowers of passion. Pedro's age, the evils of the earth, the good of the same earth. Consider, too, the will of heaven, which watches over all creatures who love each other, except if just one loves the other, because then heaven is an abyss of iniquities, and this image is meaningless" (*Esau and Jacob*, 52).

The noble madnesses of Quincas Borba and Rubião lead them to cross the fateful abysses into illusion, whether determined by nature or circumstances. The mad philosopher explained the system of *Humanitas* to his caretaker Rubião before returning to Barbacena: "Quincas Borba was not only mad, but he knew that he was mad, and that remnant of awareness, like a dim lamp in the midst of the shadows, greatly complicated the horror of the situation" (159). When he thinks his delirium is starting, his "suburbs of death," as he puts it, before departing from Barbacena to wrap up business in the capital he turns his eyes inward and sees his own brain thinking, and he departs like a soul that has fallen into an abyss: "He was leaving them behind on the good soil of Minas like the last sweat of a dark soul ready to fall into the abyss" (8). Once in Rio de Janeiro and stunned by his passion for Sofia, Rubião soon began to fantasize—perhaps a royal title, a marriage—and he conversed with the dog Quincas Borba, who barked at him to get married: "'Quincas Borba, do you still remember our Quincas Borba? My good friend, my great friend. I was his friend too, two great friends. If he were alive, he'd be the best man at my wedding, at least he'd give the toast in honor of the happy couple—and it would be with a cup made of gold and diamonds that I would have made especially for him. . . . Great Quincas Borba!' And Rubião's spirit hovered over the abyss" (82). Once on the other side of reason, Rubião oscillated for a time between his illusions and fantasies and short periods of release, and he is compared to a man trying to climb his way out of an abyss but invariably destined to fall and lose himself in its deepest recesses: "When Rubião would come out of his delirium, that whole wordy phantasmagoria became a silent sadness for a moment. His consciousness, where traces of his previous state remained, forced him to get rid of them. It was like the painful ascent a man was making from the pit, climbing up the walls, tearing his skin, leaving his nails behind in order to reach the top and not fall back down again and be lost" (179).

Death and suffering add more poignantly to the unknown dimensions and questions. Brás Cubas witnessed the death of the ship captain's wife, Leocádia, and insincerely praised the elegy the captain composed in her memory; when his own mother died after a long agony Brás had no answer to the inexplicable randomness and pain of death: "Why? A creature so docile, so tender, so saintly . . . why did she have to die like that?" For the first time, he "peered into the abyss of the Inexplicable," however spoken with his usual supercilious presumption (24). In *Esau and Jacob*, the agony of death is given its pathetic place on the world's stage when Natividade dies after a few hours of agony, leading Ayres to compose his own miniature "delirium," which is a universal overview of death across time: "Adding up all the hours of death throes that have transpired in this world, how many centuries would they make? Of these, some would be terrible, others melancholy, many desperate, few tedious. In sum, death comes, however long it delays, and plucks its victim away, either from the weeping or the silence" (120). Ayres has just dreamed that Fidélia came to visit him seeking advice whether she should marry or remain a widow; he offered himself, and she agreed: "You are the very one I had in mind." The shock of realizing that his fervent wish was only a dream led him to look beyond his own existence and indeed beyond all present and future events, to foresee that all are devoured in the abyss of time, such that he endorses and repeats Joseph Ernest Renan's exclamation proclaiming devouring to be the only universal law: "Twenty years from now I shall not be here to repeat this reminiscence; another twenty, and there will no longer be a survivor among the journalists, or among the diplomats, or only a rare one, a very rare one; twenty more, and no one. And the earth will continue to whirl round the sun with the same fidelity to the laws that govern them, and the battle of Tuyuty, like Thermopylae, like Jena, will cry out from the depths of the abyss those words of Renan's prayer: 'O abyss! Thou art the only god!'" (May 24, Noon). Brás Cubas had anticipated Ayres in his flippant chapter of maxims: "We kill time; time buries us" (119).

Breaking the Frame:
The Rhetoric of Substitution

Uma vez que não entendiam: reler-me ou calar.
[Given that they didn't understand: reread me or be quiet.]

—Eça de Queirós, *O Primo Basílio*

O espelho partiu / a moldura ficou.
[The mirror broke / the frame remained.]

—Ana Hatherly, *Fibrilações*

THROUGHOUT HIS FICTION Machado de Assis plays with discontinuities. Among those are his frequent conversations with the reader, who is called upon to remember details, to refer to previous chapters, and to solve puzzles. For example, the reader is challenged unexpectedly to remember what happened in a certain earlier chapter, to digest apparently useless and meaningless form and content, and to interpret adages and apostrophes requiring knowledge of broad literary and philosophical information. Narrators apologize for approaching the limits of propriety or for tiring their female readers, and Brás Cubas famously accuses readers of being the biggest defect in his book. The narrator in the story "O segredo do Bonzo" ("The Bonzo's Secret," 1882), a parody of Portuguese religious orders in Japan in the style of Fernão Mendes Pinto, explains the sleight of hand used by the Bonzos to proselytize and gain converts to their doctrine: "I don't think you've captured the true meaning of the doctrine. We aren't supposed to instill in others an opinion that isn't ours, but rather make them believe we can do something we can't do. That is the essence of it."[1] Through such discontinuities, Machado practices a rhetoric of dissimulation and substitution, and he once even imagined the freedom of writing a book without readers.

In addition to playing with the reader, he dots his chapters with un-expected motifs, what could be called Machado's things, being various objects or creatures that he personifies and to which he grants autonomous volition. Their strange actions play out in rhetorical parables reminiscent of moral tales and fables in the tradition of the *Panchatantra*.[2] Stylistic discontinuities further give to his fiction a pointed self-awareness that is allusive, atemporal, and nonlinear. The rhetoric of metonymy displaces observation by converting actions into moral examples, allegories, and aphorisms. José Guilherme Merquior described how dissimulation and inferred meanings are communicated solely through plastic intention: "In *Quincas Borba*, where the motive of dissimulation already announced *Dom Casmurro*, Machado's art is composed of the rhetoric of inference. In this hidden style, metonymy rules: the register of effects suggests their causes, without explaining them. For example: Palha's constrained embarrassment when Sofia tells him about the declaration of love she received from Rubião is communicated through a laconic reference to his gestures" (24). In the story "Capítulo de Chapéus" ("A Chapter of Hats," 1883), Mariana is attempting with all her charms and arguments to get her husband, Conrado, to change the hat he has always worn, and he has just confided that there is a philosophical principle that will not allow him to honor her request. In reaction, Mariana bit her lip, picked up a knife, and began to tap on the table. Conrado understood her gesture and would not allow her to continue, delicately taking the knife out of her hands.

The shuffling of time regularly involves references to chapters almost certainly forgotten by readers, chapters that lie outside of the biographical account and may have been written either before or after the rest of the book. The final chapter of *Dom Casmurro*, for example, "Well, and the Rest," remits readers to chapter 3, "The Information," proposing a relationship that implies the same degree of association and the same inexorable development as a fruit in its rind, the phrase Bento uses as his final metaphor to convince readers of his wife Capitu's guilt. Thus, the act of reading the novel mirrors the *mise en abîme* of the narrator's argument, displacing the continuity of reading enough to suspend analysis and replace it with a concentration of repetitive symbolic keys serving his argument and consonant with his differential logic. On this point, Machado, through Ayres as author-narrator, refines his perverse and malicious play with readers, from whom he has no high expectations, as if defying them to unravel his narrator's intentions: "If no one understands me, I can wait" (*Esau and Jacob*, 38). Readers who are intent on discovering interpretive keys in the recovery of chapters rapidly passed over will find themselves obligated to reconsider their ideas and to reboot their reading, in view of the layered yet fixed structure of the memoir and in consideration of the fatal yet variable events being recounted.

In the chapter "The Dalmatian Revolution," Brás Cubas tells how an unexpected, apparently irrelevant event in an abstract, faraway land could play a crucial role in his life. In fact, Brás is facing his own revolution because Virgília's husband, Lobo Neves, has just accepted a position as provincial governor, and Brás's lover Virgília will be sailing away with him. Brás notes that she secretly felt some pleasure over the prospect of higher political position and a title, even if it involved ending their long affair. Meanwhile, a certain count from the legation of Dalmatia had been attempting to take advantage of her love of nobility. He was a nobleman who pursued her for three months, and Brás was concerned that he might actually turn her head and overcome her newfound virtue. Suddenly a bloody revolution broke out in Dalmatia, overcoming the government and emptying the embassies. Brás balanced the horrors of the revolution against the removal of the dangerous count and found that he actually blessed the tragedy, with the moral excuse that "Dalmatia was so far away!"[3]

Discontinuity is treated metonymically in the episode of Bento's unfinished sonnet, based on the comical conceit that one can be cured of wanting to write in youth but not if the fever strikes later in life. Bento's sonnet is a symbol of the very memoir, which is the story of his unexplained life, as well as an allegory on the construction of meaning.[4] The background comes from the preceding chapter on two of Bento's acquaintances in the seminary, one who has forgotten the verses he wrote in the style of the religious romantic poet Junqueira Freire when Bento reminds him, and another who, to the contrary, has carried his "opusculum" titled *Panegyric of Saint Monica* around with him all his life. It takes him back to his youth and is the sole anchor in his life, representing continuity in the face of ever-changing times. Bento never finished his own poem, although a first line came to him spontaneously (*"O flower of heaven! O flower bright and pure!"*); he decided to make it part of a sonnet and composed the final line (*"Life is lost, the battle still is won!"*), finding it sublime, but he could not compose the twelve connecting lines in the middle. The thought that if he just started to write the other verses would come to him leads to nothing. To fill out the chapter, he writes paragraphs about the possible meaning and logic of his lines, even deciding to alter the meaning of the last line by transposing the verse and its meaning (*"Life is won, the battle is still lost!"*). The chapter is a hilarious parody of writer's block and of the obscure interpretations writers attribute to their least expression, but in terms of displacement it embodies the missing middle. It is an allegory on the necessary but unsubstantial connections made between all beginnings and ends, just as Bento is doing with his past life in these memoirs. There is no necessary connection, their content is debatable, and all readers will fill in the missing middle according to their own talents and ideas.

Machado's pattern of discontinuity forms part of his modern understanding of the relationship of the present to tradition and innovation, found in the hundreds of historical, literary, and philosophical references in his writings. His method of discontinuity and his alteration of references cited in the works can be supported by the analysis of legal discourse written by the jurist and professor of legal theory and history António Manuel Hespanha, who points out that the concept of continuity has been accepted non-critically as a preposition from which to legitimize history. Present knowledge is generally presumed to have roots in the past, from which it has received its fundamental categories, each epoch basing itself on a rereading of inherited tradition. Hespanha affirms, to the contrary, that this is a weak, incomplete understanding of the idea of continuity, since the successive use of texts over time invariably creates new meanings and contents through interaction, which would create reinterpretations. In an essay on the development of a canon of Brazilian and world literature, João Alexandre Barbosa states that, inescapably, literary understanding becomes effective only when informed by historical variation, including the different critical reflections that literary works have provoked over time.[5] Brás Cubas's theory of editions reconfirms this point: "Every season of life is an edition that corrects the one before and which will also be corrected itself until the definitive edition, which the publisher gives to the worms free of charge" (27). Thus, texts inherited from the past can never be the same because they are constantly subjected to changes in new circumstances, and they are not, as assumed, independent of history or unchangeable entities.[6] Belief in their unchangeable meanings or in the inviolable intentions of "founding fathers" leads to a flattening or even to a negation of historical depth, in Hespanha's reading, and promotes an idea of the past that trivializes its difference. Past ideas, feelings, and ways of thinking separate those periods of time profoundly from the present.

In the history of law the idea of continuity has been essential to establish methodology and assert its timeless correctness (*ratio iurus*). The supposition of a nondebatable juridical tradition of reference has been the basis for legitimizing legal knowledge and expanding it to other cultures and areas outside of Europe. Any questioning or challenge to this concept of the immutability of tradition and direct inheritance of unchanged meanings could destabilize accepted values of juridical culture: "If firm convictions in the rationality of law and legal knowledge were to be substituted by relativism, by the idea that the values and methods of law depend on inexplicable discontinuities, then the project of universalizing lettered juridical culture would certainly be threatened."[7] To recuperate original meanings, on the other hand, would require a careful excavation of layers of meaning, as in archaeology. To do so would mean to recuperate the strangeness rather than the familiarity of what was said and to reread each word, concept, and proposition not with our logic but through a reconstruction of the logic of the original text in its time. As a result of this process, what has been made banal through repetition finds new and unexpected meanings in a reconsideration of tradition and, as a result, "The past, in all its scandalous diversity, is reencountered" (65). Machado's story "The Devil's Church" makes a comparable argument, when God rebukes the

Devil on the founding of his reverse church: "You are banal, which is the worst thing that could happen to a spirit of your kind. Everything you're saying or may say has already been said and re-said by the moralists of the world. It's a hackneyed subject, and if you haven't enough resourcefulness or originality to restate it in a new light, it would be best for you to be quiet and forget about it." Machado was engaged in a critical rereading and reinterpretation of the past that questioned the legitimizing framework of empire, or indeed of any legal, political, or philosophical system.

In terms of style, the extensive use of discontinuity, surprise, dissimulation, and allusion—even madness and nonsense—forms part of a different construct of sense that arises from the experience of estrangement, especially evident in Machado's non-chapters or empty chapters. Style provides its own distance from and perspective on reality. In the story "Último Capítulo" ("Final Chapter," 1883) Matias considers the adverb *happily* to be an anomaly in his life: "Continue reading and you will see that the adverb belongs to stylistics, not to life; it's a matter of transition, nothing more." From the *Posthumous Memoirs of Brás Cubas*, "The Old Dialogue of Adam and Eve" is composed entirely of punctuation; the chapter "Epitaph" reproduces the wording on Nhã-loló's tombstone; and "Uselessness" confesses itself in one sentence to be a useless chapter. The practice can be thought of as a kind of wit that disrupts commonplaces and leads to unexpected perceptions. In music, Rosen describes a comparable effect in modulations within the classical style, which produce meaning out of irregularity: "If wit can take the form of a surprising change of nonsense into sense, a classical modulation gives a splendid formula: all we need . . . is one moment when we are not sure what the meaning of a note is . . . indispensable, of course, is the irregularity of the phrase rhythm . . . and the tone of witty conversation that characterizes the thematic material" (52). Applied to rhetoric and literature, the word that coordinates two disparate meanings confuses verbal concordance, subordinates meaning to syntax, and disrupts linear reading. After a short adjustment, what was out of place— the buffoonery and comic play—seems suddenly and perfectly to express the subtle wit the author intended. The process may be compared to modulation to a distant key, which often invokes an unexpected musical logic, before a return to the tonic. Zulficar Ghose explains how intrusions, absurd humor, nonsense, and asymmetry lead to a deeper depiction of reality and to a greater degree of verisimilitude than are found in conventional narratives:

> Machado developed the elements of his style in the *Posthumous Memoirs of Brás Cubas* which he then used to perfection in *Dom Casmurro* and with great assurance in the two novels that followed. He mastered the construction of short chapters as in Sterne's *A Sentimental Journey*. Then he introduced a second element—apparent irrelevance, a method not unlike Polonius's instructions to Reynaldo, telling him to proceed by "encompassment and drift of question" and by "indirections find directions out." Sometimes an entire chapter will be an absurd episode humorously presented with trivial details that are apparently unrelated to the main action; some readers must find such seemingly self-indulgent intrusions somewhat trying if not plainly irritating—what merit, for example, could they discover in a chapter that has only the sentence, "And, if I am not greatly mistaken, I have just written an utterly unnecessary chapter"? But it is precisely these chapters that contain clues to a larger understanding of the text and also suggest a truer depiction of reality than is to be found in those conventional narratives which rigidly exclude that which is not obviously "relevant." Machado himself says as much in one such chapter: "How much better it would be to tell things smoothly, without all these jolts!"[8]

In the story "The Captain of Volunteers," Simão notes how Maria would have tearfully confessed her secret meetings with him to her steady companion X through a language of indirectness: "She would probably use circumlocutions and synonyms, vague and truncated phrases, and at times only gestures."

Machado's Things

Machado's disjointed rereading of the past accompanies a further innovation in his approach to writing, which is his practice of breaking the literary frame. Machado catches the reader unaware by practicing radical breaks in the narrative frame to reach beyond a linear concept of the experience of reading. His purpose is to help the reader find the strangeness rather than the familiarity of the text. Fetishistic objects are spread throughout his fiction to break the frame of narration both through their allegorical function and through their strange, illogical intromission into the story line. Machado's pendulum, as independent actor, joins this extensive list of objects, body parts, and assorted creatures that appear in all of Machado's fictions— poultices, legs, trapezes, hats, flowers, balls, benches, chairs—that are personified and seem to govern humanity with a mysterious independent will and force all their own. They include the most typical symbols of destiny in Machado's works: the black butterflies, the rats and worms that chew books, the winds and waves of the sea, starlight, ants, and swallows. The narrator of *Quincas Borba* explains the partnership between men and things, calling it one of the most interesting on earth: "The expression 'Talking to his buttons,' which looks like a simple metaphor for 'Talking to himself,' is a phrase with a real and direct meaning. The buttons operate synchronically with us, forming a kind of senate, handy and cheap, that always votes in favor of our motions" (*Quincas Borba*, 142). The repertoire of animated objects originates in the fable and moral tale, although in Machado's writings they are invoked as if their function were primal, disconnected from the surface meaning and the context. In *Quincas Borba*, when D. Fernanda and Maria Benedita rise from the bench where they have been seated to discuss Maria Benedita's secret passion to attend to a distraught Teófilo, the bench feels a sudden freedom: "There remained the bench alone, now free of the women, feeling the full rays of the sun, that doesn't fall in love or make speeches." In the short story "The Mirror," the idea of an external soul is embodied in things that come to circumscribe and control the protagonist's existence: "a polka, whist, a book, a machine, a pair of boots, a cavatina, a drum, etc. . . . losing the external soul means losing an entire existence."

All through the novels there is a rhythm and sequence of unusual, unexpected things—objects, insects, body parts, animals, natural phenomena—each assigned an independence and will of its own, all of which synthesize nuclear ideas by a rhetoric of substitution. These objects express both plastic intention and taboo in Machado's prose theater: their physical presence substitutes for the missing subjects and incomplete ideas they deceptively replace, whether of moral, philosophical, or allegorical import. Their relationship to a field of meaning in the novels is not immediately apparent and is purposefully estranged. As mysterious objects removed from context, like Carlos Drummond de Andrade's stone in the middle of the road, they play a role assigned to fetishistic objects.[9] They ward off taboo by deflecting forbidden subjects onto acceptable substitutes. Machado's things concentrate their power and magical effects, and their very purpose in the narrative seems puzzling and mysterious to the narrators. Their strange fetishistic presence gives them the power to concentrate latent or underlying theories and ideas, acting as intermediaries or substitutes whose relationship to their occult subject matter must be explored by the reader via the rhetoric of substitution, in which one term is very distantly related to another. Brás must answer the trapeze in his brain on which all his ideas hang. The ideas go through daring antics, waving their arms and legs to attract his attention; finally confronting him, an idea takes the shape of an X and challenges him in the words with which the Sphinx proposes an enigma that Oedipus must solve: "Decipher me or I'll devour you" (2). José Pereira da Graça Aranha explains how maxims and Machado's things work together in his fiction to make them more penetrating and suggestive: "The words, the verb, the expressions that dress his things are his imaginary game, his gymnastics in a secret room. After letting the sentence drag along, the marvelous illusionist makes it jump suddenly and likes the jump, an intentional acrobatics that entertains and enchants us."[10]

In one of the most prominent episodes in the *Posthumous Memoirs*, a black butterfly enters Brás Cubas's room. Brás had become enchanted with young Eugênia, the sixteen-year-old daughter of D. Eusébia, for her composure and grace. He envisioned a butterfly with golden wings and diamond eyes flying behind her sparkling eyes, when to the contrary a black butterfly fluttered onto the veranda, scaring both women until Brás shooed it away with his handkerchief. In the following chapter, a black butterfly entered his bedroom and settled on a portrait of his father. Brás had previously felt a desire to be a father when he witnessed D. Eusébia give a tender kiss to her daughter; here, he detects a mocking attitude in the black butterfly, aimed at his fascination with Eugênia, and swats it with a towel. The creature takes a few seconds to die in his hand, and he feels remorse, finally placing the blame on the inexplicable or unfathomable nature of things with a question: "Why couldn't it have been blue?" Referring subconsciously to his lost chance at fatherhood, his question foreshadows Brás's existential question about Eugênia when he discovers that she has been lame since birth, a golden butterfly blackened by physical disability, and questions: "Why beautiful if lame? Why lame if beautiful?"

After this rhetorical substitution, Brás's hidden wish to be a father is expressed in another mythical allegory of origin, a genesis myth that is a miniature version of his earlier delirium and again a critique of Pandora as creator and destroyer. He imagines that the butterfly had never seen a man and after observing his colossal stature supposed he was the inventor of butterflies. The portrait would then be the father of the inventor of butterflies. The missing triad of this generative father-son myth, the Holy Ghost, is supplied by the blue immensity of the sky, the flowers and green leaves that had given joy to the butterfly's adventures. Its spiritual universe came to a brutal end by human hand with the blow of a towel. Brás considers that his act proved his superiority to butterflies, as if he were master of the natural world; however, he soon repeated his question about the nature of fate and rationality in this world: "I think it would have been better had it been born blue." Nature and culture are again placed in comical opposition, like an interlude of opera buffa, through Brás's symbolic actions and questions.

Brás's greatest project is the dream of inventing a poultice to cure melancholic humanity. Besides philanthropy, his goal is eternal glory in the three words "Brás Cubas Poltice" that will be printed on every box of medicine and every announcement—a beneficial invention that will resolve an eternal dilemma of humankind. Melancholia is associated with the four humors of Hippocratic medicine, representing black bile alongside yellow bile, phlegm, and blood, and traced historically to Hippocrates's treatise "On the Nature of Man." Brás's two intentions may reflect a dual interpretation of melancholia over time; whereas Hippocrates regarded it as a disease indicated by symptoms of fear and despondency, Aristotle considered it a positive indication of artistic, intellectual, or philosophical temperaments. Connected to the planet Saturn, melancholia came to be associated with communication with nether regions and the immaterial world. More relevant to Brás, renaissance Neoplatonism linked melancholia to love, which sentiment it could provoke and dominate, making Brás its easy and noble victim. According to the literary scholar Vítor Aguiar e Silva, melancholia produces recognition of the fragmentation, caducity, fragility, and uncertainty of the present and instills a dynamic return to the original world of the Father.[11] Machado follows Camões, who represented the most extreme expression of melancholia in the second half of the sixteenth century in his anguished awareness of the absurdity and disconcert of the world, which no spiritual values could make coherent: "There love has hidden a flaw that kills and can't be seen / For some days he's put in my soul / what I don't know, or from where it comes / or how it arrives, or why it hurts." Machado makes his presentation of melancholia satirical, however, following the tradition of Menippean satire in Richard Burton's *Anatomy of Melancholy*, the subject of parody in Sterne's *Tristram Shandy*, cited by Brás in his note "To the reader." Machado assumes Burton's digressive style, his encyclopedic references, and his satirical tone and humor. Taken from Burton as well is the notion that melancholy is an attribute of mortality to which all are subject and no one can escape: "That idea was nothing less than the invention of a sublime remedy, an anti-hypochondriacal poultice, destined to alleviate our melancholy humanity" (2). Brás's remedy that he never invents sets a comical mode for a memoir of relived experience, including the fantasy of imagined outcomes, naturally melancholic since it was written after death.

Brás dedicates a chapter to "Legs." After venting his rage at Virgília for not running away with him as he proposed, he has calmed her by confessing that his madness and insanity were caused only by his love for her. At that moment the baroness arrives with Brás still in the house, and her verbal exuberance is full of inferences about love affairs and praise for the elegance of Candiani at the opera. Brás excuses himself and once on the street becomes preoccupied with the suspicions of all those in the house, particularly those of the experienced baroness. His legs are his protective subconscious mind, as they carry him down the street automatically without his realizing it until he finds himself in front of the Hotel Pharoux, where he had the habit of dining. The two legs carried on a dialogue as if in a subconscious theater: "He's got to eat, it's dinnertime, let's take him to the Pharoux. Let's divide up his consciousness, one part can stay with the lady, we'll take over the other part so that he goes straight ahead, doesn't bump into people or carriages, tips his hat to acquaintances and, finally, arrives safe and sound at the hotel." Machado forms a theory of the subconscious mind that remains lucid during Brás's somnambulism. When he comes to, Brás exclaims, "Blessed legs!" and decides to immortalize them for being the invisible half of his divided consciousness.

Rolling balls form a comic metaphysical theory in the chapter "What Aristotle Left Out," through which Machado shows his interest in involuntary and subconscious forces. Like a carom shot in billiards, Brás puts his life in motion: "Put a ball in motion. . . . It rolls, touches another ball, transmits the impulse, and there you have the second ball rolling like the first." The first ball, Marcela, touches the second ball, Brás Cubas, which touches the third ball, Virgília. Brás's scenario illustrates how extremes come into contact even though they have had nothing to do with each other. This story is a corollary to the pendulum clock with no hands in that the extremes become connected through the transmission of an underlying, unseen force. The result is unintended and almost oxymoronic since human aversion when touched by an outside force in this case produces solidarity. In *Esau and Jacob* Flora is compared to the goddess of dance,

Terpsichore; however, her indecision between the suitors Pedro and Paulo does not progress beyond dance and contra dance, leaving her bored and dubious. The narrator Ayres interrupts to exclaim about the ungovernable forces by which things collide and are repelled by others, in which only the passage of time is the constant backdrop for human action: "What a multitude of factors in life, reader! Some things are born from others, bump into each other, repel each other, are confused with one another, and lose each other, and time marches on without losing itself" (48).

The "theory of the nose" divides time between motion or stasis and life between multiplication and equilibrium. On the question of the purpose of the nose, the narrator rejects Dr. Pangloss's explanation that it was created for the use of eyeglasses in favor of the nose as a point of concentration and meditation, as practiced by the fakirs who spend long hours detached from the world trying to grasp celestial light by looking at the tips of their noses. Contemplation is the equilibrium of societies, he says, as each man has the need to search for celestial light; yet a world of people contemplating noses would die out. Time inhibits and restricts contemplation through two capital forces, love and multiplication of the species versus contemplation and equilibrium. Those two opposing forces can be brought into equilibrium through another of Brás Cubas's theories, the sublime law of the equivalency of windows, by which actions are universally reciprocal: for each closed window another must be opened. In the chapter "Mine," Brás has found a gold coin, a half doubloon in the street, which he thinks should be his. Ethics, however, tells him that the coin has an owner and perhaps a needy one, so he sends a letter off to the chief of police asking his cooperation in returning the coin to its owner, for which letter he gains wide local notoriety. In the next chapter he finds a package on the beach containing not one coin but five *contos* in good banknotes and coins, "all clean and in neat order, a rare find." Brás fears that some servants have spied on him but, becoming convinced they have not, keeps the package. While depositing it in the Banco do Brasil he is congratulated on the matter of the one gold coin he returned. Once again it is a matter of multiplication versus equilibrium placed in comic and hypocritical reciprocity.

Creatures are heard giving advice to humans. Brás Cubas listens as a bat climbing to the roof of his carriage speaks to him to correct his impressions that he has been rejuvenated by a newfound youthful energy. Seeing Virgília at a ball for the first time since her return to Rio de Janeiro, Brás is stunned by her mature beauty and by the aura of his amorous adventure; he feels like dancing the polka under the chandeliers and in the bubble of conversation. When he entered his coach, his fifty years were waiting for him, and he felt the numbness of fatigue. The bat tells him the undesirable truth: the rejuvenation was in the room, the brilliant objects, the people, but not in himself with his fifty years. In *Dom Casmurro*, a young Bento Santiago listens to a coconut palm, birds, butterflies, and a grasshopper magically tell him that a youth is supposed to get into corners with girls of fourteen. After Capitu challenges Bento with a series of questions about his loyalty to her versus his mother and receives insincere answers, she carves the word "liar" in the dirt. Bento claims not to understand the reason for the word, his head is a vacuum, and he fears that someone else may see it. At this moment some swallows fly over the garden and head toward the Morro de Santa Theresa. When the two reconcile and Capitu invents an innocent but false reason for having raised her questions, Bento finds her even more captivating, and at that moment the swallows return from the opposite direction. The passage of the birds contrasts their freedom of flight to the couple's oscillation between truth and illusion, fear and affection. When Bento is trying to complete his sonnet he thinks of opening a window, in the hope that fireflies in the night would look like rhymes and would write out the verses he was unable to conceive, ready-made with rhyme and sense. When Counselor Ayres converses with Tristão over breakfast at Paneiras, two great black birds cut through the air at the moment Tristão pauses in his first confession to the counselor of his love for Fidélia and his doubts that it will be corresponded. Ayres is discreet and smiles, possibly because of his own hidden affection for Fidélia and Rita's wager, unknown to Tristão. For him, the black birds are a couple, he pursuing and she saying no. By suggesting to Tristão that perhaps Fidélia already loved him, Ayres knows he has overstepped the bounds of discretion and of his metaphor.

After Estácio has pleaded with Helena to delay her marriage to his friend Mendonça, a union recommended by Father Belchior to cut off the passion that brother and sister felt for each other, the two are silent. Estácio absentmindedly takes a twig and breaks up the silent march of a column of ants bearing green leaves. The ants flee, while others try to press on. Helena seizes the twig, and Estácio ends the scene by openly opposing her marriage to Mendonça because he considers it to be an inglorious and unnecessary sacrifice, and secretly because of the passion he nourishes for her. The ants had meanwhile returned to their precise formation. Estácio compared them to his ideas and concluded that he too needed a twig to scatter them so they could re-form with less confusion. Another caravan of ants appears, on the windowsill in *Quincas Borba*, when Rubião is annoyed by the vision in which he threatened the seamstress and also by his assumption that Sofia is having an affair with Carlos Maria. In a reprise of Brás Cubas's episode with the black butterfly, Rubião takes a towel and swats the ants, killing many of them. Since they stand for Sofia, he comes to imagine that some of them have attractive bodies and figures, whence he regrets his action. A cicada's singing distracts him, and the narrator accuses the reader of thinking that the song is sufficient consolation for the dead ants. Machado has reversed a fable of Jean de la Fontaine, "La cigale et la fourmi," so that rather than invite the ants to dance, the cicada announces their deaths and says laughingly, "Vous marchiez? J'en suis fort aisé. Eh bien! Mourez maintenant" (Are you walking? Fine with me. But now it's time to die). Rubião may regret his act, but he cannot restore life to the dead any more than he can reverse or truncate the passions he has envisioned in his imagination. In her confusion about the implication of Rubião's invitation to go riding to Tijuca with him—thinking of being alone with him, with the city at a distance and open sky above, she had imagined she felt a kiss on the back of her neck—Sofia interrogates roses and other plants in her garden. Two roses that Rubião had been admiring engage in a dialogue, a debate over her best course of action. The first rose sanctions her anger, thinks Rubião is not worth her love, promises other suitors, and urges her to forget him; the second rose notes Rubião's fidelity and devotion, his patience in waiting seemingly forever for her, his discreet and blameless character, advises Sofia to take him as a lover if she needs someone outside of her marriage, and accuses her of being unjust (141).

Machado writes that a pair of spectacles is required for his readers "to penetrate what is less clear or totally obscure" (*Esau and Jacob*, 13). Those spectacles are the novel's iconic image, presiding over other specific clues the author has provided for the reader to open the text. In the case of *Esau and Jacob* it is a verse from Dante, and in other novels it may be a quotation from Shakespeare or from an opera libretto. The spectacles will also help the reader to see the pieces in the chess game that Machado plays with them. Machado defines reading as both collaboration and an exchange of pieces with the author–chess player. Thus the spectacles, like 3D glasses, focus the image and separate the clues from the remainder of the narrative game.

The Rhetoric of Substitution

To encourage an estranged reading, Machado employs a rhetoric of substitution composed of classical figures, including metonymy, synecdoche, metalepsis, syllepsis, and zeugma. For example, an object is not called by its name but is modified by another name that may be far removed yet associated with it, or a single verb coordinates two related or antithetical objects or meanings. In the short story "Uma senhora" (A lady, 1883), the narrator describes the beautiful D. Camila as looking much younger than her thirty-six years, as if she were still in the "casa" of her twenty-ninth year; noting that "house" is only a common way of speaking, the narrator turns on the same word from the topic of age to the house from which D. Camila is trying to excuse herself in order to escape the continual music, dancing, and games her hosts are using to keep her from leaving. In a chronicle, Machado explains the double use of the word "meteor": "If I say that life is a meteor the reader will think I'm going to write about philosophy, when I'm only going to tell about the *Meteoro*, an eight-page journal that announces: 'The *Meteoro* has no pretension to last'" (November 1, 1877). Through the use of these devices, Machado switches descriptive meaning to a higher plane of abstraction involving wry humor; vocabulary is a springboard for reaching wider frames of reading and interpretation. On the basic level of composition of sentences, these resources formalize dissimulation, substitution, deception, and displacement. They constitute an organizing principle that juxtaposes Brás's atemporal view from eternity with a linear account of his life since birth.

Narration on contrary spheres constitutes one of the pillars of comedy in Machado's works because of the tension produced by the coupling of contrary objects of a verb or the preposterous junction of two remotely comparable things and ideas. In *Dom Casmurro*, Bento compares a loving portrait of his parents to a lottery ticket: "What you read in the face of both is that if conjugal felicity can be compared to the grand prize in a lottery, they had won it with the ticket they purchased together. I conclude that lotteries should not be abolished" (7). The rhetoric of substitution makes it possible for Machado to organize the jumps and incongruities in narrative voice that allow Brás Cubas to have a voice to recount his life, for example, and at the same time completely transform the genre of memoirs by making it atemporal, by overlapping linear and omniscient accounts.

Through these rhetorical devices Machado is able to advance comparable techniques used almost two centuries before by Maistre and Sterne, both cited by Machado in the introduction to Brás Cubas's memoirs. *Voyage autour de ma chambre* provides a model for the constriction of death and the liberty of memory in Brás's memoirs, since Maistre wrote his book while imprisoned in Turin for six months as the result of a duel. Although he is confined in a small space, his room expands with his imagination and the different proportions and angles he gives it:

> My room lies in the forty-fifth degree of latitude . . . it extends from east to west, and forms an oblong square of thirty-six steps along the wall. But I shall make many more steps during my journey, for I shall cross my room in all directions, without rule or method. Zig-zags may also occur, and I shall, if it be necessary, describe all sorts of geometrical figures. . . . While traveling within my chamber, I seldom go in a straight line, but from my writing table I repair to a picture which stands in one corner;

I advance obliquely towards the door; and . . . if I meet on my
way with a chair, I make no compliments but throw myself in
its arms. . . . The hours glide away and fall silently into eternity, without making us sensible of their passage.[12]

In a chapter of *Quincas Borba*, Machado makes fun of methodical books
that are unlike his own: "Here's where I would have liked to have followed
the method used in so many other books—all of them old—where the subject matter of the chapter is summed up: 'How this came about and more
to that effect.' There's Bernardim Ribeiro, there are other wonderful books.
Of those in foreign tongues, without going back to Cervantes or Rabelais,
we have enough with Fielding and Smollett, many of whose chapters get
read only through their summaries" (112).

In the preface to *Tristram Shandy*, Sterne repeats the contrasting
rhythm of reality and imagination, restriction and movement in his novel:
"I will tell you in three words what the book is. It is a history. A history! Of
who? what? where? when? Don't hurry yourself. It is a history book, Sir
(which may possibly recommend it to the world) of what passes in a man's
own mind."[13] The text begins with humor by contradiction in contrasting
a Greek epigraph by Epictetus, "Not things, but opinions about things, trouble men," with a character who takes no personal responsibility and
blames his parents for his misfortunes. Machado's major difference from
these earlier authors' works is that he is affected not by time but by eternity: he accomplishes this advancement by using the voice of a purported
dead man to break the literary frames and conventions of his time.

As a dead narrator, Brás exists in eternity, yet he seems to be alive
enough to tell a successive linear, if digressive, story that is legible to living
readers. He switches fluidly from the concrete sphere of past events and social contacts of daily life to an abstract sphere of meditation, reference, and
observation, free both of prejudice and of discretion: he knows from experience that "there is nothing as incommensurable as the disdain of the dead,"
yet people carry watches in order to know the exact time of their deaths or
even of the end of the world. These tensions compose his irony and sup-

port his serene, reflective, and fatal philosophy. The rhetoric of substitution throughout his fiction allows for external actions or figures to represent unseen yet effective levels of meaning.

In *The Hand and the Glove*, Estévão awakes after spending the night at Luís Alves's house on Botafogo beach; washed and dressed, he goes into the garden separated from the estate next door by a fence. Amid the fragrance of flowers and the singing of birds, he is distracted by a bathrobe that comes out of the house next door, as that was all he could see. Estévão thought the bathrobe was about to have a soul, and he strained with excitement and curiosity to see who it was, but the bathrobe continued walking along on its own. Estévão tried to see within and beyond it but was left with only suppositions and literary reminiscences: perhaps it was a seraphim of Friedrich Klopstock or a fairy godmother of Shakespeare, he mused? His memory made the bathrobe ethereal and transparent, although he could not see beyond its white muslin fabric and sapphire buttons. The bathrobe is a synecdoche for Guiomar, whom he will soon meet.

Brás Cubas chooses as a metaphor the nature and effects of sedimentation to mirror his rival Lobo Neves's "moral geology . . . the layers of character that life alters, preserves, or dissolves according to their resistance." The fundamental layer, a certain dignity, is made of rock that keeps him out of political deals, while earth and sand fill out the composition as an example of volubility, which he calls life's perpetual torrent. He has added the adjective "perpetual" both to refer to the rather coarse and questionable nature of Lobo Neves's activities and to describe its constant excess in what Brás comically calls "young, hot countries" (87).

Quincas Borba, the mad philosopher, gives his name to his dog—"a dog, a handsome dog, medium sized, the color of lead with black patches"—for two reasons. The dog illustrates his philosophy of *Humanitas*—given that the principle of life exists everywhere, it also exists in his dog—and if he should die first his name will live on in the dog. Quincas's great book of doctrine would doubtless make him immortal, he says, yet he thinks of those who cannot read, and for them he leaves the direct bond of a creature with his name. Rubião becomes convinced that the barking Quincas carries on the life and ideas of his master, as he lectures his guests while on the border of sanity:

"The truth is that there's a great man inside him," he said. "The philosopher, the other Quincas Borba," the guest went on, looking around at the newer ones to show the intimacy of his relationship with Rubião. But he couldn't keep the advantage to himself because the other friends from the same period repeated in a chorus: "That's right, the philosopher." And Rubião would explain to the newcomers the reference to the philosopher and the reason for the dog's name, which they had all attributed to him. Quincas Borba (the deceased) was described and spoken of as one of the greatest men of his time—superior to his fellow countrymen. A great philosopher, a great soul, a great friend. And at the end, after a moment of silence, rapping with his fingers on the edge of the table, Rubião exclaimed: "I would have made him a minister of state!" (133)

Natividade, in the first scenes of *Esau and Jacob*, visits the old *cabocla* at the Morro do Castelo to learn the fortunes of her twin sons. She was so elated with the prophecy that on passing Misericórdia and São José streets, she selected a new two-thousand-*réis* bill and put it in the bowl of an alms collector. The collector shouted two blessings and wished that they be multiplied with all the happiness of heaven and earth. The note was crisp, clean, real, and valuable; he thinks it must have been intended for him. Years later it is Nóbrega, the poor collector, who is in the coachman's seat. He had traveled and returned with some wealth, which again increased greatly. Beset both with fear and nostalgia, Nóbrega revisits the Rua São José and envisions the two-thousand-*réis* note floating in the air, which functions as one of Machado's pendulums. He considers it a gift from his saint, Saint Rita de Cássia herself, since the portion that he spent was multiplied. When he first received the note, he attributed the gift to a clandestine amorous adventure, and now it is he who will seek to court Natividade. While in his reverie, he hears a woman beg for alms; rather than a few small coins, Nóbrega searches for an old two-thousand-*réis* note and hands it to the astonished woman, who kisses it in gratitude. Nóbrega is touched by his own spontaneous act of homage to his past memory, to the point that he imagines that the note he had just given to the woman was the same one he had received years before: "Perhaps it was the same one!" (76).

Paired chapters in the *Posthumous Memoirs* are constructed on the disparity by which different terms relate. Dona Plácida is a poor old woman who had worked for Virgília's family until she married; now Brás calls her to care for the house in Gamboa in which he and Virgília will carry on their affair. Dona Plácida struggled to overcome her moral objections, wept, and avoided looking at Brás during the first two months. Brás overcame her scruples by making up a "novel" with stories of his great love, the husband's cruelty, the father's resistance, and so on, which Dona Plácida accepted through obligation. To solidify the fiction, Brás gave her the package of five *contos* he had found in Botafogo as security for her old age. In the next chapter Brás feels the tedium of the book and nostalgia for this episode of his life, which will fall like all the other splendorous leaves of a season. The chapter telling of Dona Plácida's tragic life story begins with the little silver coins the couple placed in her pocket to assure her acquiescence. In her life she was fated to work for survival and fear of ending up a beggar on the street: "You don't get this way by chance, sir. God knows how you get this way" (74). In the connected chapter, Brás imagines her conception in a theatrical scene involving a sexton and a lady in the cathedral. Empty sexuality is the motivation for her existence, and when she asks those parents why they called her into being, their answer is a corollary of Brás's call to her: "We called you to burn your fingers on pots, your eyes in sewing, to eat poorly or not at all, to go from one place to another in drudgery getting ill and recovering only to get ill and recover once again, sad now, then desperate, resigned tomorrow, but always with your hands on the pot and your eyes on the sewing until one day you end up in the mire or in the hospital. That's why we called you in a moment of sympathy" (75). Years later Virgília writes to Brás asking him to visit Dona Plácida, who is very ill, and have her admitted to the hospital. Once again, paired chapters contrast his reaction: remembering the five *contos*, he imagines that Dona Plácida has squandered her fortune on parties and her current address to be a humiliating alley. There he finds her in rags and poverty; there, she will be found dead the next morning. Brás judges Dona Plácida's life solely by her temporary usefulness to him in sustaining the effervescence of his affair with Virgília; in the paired chapter he confirms her ill-fated life with the story of a stonemason who pretended to be in love with her, married her, took her money, and fled. Without sympathy, he calls this chapter unnecessary, as it repeats all the evils that have plagued Dona Plácida since her ill-fated birth.

In *Counselor Ayres' Memorial*, on November 11, 1888, Fidélia is in her garden with brush and palette in her hands. She modestly asks Counselor Ayres not to look, a request to which he acquiesces immediately and answers with the required polite admiration. This is the first time he has observed a female artist, and he finds her charming and without airs of self-importance. Tristão arrived and also praised her work, more effusively, although his compliments did not elicit any smile or sign of special appreciation. Ayres, who suspects a special relationship to be developing between them, finds her concentration on the seascape she is painting has made it seem as if there is no conversation going on. He is puzzled by her silence and her close attention to the painting in their company and wonders if it is love of art or another hidden attraction that motivates her. His thought applies to Machado's full fictional world: "The secret motive of an action many times escapes the sharpest eyes" (November 11).

SEVEN

Machado's World Library

Leio por instruir-me, ás vezes por consolar-me. Creio nos livros e adoro-os.
[I read for instruction, at times for consolation.
I believe in books and adore them.]

—"Job," *Diário do Rio* (March 1867)

Uma infinidade de ecos, que pareciam as próprias vozes antigas.
[An infinity of echoes . . . the voices of the ancients.]

—*Esau and Jacob*, chapter 33

Não se usavam almanaques. Vivia-se sem eles; negociava-se, adoecia-se,
morria-se, sem consultar tais livros. Conhecia-se a marcha do sol
e da lua; contavam-se os meses e os anos; era, ao cabo, a mesma
coisa; mas não se nomeavam dias nem meses, nada; tudo ia
correndo, como passarada que não deixava vestígio no ar.
[Almanacs were not used. One lived without them, negotiated, fell ill, died,
without consulting such books. The march of the sun and moon were known;
months and years could be counted; it was, all told, the same thing;
but days and months did not have names, nothing; things kept going,
like a flock of birds that left no trace in the air.

—"How almanacs were invented"]
—"Almanaque das Fluminenses," 1890.

ONE HUNDRED YEARS BEFORE MACHADO, Denis Diderot
and Jean Le Rond d'Alembert were writing, editing, and compiling an encyclopedia covering all branches of knowledge, describing the taxonomy
of human memory, reason, and imagination with the support of more than
thirty French *encyclopedistes*, intellectuals seeking to expand learning and
reason for an enlightened and transoceanic republic of letters.[1] Their ideal
and purpose were transcendental: "The goal of an *Encyclopédie* is to assemble all the knowledge scattered on the surface of the earth, to demon-

strate the general system to the people with whom we live, & to transmit it to the people who will come after us, so that the works of centuries past is not useless to the centuries which follow, that our descendants, by becoming more learned, may become more virtuous & happier, & that we do not die without having merited being part of the human race."[2] Machado applied the vision of a comprehensive encyclopedia to the compilation of a personal world library of texts composed of all the books read and discussed by the intellectuals of his day, and he incorporated that library into his fiction as counterpoint to narrative.[3] His character Rubião in *Quincas Borba* became the author of an imaginary library by editing and correcting so many phrases that "he ended up writing all the books he'd ever read" (113).

Rubião's fantasy marked a change in the critical devouring of the universal cultural heritage: his imaginary authorship is an appropriation and deconstruction of the world library, carried out with desacralizing humor, satire, and a differential nationalism that absorbs and transforms the universal library. In confusing the particular with the universal, Rubião's delirium reaffirms the scope of libraries: "Isn't a private library simply a universal legacy pretending to be an individual one?"[4] In the short story "O Cônego, ou metafísico do estilo" ("The Canon, or Metaphysics of Style," 1885), Canon Matias plans his unwritten sermon in a vast, unknown world of words and ideas in which remote voices overlap in an obscure yet grand unity, drawn from such diverse sources as Plato, Spinoza, and St. Thomas Aquinas, yet all are guided by a secret affinity. Matias attributes sex to parts of speech, thus nouns and adjectives come together to form both discourse and intercourse by the force of their own physical and sexual attraction. Coming from a wide world of knowledge, they draw upon theology, philosophy, liturgy, geography, history, ancient and modern examples, dogma, and syntax. All are attracted by a fatal natural law of grammar and procreation across the ages. Machado's world library is spawned from this vast unknown world, bringing together the voices of the ancients, whether in harmony or discord, to form a Song of Songs that is the repository of human knowledge and experience.

Machado's readers receive a startling piece of advice on the first page of *Dom Casmurro*: "Don't consult dictionaries." Bento Santiago explains that the term "casmurro," applied to him by a young poet on the suburban train, does not have the same meaning that dictionaries give to the term, which is a stubborn or introverted person, rather than the obstinate, irritated person that the poet characterized. His advice becomes very instructive if applied to the encyclopedic citation of sources spread by the hundreds throughout Machado's works. Those copious references go through a comparable process of decontextualization; they lose their historical or literary specificity when recalled and applied to Machado's world. The reader-researcher is obligated to play the role of archaeologist, first searching for the meaning and context of the historical references, only to find the allegorical or symbolic clues or threads of comparison ready to be applied to a fictional situation in order to uncover or interpret Machado's intended deeper meaning of an action, passage, or character. Taking on the role of archivist of readings and references from the encyclopedia, Machado occupies a position superior to that of his readers in that he directs and controls the redirection of the Western archive while he adapts it to his fiction. His references alter the very act of reading, while drawing in the reader as an accomplice and participant. Machado takes readers on a tour of literature, a voyage around his literary room to get to know his favorite titles from the collections of world literature at his disposal in Rio de Janeiro.

Machado's world library of references and citations is a hybrid mixture of a long list of books and authors since biblical and classical times, which he blended because he recognized that identical themes and expressions of philosophical truth are found in all eras. The mixture is nonlinear and free of chronology. His fictional works became repositories of this information and knowledge, which he cited or creatively altered, modified, falsified, or parodied in order to draw comparisons and to promote reflections on his subjects from a position outside the text. He freely makes fun of Hamlet: "Há entre o céu e a terra, Horácio, muitas coisas mais do que sonha a vossa vã dialética" (Between heaven and earth, Horatio, there are many more things than dreamt of in your vain dialectic); "Há entre o Palácio do Conde dos Arcos e a Rua do Ouvidor muitas bocas mais do que cuida vossa inútil estatística" (*Quincas Borba*, 169; Between the Conde dos Arcos Palace and the Rua do Ouvidor there are many more mouths than counted in your useless statistics) (July 2, 1893). Machado's biographer Raimundo Magalhães Jr. labeled him a "distorter of citations":

> He gave in to an irrepressible impulse and transferred to his manuscript first a passage from Coriolanus or from Shakespeare's Hamlet, then an idea of Pascal, or a verse by Molière, of Corneille, of Racine, of Boileau, of André Chernier, of Mareline Desbordes-Valmore, Lamartine, Hugo, Musset, and so on, if not also from Dante, Shelley or Longfellow. When he began to study German, he couldn't resist putting some verses by Goethe in a footnote to a chronicle, ending with a Latin quotation. . . . Molière, however, was always his great favorite. There he got all his inspiration and ideas. He often quoted his verses, whether from *Tartuffe*, *Le Misanthrope*, or *Les Femmes savantes*, and a few prose passages besides. In the choice of pseudonyms, he also paid homage to Molière by taking the name Lélio, one of the main characters of *L'Étourdi* and *Sganarelle*.[5]

Machado incorporates his literary education into his works in the form of such a personal world library, and his writings coexist and dialogue with authors and works from his wide literary knowledge that impressed him. They are crisscrossed with references and allusions to and quotes from dozens of authors and works representing what was then known and thought to be world literature. His sources were the knowledgeable literary circles he frequented in Rio de Janeiro, the theater, and the reading rooms where he read classics, major works, history, philosophy, and everything he could find in French and Portuguese literatures. His novels and stories depicting life in nineteenth-century Rio de Janeiro are filled with references from his substantial reading that complete, alter, and complement the original texts. Machado sought to apply his citations by altering them in the light of the context, often with distance, irony, and subtle emendations. Embedded in fiction, the library is a good example of temporal and conceptual blending, allowing the reader to judge the familiarity of distant relationships. It collapses time, promotes comparison of ideas and concepts, and documents Machado's understanding of life as a series of themes and variations.

Preceding Borges's "Biblioteca de Babel" by half a century, Machado's library is not futuristic or combinatory, but it is magical in that it allows a sweeping overview of time. Amassing a library of world literature for Machado is comparable to Brás Cubas's ride over the centuries of time on the back of a flying hippopotamus, witnessing the spectacle of human experience, or to the crystalline globe of the universe in which Tethys revealed the future of Portuguese voyages to Vasco da Gama. The library is another of Machado's eternal points of view, since it was thought to synthesize all that had been thought or written or was likely to be so. Machado stated openly in a chronicle of 1867 that he believed in books and even adored them, and over the decades he accumulated a large library at his bungalow in Cosme Velho, even though he enjoyed the use of libraries in Rio de Janeiro. In Cosme Velho he could live and write both in reality and in the imagination, as Borges did in the neighborhood of Recoleta in Buenos Aires in the next century, as recollected by Maria Kodama: "It is a real Library of Babel, full of old books, their endpapers scribbled with notes in his tiny hand. . . . Sometimes, following Borges, I wonder which one is real: the world I see from the window, bathed in afternoon splendor or sunset's soft glow, with the house that once belonged to Borges in the distance, or the world of the Library of Babel, with its shelves full of books once touched by his hands?"[6] The Alexandrine world library could have been re-created, following Borges, in authors' collections throughout the Americas, as Haroldo de Campos writes, in the Alfonso Reyes *capilla* (chapel) in Mexico City, in Mário de Andrade's library on Lopes Chaves Street in São Paulo, or in Lezama Lima's old house in Havana.[7] Although part of Machado's collection was lost after his death, Massa located 723 books in eleven fields of knowledge: Greek, Latin, the Bible and religion, Oriental, Italian, Spanish, Portuguese, Brazilian, English, German, French, general history, philosophy, and psychology. One of his intellectual goals was to read the universal classics in their original languages.

One feels, comments Grieco, that Diderot was one of Machado's favorite readings because "so many features of his fiction are recognizable in

Machado." Literature and philosophy provide a framework of wide latitude for the multitude of references that pass through the two authors' minds. In Diderot's *Le Nevue de Rameau*, first published in a translation by Goethe in 1805, a narrator ("Moi") and the nephew of the title ("Lui") engage in a comic dialogue, a self-reflexive contest of wit full of allegory and allusion. Signs of Machado's fascination with this work may be seen in the narrator's intense interest in chess at the Café de la Régence; in the unreliable, contradictory, ironical dialogue form; and in the nephew's resemblance to a picaresque and witty provocateur. The book's epigraph from Horace, *Vertumnis, quotquot sunt, natus iniquis* (Born under the baleful influence of Vertuminis), links the work to the Roman god of chance, to satire, and to comic writing. Diderot's novel *Jacques le fataliste et son maître*, published posthumously in 1796 and known in a partial translation by Goethe, would have interested Machado for its journey motif, its many contradictory characters who make up their stories, and its grounding in a philosophy of determinism approaching fatalism. Diderot confessed that he lifted a part of Jacques's story directly from Sterne's *Tristram Shandy* (published 1759–67), perhaps as a kind of homage but nevertheless creating a bond that could be extended to a group of international writers working with similar ideas and techniques, all of whom were among Machado's major influences and whom he continually cited. Magalhães tries to trace part of the web of writing that links authors who use borrowing, quotation, and invention, leading to Machado de Assis: "Carlyle's Dr. Teufelsdröckh comes from Laplace and the *Alcoran*, as well as *Robinson Crusoe* and the *Belfast Town and Country Almanack*, and Mariana's husband Conrado, in Machado's story 'A Chapter of Hats,' comes from Darwin and Laplace. And both Carlyle and Machado allude to celestial mechanics, citing Laplace. Even Carlyle's nonsense of mixing the *Alcoran* and Laplace with the *Belfast Almanaque* is matched by the mixture of that volume with Darwin's *Worms* in Machado de Assis" (Magalhães Jr., 218). Sérgio Paulo Rouanet notes that Diderot and Sterne met in Paris, where Diderot expressed his admiration for the Irish writer and the novel from which he would later borrow; meanwhile, while imprisoned in Turin, Maistre composed travel memoirs that would later inspire Almeida Garrett to write his *Viagens na minha terra* (1846), based on an excursion in Portugal from Lisbon to Santarém. All of these titles involving the travel-biography theme and the capricious control of a narrator over his readers converge in the *Posthumous Memoirs of Brás Cubas*; other points of contact include temporal and spatial disposition, subordination of historical time to narrative time, changes in pace, fragmentation, graphic discontinuities, a dialectic of the comic and serious, and use of satire.

Machado de Assis wrote for profoundly literary reasons. While his references brought to bear the scope of a world library, most of his novels were based on a single phrase or idea culled from the great authors he admired, particularly Shakespeare (*Othello* and *Hamlet*), Goethe (*Faust* is the work most applicable to the novels), and Dante. He created original Brazilian contexts with which to develop these motifs, often reversing or inverting themes and situations. In the preface to his first novel, *Resurrection*, Machado acknowledged that he wrote his novel to illustrate a phrase from Shakespeare: "My idea when I wrote this book was to put into practice Shakespeare's thought: "Our doubts are traitors, / And make us lose the good we oft might win, / By fearing to attempt" (*Measure for Measure*, 1.4, 1604). The citation became the novel's epigraph. Machado used the practice of quotation in the epigraphs of his last two novels also. *Esau and Jacob* begins with a quotation from Dante, "Dico, che quando l'anima mal nata . . . ," that refers to the evil-born who come before Minos in the second circle of hell to await his judgment and learn their places. It sets an ominous reference to the twins Esau and Jacob, who were already fighting in their mother's womb. The plot develops as an allegorical and literal elaboration of a line from Goethe's *Faust*, which Ayres urges Flora to quote to express her situation: "Zwei Seelen wohnen, ach! in meiner Brust" (Oh, two souls live in my breast!) in her irresolvable love conflict between Natividade's twins Pedro and Paulo (LXXXI).

Counselor Ayres' Memorial is even more densely symbolic and referential in its literary construction. The novel is a contemporary enactment of two epigraphs from the medieval Galician-Portuguese lyric on two central themes: ordering ships made to travel over the seas and a young woman's farewell to her mother as she departs to meet a distant lover. The two quotations condense and foreshadow the story of Fidélia and her final departure from Brazil by ship. After his sister Rita challenges him to marry the widow Noronha, Ayres takes his volume of *Faust* off the shelf and reads the relevant passage: "The contest between God and the Devil over poor old Faust, servant of the Lord, and of his inevitable destruction at the hands of the Clever One" (January 10). This quotation clarifies Ayres's personal struggle with death and desire. Ayres adds a third level of reference from Percy Bysshe Shelley's line, "I can give not what men call love," from the poem "One Word Is Too Often Profaned" (1822), which he first misreads, then repeats at significant moments throughout his memoir so as to incapacitate his desire through a kind of devilish, paralytic incantation. On a symbolic level *Counselor Ayres' Memorial* is intended to be a thematic and character development based on the bet between God and Mephistopheles in Goethe's celebrated verse play (part 1, 1808; part 2, 1832), which Machado certainly saw in Charles Gounod's operatic version (*Faust,* 1859) performed in Rio de Janeiro in 1871 and 1886.[8]

The other six novels carry no epigraphs but choose to reveal their sources through symbols or direct references in the texts, in which Goethe's works continue to play a major role. In *The Hand and the Glove,* a young Estévão opens a page from *Die Leiden des jungen Werthers* (1774, *The Sufferings of Young Werther*) by Goethe, which characterizes the suffering from love that intensifies his own fragile emotions; a Shakespearean title, *All's Well That Ends Well* (1602), predicts the novel's outcome, as Guiomar is permitted to marry the suitor whom she has secretly chosen. In *Quincas Borba,* Rubião uses his newfound wealth to decorate his mansion in Botafogo with, among other things, two figurines, one of Mephistopheles and the other of Faust, purchased at the suggestion of his supposed friend Palha, who would appropriate his fortune and abandon him to poverty and madness: "Silver, gold, those were the metals he loved with all his heart. He didn't like bronze, but his friend Palha told him it was valuable and that explained the pair of figures here in the living room, a Mephistopheles and a Faust" (3). Dom Casmurro, in beginning his tale of regret, cites advice he has heard from busts painted on the four walls to take up his pen and write in hopes of reconstituting lost time as a form of consolation. Bento recognizes that the purpose is to provide him with an illusion, which he compares to Faust's: "Perhaps the act of narration would summon the illusion for me, and the shades would come treading lightly, as with the poet, not the one on the train but the one in *Faust*: ah there, are you come again, restless shades"? (2). Bento reveals another major literary source of his memoir in the final chapter, when he quotes Ecclesiasticus 9:1 only for the rhetorical purpose of disagreeing with its logic: "Love your wife, but don't act jealous—do not teach her lessons in how to harm you." Bento finds harm in his wife's nature rather than in his emotions, yet despite his allegation he has become a restless Faustian shadow in pursuit of absolution.

The *Posthumous Memoirs of Brás Cubas* is the novel with the greatest number of literary citations, which come piled one upon the other like a cascade, particularly in the introduction and in Brás's thematic-biographical exposition. The note to the reader covers Stendhal, Sterne, and Xavier de Maistre. Bras's story of his demise cites Moses as author and travels from the Grecian river Ilissos to Africa by way of the undiscovered country of Hamlet. His anti-hypochondriacal poultice can be traced to Diderot's *Jacques le fataliste et son maître* ("l'emplâtre est un incident, l'histoire est le récit de tout ce qui s'est passé"), Balzac's César Birroteau, and to Louis Reybaud's *Jérôme Paturot à la recherche d'une position sociale* (1846). Brás's self-description as two-faced only fails to name Janus. To explain his *idée fixe* he invokes Cavour, Bismarck, Suetonius, Claudius, Seneca, Titus, Madame Lucrezia Borgia, Ferdinand Gregorovius, the pyramids, the battle of Salamina, the Augsburg Confession, and Oliver Cromwell. Cain, Hezekiah, and Pandora are complemented by references to Buffon, Corneille, Molière, and Napoleon. Portuguese literature comes into play with references to Manuel Maria Barbosa de Bocage and playwright Antônio José da Silva. The miscellany continues with Shakespeare, Klopstock, and *The Arabian Nights*. It is a bricolage from many different authors in which, so thinks Grieco, "the author least present is the Brazilian" (1960, 23). Yet Machado is director of a symphony, which is his world library and personal literary archive, much more than a single instrument or book because of his involvement in a complex score and multiple texts. What impresses readers is not the sheer number of references but rather the skill, irony, and psychological insight brought to bear by Brás Cubas—with some outside assistance from Machado de Assis—to assemble his past life from reference and archetype. His is a question not of influence, but rather of assimilation and invention. The *Posthumous Memoirs* marks the point at which Machado fragments his authorship in both voice and style by passing it on to internal writers. In this way Machado can devote his attention to form rather than story, and he can refine his presence outside the text and even, philosophically, outside of time and history.

In *Quincas Borba*, Machado builds a story parallel to that of his characters derived from classical myths, yet his allusions are much more disturbing and immoral than those in the novel's plot, suggesting a more complex psychological situation than might appear in the story alone. The character Palha, for example, is described as "a kind of King Candaules, more personal on one side, more public on the other." The allusion is to the reputation of King Candaules of Lydia, betrayed by his wife, whom he put on display and forced his prime minister to see nude. As a result, the wife convinced the minister to kill the king and marry her. Palha did in fact display Sofia in décolletage as a social and financial ploy, and his sadistic nature emerges in the dreams of Sofia and Rubião, although neither has the courage to denounce Palha because they are in different ways accomplices to his enrichment schemes; at the same time, Palha's pathological control of his wife and of Rubião disguises his sadism. Rubião's declaration of love to Sofia catches the attention of the night sky and is referenced in the myth of Diana and Endymion. The goddess sees the sleeping Endymion in a cave and falls in love with him, visiting him every night. They have fifty daughters and a son, which here represent the fecundation of the night sky.

One of the advantages Machado enjoyed as a Brazilian writer was his access to and knowledge of Portuguese literature. He read and was educated by Portuguese authors in Rio de Janeiro, and his fiction and criticism extend from the medieval Galician-Portuguese lyric to his critical debate with Eça de Queirós over the novel *O Primo Basílio*, published in *O Cruzeiro* on April 16, 1870. He invokes major authors of Portuguese literature to support the context and even the geography of his fiction. He cites

Fernão Mendes Pinto, the author of the *Peregrinação* (1614), a work based on travels in Asia, in a story set in the Orient. Bernardim Ribeiro, the author of the first pastoral romance, *História de menina e moça* (1554, *Maiden and Modest*), the Renaissance poet Sá de Miranda, and Portugal's most celebrated writer, Camões, become references. Machado weaves in several of the famous episodes of Camões's epic poem *The Lusiads* to color his context. In *Esau and Jacob*, Natividade sails the seas of the Portuguese discoveries in episodes comparable to those in *The Lusiads*: "The Cape of Storms turned into the Cape of Good Hope, and she conquered her first and second age of youth, without the winds capsizing her ship or the waves swallowing it . . . there were yawns of Adamastor. She quickly mended the sail and the giant was left behind with Thetis, while she continued on course to India" (19). Adamastor's failed and tragic attempt to court the goddess Thetis, who taunts him eternally after turning him into a giant rock, colors Ayres's loss of Natividade, who sailed past him years before and continued to reject him as a suitor of her husband's sister. Ayres conjectures that the twins Pedro and Paulo may have attracted the attention of many young ladies, whom they would certainly have defended "like the medieval knights who defended their ladies" (18), a reference to the Portuguese knights who traveled to England in the 1390s to avenge the honor of certain English ladies. In his memoirs, Ayres ironizes his observation that Tristão has fallen in love with Fidélia on the same reference: "When I was a young man, we said *smitten*; it was more forceful, but less graceful and did not have the spirituality of the other expression, which is classic. *Making love* is banal; it gives the idea of an occupation for idlers and sensualists; but *fallen in love* is bonny. 'Battalion of the fallen-in-love,' that troop of Portuguese knights who fought for love of their ladies" (November 12).

Bento Santiago makes subtle references to *The Lusiads* almost as casual remarks or asides, so that the reader may risk dismissing their central importance. He compares Capitu's captivating eyes to the force of the tide and describes her by writing the name "Thetis" before crossing out the word. Thetis is the goddess who turns Adamastor into the stony cape forever, rejecting his passion: "Even before I was speaking of her eyes like the tide, I wrote Thetis—then crossed it out. Let us also cross out nymph" (33).

His subconscious has portrayed Capitu as unrelentingly cruel, using commanding force over him as Thetis did to Adamastor. Bento infers that he would happily have preferred to cohabit with the nymphs of the Camonian "isle of love"—the erotic paradise of the ninth canto to which the Portuguese sailors with Vasco da Gama are led by Venus as a reward for achieving their goal—if his idealization had not been made obsolete by modern times: "But times changed everything. The ancient dreams had been pensioned off, and the modern ones dwelt in a person's brain. And these, though they tried to imitate the former, could not do it: the isle of dreams, like the isle of love, and all the islands of all the seas, are now the object of the ambition and rivalry of Europe and the United States" (64).

Machado pays homage to the short story "José Matias" by Eça de Queirós, published in the *Revista Moderna* in 1897, by inserting a parallel episode into *Esau and Jacob*. The unfortunate clerk Gouveia wishes to court Flora but is too shy to express his love, even by letter; instead, he stays on the sidewalk opposite the house where she lives looking fixedly at it, trembling. When it begins to drizzle, Gouveia prefers to stand in the rain rather than to take shelter, "ready to die for his lady as in the times of chivalry" (95).

Throughout his fiction Machado weaves Shakespearean meaning into the psychology and character of his principal actors. Shakespearean plays provided not only augurs of fate and tools for psychological probing; Shakespeare spoke as a representative of eternity and universality, such that no topic of this world could be compared to their lasting, inherent human value:

> Cuba, what does Cuba matter to me now? . . . African wars, Asiatic rebellions, the fall of the French cabinet, political agitation, the proposal to suppress the Senate, the Egyptian budget, socialism, anarchy, the European crisis that makes the Earth shudder and only doesn't explode because nature, my friend, hates that verb, but it must explode, certainly, before the end of the century, what does all that matter to me? What do I care if Christians and Muslims on Crete are killing each other, according to what telegrams of the 25th say. And the

accord signed the day before yesterday between Chileans and
Argentines, and just yesterday was undone, what do I have to
do with the blood that flowed and that will flow? . . . The
Monroe doctrine, which is good as an American law, is nothing compared to that embrace of English souls in the memory
of its most extraordinary and universal representative. One
day, when there is no more British Empire or North American
republic, there will be Shakespeare; when English is no longer
spoken, Shakespeare will be spoken. What will all the current
disagreements be worth then? The same as those of the Greeks,
who left us Homer and the tragedies. . . . The celebrations of
the human soul have come to an end." (April 26, 1896)

Machado introduces parallels with Shakespeare through the tragedies *Ham-
let*, *Othello*, *Macbeth*, and *Romeo and Juliet*, while also making use of *The
Tempest*, *The Merchant of Venice*, *Richard III*, *Coriolanus*, *As You Like It*,
Measure for Measure, and *The Merry Wives of Windsor*.

In *Quincas Borba*, Rubião romantically asks Sofia to look at the stars
of the Southern Cross at the same time every night. References to Othello,
legion in the novels, here invoke the passage in which Othello speaks to
chaste stars, which are not guilty as he thinks Desdemona is, yet whose light
will be forever lost when he kills her. Jealousy equally drives Rubião mad,
although the chaste stars he observes reflect only the unreadable reaction
of Sofia to his declaration, "Now one way, then another." Sofia's own ego
is reflected in her jealousy of Rubião, to whom she denies any connection,
when she resists telling her cousin to marry him. Jealousy here takes on another cruel role, which is to "contrive this other jealousy in a person who
didn't want to release what she didn't want to possess." The same pattern
returns in *Esau and Jacob*, when Natividade resists her sister's possible marriage to Counselor Ayres, who was once her beau; in his own veiled response,
certainly a sly challenge to her veto, Ayres reveals to her his romantic interest in her sons' girlfriend, Flora. When Rubião is daydreaming about a
marriage that will take his mind off Sofia, there is a reference to *The Tempest* at the point when Prospero creates a magical spectacle for Miranda,

his daughter, and Ferdinand in honor of their engagement; Rubião's possible false wedding is compared to Prospero's masquerade, revealing just how deeply Rubião has wandered into fantasy.

Machado's dark themes are centered on *Othello,* which had fascinated him since 1861. The play underlies a central theme of *Dom Casmurro*: in the chapter "A Touch of Iago," Bento turns pale and becomes cruelly jealous when José Dias blithely reports in a visit to the seminary that Capitu, whom he calls a "giddy creature," is being courted by neighborhood gentlemen. Bento gnaws on the words and convinces himself of her betrayal—a pattern that will be repeated—while imagining her at the window of her house. In a confused whirlwind he dreams of running there, seizing her, and forcing her to confess, before he exits his obsession and relents, yet the impression is cast in his mind and, more important, in the reader's. This chapter prepares what will follow, when Escobar returns from the grave in the person of Bento's son Ezequiel, who resembles him. Bento's accusations against Capitu have been formalized, and a "certain idea," his "project," comes into his mind. Only when he thinks of his childhood house does he think of relinquishing his obsession and remaining there, engraving the house within himself, as he does when he has a replica of the house constructed in his old age in an attempt to recover that special moment of return to innocence. Once again, however, a distraction or coincidence restores Bento to his delusional obsession: he goes to the theater and sees *Othello,* which only confirms his suspicions of false paternity, illegitimacy, and betrayal, although Bento would have readers believe he was only slightly familiar with the play's theme and had never read or seen it, even though he had effectively played the part in chapter 62: "I went to the theater in the evening. They happened to be playing *Othello*, which I had never seen or read. I was familiar only with its theme, and rejoiced at the coincidence. I watched the Moor rage because of a handkerchief . . . since I could not escape the observation that a handkerchief was enough to kindle the jealousy of Othello and fashion the most sublime tragedy of this world. . . . These were the vague and muddled ideas that passed through my mind as the Moor rolled convulsively and Iago distilled his calumny. . . . The last act showed me that not I, but Capitu ought to die. I heard the prayers of Desdemona, her pure and loving words, the fury of the Moor, and the death he meted out to her amid the frantic applause of the audience" (135). At this point, Bento plays a Shakespearean role ("Let them call me assassin if they like . . . my second impulse was criminal"); being incapable of facing Capitu, he decides to poison his young son but relents at the last moment, just as he always does from a number of perverse fantasies. To get his way, Bento bends one of the novel's utopian themes to his own devices—the voyage to Europe—which now becomes an exile til death for Capitu, Bento's way of justifying his fixed idea by hiding it behind a common façade of innocence, the European voyage.

Brás Cubas finds himself caught between the satiety of his desire for Virgília, after the annoyance of an anonymous letter sent to Lobo Neves and the deception required to refute it, and the titillation of Nhã-loló, whose name is Dona Eulália, a charming young girl whom his cousin Sabina selected for him. Contemplating how chastely a dress covered her knee, Brás arrived at yet another of his grand theories about human nature and society based on the pendulum's action: "that nature foresaw human clothing, a condition necessary for the development of our species. Habitual nudity, given the works and cares of the individual, would tend to dull the senses and retard sex, while clothing, deceiving nature, sharpens and attracts desires, activates them, reproduces them, and, consequently, drives civilization." Here, Brás may anticipate Freud, but he turns his theory toward Shakespeare to conclude, "A blessed custom that gave us *Othello* and the transatlantic packets." He refers to the eroticism of the play, performed in Brazil by European theatrical companies who arrived by ship. Brás then adds a paragraph that at the same time he suppresses because it comes dangerously close to a comment on female sexuality, both central and centrifugal in Virgília, who has just given Brás a cold kiss of death. He describes the alternative, Nhã-loló, both as Pascalian angel and beast: angel because of "the heavenly things she says"; however, he suppresses the chapter to avoid describing her opposite nature, which by implication lies in the eroticism of a revealed knee and the sex incited by human clothing. Brás's unspoken revelation completes the erotic circle now being closed with the cleverly deceptive, yet now symbolically naked, Virgília.

In *Quincas Borba*, *Othello* underlies the energized yet empty love triangle of Rubião, Carlos Maria, and Sofia. When Rubião and Sofia leave the party to look at the moon and the stars from the terrace, he becomes suddenly and uncharacteristically loquacious and poetic in his declaration of love to Sofia, who must pretend not to understand what he means. The stars are laughing, insists the narrator, who assures the reader ironically that they are stars unlike those in the scene on the terrace: "Chaste stars! That's what Othello the terrible and Tristram Shandy the jovial call them. Those extremes in heart and spirit are in agreement on one point: the stars are chaste" (40). Once again, the chaste stars from act V, scene 2 ("Let me not name it to you, you chaste stars!"), replace what cannot be spoken, which is Rubião's sexual intention here displaced to the stars of the Southern Cross.

In *Resurrection*, the blunt Félix blurts out his suspicions to Lívia: "He did not adopt Yago's method, which struck him as risky and childish; rather than insinuating suspicion into Félix's ears, Luís Batista placed it before his eyes" (9). In *The Hand and the Glove*, persons from towns in the interior of the state come to the capital in search of the music of Rossini's *Othello* as sung by the famous soprano Emmi La Grua: "Today . . . I am here thirsting for music. Vassouras has neither a Lagrua nor an Othello" (2). In *Helena,* some days before Helena's father, Salvador, receives a letter from his wife, Angela, explaining that she has run away, he has a premonition in the form of a quote from *Othello* from an English sailor as he voyaged from Porto Alegre to Rio: "A few days before, on board ship, an English engineer on his way from Rio Grande to this city had lent me a dog-eared volume of Shakespeare. . . . 'She has deceiv'd her father, Brabantio said to Othello, and may do thee' " (25).

In the story "O Diplomático" ("The Diplomat," 1884), Machado arranges a fate worse than Othello's for Rangel, a scribe who cannot bring himself to declare his love for Joaninha and during a party one night loses her to an unknown newcomer, Queirós. Rather than exact his revenge on Joaninha/Desdemona, Rangel is obliged to swallow his hatred for Queirós and serve as best man in their wedding six months later as a consequence of his unchangeable pusillanimous character.

Macbeth, and the famous expression of Lady Macbeth, comes as a refrain in the novels and stories. In the short story "Uma Senhora," for example, the eternal vanity and youthful beauty of D. Camila leads her to reject all of her daughter's suitors; indeed, when the two women go out they are thought to be sisters. In time, however, when her first white hair appeared D. Camila yanked it out with a passion comparable to Lady Macbeth's murderous monologue, as if conscious of the tragedy and crime of age that would compromise her beauty: "Alone, she looked once more into the mirror. . . . Out, damned spot! Out!" In *Iaiá Garcia*, D. Valéria secures permission from Estela's father, Antunes, to supply his daughter with a dowry, in the hope of arranging a marriage that would divert the passion that her son Jorge nurtured for her: "This favor seemed to her a sort of damage which Jorge's mother was liberally paying her, a cleansing water which would wash from her lips the kisses she was making an effort to extinguish, like Lady Macbeth, with her bloodstain: 'Out, damned spot!' That was her estimation of the situation: it was also her grief." In *Dom Casmurro*, when Bento Santiago comes home with a law degree from São Paulo, his marriage to Capitu is assured. "You will be happy, Bentinho!" is the wish that Bento whispers, thinking it to be a voice he hears from a fairy. There follows an ominous foreshadowing that juxtaposes this fairy wish with the fate of Macbeth, as Bento surmises that the fairy must be a cousin of Scottish witches: " 'Thou shall be king, Macbeth!—Thou shalt be happy, Bentinho.' After all, it is the same prediction, to the selfsame tune, which is universal and eternal" (100). The tragic, murderous end of his marriage is thus foretold even before it has taken place.

The story "Aurora sem dia" (Ever-expected dawn, 1873) comes close to self-parody of Machado's own literary coming of age. The young Luís Tinoco woke up one morning a writer and threw himself into the task, producing a sonnet before lunch, although missing a few required syllables. There followed a sentimental ode. Both were published in the *Correio Mercantil*, which Tinoco carried around with him to show off. He began to put on airs of a theatrical skepticism, quoting Byron and Dante without ever having read them. Once those gates were opened, he continued to cite a collection of literary names and allusions without knowing anything about them: "It was not necessary for him to have read Shakespeare, for example, to talk about to be or not to be, about Juliet's balcony or the tortures of Othello." He went beyond Shakespeare to Aspasia, the companion of Pericles, then descended to local references, Padre Caldas and Lindóia, the heroine of Basílio da Gama's epic *O Uraguai* (1769). With experience, Tinoco came to realize that all his writings had been ridiculous. Old Anastácio had warned him: "You must have read *Macbeth*. . . . Careful with the voice of the witches, my friend." Tinoco finally abandoned writing entirely in favor of drinking a cup of coffee in silence.

Machado saw the world through books and as a book, and he was aware of their positive and negative potential and also concerned about their reception. Brás Cubas says insincerely that he does not want to provide food for future critics. In "The Bibliomaniac," he parodies a fixation with books and their meanings that causes any collector to ignore every political or social event of importance: "He reads, rereads, reads again, disjoins the words, takes out a syllable, then another, and another still, and examines the remaining ones inside and out from all sides, up against the light, dusts them off, rubs them against his knee, washes them, and nothing doing. He can't find the absurdity" (72). Having failed as a reader and critic, the bibliomaniac contents himself with writing a brief report on the finding of first editions and the sublimity of ownership and collecting, thumbing through his books lovingly. Even Brás Cubas in his delirium was transformed into a single morocco-bound volume of St. Thomas Aquinas's *Summa Theologica* with silver clasps and illustrations. When Bento attempts suicide with poisoned coffee, he thinks of literature, citing the case of Cato, who read and reread a book of Plato before killing himself. While thinking of the nobility of imitating Cato, Bento forms a maxim about the positive numbing effect of books: "I believe more people would put a term to their days if they could find this sort of moral cocaine in good books" (136). Books do nothing if not reflect the disconcert of the world, as the narrator of *Esau and Jacob* explains with devastating humor: "Discord is not as ugly as they say, my friend. It is neither ugly nor sterile. Count only how

many books it has produced, from Homer to the present day, not excluding . . . not excluding what?" (36). Machado goes beyond irony in his lack
of confidence in humankind's desire to share his love of books or, for that
matter, to learn anything from them or even to understand their purpose.
The Italian tenor in life's opera between God and the Devil in *Dom Casmurro* confirms the pure and ultimate truth of the production: "One day,
when all the books have been burned as useless, there will be someone,
maybe a tenor, most likely an Italian, who will teach this truth to men. All is
music, my friend. In the beginning was the do and the do became re, etc" (9).

For Machado, the life of books is parallel to human life: "One should
remember that the life of books is as varied as that of men. Some die at twenty,
others at fifty, others at one hundred, or at ninety-nine. . . . With the turn
of the century, many end up in libraries where they will be picked up by
the curious, from where in part they may go into history, in part into
anthologies. Well, this prolonged life, whether short or long, gives them a
little shred of glory. Immortality is reserved for the few."[9] Books are a beginning, the genesis and the regeneration of thought and life. Machado revi-
talizes world literature by connecting it through art and philosophy to
fundamental truths about humanity and existence.

EIGHT

Time's Invisible Fabric: Telling What Cannot Be Said, Saying What Cannot Be Told

O tempo é um tecido invisível em que se pode bordar tudo, uma flor, um
pássaro, uma dama, um castelo, um túmulo. Também se pode bordar
nada. Nada em cima de invisível é a mais sutil obra deste mundo, e acaso
do outro. [Time is an invisible fabric upon which one can embroider
everything: a flower, a bird, a lady, a castle, a tomb. One can also embroider
nothing. Nothing, on top of the invisible, that is the most subtle work
of this world and for that matter, of the other.]

—*Esau and Jacob*, chapter 22

MACHADO CONFIRMS HIS STATUS as a master of the short story
through plastic gestures, what he called plastic intention, applied like a
painter or an actor: "I like to pick up the least and hidden things. Where
no one sticks his nose I like to put mine, with the straight and sharp curiosity that discovers what is hidden. From there it follows that, while the
telegraph gives us such grave news as the French tax on the lack of children and the suicide of the Paraguayan chief of police, things for one's eyes,
I squint mine to see tiny things, things that escape most people, things just
for the nearsighted. The advantage of being nearsighted is to be able to focus on things that the grand vistas don't notice."[1] In the short story, Machado is a miniaturist, with light brushstrokes guided by close intellectual
focus and irony. Inflection, inference, suggestion, dissimulation, impression are among the tools Machado employs to produce the harmonious
asymmetry of his stories, unveiled in the mystery of seemingly common circumstances which he observes up close with myopic concentration. Far-
sighted readers must supply the grand vistas and sweeping themes and
conclusions only suggested in the original. Mastery of the art of storytell-
ing, Machado writes, is to conceal what is actually told: "The art of saying

things without seeming to say them is so rare and precious that I cannot resist the urge to recommend two recent examples. One of them is actually a decree. . . . The second model of this art of writing is the program of the Instructive and Beneficent Association" (March 8, 1885). The examples he cites with his customary irony say things naïvely without actually being aware of what they are saying, or even that they are saying anything at all. Machado, on the other hand, makes a conscious art of saying without seeming to say anything. His narrators tell stories in the form of unanswered questions posed for the reader's consideration. Perhaps the best example of concealing what is told—or of unaware telling—drawn from his 226 short stories is the celebrated story "Missa do galo" ("Midnight Mass").[2]

In just three short sentences Machado puts forward a fantastic incident that perhaps can never be totally understood—such is the narrator Nogueira's conceit. Perhaps it never even occurred, not with the implications seemingly attributed to it or in the way Nogueira as a mature narrator struggles to understand a strange, puzzling situation that stuck in his memory when he was a youth. It is only with age that he has come to reexamine a conversation so strange and mysterious that it has stayed current in his memory and now motivates him to put pen to paper. He begins, "I could never understand the conversation I had with a lady, many years ago, when I was seventeen and she thirty." This crucial sentence condenses everything that follows, and it conjugates the archetype of innocence and experience. Piety and conception are likewise joined symbolically in the call to midnight Mass in the Brazilian title, a cock crowing, "Missa do galo." We do not know Nogueira's current age, but time has allowed him to ruminate on the old conversation and finally to express his puzzlement openly. He seems to be speaking rather than writing, and he re-creates the scene with dialogues, as in an intimate theater. There is no certainty that the narrator, now some twenty years older, actually has any better understanding of what he now recognizes as a potential incident pregnant with previously unperceived meanings. As readers, we have only his suspicions and his admission, or protest, of youthful innocence. The phrase "I could never understand" may mean that he is still in the dark, only now suspicious of possible deeper meanings that escaped him and perhaps remain obscure.

It is as if he presents the case to the readers to resolve, to overcome his doubts and confusion, and to confirm his ultimate illumination. The reticent narrator is in any case reluctant to dismiss his doubts and to accept the implication that he was the object of unsuspected erotic desire, while innocently waiting to attend the yearly Mass celebrating birth after immaculate conception. The narrator does not say he now understands the old conversation; to the contrary, he implies a continuing innocence that is disturbed by the possibility, which he now suspects, although it may not pass beyond an inkling, of an erotic objective in his conversation with the "senhora" of the house where he boarded. It is also possible that the narrator now fully understands what happened or did not happen with the lady yet demurs saying so openly out of tact, prudery, or even to enhance the mystery of his story. A precursor of Bento Santiago/Dom Casmurro, Nogueira aims his story at protecting his innocence and projecting erotic intentions onto the lady. His is likewise a story about an episode more absent than present, a potential and significant experience he missed even as a principal; nevertheless, neither his "diaphanous fantasy," to borrow Eça de Queirós's phrase, nor the latent events of the night could divert him from attending the great Mass of the court or subvert his youthful piety and innocence. He seeks both to read the incident as remembered in all its hidden depth yet to maintain a level of uncertainty, while finding a language to relate what cannot be told or perhaps even admitted in the society of his day. The reader sees him as unprepared to accept the full weight of the story as remembered, yet the theme of repressed erotic desire and seduction, never mentioned as such, is hidden openly in his initial statement of their respective ages, genders, and status.

The narrator's fascination with this particular incident years earlier is related to Conceição, the lady of the house where he lodged, who is thirteen years his senior and with whom he conducted the conversation. Conceição, a name that means "conception," was the second wife of the scribe Meneses, who had previously been married to one of the narrator's cousins. Conceição had been married to him for four years, without conceiving. It was a custom for students from the interior—the narrator was from Mangaratiba—to reside with relatives in the capital for their period of studies; thus the narrator's tie was with Meneses, although through an absent, possibly deceased first wife. We are not told what happened to her, and perhaps the narrator never knew. Without alleging any greater understanding of the mysterious night, the narrator fills in particulars of that time and circumstance from memory, including some dissimulations that he now understands and other events that remain unexplained. He confesses his naïveté about Meneses's habit of going out "to the theater," returning only the following morning; once when the youth asked to go along, everyone laughed behind his back. Now he understands the euphemism and explains that Meneses spent one night each week with a lady separated from her husband, a realization that serves to differentiate the youth's total innocence from the narrator's retrospective sophistication. Accordingly, Conceição, who at first suffered, had no choice but to accept the situation and even to find it normal. Thus the stage is set for the childless, neglected thirty-year-old Conceição to converse with the young boarder.

It was ten thirty on Christmas eve, a night symbolizing fertility and birth in Catholic Brazil, and the young narrator had arranged to go with a neighbor to midnight Mass at the cathedral. He preferred not to sleep and agreed to wake his neighbor at midnight, so they could attend the Mass. From the beginning, the piety of religious service and the simple room where the youth is waiting are contrasted to the oneiric and fluid eroticism of the passing hours, spent completely taken with Alexandre Dumas's *The Three Musketeers* (1844), riding on D'Artagnan's thin horse, and extending to the symbolism of laconic conversation, erotic desire, and memory. As he puts it, the house was asleep by ten thirty; when he heard the clock strike eleven he heard steps in the hallway, and thus began the ghostly, somnambulistic fantasy, a Shakespearean hallucination that would be interrupted only when the narrator's friend had to rap on the window to wake him from the reverie.

Conceição's shadow seemed to haunt the doorway as she appeared in a white gown loose at the waist. She will ask him in a few moments if he is afraid of souls from the other world. Here, the narrator mixes his memories of the scene with suspicions arising at the present time of writing: Conceição had told the youth that she woke up naturally from sleeplessness, yet he saw no evidence in her eyes that she had been asleep. He wondered if her lie was a polite excuse to keep him company, and again he noted her reputation as a "good, very good," even saintly person, thereby placing a seed of doubt in readers' minds. He makes a point of noting her strange negative answer to his question whether she had been bothered by sleeplessness before she came into the room: "I didn't understand her negative reply; it could be that she didn't understand it either." Their conversation went no further than normal polite comments about the wait, wandering to questions about the novels he liked to read. The narrator, recalling the simple conversation, was occupied in observing Conceição's plastic expression at the time: her head reclined on her shoulders, her eyelids were half shut, she was looking constantly at him, she moistened her lips with her tongue, straightened her head, held her chin in her hands, placed her elbows on the arms of the chair, and continued to look fixedly. The narrator draws the reader into a return to his youthful experience, even though in retrospective memory the description of Conceição is calculated for effect. Either the narrator hides his manipulation or remains unaware of the implications of the youth's intense observation of Conceição.

Two interior scenes, intensely plastic, strengthen the bond that was arising between the lady and the youth. In the first, she commented that she was getting old, words immediately and fervently contradicted by the youth, before she began a pensive stroll around the room, wandering aimlessly, examining a bit of curtain, and straightening a few objects before picking up the conversation with the same questions she had asked before, as if distracted or preoccupied. The second scene was propitiated by the youth's excitement when her sleeves fell open and he saw more than half of her naked arms. He had seen others, the narrator confesses, but at that time it was not common for women to uncover their arms. He began to ramble animatedly on such topics as the luxury of the Mass at court compared to festivities in the interior and other topics he added extemporaneously. The youth seemed unaware of his motivation for engaging in this effusive conversation, yet he made her smile and returned to a close observation of her features: her white teeth, dark eyes, long nose, the interrogative air it gave her face. Their intimacy intensified when she asked him to speak more

quietly because "Mama could wake up." The narrator enlarged on Conceição's plastic expressions: she became serious and wrinkled her forehead; she sat down beside him, he caught a glimpse of her slippers; he
moved to a chair; their faces came close together, and both laughed about
the coincidence of being light sleepers. Conceição made light of tossing in
bed; she crossed her legs, tapped the cords of her robe on her knees, stood
up, put her hand on the youth's shoulder so he would remain seated, shiv-
ered, turned her back, sat in a chair, and looked into a mirror. Her eyes
closed for a moment after she noticed that the youth had become enchanted
with her. In this mixture of reverie and fantasy, the narrator returns for an
instant to become an enamored youth, confessing that in his story he contradicted himself and became confused. He is close to confessing the
youth's desire, which has reappeared in his mature memory.

Conceição, saint and lover, is symbolized in drawings she observes
on the walls, two placed by Meneses and one of her own. One was of Cleopatra, a suicide in defeat; Conceição comments that the drawing is stained
and that she would prefer images of saints; she compares her husband's
drawings to those seen in barbershops, where she imagines men talk of girls
and courtship and admire beautiful figures. Nogueira comments that Conceição must certainly have never seen such places, the second doubt subtly raised in the reader's mind. Conceição's image was a sculpture of her
godmother, Nossa Senhora da Conceição, kept in her oratory. Having
drawn this contrast, the narrator raises his third doubt: he remembers the
Mass and becomes anxious about the time, but Conceição has begun to
tell him about her devotions as a maiden, mixing all her reminiscences in a
long narrative. The youth considers himself caught in her magnetic spell,
his feelings shaken and speech muted. It would be impolite to interrupt
her and perhaps dangerous to break her spell, but at the same time he is
unsettled and confused by her intimate confession. He could not avoid her
eyes, and whether willingly or unwillingly the conversation slowed, complete silence overtook the room, and the two remained completely still.
The scene was complete.

With Conceição lost in a reverie, the youth could hear a mouse gnawing in the study, from an underworld of decay and dissolution coming from

Meneses, undermining the somnolent romance and its moment of fantasy. The perverse eroticism of Meneses's "opera" interrupts the "Mass" when the mouse's gnawing disturbs the pious silence of the lady and the youth. In her ghostly reverie, Conceição had returned to her own days as a maiden through a reference in the text to "menina e moça," the pastoral romance by Bernardim Ribeiro that begins with a young girl narrating her abduction from her mother's house when she was too naïve to know the reason: she saw many things change into others and pleasure transformed into pain. With this crucial reference, Conceição summarizes her unfortunate situation in her marriage to Meneses and above all reveals her sympathy and understanding of Nogueira, the narrator, who has likewise left his mother's house for a distant place and remains unaware of life's painful, erotic realities.

One of the reasons the mature narrator is disturbed by his recollection may be the suggestion planted in this reference: her lament of victimization is the initiation that he was as yet incapable of understanding to a form of Eros the opposite of the spirituality whose fulfillment he was waiting to celebrate at Mass. As mature narrator, he is perhaps unsettled by his male incomprehension that failed to gauge the depth of her regression into the purity of symbolic memory, even as he closely observed her gestural, non-verbal communion with her lost innocence, with the impossible reality of the house that was haunting her that night. Heavily downplaying the hypnotic effect of her form and gestures, even his own projection of desire in a youth coming of age, the narrator takes protective recourse in a stereotypical reading of Conceição, inventing an erotic overture only confirmed by his dry comment on her subsequent remarriage, revealed in the story's final line. He reduces her to terms he knows how to understand, certain that he escaped entrapment and enchantment by a seductive ghost, thanks to the rap on a window, saved just in time by another, sanctioned form of conception, birth, and adoration. During her promenade, Conceição was for some moments the ghostly augur of his inevitable loss of male innocence.

The youth is freed from the goddess's spell when his companion raps on the window; she admits freely her fault for their having lost track of time and even finds it funny that Nogueira, who was going to wake his

companion, had to be wakened himself instead. Two kinds of awakening
are involved at this point, the literal one of the story's theme and the oneiric one of Conceição's séance and discourse while lost in past memories.
During the Mass, the figure of Conceição arises in the youth's mind standing between him and the priest, which the mature narrator attributes to
fancies of a seventeen-year-old, for whom Conceição was a kind of fourth
musketeer; however, the next day Conceição showed no sign of having remembered the evening as he did, and soon the youth returned to Mangaratiba. The story's final phrases, like the beginning one, contain and
consume the entire text: "When I came back to Rio in March, the scribe
had died of apoplexy. Conceição lived in Engenho Novo, but I neither visited her nor met her. I heard later that she had married her husband's legal
secretary." In this unsatisfactory and inconclusive concluding statement
by the narrator there is only the plain patriarchal recognition of Conceição's status as marital property in the prosaic eroticism of a legal secretary. Lost in the distance is the reverie of piety and adolescence, of a
conception still innocent of the ways of the world. The story of his narrow
escape widens to tell a story he could never tell because he has no deep
understanding of it; thus he can tell only what cannot be told. Machado
stands in the wings taking advantage both of the limitations of his narrator and as master of the truths that have puzzled him for so many years but
that go beyond his capacity to comprehend.

MACHADO CREATED STRONG female characters in his fiction,
and through them he explored the theme of female sexuality in a rigidly
patriarchal society. Unreliable male narrators portrayed this taboo subject by recording their observations and interaction with women in the
social world of Rio de Janeiro, generally with sympathetic, if distanced
and uncomprehending, points of view. While some male characters saw
themselves as victims of a female sexuality they could not comprehend,
women were left to feel the pain or pleasure of their confined social positions. Female sexual taboos in Machado's fiction focus mainly on adultery,
with some allegations of incest and fornication, although his narratives
specialize in male doubt and remorse. Women were marriageable after

reaching the age of twelve during the Empire; at the age of thirty, a woman was usually considered too old for romantic interest, and the expression of female sexuality was highly constrained by social habits.

Rustling leaves at the conclusion of the story "Dona Paula" (1884) evoke the omnipresence of time and its unexpected role in the reconstitution of memory and the fortunes of Eros; their sounds signal the transformation of a common situation into one of mystery and estrangement. Dona Paula's young niece Venancinha has gotten into marital troubles and called on her aunt for assistance. She had quarreled with her husband, Conrado, to the point of separation, and she was desperate. He had seen her dance with another man twice and converse with him for a few minutes, and the next morning he accused her harshly. Dona Paula, entertaining some suspicion and curiosity, went to visit Conrado at his law office to straighten out the matter. It seemed that there had been other incidents, and the two finally came to an agreement that Venancinha would spend several weeks in temporary exile with her aunt in the Tijuca district. There, Dona Paula would lead her back to observing the habits of a perfect wife. When Dona Paula first heard the name of the other gentleman, Vasco Maria Portela, however, she turned pale; he was not the former diplomat with whom she once had a torrid affair, now a baron and living in Europe, but his worthless son. The person thinking of Vasco during the ride up to Tijuca was Dona Paula, feeling the echo of her youth, now lying in ruins for thirty years, far from the times of her affair and of operas starring the famous French contralto Rosine Stoltz (1815–1903), the emperor's favorite, who, availing herself of a generous subsidy from the emperor, performed in Rio de Janeiro for several seasons after her long affair with the director of the Paris Opéra, Léon Pillet. Dona Paula's passion for the diplomat Vasco was a similar adventure of a lifetime:

> They fell in love and got their fill of each other, in the protective shadow of marriage, for some years, and as the passing breeze keeps no record of men's words, there's no way of telling what was said of the affair in those days. The affair ended; it was a succession of sweet and bitter moments, of delights, of

tears, of anger and ecstasy, various potions that filled the lady's cup of passion to the brim. Dona Paula drank it dry and then turned it over so she could drink no more. Satiety brought abstinence, and with time, it was this last phase that left its mark on public opinion. Her husband died, and the years came and went. Dona Paula was now an austere, pious person, well respected and esteemed.[3]

Once in Tijuca, Dona Paula began her duplicitous moral lessons, and when a tall stranger rode by on horseback Venancinha confessed to her aunt the full story of her passion. Without being able to say a word or make a gesture, Dona Paula unexpectedly relived her own past, for she never remarried after the passionate affair of her youth with the now-retired diplomat. Venancinha's catharsis led to a plea for forgiveness and a promise to forget the young man and return dutifully to her husband. While listening rapturously to the niece's confession, Dona Paula revisited her raging emotions of yesteryear after speaking severely to her niece of chastity, public opinion, and spousal duty. Acutely aware not only that her time had passed irrevocably, but also that she had once again denied life's great passion that time had seen fit to transfer to Venancinha, she could only stare at the wind and rustling leaves. The old servants in the kitchen, observing her strange reminiscences, sensed her distress and gossiped that she was never going to get to bed that night. The leaves voiced her disintegrated moral certitude while pointing to puzzling, mysterious forces beyond human comprehension that cross over time and generations.

In the story "Singular ocorrência" ("A Strange Thing," 1883), an unidentified narrator tells his confidant the strange story of Marocas, whom they see stopping to give alms in a churchyard. They observe a kind of regal quality in her bearing. Strangely, to guess her profession years ago when she was a young beauty, the narrator asks his companion to keep going back through all the professions until by elimination he comes to hers. His oblique approach to the topic of prostitution reveals how one of the most common situations for women in Rio de Janeiro, dictated and even demanded by the rigid hierarchies of society, was at the same time a taboo. Beauty and bearing often dissimulated exclusion, as the narrator reveals that Marocas had never learned to read. To write the story of Marocas as a woman and a personality, Machado relies on the opera and theater, from which he draws the models for all his female characters; he makes her one of the courtesans who had free rein at the Theatro Gymnasio, where *Camille,* or *La Dame aux camélias,* by Alexandre Dumas fils was playing. There, she entertained and lavished all her attentions on her many wealthy clients. Andrade, a friend of the narrator who had come to Rio from Alagoas with his beautiful wife and two-year-old daughter, became enchanted with her; when she wept during the last act, his passion was complete. After their attachment had become very deep, on an occasion when Andrade took his family out of town to a festival in Gávea on St. John's day, Marocas's behavior followed the pattern of another play she had just seen, *Je dine chez ma mère,* by Adrien Decourcelle and Lambert Thiboust, which premiered in Paris in 1855. The main character of the play is the courtesan Sophie Arnoult, who is left alone on New Year's Eve by all her admirers with the excuse that they must dine with their mothers. Since Marocas had no family, she told the men she would dine with a portrait of Andrade, which all thought to be a winning gesture.

On his return to the city, however, Andrade learned that a despicable character, Leandro, always begging for money, had recently enjoyed an affair, and after inquiring further he learned that the woman lived on the same street as his Marocas. After a dramatic confrontation involving the three, featuring a degrading payment to Leandro for his denunciation, Andrade left stunned and angry as Marocas wept in desperation and threatened to take her life. Before long, himself in desperation, Andrade led himself to believe that the whole scene had been artificially arranged as a test of his love; her disappearance furthered his anxiety. He ignored his friend's advice to devote his attentions to his wife and daughter and pursued Marocas to a boardinghouse in Jardim Botânico, where they had a tearful reunion, and the incident was never mentioned again. Andrade bought her a house, and they remained together until his death in the North some years later, after which she considered herself to be a widow. When asked to explain Marocas's single and unusual lapse in sexual behavior, the narrator's confidant suggests an explanation from naturalistic theater: "There's an explanation from the theater—by Augier, I think—that could explain the adventure: a longing for the gutter." Through this reference the pendulum swings from the story of Camille, a courtesan saved by love, to Émile Augier's Olympia, in the play *Le marriage d'Olympe* (1855), who represents the opposite argument, to the effect that all fallen women succumb to a "longing for the gutter." The narrator corrects him, however, and attributes her behavior to two causes: the first raises a question of the confining nature of the social position of women in nineteenth-century Rio de Janeiro. The historian Emília Viotti da Costa comments on the relative freedom and constraint that characterized the lives of women in the capital during the Empire:

> Upper-class women also enjoyed more freedom in the cities. . . .
> In Rio de Janeiro . . . and other big cities, they were allowed to
> attend the theater, balls, and other public events. At the court,
> where the cream of society gathered, Maria Graham, an English
> traveler who visited Brazil at the time of independence, met
> women who, in her opinion, could have felt at home in the most
> sophisticated salons in Europe. But those were exceptional
> women. Since most women were still restricted to domestic func-
> tions and interacted primarily with slaves, the education pro-
> vided them continued to be poor, and travelers still marveled
> at the Brazilian custom of segregating wives and daughters. Life
> was freer for lower-class women. In spite of the ordeals they
> faced, they enjoyed a freedom of movement and a degree of in-
> dependence unknown to most upper-class women.[4]

The narrator comments on the social abyss that separated Leandro from Andrade. Read in this context, Marocas's sexual adventure represented a moment of freedom or difference that was available to women only by changing or transgressing social class, as her dependence on Andrade for money and education was total. Many of Machado's heroines look for sexual opportunities outside of their high or official social status: Virgília, in the *Post-*

humous Memoirs, in spite of her highly placed husband and son, carries on a long, intense affair with Brás Cubas, who refuses to assume any defined social role except that of rebel, although he is wealthy. Sofia, in *Quincas Borba*, is almost literally an object belonging to her rapacious, capitalistic husband; her fear of him does not allow her long flirtations with Rubião to leave the realm of fantasy, although she accepts his many jewels while remaining in the grasp of a husband made of "straw"—Palha. The second reason the narrator gives for Marocas's lowly affair is purely Machadean and expresses perfectly his sense of life's irony: "Chance . . . in the form of a god or a devil . . . well, it was just one of those things!"[5]

The omniscient narrator of "Uns braços" ("A Pair of Arms," 1885) tells in retrospect the story of Ignácio, when he was a fifteen-year-old student who in 1870 had come to the Rua da Lapa in the capital from a small town in the interior to board for his apprenticeship. To avoid the insults and reproofs of the lawyer Borges, for whom he was obliged to work as an assistant, Ignácio fixed his gaze on the bare, rounded, plump arms of Dona Severina, an image imprinted hypnotically in his mind. Dona Severina, whose name reflects the severe routine and manners of the household to which she was subjected by the lawyer, was a woman of twenty-seven who had lived "maritally" with Borges for years. To Ignácio, whose only contact with the family was at the table, Dona Severina's arms were a semiotic symbol of salvation: they formed a parenthesis, and in the phrase without words that Ignácio read between that parenthesis, he found gratifying and pleasurable release. Dona Severina regarded her bare arms as a sign of the simplicity and rudimentary character of her life, as she had worn out all of her long-sleeved dresses: she wore no ornaments, no earrings, only a tortoiseshell comb her mother had left her and a dark scarf around her throat. She was thus at the height of her maturity as a woman. To Ignácio, her arms were a consolation for the solitude and silence of his new life, and the sight of them three times a day was enough to keep him in the city.

Dona Severina noticed Ignácio's attachment, and after close observation was certain she was being admired and loved by the handsome youth, a welcome idea that she controlled by reminding herself constantly that he was only a boy. Meanwhile, Ignácio was reading a medieval romance that had been adapted by Brazilian folk chapbooks, the story of Princess Magalona.[6] In the story, an only son, Pierres, asks permission of his parents to travel widely in the world to find Princess Magalona to discern whether she is beautiful. For Ignácio the young reader, Magalona and Severina became one and the same. Having left home for his quest in the world, Ignácio identifies with Pierres, and the image makes of Severina a princess, whereas both the youth's romance and Severina's close attention belie the commonness of their daily reality. On a Sunday when Ignácio is off from work, a day he calls a "wide, universal Sunday," he falls asleep and in a dream receives a kiss from his Magalona. Yet there is another side to the story, also a function of subconscious dreaming, that recounts Dona Severina's sexual fantasy. When she saw Ignácio asleep in his hammock, the book on the floor and a blissful look on his face, her heart beat violently. She was unaware that her movements were being repeated in the boy's imagination and dream: she could have seen herself bending over, taking his hands into her arms, saying a few words that neither were aware of, and again bending over and pursing her lips to give him a kiss on the mouth. Whereas the youth continued with his dream, Dona Severina was shocked and ashamed by the reality of what she had just done, as if she had been in a trance. Her desires and fantasy had overtaken her, and she feared that perhaps the youth was only pretending to be asleep; the reality of her fantasy had frightened and shaken her. When Ignácio came down to dinner, he found the famous arms covered with a shawl, and Borges delivered the news that the youth would have to return home. Ignácio thought he was being dismissed because he had offended Dona Severina, yet throughout his later life he never felt anything so intense as the sensation he had dreamed that Sunday in the Rua da Lapa coming from what he remembered as nothing more than a dream. The narrator interrupts the story to remark on the advantages if people were able to see each other's dreams, yet he admits that the society and psychology of empire would not have supported such a magic mirror, nor would most societies. The enduring pleasure bestowed by Ignácio's dream and Severina's actual kiss depended absolutely on the veil of fantasy, difference, and prohibition. In both cases, fantasy lifted them out of their subordinate, confined positions into the realm of chivalric quest and pleasure.

In the story "A desejada das gentes" ("The Cynosure of All Eyes," 1886), the opera is Bellini's *I Puritani* (1835), which is also based on chivalric literature with a libretto by Count Carlo Pepoli.[7] In the opera, Elvira becomes deranged, thinking herself abandoned by Arturo, whom she has chosen over Riccardo, and returns to her senses only in act 3. In Machado's story, the "divine Quintilia" reflects these chivalric qualities, as "her laughter [was] the clarion calling the knights to combat." Telling the story is a counselor of state as he strolls along with a colleague past the foreign ministry, remembering his strange passion for Quintilia, who, like the Quintilian book of rhetoric, *Institutio Oratoria* (AD 95), substituted discourse for romance. She had been considered the most beautiful girl in town, and her wealth was also a point in her favor. The counselor met her when she was thirty; during the two acts of the Puritans, he had heard a group of youths talking about her mystifying celibacy; later he lost a close friend, Nóbrega, soon after his suggestion that the two fight for her. When Quintilia told Nóbrega to desist, it became a death sentence for him; the counselor had already noted at the time a coldness in Quintilia and found no mysteries or depth in her eyes. She became serious in his company and met him for hours of long conversations, whereas the counselor was hoping to marry her. When they were united in sympathy by the death of his father and her uncle, the counselor proposed, but Quintilia insisted strictly on friendship and conversation, nothing more, ignoring the counselor's resentment, anger, and feeling of humiliation. She held a strange power over him, obliging him to accept a serene friendship entirely opposed to his hopes. He observed in their conversations and in her reading material that she was incapable of understanding love or passion. After she contracted an incurable spinal disease, only when she was sure she would soon die did she agree to marry him, and after the ceremony he spent two days watching her die, only to embrace her for the first time after death. Now, in talking about the tragic case, the counselor's companion accused him of practically speaking in verse, as what he called this "very individual case"

of physical aversion to marriage split her in his memory into something
less than human but also the divine hope of youth. To explain the pain she
caused him at that time, the counselor compares her to the Puritans or, by
implication, to unattainable damsels captive in the towers of chivalry.

Female sexual perversity is more dramatically portrayed in "Primas
de Sapucaia!" ("Those Cousins from Sapucaia!," 1883), a story founded on
the strange workings of fate and of dreams. The narration in first person is
by an unnamed deputy in parliament whose attraction to a mysterious lady
seen under a parasol going up the Rua da Misericórdia is frustrated by his
obligation to oversee two cousins from the interior, Claudina and Rosa, ac-
cidental cousins brought to the capital by chance who frustrate the narrator's opportune moment to get his hands on the lady. In the deputy's
daydream, in the style of a Brás Cubas, he imagines amorous encounters
with a lady he calls Adriana, who had married an older man only to obey
her family. Their rendezvous would take place in a little house he rented
on the outskirts of town, where the narrator would teach her both love and
betrayal. As in the case of Quintilia, Adriana's eyes foreshadow the story's
outcome, as they are large and round like the bull Juno. Brought back to
reality, the narrator finds that it takes several weeks for Adriana's image to
fade. A year later the deputy meets the lawyer Oliveira on the train to Petrópolis and cannot believe the power of chance. Oliveira has rented a house in
the Renânia neighborhood after taking a woman named Adriana from her
husband. Invited to visit the couple, the deputy verifies that the woman is
the "Adriana" he had admired in the streets and in his fantasy. When he
again met Oliveira in Rio de Janeiro after the season in Petrópolis, he found
him taciturn and despondent, a mood that at first caused the deputy a bit
of devilish pleasure. His reaction changed to horror, however, when he heard
the account of the humiliation Adriana had visited upon Oliveira, the misery of incompatible natures condemned to live together, fighting perversely
but unable to separate. To Oliveira, rather than to the deputy, Adriana
had shown herself to be cunning, willful, spiteful, and vulgar, paralyzing
him with her bullish eyes. In her case, sexuality was aggressive and subju-
gating, a case in which delicate beauty was only a deceptive gesture of
entrapment.

In the story "Captain of Volunteers," Simão de Castro first saw Maria at a masked ball in the old Theatro Provisório (built in 1852, later renamed Theatro Lyrico Fluminense). As in the case of the counselor in "A desejada das gentes," one of Simão's friends, Barreto, had challenged him to win Maria, who lived with a man called only X and had a small daughter. In a situation reminiscent of the lawyer Borges in "Uns braços," X lived "maritally" with Maria and had no wish to marry. To Simão's surprise, it was Maria who gave him secret looks and kisses, and soon they were meeting discreetly on the boat to Niterói, full of hopes and excitement. Like Dona Severina, however, Maria abandoned her fantasy and confessed the dalliance to X, who punished her severely yet obliquely by enlisting as a captain in the Paraguayan War. Maria covered her arms, as it were, by shutting Simão out of her life and following X to the South, where both died. Theater, fantasy, and the pleasures of courtship could not break the social and psychological bonds that fatally bound Maria to X, even or perhaps especially in the face of his unusual and cruel extortion, accepting a commission in war as if it were a noble gesture, yet whose sole purpose was to punish Maria for her flirtation through his suicidal and unanswerable sacrifice.

In *Esau and Jacob*, Dona Cláudia's husband, the politician Batista, lost a governorship and suffered the calumnies of a slanderous political attack; the crude names he was called she savored as the essence of life: "She also felt pilloried and this made her feel voluptuous, as if it were lashes or a whip on her own skin; it gave her a better appetite at lunch" (30). When she read insults in the newspaper, the ugly names were like whips that tore her flesh and gave her an excited pleasure. Sofia, in *Quincas Borba*, allows her fantasies to come to the surface only in the symbolic meaning of her dreams. In a nightmare she found herself writing the name Carlos Maria, the young man who fascinated her, in the sea. Carlos Maria approached her and began to speak the same tender words she had heard from Rubião, who was courting her temptingly. She was listening with pleasure, riding in a carriage, when several masked figures arrived and killed the coachman and Carlos Maria. The masked ringleader told Sofia he loved her more than the other two and gave her a kiss full of blood. She screamed and awoke, and there was her husband, Palha, beside the bed.

Sofia was afraid he might have heard part of her dream, so she murmured half jokingly and half sad, "I dreamed they were killing you." Her husband, who was masochistic, was pleased, but Sofia must have recognized that she had reversed the equation: it was she who was being killed by this controlling husband. Dona Tonica, who at a dance had observed Sofia's flirtation with Rubião, in whom she herself was interested, reacted violently to being displaced: "That lady still had an urge to strangle Sofia, to trample her, tear out her heart in pieces, telling her to her face the cruel names she'd attributed to her husband. . . . All of it was imagined" (44). Rubião had his own dream that confirmed Sofia's intimate analysis of her situation: Sofia and Maria Benedita were dressed only in skirts, and Palha was lashing their bare backs with a cat-o'-nine-tails with iron tips. They were crying out, begging for mercy, and dripping with blood. Rubião ordered Palha to be hanged and placed Sofia in his carriage, where she was instantly glamorous, glorious, and dominating.

As his fiction developed, Machado allowed his heroines more agency and difference. Throughout, the expression of female sexuality was contingent on class and social restrictions but undoubtedly motivated by the double standards of a patriarchal society in which males had unrestricted access to courtesans and lovers. Lower-class women, as Viotti da Costa concluded, had relatively more freedom of behavior, yet the line separating ladies and courtesans in the theater or even in social gatherings was fluid and much influenced by wealth and beauty. Machado's Rio de Janeiro parallels and in many cases predicts Freud's Vienna after 1891 through the exploration in his fiction of female repression, wish fulfillment, unconscious states, dreams, libido, guilt, the shame of sexuality, and the death wish. The open expression of female sexuality involves transgressing or violating some of society's legal or moral codes, while remaining taboo, both in the sense of a sacred and an accursed value of the patriarchal state.

AN INDESCRIBABLE EXISTENTIAL EMPTINESS, provoked by the dual nature of identity or self-definition, is the eerie theme of "The Mirror," with its unsettling subtitle, "Sketch for a new theory of the human

soul." The story is told by a normally silent member of a group of five gentlemen who gather to discuss highly transcendental and metaphysical questions, solving arduous problems of the universe, as Machado sarcastically
characterizes their objective. Almost an outsider, Jacobina is reluctant to
participate because he rejects the very conflictive nature of argumentation,
preferring to contemplate spiritual and eternal perfection: these are the poles
of the fatal pendulum hidden in his experience. Jacobina is described as
being "casmurro"—stubborn, capricious, obstinate—and linked to the Cyn-
ics in his use of an autobiographical incident to illustrate his insight into
not one but two souls he sees in every person, one that looks from the inside out and the other from the outside in. Jacobina's terrifying personal
story illustrates how what he calls an external soul, fixed in some object or
activity, comes to substitute for and finally eradicate internal, self-conscious
identity. The almost anonymous telling of the story—Jacobina speaks as
a ghost of a former self—undermines the very existence of narrative point
of view.

His memoir returns to the day when, at the age of twenty-five, he became a lieutenant in the National Guard. Through the pride of family members and the distinction of his nomination, the rank began to circumscribe
and dominate his existence as a person, especially when he was dressed in
the uniform awarded to him as a present by his friends. His identification
with this newly acquired identity was put to a strange test when his aunt
D. Marcolina, who lived some distance away in an isolated rural location,
insisted that he visit her in his uniform. Making a fuss and addressing him
only as "Senhor alferes" (Mister lieutenant), D. Marcolina placed a large,
richly decorated mirror in his room, a fine piece inherited from the time of
D. João VI's court. This magic looking glass, augmenting the attention and
adoration afforded the new lieutenant, absorbed any part of his humanity
or nature that existed outside the uniform. His was, furthermore, a rank
without authority: the adulation of the slaves was a pretense for distracting
his attention so that they could desert, and the lieutenant was left abandoned
in the solitary country house, waiting for days and weeks for his uncle to
return. His sole companion was a clock, whose ticktock ticktock sounded

to him like centuries passing and whose pendulum wounded his interior soul like a call from eternity, reminding him of Longfellow's poem "The Old Clock on the Stairs" hauntingly repeating, "Never, forever!—Forever, never!" Jacobina found himself in a silent dialogue with the abyss.

Rather than fear, he faced a strange sensation of emptiness, as if he were sleepwalking or dead, a mechanical doll. He became lost in a vast, infinite silence broken only by the clock's ticking, and he was incapable of breaking the hypnotic spell. His activities were reduced to reciting verses, some physical exercise, and scribbling incomplete fragments on paper in black ink to pass the time. More frighteningly, when he stood before the ancient mirror, his image was fragmented, nothing more than a jumble of lines, dispersed and mutilated. Jacobina was losing his mind along with his identity, until he remembered the uniform. After dressing in his lieutenant's uniform and standing before the mirror, it recognized him; as long as he sat before it in his uniform he was capable of reading, meditating, looking around, and in this way he survived another week of solitude in this anonymous state without feelings. The horrible, unsettling realization of his captivity infiltrated and lodged itself in the storyteller, who at this absorbing point in telling his story fled the room before his four listeners could realize he was absent. With the narrator's flight, the reader is left to break the spell and complete the story, which was abandoned in a kind of suspended animation, and to contemplate its profound effect. Jacobina's explanation was not sufficient to neutralize the loss of his identity or to regain all that he had ceded to the uniform and transferred into the mirror. The reader is left to ponder the inexpressible and infinite emptiness of time set against the momentary distractions and pretensions of philosophical argument.

Two stories about composers, "Cantiga de esponsais" ("Wedding Song," 1883) and "Um homem célebre" ("A Celebrity," 1888), evoke the strange mystery of life's dialectics, fateful pendulums that seem out of sync, in cases that illustrate what appear to their protagonists to be inexplicable injustices, indeed ironies of what life permits to some yet denies to others. The stories are inverse moral lessons, recasting the unfounded hopes of which Camões writes in his sonnet: "I gave Fortune good cause to castigate/hopes that in the end had little purchase." Machado's protagonists, to the contrary, do not understand either why fate has selected them for punishment or why their hopes have been reassigned or transferred to other realms, almost as if fate had mixed cognitive domains or circuits had become crossed by capriciousness or error.

Asymmetry and the impasses of destiny come to the fore in the stories. "Wedding Song" takes the reader back to 1813 in the Carmo Church, where sung Masses once united the public in celebration of musical arts. Romão Pires, the well-known conductor, a man of sixty, embodied a world divided: personally he was slow, circumspect, sad, absorbed; but when he conducted a Mass by José Maurício Nunes Garcia his face lit up as if the piece had been his own composition. In fact, Romão had a vocation for composing, and many original operas and Masses lodged in his imagination, but he lacked the capacity and talent for putting them down on paper, which made his life sad to the point that he had given up trying to extract a score from his vague ideas. Romão did have an ideal composition, however, a responsive song he had begun to compose three days after getting married, in 1799; when his wife died three years later, Romão tried to finish his song in her homage, but notes failed him, like a bird in a cage, and he grew ill. A doctor recommended that he forget music, but as he grew worse he decided to take out the unfinished piece in the hope of leaving it as a testimony to his love. Again, he sat at the harpsichord, but no inspiration came, not even something superficial. Looking out his back window, he saw a young couple in love, looking into each other's eyes; at the moment Romão was tearing up his music in frustration, he heard the young woman begin to sing extemporaneously, unconsciously, a tune never sung or heard before, not only a beautiful musical phrase but precisely the composition he had been trying to write all those years. He listened in sadness, shook his head, and died that night.

"A Celebrity" returns the reader to November 5, 1875, to a party at the house of the merry widow Camargo, her last, as she died hardly two months later. She asked the obsequious Pestana to play one of his famous polkas. Pestana grimaced and went dutifully to the piano, while joy spread around the room, gentlemen rushed for partners, and the event was the talk of the town. The ladies could hardly believe that the young man, dark with long, curly black hair, a guarded look, was the composer Pestana; he grew increasingly annoyed with the attention and took an early leave. In the streets, he passed another party where one of his polkas was being played, and he even met two men in the street who were brightly whistling the same polka. He fled home in a panic.

There he had an old slave who cared for him and a house inherited from his father from the time of Emperor Pedro I. On the wall were portraits of his father and of a priest who had given him a classical musical education, along with portraits of Domenico Cimarosa, Mozart, Beethoven, Christoph Gluck, Bach, Robert Schumann, and a few others. His piano was open, like an altar, and his sacred text was a Beethoven sonata. Pestana lived only to be a classical composer. He spent the evening looking at the portraits, going to the piano, waiting for inspiration that never came. Even the stars seemed to him to be notes in a possible composition. While he had fame and the attention of young women for his famous polkas, he only despaired and asked the heavens why he could not write one immortal page to compare with his ideal.

At the slightest suggestion he could run to the piano and perfect magnificent polkas, all published and given strange political titles by his editor. Soon he was again overcome, however, by nausea and hatred for his natural talent and easy success. He turned against his muse and was overcome with self-hatred and remorse. One of his young admirers came to find out that he had married a singer whom he heard in the São Francisco de Paula church, thinking that his celibacy might be responsible for his musical unproductivity. When he asked her to play his "Ave Maria," she recognized it as an unconscious copy of Frédéric Chopin, and Pestana wandered, mortified and hallucinated, like a crazy person through the streets. After his wife died of tuberculosis, Pestana devoted two years to a Requiem Mass, which he abandoned unfinished; living in poverty, his only recourse was to return to the composition of polkas. They were as prolific and famous as ever; there had been no diminution of his innate sources, and with each polka his depression increased. As he lay dying, his editor urgently requested a polka for the conservatives who were coming to power. With black humor, Pestana made his first and last comment on life's pendulum, offering to compose two polkas: "Look, since it's quite likely that I'm going to die any day now, I'll make you two polkas right away—the other can be used when the liberals come to power again." Thus the greatest polka composer of his day died in disgust, a man set against himself and his fate.

ETHICS IS A FORM OF QUESTIONING philosophy in Machado's stories, where the author's ultimate interest lies in probing the oscillating nature and meaning of the world and of experience. Machado subjects all of human behavior, its desires, motivations, and habits, to the eternal laws of fate, recounted in the asymmetric situations and contexts in which its principles can be observed in play. Moral conflict and deceptive human psychology form the nucleus of "The Nurse" ("O enfermeiro"), which could be considered Machado's version of "Crime Without Punishment." Machado returns to his pattern of narration by a remorseful aged man with only eight days to live, who writes to seek pardon from his readers for unspecified deeds or crimes committed during his life. Forty-two years old and tired of his job copying ecclesiastical documents and Latin citations, Procópio Valongo accepted a position in the provinces as nurse to a Colonel Felisberto. On arriving, he encountered a rigid, demanding, rough man who was the opposite of himself, the gentle, caring scribe. The colonel received him as if he were a thief and began a never-ending campaign of mistreatment and abuse, beating Valongo with his cane and a host of injurious verbal reproofs. His excuse was his advanced age, and he asked the nurse if he believed in souls from the other world. When the ill treatment intensified in a terrible scene on August 24 in which the colonel threatened to shoot him, Valongo definitely decided to return to the Royal Court. Later that very evening, Valongo was reading a romantic novel by Charles Victor Prévost while waiting to give the colonel his medicine at midnight when he was startled by screams. The delirious colonel threw a syringe that struck Valongo's face; reacting to the pain, the nurse grabbed the patient by the throat, and the next thing he knew the colonel had expired. Naturally he did everything possible to bring him back to life, but to no avail. He soon heard accusing voices in his head crying, "Assassin! Assassin!"

Valongo was lost in the silence of the night, facing his betrayal of trust and unconscious aggression. His earlier implicit request for pardon from the reader was based on the abuse he had suffered at the hands of the punishing colonel; now his defense found its justification in natural human accommodation. Valongo decided to tell a slave that the colonel had died during the night and sent word through him to the vicar and the local doctor. With the help of the nearsighted old slave, he wrapped the colonel in a sheet and closed his casket with tremulous hands. Like a character in Dostoevsky, Valongo found it impossible to hide his crime as he walked through the streets, overcome with disquiet, affliction, and hallucinations, his eyes fixed on the ground. Release came only though moral rationalization and relativism. When others showed no interest in the colonel's death, even finding some good qualities in him, Valongo joined in the chorus. Even as a nonbeliever, he ordered a Mass for Felisberto, distributed alms at the church door, and told amusing anecdotes to soften the village's loss in his dissimulation of guilt.

After the reading of the will, Valongo, who had returned to Rio de Janeiro, found himself the universal heir to the colonel's fortunes, and he was horrified. At first he thought of refusing the inheritance but later feared that a refusal might incriminate him in the death. He would revalidate the gift through donations and virtuous acts, and in that frame of mind he returned to the village. The colonel's ghost followed his every step, and he relived the night of the crime in his imagination. The next step in his defense came naturally by convincing himself that he had acted in self-defense. Valongo was heartened by the general denunciation of the colonel by the townspeople via a lengthy list of his hard, cruel, and perverse acts. On this basis he also reduced his donations and capped the event by ordering a Neapolitan marble tomb for the colonel. With the passing of years and his own approaching death, Valongo returned to his story but added the exculpatory proviso that in telling the story he may have exaggerated his role in the colonel's death, which might have been no more than a fatality. His remorse, guilt, and need for pardon had been weakened both by time and by the human talent for rationalization. He had practiced his plea with such naturalness that it was ironically and incisively undermined and denounced by Machado in Valongo's final misquotation of the Sermon on the Mount: "Blessed are those who possess, for they shall be consoled." The name Valongo is itself a reference to the area of Rio de Janeiro occupied since the eighteenth century by slave merchants, and the relevance to this story is that Valongo is treated as a slave by Colonel Felisberto. In that context Valongo's reaction to abuse has a potential justification, but it is not enough to overcome the inherent human sense of guilt, remorse, and the perverse sense of cruelty felt by Valongo in his exoneration by the public.

One of the most devastating cases of moral choice and social criticism is found in Machado's story "Pai contra mãe" ("Father versus Mother," 1906), which is a resounding denunciation of slavery and the skewed mechanisms of a slave society. Poverty and slavery combined lead to a fatal moment of crisis and of choice in which survival and ethics come into direct conflict. The story is based on duplicity of roles and questions of whether grotesque, cruel acts can ever contribute to the building of a human social order. Because of the nature of slavery, slaves frequently run away, so Machado wryly observes—and large encampments of fugitives had existed in the interior since the seventeenth century—and catching them was the profession of impoverished men or those who thought they were enforcing a system of property rights. Cândido Neves had been lucky at that occupation and made some money; yet when he married Clara and they had a child, profits dried up and there were no more slaves to catch. Impoverished, the couple was faced with abandoning their baby to an orphanage. Just as Cândido is carrying the baby to its fate, in the street he spots a runaway slave woman, Arminda, carrying her unborn baby. When accosted and captured, she explains that her cruel master beats her severely; there is a struggle, and Arminda is dragged through the streets and returned to her master. As Cândido receives his large reward, Arminda miscarries then and there in front of him. On hearing the account, Cândido's aunt criticizes the slave woman severely for the miscarriage, yet Cândido can only bless her for running away. The story closes with his motto, "Not all babies have the luck to be born!" Machado's narrative control of the story reaches well beyond the ironic or sardonic attitudes for which he is usually known and praised. Here, he has reached a point beyond words, for there is a profound level of truth in

Cândido's self-serving motto. To be born, as to live, is a struggle, as the science of the day proclaimed; yet that is hardly the whole story. Grotesque and cruel acts, implicit in a social order that proclaims itself humane, also intervene beyond ethics, and Cândido invokes them with a blindness and self-interest protected by the social order and contentment in the sacrifice of the weakest. In telling what should never have had to be said, Machado's story is one of the strongest and most profound indictments of slavery to be found in Brazilian literature.

PART THREE

Three Exemplary Modes

Theater and Opera: Machado's Operatic Theater of the World

Pomos hoje no teatro do Mundo esta nossa História.
[Today we place our History in the theater of the World.]

—Antônio Vieira, *História do futuro*

Tous les grands divertissements sont dangereux pour la vie chrétienne; mais entre tous ceux que le monde a inventés, il n'y en a point qui soit plus à craindre que la comédie. C'est une représentation si naturelle et si délicate des passions, qu'elle les émeut et les fait naître dans notre Coeur.
[All great diversions are dangerous for a Christian life, but among all those the world has invented none is to be so feared as that given by theater: it creates a representation of human passions so natural and so subtle that it excites and engenders them in our heart.]

—Pascal, *Pensées*, 11, 1655–62

"LIFE IS AN OPERA BUFFA with intervals of serious music," proclaimed the character Luís Batista in Machado's novel *Resurrection* (1872) on the eve of his friend Félix's expected marriage to Lívia. Luís was encouraging him to partake in one last amorous adventure, the equivalent in his musical imagination of a Carl Maria von Weber melody before the marital curtain was to lift on Jacques Offenbach. Machado's early involvement in the theater and opera, his own original plays and translations, may not have left a lasting influence on Brazilian theater, according to his bibliographer J. Galante de Sousa, yet the theater and opera, their atmosphere, characters, and conventions, were a constant and profound presence that left an indelible mark on his fiction, visible in every major work throughout his career.[1] When Maria Benedita leaves on her wedding voyage with Carlos Maria in *Quincas Borba*, D. Fernanda, who has masterminded their attachment, feels so fresh and overjoyed that she sings an Italian tune, "perhaps this aria from *Lucia: O'bell'alma innamorata.* Or this piece of the *Barbeiro: Ecco ridente in cielo, Già spunta la bella aurora.*" In *Helena*, the heroine confesses flirtatiously to Estácio, thought to be her brother, that she has stolen a book from his bookshelf, *Manon Lescaut*:

> "Oh!" exclaimed Estácio. "That book . . ."
> "Odd sort of book, isn't it? When I saw what it was like I closed it and put it back."
> "It's not a book for young unmarried ladies . . ."
> "Nor, I think, even for married ladies. . . . Anyway, I read only a few pages. Then I opened a geometry book . . . and, I confess, a desire came over me." (6)

In a letter of 1863 to Quintino Bocaiúva, Machado described theater as a laboratory for writing: "To progress from these simple groups of scenes to wider comedy, where the study of characters is conscious and sharp, where observation of society is joined to practical knowledge of the possibilities of the genre, such is a worthy ambition for youthful enthusiasm, which I have the immodesty to confess." He was led to write in his penultimate decade, "I am interested in music, only music, above all music" (July 5, 1896). In 1899 the composer Alberto Nepomuceno wrote a musical version of Machado's poem "Coração triste falando ao sol," the eighth poem of "Lira Chinesa" from *Phalenas* (1869), recorded with the pianist Arthur Napoleão, Machado's close friend.[2]

The musicologist André Heller-Lopes reports that attendance at the opera became an obligatory daily routine in Machado's day, and writers were deeply involved in operatic life. European music was accepted as national, while local music was considered to be exotic. Among the frequenters of the Alcazar Lyrique was the cream of Carioca society, filled with senators, deputies, and the rich.[3] Giuseppe Verdi's *Macbeth* was produced on March 25, 1852, and his *Ernani* on May 19, 1854.[4] Opera buffa was represented in Machado's adolescence by Vicenzo Fioravanti's and Andrea Passaro's *Il Ritorno di Columella* (1858). In 1859, according to Heller-Lopes, the Theatro Lyrico pursued its season of Italian operas producing works by "Bellini, Donizetti and Verdi, such as *I Puritani, I Martini, Lucrezia Borgia, Il Trovatore, Rigoletto*, and *Ernani*" (148). That year the Cariocas were fascinated by Bellini's *Norma* because of the soprano singing the title role, Augusta Candiani.[5] In a later column Machado wrote about her "resurrection" in a triumphal return to Rio de Janeiro in 1877, once again to perform *Norma*: "Candiani is unknown to the current generation. But we older people still remember what she did, because I was (*me, me adsum*) one of the horses of the moment pulling the prima-donna's carriage on the nights of the beautiful Norma! Candiani did not sing, she put heaven in her mouth. When she sighed, Norma was enough to make people beside themselves. The Fluminense public, suckers for melody like monkeys for bananas, was lifted to lyrical auroras. They heard Candiani and lost all sense of reality" (July 1, 1877). In the *Posthumous Memoirs of Brás Cubas*, Virgília is delighted when her husband, Lobo Neves, produces tickets to the opera featuring Candiani.

Luís Batista's aphorism further captures the concise, ironic skepticism that was one of Machado's characteristics, anticipating Falstaff's final chorus on human folly, "Tutto nel mondo è burla" (Everything in the world is a jest).[6] Machado wrote as if he were the artistic director of a social and allegorical theater of Rio de Janeiro, drawn from the comic operas and French *comédies lyriques* for which he had written libretti. French theater was more commonly produced than Brazilian in theaters in Rio de Janeiro, and Machado attested to its abundant presence in the city: "A man who is born, lives, and dies in Rio de Janeiro can be certain of finding a good selection of Parisian theater in five or six theaters in his native city" (1877). He describes life as a natural opera performance: "Luck is everything. Happenings weave together like plays in a theater; and they are acted the same way. The only difference is that there are no rehearsals; neither the author nor the actors need them. Once the curtain goes up, the play begins, and all know their roles without having read them. Luck is the point" (December 30, 1894). Machado dramatized the fallible city-world he observed with the distance of a critic, the aplomb of an artist, the sympathy of a comprehending audience, and the moral lessons of an aphorist.

The theater built for the Brazilian National Exposition of 1908, the year of Machado's death, illustrated the dominance and continued popularity of comic opera by incorporating musical motifs in its decoration: "A bar of music forms the frieze, the notes being marked in female figures; and the walls of the gallery are decorated in masques, comic silhouettes and other fanciful designs. The idea carried out in the decoration is a recognition of the popular music of Brazil as expressed in its comic operas and street songs."[7]

"Ao teatro! Ao teatro! Oh! que é sublime!" exclaimed Machado in 1856. Both Machado's literary education and his apprenticeship as an author were very closely tied to the theatrical and operatic world in Rio de Janeiro, an experience whose lasting impressions carried over into his fictional writings: "No, the theater isn't an industry . . . let's not reduce ideas to the level of merchandise. The theater isn't a bazaar. . . . Isn't the theater a school for morals? Isn't it a pulpit? Victor Hugo says in the preface to *Lucrezia Borgia*: 'The theater is a tribune, the theater is a pulpit'" (December 16, 1861). Machado's first novel quotes the play *Os estrangeiros* (1559) by the Portuguese author Francisco de Sá de Miranda to describe Viana, a social parasite ("good face, good hat and good words, costing little and worth a lot"). In *Resurrection*, Félix was in the orchestra when he saw Lívia and Vianna in the loges (4). Helena's father, Salvador, made his living for a time copying plays and actors' parts, and he described her mother resentfully as "half nun and half ballerina" (25). In *The Hand and the Glove*, after Estévão's first encounter with Guiomar, he saw her again at the Lyrico for Bellini's *La Sonnambula* (1831) and at the Gymnasio for Théodore Barrière's *Les Parisiens de la Décadence* (1854) (6). Characters throughout the short stories frequently attend and meet in theaters. In a chronicle Machado comments on the French opera company's performance of Daniel Auber's *Les diamants de la couronne* (1841): "One can say that the first lady of comic opera is the first artist in the dramatic and musical sense . . . she has the grace of her gestures and the precise knowledge to carry out the dramatic art of her role" (October 12, 1861).

The arrival of D. João VI with the Portuguese court saw the inauguration five years later of the Real Theatro de São João, which attracted Joseph Antoine Louis Lacombe's dance company and Marianna Torres's Portuguese theater company. The Real was rebuilt as São Pedro de Alcântara after a fire in 1824 and featured prominent Portuguese actors and dancers. It was again rebuilt and rededicated in 1857. The Theatro São Francisco de Paula (1833), called Gymnasio Dramatico, saw the comic opera *O Primo da Califórnia* by the Brazilian Joaquim Manuel de Macedo premiered on April 12, 1855; and in 1831 at the Theatro Constitucional Fluminense (later known as the Atheneu Dramatico), director João Caetano developed an important Brazilian dramatic company.[8] During the period of short-lived opera academies at the apex of Machado's involvement, the city gained many new theaters, including the Imperial Theatro D. Pedro II, the Lyrico Fluminense, Theatro Gymnasio Dramatico, the Theatro Cassino Franco Brasileiro, and the Théâtre Lyrique Français.[9] Attesting to his lifelong attachment to the theater, Machado returned to the genre to write the late comedies *Não consultes médico* (1896) and *Lição de botânica* (1905). *Não consultes médico* was produced at the Brazilian National Exposition of 1908 in celebration of the centenary of the opening of Brazilian ports to international commerce.

Carl Schlichthorst, a German engineer who arrived in Rio de Janeiro in 1824 and wrote a critical account of his two-year residence—he added a pointed "once and never more" to his title—gives a lively panoramic description of the city's theatrical life, audiences, and performances: "Theatrical shows can generally be divided into three parts: They start off with tragedies or grand opera. Then there is a dance scene. Finally, a farce. As a rule, operas are sung in Italian and repeated frequently, as in Italy. We are always hearing *Tancredo*, *Aureliano in Palmira*, and *Semiramis*. Comedies are generally translated from French. Schiller's *The Bandits* met with great success" (122–23).[10] He describes ritual behavior when the monarch is present:

> On the Imperial box one sees the coat of arms of the Empire of
> Brazil, supported by geniuses. Beautiful curtains of blue silk
> richly trimmed in gold tastefully veil the stage, opening only to
> the sides when the emperor arrives. These days an honor guard
> of 100 men, with a flag, is posted in front of the theater, and

sentinels guard the corridors and the main floor, leaving a dis-
agreeable and bothersome impression. At times, the public sa-
lutes the monarch on his arrival with a Viva! They then play
"Brava Gente Brasileira," a kind of national hymn that the Portuguese parody mercilessly. Both during the acts and the inter-
missions all hold their hats in their hands. This also happens
when the emperor is not present, because of the ladies. (123)

Most important with respect to the characters and interior scenes in the
novels and short stories of Machado de Assis, Schlichthorst differentiates
between the action on stage and action in the audience: "What is produced
on stage cannot by any means be compared with what happens in the boxes,
where the enchanting Carioca ladies, with indescribable style and grace,
the privileged inheritance of their peninsular ancestors, accept the hom-
ages and gallantries of their admirers." He describes scenes of elegant society women entertained alongside richly dressed and very costly courtesans
in the rows of theater boxes:

Those sensitive delicacies of the tropical world fill the boxes,
forming four semicircles full of color and life. The light golden
filigree work in front of them does nothing to detract from the
enchanting eyes that nature gave them or the art with which it
decorated them. One sees their full splendid figures from
head to foot, richly dressed with the most beautiful fabrics,
covered with gold and diamonds, with their beautiful and
well-shaped faces, shaded by swinging feathers. Each of their
gestures, looks, and smiles is animated by the Graces. Everyone unconsciously turns his back to the play and gets more
enjoyment out of the entr'actes being performed by the spectators rather than what happens on stage. The truly distinguished society of Rio de Janeiro would consider it a serious
lack of decorum to pay any attention to the stage. In the boxes,
gentlemen animatedly entertain their ladies who are conversing
or playing with their fans. Only the dances manage for a short

time to interrupt those conversations. The audience is absolutely absorbed by the ladies.

As brilliant as these reunions in the theater may be, one would commit a great error in thinking that all of those well-dressed ladies are Princesses and Countesses. One can affirm without fear of error that half of them belong to a league of public women or others who live by philosophical ties. As I have had occasion to say, Brazil is a paradise for these creatures. The prices are so exorbitant that one pays for their favors that I fear being called a liar if I revealed them. The true Brazilian finds that the dangerous pleasures offered him by such Circes are well worth 40 or 50 *mil-réis*. Even the most common prostitutes demand high prices, since they are white, which permits them a luxurious ostentation that, so to speak, ennobles their lowly occupation. (123–24)

Writing some thirty years before Machado entered Rio's theaters, Schlichthorst paints Rio's society as unsophisticated and undiscriminating, characterized by passionate flirtations and trivial entertainments without a high art of conversation: "Brazil is a country where social life is still in its infancy and where there is not a very great difference between a decent lady and a loose woman. There are truly no great social circles or art of conversation. In their gatherings they sing, some pairs dance by themselves, and time passes in flirtations with fans and the exchange of passionate glances. . . . At the theaters, all the women have an equal right to enter and, in what can be seen of their dress and comportment, there are no differences between the two classes. In the streets, no one feels any shame in greeting a courtesan" (124–25). In the 1850s the Theatro Lyrico Fluminense was the center of the city's operatic world, the scene of productions of Verdi's *Macbeth* and *Ernani*. Of the operas and zarzuelas produced by the Imperial Academy of Music before its extinction in 1860, Machado wrote the libretto for the production of *Pipelet*, an opera in three acts, episodes extracted from *Les Mystères de Paris* by Eugène Sue, music by Ermanno Wolf-Ferrari. The Theatro Gymnasio Dramatico, the place for realistic theater, was where Machado admired the Portuguese actor Furtado Coelho in plays by Alexandre Dumas fils, Émile Augier, Octave Feuillet, and Barrière.[11] Machado's first volume of plays (1863) was patterned after this realistic theater but was considered by Quintino Bocaiúva to be more suitable for reading than staging. Nevertheless, by 1866 five of his plays had been produced: *O caminho da porta*, *Gabriela*, *O protocolo*, *Quase ministro*, and *Os deuses de casaca*.[12]

Machado's essay of 1879 on the playwrights António José da Silva and Molière testifies to the importance he attached to popular musical theater. It is a study of the short-lived career of Silva, a Jew born in Brazil, who became a victim of the Inquisition in Portugal "in the bonfire of 18 October 1739" because of his satirical plays. The critic João Ribeiro defined Silva's work as a mixture of comedy and opera as well as different national popular musical traditions: "This brilliant poet's invention was to attach to a Spanish kind of comedy something from the Italian opera, joining national and Italian music, or arias, in the dialogues of his plays. Thus he contrasted to foreign opera the popular and national, less cultured or scientific but much more profound because it was part of the roots of the soul and of the popular tradition." Machado would have agreed with this assessment: he too commented on the influence of Italian operas on António José. Machado placed his theater in the style of Molière, noting in the comedies "much spontaneity, lively dialogue, graceful style, variety of situations, and a certain scenic awareness," qualities which, while inferior to those of Molière, were still admirable. He kept them in mind for his own scenes and dramatizations, as authenticated by his revision and publication of the essay in 1906. Machado inserts lines from António José into a comic scene in the *Posthumous Memoirs*, for example, in which Dr. Vilaça courts Dona Eusébia in a garden, expressing his passion with a remembered literary fragment: "Don't weep my love, don't wish for the day to break with two dawns," which the boy narrator Brás later discovered "to be from an opera by António José da Silva, the Jew" (12). Brás's discovery may have played a role in his later rejection of Eugênia, the illegitimate daughter of the couple the young Brás disturbs in the garden. Characters and quotations based on opera become a characteristic of Machado's fiction.

Machado singled out plastic expression ("intenção plástica"), that is, meaning conveyed by nonverbal, gestural, and physical means, as perhaps the most important influence on his works from theater and opera. Machado incorporated the procedure into his stories and novels on a subtle symbolic level. In *Quincas Borba*, for example, Rubião is seen at the beginning tapping the tassels of his robe against his knees, while feeling that he wasn't yet entirely happy and thinking about the beautiful Sofia: "He reconstructed in his head some mannerisms, some looks, some unexplained swaying of the body which had to mean that she loved him and that she loved him a great deal!" (3). As Merquior observed, when Sofia recounted to her husband the amorous advances she had received from Rubião, Palha's gestures conveyed his constrained reply. In *Esau and Jacob*, when Natividade and her husband, Santos, were out riding in a carriage, she answered his question without words: "If she said anything, it was so brief and muffled that it was lost entirely. Perhaps it was nothing more than a glance, a sigh, or something like that" (6). The reader is asked to guess the cause of her mysterious expressions and the couple's intertwined fingers, before being told at the end of the paragraph that Natividade was pregnant and had just told her husband.

Plasticity becomes a prime communicator of character, intent, and unspoken meaning in Machado. Settings that may seem gratuitous are often significant: the new sofas in Palha's living room, for example, signify that his acquisition of new furniture is the sign of an ascension in his fortune, which could only have been the result of his exploitation of Rubião's financial investments as director. When he suggested to Rubião that they untie their financial links, the reader understands that Palha has already depleted the funds, and his phrase effectively loosens Rubião's standing and stability, a fiduciary step to his fall into madness, vertigo, and delirium. Color plays both a plastic and an allegorical role in *Esau and Jacob*: "I haven't told you yet that Natividade's soul was blue. There I'll leave it. A sky blue, bright and transparent, that sometimes clouded, rarely stormed, and never darkened by night. . . . It was her immunity, having passed through life intact and pure" (19). In the short story "Final Chapter," colors are assigned to the character of historical and literary personages: "Rufina (permit me this chromatic figuration) did not possess the black soul of 'lady' Macbeth, or the red one of Cleopatra, or the blue one of Juliet, or the cream one of Beatriz, but a gray and subdued one like the multitude of human beings."

Theatrical comparisons animate the major novels. Brás Cubas declares that his brain is a stage on which all kinds of plays are performed: "Sacred dramas, austere, sentimental, crazy comedies, straggly farces, autos, buffooneries, pandemoniums, sensitive souls, a barrel full of things and characters where you can see everything, from Esmirna's rose to the rue in your garden, from Cleopatra's magnificent bed to the secluded beach where the beggar shivers in his sleep. Varied types and kinds of thoughts happen there. The atmosphere is not only for the eagle and hummingbird; there is also room for the slug and the toad" (34). The politician Lobo Neves compares his fading ambitions to a call from the stage, which had once captivated him when he saw it from the audience: "I had seen the theater from the audience's side and, I swear, it was beautiful. An imposing scenario, life, movement and grace in action. I signed up; they gave me a role" (58). In *Quincas Borba*, Sofia is pouting over a letter that is provoking her doubts about Carlos Maria, object of her curiosity and flirtation, and she has closed herself in a cedar box, as it were, as if she were dead. From that place, a swarm of new notions emerges to replace the old ones: "They emerge criticizing the world the way spectators come out of the theater criticizing the play and the actors" (159).

In *Dom Casmurro*, Bento introduces the chapter comparing life to an opera as if everything that had happened up to that point were only a preparation or prelude for a performance: "Truly that was the beginning of my life; everything that had happened before was like make-up and costuming of people who were going on stage, lights coming on, fiddles tuning, the overture. . . . Now I was going to begin my opera." Bento sets up an elaborate description of destiny as theater, as if he were but a pawn in a predetermined performance, unaware of or unable to control its outcome: "As certain that destiny, like all dramaturges, does not announce the incidents or the outcome. They come when it is time, until the curtain falls, the lights go out, and the spectators go to sleep." In feigned innocence, he proposes that plays should begin at the end, so the audience would understand the themes and complications at the outset, "because the last acts would explain the outcome of the first, a kind of conceit, and on the other hand I could go to bed with a good impression full of kindness and love" (72). Bento disguises his own role under a window when Escobar departs from his childhood home amid tearful and affectionate good-byes that are questioned by Capitu ("Who is that great friend?"). Bento turns the reader's attention to a horseman who had passed by Capitu's window, perhaps in hopes of courtship, by proclaiming that destiny had positioned his viewpoint; however, he disarms its very serious effect by telling it as a joke. The comparison nevertheless is telling: "Destiny is not only a dramaturge; it is also its own foil, that is, it tells the characters when to go on stage, gives them purpose and other objects, and at the right times executes a thunderclap, a carriage, a shot. . . . Thus my position underneath Capitu's window and the passage of a horseman is explained" (73). By means of this unlikely explanation of a fortuitously theatrical position, Bento used destiny to transform his role from guilty defendant to avid prosecutor.

Counselor Ayres, the purported author of Machado's last two novels, gives the theater a prime role in his writings. Opera determines his generous philosophy of life as an experienced man of the world (*"Perdonno a tutti,* as in opera," *Memorial,* January 14), and the libretti are scripts for all the world's renewed dramas and passions. Ayres compares the growing love between Tristão and Fidélia, which thwarted his own hopes, to a repeated theatrical drama of passion: "There is nothing like the passion of love to make what is common original, and new what is dying of age. That describes the engaged couple. . . . That love drama, which seems to have been born from the perfidy of the serpent and disobedience of man, still produces floods in this world. Poets at one time or another lend it their tongues, among spectators' tears: that is all. The drama is performed every day and in every way, new as the sun, which is also old" (March 13). Ayres's chapter on the entr'acte (titled "Between one act and another") is his allegory of the world as an indeterminate and deceptive moment of passage. Reality and fantasy are to be found both in the audience and on the stage:

While the months pass, pretend you are in the theater, between one act and another, conversing. Inside they are preparing the stage, the artists are changing costumes. Don't go there: allow the leading lady in her dressing room to laugh with her friends about what she cried about here outside with the spectators. As for the garden they are preparing, don't turn your back to it; it is an old canvas without any painting, because only the part turned toward the spectator is green with flowers. Allow yourself to remain out here in this lady's box. Examine her eyes; they still have the tears caused by the lady in the play. Speak to her about the play and the artists. That it is hard to understand. That they do not know the parts. Or then that it is sublime. Then look around the boxes with your binoculars, distribute justice, call the beautiful beautiful, the ugly ugly, and do not forget to tell anecdotes that make the beautiful less ugly and virtues that beautify the ugly. The virtues should be great and the anecdotes entertaining. Some comments are banal, but banality in the mouth of a good narrator becomes rare and precious. And you will see how the tears entirely dry up and reality takes the place of fiction. I speak in images; you know that everything here is the pure truth without tears. (*Esau and Jacob*, 46)

Natividade's elegant life before her pregnancy included "a box in the Lyric Theater, not counting the balls at the Fluminense Casino" (6). Ayres used a melodramatic opera anecdote to disguise his anguish over the question of courting the beautiful young Flora, who he had just admitted was pretty. In the company of ladies on the way to Petrópolis, he indulged in dramatic hyperbole to cover his feelings by relating a Neapolitan anecdote: "But there, on the road, among ladies, he confessed that he had killed more than one rival. That if he remembered correctly, he must be carrying seven corpses. He praised his dagger . . . he had been obliged to give it as a present to a bandit, his friend, when the man proved that he had just committed his twenty-ninth murder the day before. 'Here's for your thirtieth,' he said, giving him the weapon. A few days later, he learned that the bandit, with that dagger, had killed the husband of a lady, and later the lady, whom he loved hopelessly. 'I left him with thirty-one first degree murders.' The ladies continued to laugh. Thus he was able to divert the conversation from Flora and her lovers" (92).

In *Counselor Ayres' Memorial*, the passion between Fidélia and her first husband, Eduardo, began at the theater, in a story told by Ayres's sister Rita: "The first time that he saw her was from the gallery of the Theatro Lyrico. He looked at her once again, she noticed him, and they ended up in love with each other. Once they found out who they were, the die was already cast, even if they had known from the beginning, because their passion struck suddenly" (February 10). Ayres relies on a complex operatic metaphor to summarize his conversation with the Aguiar couple, in which he has tried unsuccessfully through allusive comments to diminish Tristão's standing as a beau for Fidélia. Before leaving their company, Ayres surprised Aguiar by commenting on the death of a beloved dog, whose illness had brought much suffering to D. Carmo; he had learned of the death from Tristão and perhaps was trying to associate him symbolically with the buried affection the couple had felt for the animal. After he departed, while walking down the street, Ayres heard a dog barking from inside a country house, telling him with the barks that his efforts were useless: "My friend, you don't need to know the reason that has inspired my discourse; barking is like dying, dogs do everything, and the Aguiar's also barked until recently; now forget it, since it belongs to the dead" (September 18). The subtlety of these barks led Ayres to think that the barking was coming from inside his head because he had swallowed a "philosophical dog," perhaps one served by his cook? He turned the metaphor into cannibalistic discourse, as he was being devoured by his own argumentation. The coarse way in which he gained this philosophical perspective reminded Ayres of an operatic performance in Europe characterized by extremes, where it was said that a certain soprano was an elephant who had swallowed a nightingale: "I think they were talking about Alboni, large and gross in body, with a delicious voice" (September 18).

Machado wrote a series of reviews of performances by international actresses, beginning with that of Gabriela da Cunha as Margarida Gautier in *La Dame aux camélias*: "Frivolous at the beginning, then sentimental, later passionate, resigned" (January 8, 1860). He attended performances by the romantic Portuguese actress Emília das Neves, praising her ability to portray a state of madness on stage without excess or exaggeration. He praised Adelaide Ristori, Italy's greatest tragic actress, who was performing in Brazil in 1869: "Imposing figure, sculptural, severe face, sonorous and vibrant voice. . . . Her face is the lively mirror of the soul, supreme gift of theatrical art. A contraction of her face, an expression with her eyes are at times worth an entire monologue, and no one better than Ristori to possess this gift of making herself understood by gesture for those who cannot understand her language . . . each gesture, each step, each movement reveals a plastic intention and always communicates an artistic attitude." He catalogued the repertoire of her expressions: "The pain, the rage, the disdain, the love, the irony, the hopelessness, the jealousy . . . she knows how to express them with such artistic truth!"[13] Machado admired the greatest French actress of the nineteenth century, Sarah Bernhardt, who performed in Brazil in 1866, 1893, and 1895—"with all her bones and quirks, but with her genius also"—praised by Joaquim Nabuco as the "ambassador of the French spirit"; the Italian actress Eleanora Duse, in Brazil in 1885 and 1907: "I liked that devil of a woman so much that I pretended to tear my gloves in enthusiasm"; the Italian tightrope walker Maria Spelterini, who arrived in Brazil in 1877: "That pretty and agile tightrope walker, master in the art of using the tightrope, has stunned part of the population that admires her gymnastic accomplishments"; and the actress Aimée at the Alcazar Lyrique, in Brazil from 1864 until 1868 performing in the French operettas that took over the Brazilian stage with Offenbach's *Orfée aux enfers* (1858) and *La vie parisienne* (1866), the *cocotte comédienne* whom he described as "a little blonde devil, a light, slender, graceful figure, a rather feminine head, half angelic, with lively eyes, a nose like Sappho's, a mouth lovingly fresh that seems to have been formed by two songs of Ovid."

The strong, dramatic feminine characters in Machado's five major novels must certainly have been drawn from his descriptions of the international actresses he admired and reviewed. His Virgília is described

in comparable terms by Brás Cubas: "She was pretty, fresh, she came
from the hands of nature full of the sorcery, uncertain and eternal, that an
individual passes to another individual for the secrets of creation. That was
Virgília, and she was fair, very fair, ostentatious, ignorant, childish, full
of mysterious drives, a lot of indolence, and some devoutness—devoutness
or maybe fear: I think fear"; "She was one of those figures carved in Pen-
telic marble, or noble workmanship, open and pure, tranquilly beautiful,
like the statues but neither indifferent nor cold" (63). Rubião observes Sofia as if she were exhibited like a flower: "Rubião admired her figure once
more, her sculptured torso, narrow below, broad above as it emerged from
her ample hips the way a large bouquet comes out of a vase. Her head, he
was able to tell himself then, was like a single, straight magnolia thrusting
up in the center of the bouquet" (37). Bento's description of Capitu is worthy of a tightrope walker: "I could not take my eyes from that creature—
fourteen years old, tall, blooming, clasped in a calico dress that was
half-faded. Her heavy hair hung down her back in two braids with their
ends tied together, in the fashion of the time. She was dark, with large,
clear eyes, long straight nose, delicate mouth and rounded chin. Her
hands, in spite of rude tasks, were lovingly cared for: they did not smell
of fine soaps or lotions, but, washed with well water and common soap,
were without blemish. She wore cloth shoes, cheap and old, to which she
herself had given a few stitches" (13). Flora, the object of Pedro's and Paulo's affection, was compared to "a brittle vase, or to a flower that would
bloom only for a day, and would have had material for a sweet elegy. Already she had big clear eyes, less knowing, but gifted with a particular
look that was not the darting of her mother or the dullness of her father,
but rather tender and pensive, so full of grace that it would soften the face
of a miser. Add an aquiline nose, sketch out a half-smiling mouth, forming
a long face, smooth her red hair, and there you have the girl Flora" (31).
Counselor Ayres is fascinated by the alluring widow Noronha, the Fidélia
whom his sister has challenged him to marry, described as an actress of
emotion: "Fidélia had only partially left off mourning: she had on a pair of
small coral earrings; and the locket with her husband's portrait, which
hung at her breast, was gold. The rest of her dress was somber. The jewels

and a spray of forget-me-nots at her waist were perhaps in compliment to her friend. . . . She seems to have been shaped on a lathe—without this expression giving any idea of rigidity. On the contrary, she is pliant and soft. I allude only to the correctness of her body's lines, that is, the ones seen; the others are guessed at, and sworn to. Her skin is smooth and clear, and her cheeks have a ruddy glow that is not unbecoming to her widowhood" (January 25). Machado created five great actresses who played their parts in his scenarios in the same terms he applied to the Italian and French actresses who appeared on the stages of Rio de Janeiro in the 1850s and 1860s.

Machado witnessed life-changing performances by international actors also, including the first productions of Shakespeare in Brazil in 1871 with Ernesto Rossi and Tommaso Salvini, the greatest interpreters of the day. Rossi's performances in May 1871 in *Hamlet, Othello, Romeo and Juliet,* and *Macbeth* made an indelible impression on Machado, expressed in 1871 in a letter to Salvador de Mendonça: "Imagine Othello, Iago, Cordelia, Desdemona, Lear, Shylock, almost all of Shakespeare; imagine Horace, Camila, Phedra, Mirra, Luis XI, Frei Luís de Sousa, Stuart, what else? Imagine all those great characters played by three Italians, at the same time, on the same stage, right before us! *Quel rêve! Et c'est n'est pas notre destin! [What a dream! And that isn't our destiny!]*." The next year he translated Hamlet's famous monologue, published in the *Arquivo Contemporâneo,* used the title for a short story in 1876, and wove more than 250 references to Shakespeare into his subsequent fiction. João Roberto Faria connects the *Othello* that the character Bento attends in a definitive chapter of *Dom Casmurro* to Rossi's performance in 1871 and the frenzy it caused that so impressed Machado. In a column from 1865, however, Machado was already invoking the themes of jealousy and passion found in Othello and Desdemona, perhaps based on performances of Rossini's *Otello* (1816): "Everyone knows Othello, that *obra-prima* by Shakespeare, that brings to the character of the Moor all the furor of jealousy, all the ardors of passion. What a beautiful scene when Othello contemplates Desdemona in bed! Desdemona dies assassinated, although innocent; the perfidious woman lives, in spite of being guilty" (June 18, 1865).

Life Is an Opera

In the same way that "The Delirium" established an early allegorical, expansive structure for the *Posthumous Memoirs*, endowing it with a temporal dimension, "The Opera" in *Dom Casmurro* establishes allegory as a mainstay of Machado's literary world and source of its creative tensions; it propounds a parallel genesis myth explaining how this world was created as opera and music written, staged, orchestrated, and performed in contention between God and Satan. "Life is an opera," said the old Italian tenor Marcolini to the young Bento, who narrates the myth. The "overture" to this grand opera follows the metaphor of life as theater: everything about Bento's life up to this young age, he says, was like a preparation for going on stage, putting on makeup and costumes, turning up lights, and tuning violins, in preparation for the beginning of his life's opera. While viewing old portraits of his parents at the time of their marriage, Bento says, "I commenced by not being born." Such a state of potentiality applies to life as a struggle to be born—to the tenors, baritones, and bassos who fight for the soprano, and the contralto and soprano who fight for the tenor in the grand opera, with its choruses, ballets, and orchestra. After a glass of Chianti, the Italian lays out the operatic story of creation:

> God is the poet. The music is by Satan, a young maestro with a great future, who studied in the conservatory of heaven. Rival of Michael, Raphael, and Gabriel, he could not endure the priority those classmates enjoyed in the distribution of the prizes. It may be, too, that their overly sweet and mystic music was boring to his genius, which was essentially tragic. He started a rebellion, which was discovered in time, and he was expelled from the conservatory. The whole thing would have ended there, if God had not written a libretto for an opera, and thrown it aside, because he considered that type of amusement unsuited to his eternity. Satan carried off the manuscript with him to hell . . . he composed a score. As soon as he finished it, he took it to the Eternal Father. (6)

Satan's supplications to hear, emend, and perform his score were all rejected, until a weary God agreed to have it performed, but outside of heaven. A planet, Earth, was designed as a special theater and a company of men created to play all the parts plus choruses, ballets, and musicians, but God refused to attend any of the rehearsals. The ensuing rivalry or duality between the text and performance leads to a theory of contradiction, contrast, repetition, obscurity, and imbalance that foregrounds many of Machado's aesthetic principles and procedures. Critical opinion of the opera was equally divided between those who thought that the rough spots could be emended so as not to be at variance with the poet's sublime ideas and those who thought the libretto had been so corrupted by contrivance and altered meaning that it was now contrary to the spirit of the whole. Yet, the Italian concludes, the piece will last as long as the theater, until it is demolished by "astronomic expediency," and the success of the production will increase, even though poet and musicians are paid very different and unequal amounts. The opera is comprehensive, in that all elements—fire, water, air, earth—are included, and the production lasts as long as life on Earth. The musical score is conflictive in some parts, repetitive in others, there are obscure passages, and the coauthors never agree. Nunes sees in Marcolini's opera the contradictions of human existence through myth and metaphysics, the dramatic contrast between opposing and irreducible forces, which are never capable of producing complete harmony.

While it may seem to be only an amusing fantasy, Marcolini's opera is an all-encompassing chapter, a microcosm of the novel that is about to unfold. Machado proves his literary ingenuity by intimating deeper significance to his novel through a mythical account of the origin of Earth, one that distorts and satirizes Genesis and consequently casts Bento Santiago's secondary narrative into relief. Both opera and Bento's memoirs are undermined by the unreliable and conflictive relationship between libretto and music, memory and actuality, archetypal and individual authorship. If extracting truth from the opera is made impossible because of the clash between God's words and Satan's score, Bento similarly denies his readers a definitive conclusion about his innocence by being absent from and unsure of his own testimony, while presenting contradictory, prejudiced, and slanted details from his early life, education, and marriage. Bento's confessed unreliable memory conflicts with an ostensible obsession with accuracy, perhaps feigned for the reader's benefit, in a story full of missing parts. Even Bento's dislike of the color yellow may be an impression caused by forgetfulness and confusion. With a narrative so full of lacunas, the reader must reconstruct the drama and interpret the missing parts; for Bento, forgetfulness can be a device for controlling the narrative, since, as he comments, "everything can be put into books with omissions."

It is unclear in the opera whether Satan's intention is cooperation and collaboration or jealous rebellion and competition with God. Marcolini seems to favor Satan as a rebel and outcast, while portraying God as inflexible and demanding, a stubborn and truculent capitalist: Bento's struggle against entering the seminary is thus colored and prepared in terms of the opera's fundamental conflict. On the level of discourse, like the discordant opera, Bento presents a story full of lacunas he himself does not completely understand; at the same time, he exploits the pretense of not understanding, intensified by confessions of disorientation, confusion, and failure, as a rhetorical device aimed at gaining the reader's favor and sympathy, even though in reality he actually does have little deep understanding of the events he narrates. His life recapitulates Marcolini's opera: he understands some parts but not others, the music of his prose often distorts the meaning of his words, and he is both intentionally and unintentionally discordant, confusing, obscure, and replete with contradictions.

Marcolini's divine and profane comic opera inverts the biblical story of origin, so that even angels become quarreling critics, thus mirroring Bento's narrative, in which tragic events are often treated comically and comic situations tragically. Bento will carry the comparison forward by claiming that both the opera and, later, Shakespeare's tragedy *Othello* mirror his life; the master narrative is invoked in order to justify Bento's personal variation on a theme. His reference to Shakespeare's *The Merry Wives of Windsor* introduces yet another theatrical and operatic model, suggesting Capitu and Sancha in the role of merry wives and Escobar and Bento as Falstaff and Ford, the would-be seducer and the needlessly jealous husband. Both Bento and Marcolini will insist absurdly that their accounts are "pure and absolute truth," whereas Bento is quite aware that the opera only appears to be true; thinking like a lawyer, he pronounces aphoristically that "appearance is often the whole of the truth," a phrase that demonstrates to what extent he has failed to grasp the interplay between truth and invention in the opera. He is intent instead on playing a role as a character in his own opera, flaunting his own embellishments and subjectivity, either unaware of or choosing to ignore the flaws in the libretto that render it, and his account as well, hermeneutical failures.

If the world is the stage for an opera, then representation is our mode of being, and music takes the place of words in explaining the workings of the world: "Wordlessly, like a novel for the piano" (*Esau and Jacob*, 18). Bento's brief, elusive interlude, the chapter "In Heaven," dedicated to feelings of bliss after his marriage to Capitu, is in this context only half an opera; the harmony of an organic work of art, in which music and words coincide, written and composed exclusively by the artist who oversees the production and controls its meaning, runs contrary to the grand celestial opera of the world, whose baroque dynamic features a discordant performance by two diametrically opposed composers, one of whom is motivated by rebellion, blame, and jealousy. Even Bento seems not to believe fully in his newfound heaven, since he asserts that his happiness "would have given the lie to the Italian tenor's theory," not that it actually did, and being a person who is frequently overcome by fantasies and visions, Bento admits that "everything may have been a dream." Through both the allegory of the opera and Bento's uncertain moments of heavenly happiness, Machado as author invokes dialectical, unstable, and conflictive forces that impose themselves onto the world stage. Within this larger universal and global human and divine theater, Machado continues to delineate subthemes of interior allegories on the nature of his plots and their variable meanings.

In a reprise of Marcolini's opera, the theme of the flood and Noah's ark leads to a satire on immortality: "Everything brings to mind the idea of a wise modern Frenchman. By his calculations, he thinks that every ten thousand years there will be a universal flood on Earth, or at least continental, caused by displacement of the oceans caused by the planet's rotation: 'A periodic flood! What then will become of the immortality of our works? Only if one copy of the works of all poets, musicians, and artists is placed in an arc. Oh! But what kind of ark could that be!'" (November 1, 1877). The age-old depiction of love as pursuit, conquest, and surrender comes in for parody when compared to warfare: "An illustrious banality has been revealed to me: What is love more than war, in which one advances by ambushes and battles, in which there are dead and wounded, heroes and forgotten multitudes? As in other bombardments, love attracts the curious. Life, on this point, is an interminable Gloria Beach, or Flamengo. When Daphnis and Chloe were fighting, there were few ocular or binocular witnesses of idle wanderers counting the bullets" (November 12, 1893). The eternal rhythm of change is portrayed in a comic political allegory of empire and republic: "A prophet came forth in an Arabic tribe, founded a religion and formed the bases of an empire . . . strong like granite, implacable as a scimitar, infallible as the Koran. Centuries passed, men, republics, passions, and history are made day-by-day, page-by-page; human activities are altered, corrupted, modified, transformed. All the civilized lands of Earth are a vast rebirth of things and ideas. . . . One day, a half dozen libertine youths, rounded up by Jean Jacques and Benjamin Constant . . . decided . . . to open the womb of fatalism and pull out a constitution" (July 1, 1876). Machado plays on opposing functions such as death and medicine: "Why have so many medicines died? Why is it that medicines die? That is the question. . . . The solution is of a metaphysical order. Nature, interested in conservation of the human species, inspires the composition of medicines according to the pathological gradations over time. Someone already said, with great sagacity, that there are no illnesses, only sick people" (November 19, 1893). Men are given the function of grammar in a fantasy and parody reminiscent of Jonathan Swift:

> The adjective was introduced in languages in anticipation of the honorific titles with which civilization would shame naked breasts and the singular names of its ancient heroes. Example: a man using his baptismal name is a noun. If this man suddenly adds an honorary title he becomes an adjective. Yesterday's celebration left many nouns with open mouths. They said that it

was raining adjectives. But actually there was only one. And the disconsolate nouns were left to see themselves de-adjectivized, with the hope of an adjectivization later on. . . . That's also what happens to the young ladies, who are nouns, and go around looking for husbands who are adjectives. For some, days, months, and years pass before Hymen, the great writer, comes to tie together those two distant parts. (April 1, 1862)

Through an allegory about a king without subjects, Machado suggests by analogy that the ideal writer would be independent of readers: "If I entered the island of Trindade, I would begin by never leaving it; I would name myself king without subjects. There would be only three people, me, the queen and a cook. . . . King without subjects! Oh! Sublime dream! Singular imagining! A King without anyone to govern, to hear, no petitions, no annoyances. There would be no political party to attack me, to spy on me, to insult me, nor any party to worship me, kiss my feet, call me radiant sun, indomitable lion, strongbox of virtues, the air and the life of the universe" (March 11, 1894). Machado's concluding adage on the changeable nature of things, found in the short story "Those Cousins from Sapucaia!," follows his description of the page by page and day by day process of inevitable change: "Everything depends on circumstances—a rule as valid for one's style as it is for life; one word leads to another, and that's the way books, governments, and revolutions happen; some even say that's the way nature put the species together."

Worms are the unlikely allegorical actors buried in Machado's library: Brás Cubas dedicates his memoirs to the worm that first chewed on his cadaver before encountering literary worms that will ultimately consume his library. In his "theory of editions," life, like books, goes through different editions until the last one, which the editor gives to the worms without charge. In a satire on the paradoxical nature of life, Bento Santiago wants to find out how Achilles's lance can both wound and cure or how the Almighty can both wound and make whole, so he consults old, dead, and buried books to track down the meaning. He interviews a long, fat worm he finds in one of the volumes it is gnawing, an occupation of devouring that is material, universal, and existential, an end in itself: "We know absolutely nothing of the texts we gnaw, nor do we choose what we gnaw, nor do we like or dislike what we gnaw: we gnaw" (17). Machado's reference is to Charles Darwin's *Worms* (1881), based on the geologist Charles Lyell's view of nature as being in constant slow change because of the geological benefits of worms: "When we behold a wide, turf-covered expanse, we should remember that its smoothness, on which so much of its beauty depends, is mainly due to all the inequalities having been slowly levelled by worms. It is a marvelous reflection that the whole of the superficial mould over any such expanse has passed, and will again pass, every few years through the bodies of worms."[14] Machado referred specifically to Darwin's work in the short story "A Chapter of Hats," when Conrado propounds his theory on the metaphysics of hats to Mariana:

> The metaphysical principle is the following—the hat completes the man, it is a complement decreed *ab eterno*, no one can change it without self-mutilation. This is a profound matter, one that has never yet occurred to anyone. Wise men have studied everything from stars to worms, or, to give you the bibliographical references, from Laplace onwards. . . . You've never read Laplace? From Laplace and his *Mécanique celeste* to Darwin and his curious book about worms, yet they've never thought to stop and look at a hat, and study it from every angle. No one has noticed that there is metaphysics in hats.

Darwin had read papers on coral reefs and the formation of mold at the Geological Society in 1837, theorizing the power of construction in mud and soil that passes through earthworms and coral polyps. The fat readerly worm consulted by Bento Santiago is an actor in the allegory of smoothness and leveling in reading the world library. Its answer could be rewritten as pure devouring: "We know absolutely nothing of the texts we read, nor do we choose what we read, nor do we like or dislike what we read: we read." The worm's answer could also describe the roles humanity plays in the celestial opera composed and written by God and Satan and sung by the Italian tenor Marcolini in the theater of the world: "We know absolutely nothing of the arias and choruses we sing, nor do we choose what we sing, nor do we like or dislike what we sing: we sing."

TEN

Delirium, Hallucination, and Dream:
Flying Through Time on a Delirious Trapeze

Tenho uns dias, umas horas, em que dou para subir à montanha e doutrinar
os homens. A natureza, que não faz saltos, também não gosta de andar
torto, e depressa me repõe no caminho direito, que é na planície.
[There are some days, some hours, when I can climb the mountain and
preach to men. Nature, which is constant, doesn't like crooked paths,
and soon puts me back on a straight path, back on the plain.]

—"A Semana," January 27, 1895

Tal era o espetáculo, acerbo e curioso espetáculo.
[Such was the spectacle, a bitter and odd spectacle.]

—"The Delirium," *Posthumous Memoirs*, chapter 7

Um dia sonhei, eu Tcheouang Tseu, que era borboleta, e voava daqui, dali,
como uma verdadeira borboleta. Seguia consciente meus caprichos de borboleta, inconsciente de minha condição humana. De repente despertei, aqui estou
deitado, eu mesmo, de novo. Agora, já nem sei mais ao certo se era um homem
que sonhava ser borboleta, ou se só uma borboleta que sonhou ser homem.
Entre o sonho e a realidade, segundo Tcheouang Tseu, difícil é distinguir onde
um começa e outro termina, e acrescentou—existe um sonho que nos espera
a todos nós e então, só então, saberemos se sonhamos um grande sonho.
[One day I dreamed that I, Chuang Chou, was a butterfly, flying around like
a real butterfly. I was conscious of my butterfly efforts and unconscious of my
human condition. Suddenly, I awoke and am lying here, once more myself.
Now, I am no longer sure if I was a man who dreamed he was a butterfly,
or if I am a butterfly dreaming I am a man. According to Chuang Chou,
it is difficult to tell where the dream ends and the reality begins, adding
that there exists a dream that awaits us all and then, and only then,
will we know if we are dreaming the big dream.]

—Maria Martins, *Ásia maior: O planeta China*, 67

"THE DELIRIUM," chapter 7 of the *Posthumous Memoirs*, was considered to be so unmatched and imaginative that the Portuguese novelist Eça de Queirós memorized it to recite to his dinner guests in Paris in a kind of intimate evening theater. Nunes considered it to be a metaphysical farce, one of three exemplary moments in Machado's entire output. Entering into a reverie, Brás Cubas finds himself on the back of a flying hippopotamus; time and space are reversed, and he is on a delirious flight headed toward the origin of the centuries. Brás's encounter with the formidable and primordial Pandora, goddess of nature, is an allegory on the continuing debate on nature and a critique of tenets of social Darwinism. She declares, "I am your mother and your enemy." Brás rides with a trapeze in his brain, from chapter 2, and on it hangs an idea that waves its arms, takes a leap, and ends in the form of an X that challenges the reader to decipher the riddle or be devoured. Here the mystery of occult knowledge is crossed with the theme of devouring, associated with post-Darwinian concepts of nature and science. Machado compares the insatiable appetite of the public to an ancient Mexican serpent that oscillates between consuming and digesting: "Like the reptile monster that I mentioned, the public is not satisfied with simple repasts and tiny quantities; it wants good and ample provisions. Nothing notable has happened recently that could satisfy that collective mouth that gorges on everything" (January 7, 1862). Brás's idea repeats words of the ravenous Theban Sphinx, pictured as woman, lion, and bird, that swallows all who cannot answer her riddle. She represents the mysteries underlying reality as well as the march of life as a process of continual devouring. Pandora is, in Nunes's reading, the "ineluctable will to live, which sacrifices the individual through the egotistical force of the same principle of conservation with which she holds out the hope of more life" (8). The principle recurs in Counselor Ayres's meditations on Fidélia's love for Tristão and her devotion to her deceased husband: "Everything could exist in the same person, without either the widow's hypocrisy or infidelity to the next husband. That is the accord or contrast between individual and species" (*Memorial*, January 9).

Brás's trip to the origins of time opens the theme of primitivism that will occupy social and anthropological thinking into the early and mid-twentieth century in classical studies such as Sir James Fraser's *Golden Bough: A Study in Magic and Religion* and Lucien Lévy-Bruhl's *La mentalité primitive.*[1] In Machado's macabre short story "Conto alexandrino" ("An Alexandrian Tale," 1883) the medical experimenter Stroibus seeks to prove that the qualities of animals can be directly transferred to men: "A rat's blood, if given to a man to drink, will turn him into a burglar . . . the spider, if we could transfer it inside a man, would give that man the rudiments of geometry and musical appreciation. With a flock of storks, swallows or cranes, I'll make a home-loving man into a wanderer. . . . In sum . . . the animals are the letters of the alphabet; man is the syntax." The story parodies Stroibus's belief that the pain of dissection is justified for the goals of science by giving it an unexpected turn, when Stroibus and his accomplice Pythias successfully become thieves and are arrested, then subjected themselves to dissection by Herophilus, father of anatomy. In this twist, Machado sketches a chilling allegory of human psychology: the animals saved decide to celebrate and to keep laughing, until the time comes when the same thing will happen to them. Science is not immune from the universal, primitive devouring of *Humanitas.*

The delirium could be classified as a response to Darwin's *On the Origin of Species* (1859) in the style of Jules Verne's fictional journeys that he termed "Extraordinary Voyages," including *Journey to the Center of the Earth* (1864) and *Around the World in Eighty Days* (1873). Brás flies back to the origin of the centuries, which, like mythical gods, he fears, may become annoyed and crush the two travelers. The delirium constitutes a historical satire of the concept of primitive origin, to be followed in the novel by the philosophical satire of Quincas Borba's Humanism. Both concern the distant, phylogenetic origins of culture, although the delirium is dominated by the terrifying maternity of Pandora, who is Nature formless and wild: "'Don't be frightened,' she said, 'my enmity doesn't kill, it's confirmed most of all by life. You're alive: that's the only torment I want.'" She appeared passive yet immovable, strong and vital, as she continued: "Yes, worm, you're alive . . . and if your consciousness gets an instant of wisdom, you'll say you want to live." She has only scorn for the individual who, once brought into existence, is no longer of interest and subject to her variable and disinterested laws: "I no longer need you. The minute that passes doesn't matter to time, only the minute that's coming. The minute that's coming is strong, merry, it thinks it carries eternity in itself and it carries death, and it perishes just like the other one, but time carries on. Selfishness, you say? Yes, selfishness, I have no other law. Selfishness, preservation." Brás passes in flight over the panorama of the centuries; his turbulent, dizzying view confirms the laws and archetypes that have conditioned the historical present by witnessing the spectacle of the world in all its inexplicable contradictions, mixing virtues and vices, glory and misery, pain and indifference: "I saw everything . . . torments and delights— from that thing called glory to the other one called misery, and I saw love multiplying misery and I saw misery intensifying weakness. Along came greed that devours, wealth that inflames, envy that drools, and the hoe and the pen, damp with sweat and ambition, hunger, vanity, melancholy . . . all of them shaking man like a rattle until they destroyed him like a rag." It is the ultimate hippopotamus's-eye view.

A possible source of Machado's astronomical perspective on all human time and history lies in the idea of the encyclopedia and world library, as illustrated by the Greek historian Diodorus Siculus, whose *Library of History* (*Bibliotheca historica*), originally forty books, covers world history beginning with myths of Hellenic tribes and extending to Julius Caesar's Gallic Wars. One of the first literary flights, Lucian's "Icaromenippus, an Aerial Expedition," introduced Machado to the skepticism of Menippean satire. While in *The Lusiads*, cited by Machado, the goddess Thetys reveals to Vasco da Gama on a mountaintop the geographical successes of the Portuguese fleets viewed in a crystalline globe, Pandora in the delirium similarly carries Brás up to the top of a mountain: "I cast my eyes down . . . through the mist I contemplated a strange and singular thing. Just imagine, reader, a reduction of the centuries and a parade of all of them, all races, all passions, the tumult of empires, the war of appetites and hates, the reciprocal destruction of creatures and things." More immediate sources mentioned for the delirium are hallucinations in Flaubert's *La Tentation de Saint Antoine* (1874) and Giacomo Leopardi's "Dialogue between Nature and an Icelander" ("Dialogo della Natura e di un islandese," *Operette morali*, 1827). Rather than Leopardi's tragic confrontation with Nature, however, Machado's tone turns the topic of Nature's indifference to the human species into a parody of the conflict between the universal will and individual will, as dramatized in Arthur Schopenhauer's pessimistic philosophy: "My gaze, bored and distracted, finally saw the present century arrive, and behind it the future ones. It came along agile, dexterous, vibrant, self-confident, a little diffuse, bold, knowledgeable, but in the end as miserable as the ones before, and so it passed, and that was how the others passed, with the same rapidity and the same monotony" (*Posthumous Memoirs*, 7).

Having an imagination rooted in history, whether visionary, moral, or prophetic, Brás cannot fly into the future, and thus he returns to consciousness at the moment his hippopotamus changes course and is fast flying toward present time, approaching the limit of what has not yet come to be. Although the delirium is not futurism, magical realism, or science fiction, the chapter is nevertheless presented with a tone of the fantastic and astonishing; it speaks to scientific theories of the day, which must have seemed fantastic, presented in the context of an encyclopedic or panoramic perspective on human history, much like the world library Machado incorporated into his fiction. Humor in the delirium is bound up in its skepticism and ironic sense of amazement and wonder, enhanced by the suspension of belief with which Brás casts it. Machado is also not without his jokes. He could have chosen the hippopotamus as an aircraft because of its incongruous size and weight, being, among the animals, one of the least likely ever to be able to fly; but it is also possible that the hippo is an alliterative joke related to St. Augustine of Hippo Regius (Santo Agostinho de Hipona), the author of the *Confessions* (which was important to Machado), perhaps because of his location in Africa or his confessions of a hedonistic youth. The etymology of *hippopotamus* as "river horse" belongs to this association, just as the search for the origins of the Nile in the late nineteenth century represented a quest for the origins of civilization. Multiple layers of humor fill Machado's comprehensive vision of the world theater.

Indeed, Machado looked on all philosophic ideas with a mocking and ironic smile: when faced with the calamity of human experience, Brás turns his potential cry of anguish into "an arrhythmic and idiotic laugh." Nunes considers that philosophy in Machado's work is inseparable from the narrative form of discourse, which establishes a ludic relationship to philosophic ideas, treating them with imagination and recasting them as literary fantasies, laughing at philosophy with an ironic and even mordacious inflection. In the story "O empréstimo" ("The Loan," 1882), the question of first causes is reduced to the hidden meaning of vests: "There is philosophical meaning in everything. Carlyle discovered the meaning of vests, or more properly, the vestuary"; and in the story "Teoria do medalhão" ("Education of a Stuffed Shirt," 1881), a youth receives instruction on how to succeed in society: "—"No philosophy?—Let's understand each other: on paper and in speaking, some, in reality none. 'Philosophy of History,' for example, is a phrase that you should use frequently, but I won't permit you to come to any conclusions except those found by others. Flee from everything that could smell of thought, originality, etc." Machado ironizes the case of a trolley that ran over and eliminated two old people: "There's a philosophy for everything. . . . In any case, we're not going to be against electricity, we'd have to condemn all machines and, seeing that there are still shipwrecks, burn all the ships. No, sir. The necrology of trollies pulled by donkeys is long and lugubrious enough to show that control of traction doesn't have anything to do with disasters." He writes on reports of a visit to the Turkish and Christian cemeteries of Constantinople and their different concepts of death: "What do you want death to mean to a people for whom eternity is promoted for the most voluptuous pleasures that the liveliest imagination can imagine? . . . But, philosophically, are they right, or are we, sons of the Christian church? There is enough truth for both parties, and one should accept distant beliefs, so that they will not disrespect ours" (November 1, 1861).

While the delirium resembles a dream, the symbolism of its strange figures and its disjointed associations seems to be ripe for psychological interpretation as coded mental messages or meanings. Brás Cubas claims to be the first person to speak about his own delirium, and in saying that science will thank him for his contemplation of mental phenomena he parodies early investigations into magnetism, vitalism, and hypnotism by Franz Anton Mesmer and James Braid and Abbé Faria's (José Custódio de Faria) use of auto-suggestion and magnetic fields in séances. Indeed, Brás's delirium resembles a form of hypnotism, as he enters into an altered mental state lasting "for some twenty or thirty minutes," during which he takes on different forms. He is first a potbellied Chinese barber shaving a mandarin who alternately rewards and abuses him, before he is transformed into a large book, St. Thomas Aquinas's *Theologica*, with a leather binding and silver clasps. With his hands crossed over his stomach securing the clasps, he appears to be dead, and he imagines that Virgília comes to uncross them. Those interested in psychoanalytic interpretations will note the dialectical opposition of theology and eroticism—a dilemma that will dominate *Dom Casmurro*, the novel Machado will write twenty years later—and the association of a book with a deceased author. Brás's allegorical description of man flagellated by the centuries invokes mechanisms for avoiding the fatality of experience that are of psychological import: "Then man, whipped and rebellious, ran ahead of the fatality of things after a nebulous and dodging figure made of remnants, one remnant of the impalpable, another of the improbable, another of the invisible, all sewn together with a precarious stitch by the needle of imagination. And that figure—nothing less than the chimera of happiness—either runs away from him perpetually or lets itself be caught by him, and man would clutch it to his breast, and then she would laugh, mockingly, and disappear like an illusion." Just as Brás thinks he is on the verge of being able to decipher eternity, everything shrinks in a mist back to life size. Brás has no reason to believe, however, that the monotonous pattern that determines both youth and age will change or that the rapid speed of the centuries will not continue "beyond all comprehension." He begs God to save his readers from an idée fixe, referring to a form of monomania—in this case a pathological disorder stemming from a single compelling idea—advanced by Jean-Étienne Dominique Esquirol, who studied the passions as causes of insanity.[2] Brás gives contrary evidence: nature is fickle and meretricious, ideas are mobile and changeable, history is voluble, philosophy is unequal, and public actions often have private motivations (4).

The destructive power of delusional passions is a constant psychological theme in Machado's fiction. Remorse and envy have a strong presence, affecting narrators who write their memoirs out of a deep, yet repressed, regret and with varying degrees of self-knowledge. The gnawing literary worm to whom Brás dedicated his posthumous memoirs, symbolizing that regret, may be a relative of the worm in Charles Baudelaire's poem *Remords posthume*: "—Et le ver rongera ta peau comme un remords" (—And like remorse the worm will gnaw you in your sleep).[3] In *Helena*, Estácio censures himself as petty and cruel, blaming himself for a quarrel with Eugênia because he idealized her qualities to a degree that she could not maintain: "He felt something like a sting of remorse" (5). Iaiá Garcia rues the accusatory thoughts she directs toward her stepmother Estela, whom she suspects of having harbored over the years a romance with Jorge in betrayal of her husband, Iaiá's ill father, for whom the daughter feels a strong loyalty: "She spent an entire hour in that solitary pensive state, alone with suspicion and remorse—remorse also because . . . her soul would falter and tremble. . . . She hated herself" (10). The true situation is quite different, however, and Iaiá has no knowledge of Estela's noble self-sacrifice and constancy because of the persistence of her malicious suspicions. Her haunting doubt is a continuation of Félix's quandary, from *Resurrection*, and prefigures Bento Santiago's in *Dom Casmurro*.

In the story "Captain of Volunteers," Simão de Castro tells of being challenged by his friend Barreto to seduce Maria, the young companion of his much older close friend identified only by the letter X. After a promising romance on the Niterói ferry, Maria suspends her visits. Simão reads in the newspaper that X has enlisted as a captain in the Paraguayan war, in spite of his dislike of military service and disapproval of that war. After a few days' delay, Simão is received formally but coldly by X, noticing Maria's constraints as X discourses at length on the glories of his future service. He leaves Simão his last photograph, already in uniform, as a final parting gift. Maria leaves to reside in Porto Alegre and never returns to Rio; X dies in the Paraguayan war, and Maria dies sometime later in the South. Simão is left between his regret and his melancholic remembrances and with a particular sense of his lowliness in contrast to X's presumed nobility: "I can't remember any other situation in life in which I felt more estranged from myself." X's revenge had no noble cause, yet it was complete and carried out with determination to its intended consequences, mixing heroism with condescension and disdain. Simão is left with a very strange kind of admiration for X, "a special admiration, which isn't large except to make me feel small. Yes, I wasn't capable of doing what he did."

In Bento Santiago, remorse touches the most profound and sudden depths, as he is subject to ideas and impulses that do not come into his conscious mind because he represses all possible emotions, a consequence of his fear of his mother, who dominated his early development. José Dias goes to call him home from the seminary because of his mother's illness and her wish that he be present in case of her death to save her soul. Bento is overcome in the street: "My heart was pounding, my legs wobbled. . . . My desire to hear the truth was complicated with the fear of knowing it" (67). He kept on walking in a blank state, and an idea without words, like the trapeze, came into his mind: "With Mama dead, that would be the end of the seminary." Bento is horrified with himself and rushes to excuse this terrible idea as a "lightning flash" of no permanence or consequence; yet the unexpected opening of his subconscious mind left him under an intense weight of remorse. He had betrayed his filial devotion, if only for a split second in which he recognized lust and selfishness and for an instant his fear and loathing. What he cannot admit is that he had subconsciously planned for his mother's death, just as he would come to plan those of his son and wife in a similar sublimation, namely, when lost in another state of passion over the drowning of Escobar, who had become a father figure to him. Bento hopes his Uncle Cosme will die so that Escobar can take his place as his son's godfather (108), and he does wait for Aunt Justina to die so that he will not have to take Ezequiel to visit her, so that she will not pronounce the boy, as would José Dias, to be the very image of Bento (145). When his mother recovered, Bento was motivated to make another of his exaggerated spiritual promises: if God would pardon him he would say two thousand paternosters. In an earlier promise, Bento had been obligated to pay a debt to his mother, that of going to the seminary and becoming a priest, which he was determined to avoid; here, the debt to God was also unpaid, and Bento makes use of the hyperbole of his exaggerated promissory notes to detract attention from his hidden resentment.

Bento thus attempts to reestablish his goodness and innocence in the face of perverse, sublimated desire.

In a meeting with his best friend Escobar and his wife, Sancha, Bento has another "instant of madness and sin" (118). For no obvious reason he has read an "irresistible urge" of passion into his exchange of glances with Sancha, part of a subconscious mechanism by which he wishes to exchange himself with Escobar or in some way become Escobar, whom he admires excessively. When leaving the couple's company, he imagines that her eyes speak to him and that her hand lingers in his longer than usual. His impression inverts a scene with Escobar in the seminary on the theme of envy, which ends when "Escobar furtively gripped my hand so hard that my fingers still tingle" (94). Escobar's photograph, which Bento keeps alongside one of his mother, speaks to him, and he feels guilt for what he excuses as sexual intent with Sancha. His subconscious association links Escobar with his mother, who early on "gazed at me like a lost soul or caught hold of my hand for no reason at all and squeezed it hard" (11). Again, he dismissed his confused feelings about Sancha as "a swift flash of sensation" destined to fade away with night and sleep: "There are pangs of remorse that spring from no greater sin and have no greater duration." Bento continues to dismiss his sublimated desire because he cannot fathom its reason, since he has repressed its actual meaning: "It was not passion or love. Was it caprice or what?" The photograph of Escobar continues to speak to him, but he does not record or confess its message, nor does he seem to understand its powerful influence over him (118).

In *Esau and Jacob*, Counselor Ayres feels a more lyrical kind of remorse in his frustrated, self-censored desire to court the young Flora, the daughter of Dona Cláudia and Batista who is the object of competition between Natividade's twin sons. It was Natividade, in whom Ayres once had a love interest years before, who had refused to consent to Ayres's marriage to her sister, for subtle and unstated reasons, whether, as the narrator suggests, to avoid ceding him to another or to punish him for loving her. The fifteen-year-old Flora is graceful, retiring, and modest, spending whole days at the piano with her music. Ayres finds her intriguing and "an inexplicable creature"; he gallantly describes her to her mother: "But if you permit me to say something, I will say that this young lady sums up the gifts of her mother" (31). With the substitution posited, Ayres finds he has attracted Flora's attention with his mysterious adjective, "with Flora staring at him with her restless, questioning eyes, curious to know why she was or would become inexplicable." Ayres is charmed, almost overwhelmed: "Note that I like her very much. I find a special flavor in that contrast of her opposing characteristics, at the same time so human and so removed from this world, so ethereal and so ambitious at the same time, with a hidden ambition" (49). Flora did not avert her gaze until the twins Paulo and Pedro came to distract her, and at that point Ayres strongly felt the gap of years separating him from love and romance. He had become solitary, devoted to reliving the past rather than assuming a new role in the present; nevertheless, he could not bear hearing Flora laugh with the twins and departed. His feeling was, he writes, "something like remorse. Remorse at getting old, I think" (34).

In all of his fiction Machado explores the subtleties and perversions of cruelty. In his first novel, *Resurrection*, Félix confesses to having symptoms of a disaffected disposition: "One year is an eternity for my heart. No affection lasts for more than six months; when that time is up, love packs its bags and leaves my heart like a traveler leaves a hotel; then boredom checks in—my guest." In *Iaiá Garcia*, the character Luís Garcia "loved the species but spurned the individual" (1). Machado's well-known story "A causa secreta" ("The Secret Cause," 1885) presents the tale of Garcia and Fortunato, told retrospectively by an omniscient narrator after their deaths. Garcia, who had obtained his doctor of medicine degree in 1861, had begun to notice Fortunato, whom he met by chance one night in the Theatro São Januário, engrossed in a heavy melodrama full of daggers and remorse. When a resident of Garcia's apartment building was wounded by a dagger from a gang of *capoeiras*, Fortunato suddenly appeared to attend to him, looking coldly at the suffering man, much to Garcia's astonishment: "His eyes were a clear gray, the color of lead, they moved slowly and had a hard, cold, indifferent expression." Still, Fortunato's help had to be viewed as an act of dedication; the contradiction would have to be explained by accepting the human heart as a "well of mysteries." In fact, Fortunato was hypnotized by his cold, scientific curiosity: "The young man possessed in germ the ability to decipher men, to unravel human character. He had a love of analysis, and felt a special pleasure, which he called exquisite, in penetrating layer after layer of spiritual strata until he touched the secret heart of an organism." Fortunato married and invited Garcia, whom he met unexpectedly on the street, to meet his wife, Maria Luíza, a gentle, submissive young woman half his age, for dinner. After Garcia and Fortunato open a hospital in partnership, their visits become almost everyday occurrences. The point of horror comes when Maria Luíza, whom Garcia has found to be ill, hears the cries of a laboratory rat that Fortunato is torturing because it carried off one of his important papers. In ordering an end to the last stages of the torture, Garcia comes to perceive the inner psychology of his partner: " 'Punishment without anger,' thought the doctor, 'the need for a sensation of pleasure that only another creature's pain can give— that is the secret heart of this man.' " Characteristically, Fortunato cares for Maria Luíza throughout her illness, taking care of the slightest detail and sparing nothing, and she dies under prolonged torturous visions. Garcia, when left alone at the wake to watch over the corpse, comes to realize the great love for her that he had spiritualized, and he bends over to place a kiss on her forehead and then a second kiss before giving way to sobs. Fortunato, who had meanwhile come to the doorway, witnessed the first kiss as the "epilogue to a book of adultery" and, with the second, began to savor his partner's hopeless despair and pain, which to Fortunato "was long, very long, deliciously long." The pleasure of observing suffering portrayed in this story is matched by Fortunato's quick presumption of adultery; both narrative strands will reappear in a different guise in *Dom Casmurro*.

Bento Santiago goes to some lengths to disguise the cruelty that has resulted from his early life of weakness and resentment yet strangely lets slip at several key moments confessions of the pain he inflicts on himself and others. He would have readers believe that his solitary life as an old *dom casmurro* has a normal rhythm, one marked by invitations to opera in the city and by the visits of a never-ending stream of women; yet his hidden purpose is to expiate a crime, to rationalize his underground motives, and to shift blame for his actions, whose purpose and nature are veiled, often even from himself, and sublimated onto his wife, Capitu. Almost from their first acquaintance, his narrative craftily builds a case against her, culminating in a commonly accepted accusation of adultery; the seeds are planted in a childhood argument following Capitu's question whether he would come to her against his mother's orders.[4] Bento exaggerates, hoping to gain her sympathy and tears, but she proves stronger and more imaginative. Driven by spite in a losing game, he insists he will indeed become a priest; upping the ante, he requests of her that he be the only priest who gives her penance and absolution and who marries her. Capitu declines but slyly promises that he can baptize her first child. Thus, the illegitimacy of her son is established in Bento's mind by her defiance during this "duel of ironies" (um duelo de ironias): "The threat of a first child. Capitu's first child, her marriage with another then, absolute separation, loss, annihilation, all this so wrought on me that I found neither word nor gesture, but sat stupefied" (45).

In chapter 40 Bento recounts another fantasy of classical origin that further symbolizes Capitu's unfaithfulness. He remembers reading in Tacitus about Iberian mares that could conceive from the wind, and his imagination becomes a mare ready to confess to D. Glória its lovemaking with Capitu, a fanciful, windswept idea that will disqualify him from the priesthood at the same time it associates Capitu with atmospheric pan-insemination. The corollary to the motif is for Bento to classify his son as an illegitimate stranger sown by the wind, once he makes his final accusation against Capitu. That his young son appears to him in a hallucination as Escobar returned from the dead, Bento, the lawyer, craftily explains, is nothing more than proof of his victimization at the hands of the deceptive Capitu. Only a few chapters before, however, it was Bento who tried to seduce Sancha and envied Escobar's powerful arms; now he is transferring his "sin" to Capitu, distracting the reader so that her guilt will produce his exoneration.

No doubt the depths to which he descends in plotting to kill his wife and son make the struggles of his youth appear fanciful, and Bento feels the "pleasure of old sufferings," the title of chapter 77: "In telling of that crisis in my adolescent love, I feel something I do not know how to explain: somehow the sufferings of that period have become so spiritualized with time that they have melted into pleasure. This is not clear—but not everything is clear in life or in books. The truth is I feel a particular pleasure in retelling this ordeal, while it is certain that it reminds me of others which I would not be reminded of for anything." Again, Bento hides by confessing, and his assurance of truth is tied to an understatement as opaque as the experiences of his later life that it conceals and avoids. To employ the same rhetorical device, one can say that the pleasure Bento feels in retelling his ordeals is not unconnected with the pleasure Fortunato feels in "The Secret Cause" in observing and participating in suffering.

Counselor Ayres's reaction to cruelty is more variegated and proverbial since his life has been one of Faustian bargains rather than of Shakespearean visions and passions. Readers learn that he enjoyed being a bachelor, never had much interest in his wife, whom he left buried in Vienna, and thinks fondly of his dalliance in Caracas with a certain Carmen, reminiscent of the opera heroine. Ever the diplomat, Ayres is capable of seeing two sides to any question, and in the case of evil or cruelty he advances an adage to demonstrate that there are no absolutes in questions of morality and ethics and that human beings may be observed to have an undeniable taste for and find pleasure in what is bad: "There is no evil that does not bring a little good, and for that reason what is bad is useful, often indispensable, sometimes delicious" (*Esau and Jacob,* 59). He documents this observation in his memoirs by recounting one of the barbs of the quick-witted, malicious Cesária, who has attracted the counselor's admiration for her sharp tongue. Cesária sees through Tristão, who claims to be undecided between the call for him to go back to Lisbon for politics and his courtship of the beautiful widow Fidélia. Cesária dryly comments to Ayres, "He loves Fidélia, but it is plain that he prefers politics." Ayres, by way of his diary, arrives at the deeper meaning and intention of her unmasking of Tristão: "It was the melancholy of secret pleasure, or however one should express it to explain a pleasurable discovery that ought to be decently cloaked in sadness. There was in her remark a kind of condemnation of the young man, but only apparently: the true meaning was the pleasure of seeing the lady slighted" (November 30). Satire can be truthful and cruel simultaneously, and Ayres is not beneath enjoying the delicious undercurrents.

Brás Cubas's expressive delirium is only the prelude to a stream of hallucinations, dreams, and visions that haunt Machado's fictional characters and test the rationality of their expositions and control of their narratives. While presented as comic, inconsequential, and surreal, hallucinatory scenes often break the narrative frame and allow prohibited or repressed content to appear, although in metaphoric guise. Hallucinations often involve allegorical fantasies, scenarios of self-loathing or wish fulfillment, and violent, even homicidal, urges repressed in narration of events. The Spanish girl Marcela is humming a *seguidilla* while Brás is angrily pouring out his despair over his love for her, yet she remains cold: "I had an urge to strangle her, humiliate her at least, make her crawl at my feet" (17). Yet he is soon tearfully begging her not to abandon him. Brás's theatrical anger reappears when the noble lady Virgília, his lover who summed up all love and whose purpose for existing, in his opinion, was to spare him unpleasant feelings, refuses to accept his proposal to run away to a far corner of the globe. Chewing on his jealousy, Brás is ready to strangle her husband; yet at dinner with the couple he turns his coldness and anger against Virgília: "It was the first great anger I'd felt for Virgília" (63). His jealousy leads to desperate fantasies, tied to the theater where Virgília has gone that evening to hear the soprano Candiani. Brás's reaction is to increase his coldness toward her, "ready to forget her and to kill her." He imagines her in the theater with her magnificent arms bare, pained that others should see "her milky white breast, her hair in tight curls in the style of the time, and her diamonds, less brilliant than her eyes" (64). In his mind he then undresses her item by item until she is restored to his sole, naked possession.

In the short story "The Diplomat," Rangel, who reads the cards at dances and parties to reveal which woman has a secret admirer, is himself barred from finding a beautiful young companion, especially among the great ladies of the court, because of his low standing, reluctance, and shyness. Instead, he fantasizes about becoming the greatest of lovers and seducers: "In his imagination he did everything, raped women and destroyed cities. More than once he named himself minister of State, and was satiated

with courtesies and decrees. One day, December 2, he went to the extreme
of proclaiming himself emperor on returning from the parade at the Palace; for this to happen he imagined a revolution in which he spilt some
blood, little, and set up a beneficent dictatorship in which he took revenge
only on a few small annoyances as a scribe. For the outside world, however, all his great deeds were fables. In reality, he was reticent and discreet."
There is a murderous misreading in *Quincas Borba* when Rubião finds a
letter dropped by the postman written in Sofia's hand and addressed to Carlos Maria. Jealousy overcomes him: "What could be written there on that
homicidal piece of paper? Perversion, lust, the whole language of evil and
dementia are summed up in two or three lines" (99). He imagines invad-
ing the house on the ironically named Harmony Street, where he thinks
the two had met, and forcing the seamstress who lived there to confess: "He
knocked, entered, grabbed the seamstress by the throat, and demanded the
truth or her life. The poor woman, threatened with death, confessed everything. She took him to see the lady, who was someone else. It wasn't
Sofia. When Rubião came to, he felt annoyed" (90). Rubião takes on the
role of a spectator in the theater, and he imagines the scene of their confrontation when he faces Sofia with the letter in hand: "I'll take a good
look at her face and see if she's frightened or not. Maybe she'll grow pale,
then I'll threaten her, talk to her about the Rua da Harmonia. I'll swear to
her that I'm prepared to spend three hundred, eight hundred, a thousand
contos, two thousand, thirty thousand *contos* if necessary to strangle the
swine" (99).

    Bento is overcome with homicidal urges throughout his memoir, al-
though he deflects attention by confessing and dramatizing them as fantasies, placing them amid many other kinds of incidents, and characterizing
them as typical of his jealous overreactions. When José Dias answers Bento's awkward question about Capitu during a visit to the seminary by saying casually that she was a "giddy creature . . . just waiting to hook some
young buck of the neighborhood and marry him," Bento becomes unstable. He is careful to write that he exaggerated his reaction—turning pale,
feeling chilled, and weeping—but does confess that a new and cruel feeling of jealousy gnawed at his heart as he imagined Capitu gaily exchang-

ing flowers for kisses with a young horseman. The motif of the passing horseman, which recurs in Machado's work, can be compared to an incident in the short story "A Chapter of Hats." There, Mariana is frustrated by her husband Conrado's refusal to try a new, different hat, although she has been docile and acquiescent to his whims and wishes. Her older friend Sophia suggests that she has been too soft on him, and she cites the example of Beatriz, whose husband took her to the country because of an Englishman who passed by their home on horseback in the afternoons: "Poor Englishman! Naturally he didn't even notice she'd gone. We women can live quite well with our husbands, with mutual respect, nobody treading on anyone else's toes, with no fits of pique and no overwhelming ways."

Bento loses awareness in a dream in which he dashes headlong to Padua's house to seize Capitu and "command her, force her to confess." When he recovers his senses, José Dias is still talking, and Bento limits himself to asking meekly when he would be able to return home to see his mother. On his next visit the obsessive vision returns with greater vengeance, propelled by his memory of José Dias's phrase about Capitu; Bento imagines that he sees malicious glances among his relatives, and he wants to grab Dias by the collar and question him. His decision, however, is to flee to his room, talk to himself, persecute himself, roll on the bed and weep, all the while plotting revenge. Bento will not visit Capitu and once more has the extreme idea of being ordained, so that he can stand before her inaccessibly cold, serene, scornful, and contemptuous. He will further punish and desecrate her body for the perverse betrayal he has imagined: "Twice I found myself gnashing my teeth, as if she were between them." When he heard Capitu's voice in the living room, he became even more explicit: "I continued deaf, alone with myself and my scorn. And I was filled with a desire to drive my nails into her throat, bury them deep, and watch the life drain out of her with her blood" (75). This is the same Bento who will return later to the theme of Capitu's betrayal and convict and punish her with the agreement and even the praise of his readers.

Bento's vengeful scenarios are aimed at others as well. He learns that Capitu has been visiting Sancha, staying overnight, and he hears Cousin Justina gossip that the two have perhaps been flirting with some young men.

Bento immediately accepts the rumor as fact: "I did not kill her because I did not have handy either steel or rope, pistol or dagger; but the eyes I turned on her, if they could have killed, would have done the work of all four" (81). Bento then begins an exposition on the value of eyes as weapons of attack, such than one glance would halt or fell an enemy or rival. In this way he subtly prepares his association of Capitu's eyes with the tide, particularly the tide that kills Escobar, and this link will amount to further proof of her homicidal guilt. This is not the crime of which he openly accuses her; he prefers to substitute the accusation of adultery because it exacts revenge on the basis of his jealousy of an imagined liaison with Escobar superseding and substituting his own.[5]

Numb from the death of Escobar, whose photo he has kept along-side one of his mother, Bento is horrified by the resemblance of his son Ezequiel to Escobar, making him think a ghost has returned to haunt him with recollections of the man whom Bento had found inside his soul: "Es-cobar returned from the grave, from the seminary, from Flamengo; he sat at table with me, welcomed me on the stairs, kissed me each morning in my study or asked for the customary blessing at night. All this repelled me; I endured it so as not to be revealed to myself and to the world" (132). The impossible revelation would be conscious recognition of his weakness and emotional dependence on Escobar. When he is alone with his terrible se-cret, he feels an extreme desperation: "I would vow to kill them both, sud-denly or slowly—slowly, so as to transfer into their dying, all the moments of my dulled, agonized life. . . . All Capitu's artful attempts to attenuate [the evil] were to no purpose: I grew steadily worse." Bento postures that he is going to imitate Cato and drink poisoned coffee; because a photograph of Escobar happens to be looking at him, he instead offers the cup to his young son but withdraws it just as the boy is about to drink. Bento was on the verge of confessing his phantasmagoria as the grand illusion he knew it to be when he again glanced at Escobar's photograph. He reached a point of no return, as he decided that to be a man meant never to relent, and, as a lawyer, he decided to demand reparations, not for Capitu's alleged infidelity but for the cause he cannot admit, the death of Escobar. Bento becomes dizzy with the recollections and wonders, "And why did I not strangle them that day when

I turned my eyes from the street where two amorous swallows were treading on the telegraph wire?" His sentence on them is to impose exile until death by reversing the theme of the voyage to Europe that recurs through the novel—up to and including Escobar's proposed European excursion for the two couples—and turning it into a final revenge and punishment, an inverted and perverse voyage. Bento's proclivity for bizarre, fanciful, cruel visions contributes to a subcurrent of opera buffa, as he depends on others to rescue him from his petulant and revengeful imagination. With his excessive doting on his misdeeds, Bento makes of himself a foolish comic character: the widowed bachelor lawyer drawn from opera buffa outshines the role of young victim of family and society.

In *Esau and Jacob*, Dona Cláudia and Flora, while out shopping for hats, run into Paulo, who has just returned from law school in São Paulo. The scene recapitulates in many ways the preceding story of Bento. Paulo tries to entertain the ladies with anecdotes of São Paulo that are of no interest to them, and Flora gives him trivial news about her girlfriends. Everything served as a point of further digression, making obvious the lack of any real conversation between the two, and both began to stare with melancholy into the distance. The growing silence became a portent: when the ladies decided to return to a shop for some forgotten item, Flora had the feeling she was undertaking a voyage into exile until death: "Those errands on the list already had the feel of boat tickets, the ship was on its way, they would rush to pack their bags, make arrangements, say their good-byes, check into their cabins, get seasick, and then go on to that other sea and land sickness which would kill her, for certain, Flora thought" (62). Paulo, overreacting to the deteriorating situation, feels the impulse to ask Flora privately if she had thought or dreamt of him while he was studying in São Paulo. He assumes that she had not, and the thought is enough to unleash his rage: he would hurl insults at her; if she ran, he would catch her by the sleeve of her dress and strangle her. Rather, he corrects himself: he would sweep her up into a Strauss waltz or a polka. Paulo dissimulates so as to disarm his homicidal jealous urge, which he dismisses as "wild thoughts." They leave such an impression, however, that Paulo has no memory of anything else that happened to the three that afternoon.

In her inability to choose between the twins Paulo and Pedro, Flora began to have unusual hallucinations. She divided her idea of herself between heart, which she compared to Paulo's valor and impetuosity, and spirit, which belonged to Pedro's artfulness and subtlety. Left with opposing and irreconcilable sides of herself, Flora is subject to hallucinatory doubts that make her inner pendulum shift constantly from one idea to another, one side to another in a restlessness mirroring her psychological inability to decide. The narrator calls her condition a "deranged sadness," leaving Flora afraid of her own thoughts. In her hallucinatory state, Flora makes one person out of the twins in her mind, entering into a state of reverie and unconscious desire that brings about her midsummer night's dream: "But sleep came, and dreams completed the work of wakefulness. Flora strolled then on the arm of the same beloved, Paulo if not Pedro, and the couple went to admire the stars and the mountains, or the sea, which sighed or stormed, and the flowers and the ruins. It was not rare that they remained alone, in front of a patch of sky, in the moonlight, the night sky sometimes studded with stars like a dark blue cloth. It was at the window, suppose; the song of soft breezes came from outside, a large mirror, hanging from the wall, reproduced images of him and her, confirming her imagination" (80). Flora would wake up and think it was all an illusion, but she began having the illusion without the dream, in which a sole figure brought to mind her unconscious desire to embrace him, put her arms around his neck, and at that point he split into two persons. Flora was frightened by those ghostly transformations that left her in a state of amazement, perhaps suspecting they would lead to the paralysis of her will, illness, and death, as they eventually did.

Fantasies and delusions impinge on the consciousness of Machado's narrators. Brás Cubas conflates the grotesque with the sublime by confusing his unexpected encounter with Marcela, his former Spanish mistress, whose beauty had been destroyed by marks left by smallpox all over her face, with his first meeting with his intended bride, Virgília: "All of a sudden my voice died on my lips, I was paralyzed with wonder: Virgília . . . could that girl be Virgília? I took a good look at her and the feeling was so painful that I took a step back and turned my eyes away. I looked at her again. The smallpox had eaten at her face. Her skin, so delicate and

pink and pure before, just a day ago, looked yellow to me now, stigmatized
by the same lash that had devastated the Spanish woman's face. Her eyes,
which used to be lovely, were dull, her lips were sad and she had a wary air
about her. . . . I think I took on an expression of revulsion" (41). When Virgília steps away, he sees her unblemished, as she actually is—"Beautiful as
ever," he remarks; however, his first distortion mirrors his description of
her as "an angelic mischief-maker" in the next chapter and suggests the con-
tours of their future liaison. In a decisive later scene, Brás imagines he is
conversing with the embryo inside a pregnant Virgília, before her miscarriage: "The best thing is that we would both converse, the embryo and I,
talking about present and future things. The rascal loved me; he was a funny
little rogue, giving me little pats on the face with his chubby little hands or
then sketching out the shape of a lawyer's robe, because he was going to be
a lawyer, and he would make a speech in the chamber of deputies" (90).
This is the vision that belies Brás's final chapter on negatives, in which he
states that having no children, leaving to no one the legacy of human misery, is the positive balance of his life.

Bento Santiago is haunted by fantasies throughout his life, recognizing that they "weave themselves on the pattern of our inclinations and memories" (30). Even the incentive to write his memoirs comes from a spoken
message he hears uttered by busts painted on the walls, saying that since
they had failed to bring back the past he should pick up his pen to write
about times past. They voice Bento's principal obsession, which is to find
consolation for all he has lost, absolution for his crimes, and the recovery
of some of the energy and innocence of his adolescence to counteract the
weariness and monotony of his lonely, painful existence in old age. The busts
are of three Roman emperors and a king of Numidia—Nero, Augustus, Caesar, and Massinissa—names which, like the four seasons painted in the corners at the ceiling, symbolize the course of the narrator's life. Brás claims
to have no idea why these personages were selected and is quick to compare his yet unwritten memoirs with Caesar's *Commentaries*, while ignoring the significance of the other names.

Bento's mother, D. Glória, had promised God that if her second son
lived he would become a priest, and she lectures young Bento not to take

his eyes off the priest at Mass. At home he would play Mass with Capitu, him acting as the priest, Capitu as sacristan, and the host always a sweet. The invitation "Mass today?" would lead to his borrowing the host under another name and a rush through the mumbled ceremony to gain the reward. The ceremony included the phrase *Dominus non sum dignus*, which Bento never managed to repeat the requisite three times.[6] This childish, funny anecdote conceals a reference to the future romance and fecundation of Capitu, which would at the same time render Bento unworthy of the priesthood. Just the idea of a "new pleasure" with Capitu splinters Bento into satisfaction and abomination, and he begins to hear voices: "A coconut palm that saw me perturbed and divined the cause murmured from the top of its crown that it was not unseemly for boys of fifteen to get into corners with girls of fourteen; on the contrary, adolescents of that age had no other occupation, nor corners any other use" (12). Bento's fear of sin is encrypted in Padre Cabral's opinion that the neighbor Pádua, Capitu's father, brought to mind the case of Eliphaz and Job. Eliphaz suggested to Job that his suffering was the punishment for some secret sin and thus was justified. He urged Job not to proclaim his innocence but to confess his concealed misdeeds. Following up on this theme, Bento is curious to know how and why a divine wound (the seminary, in his case) can be made whole (by sanctifying romance), and he questions worms he finds in old books in an attempt to track down their meaning. The worms speak to him, telling him they know nothing about the texts they chew, they just chew, leaving Bento clueless, as he puts it, to chew comically on the thing chewed.

Bento's scheming to avoid becoming a priest while not defying his mother's will describes the situation that underlies all his inner conflicts. When he blurts out, "I love only you, Mamma," he is thinking, "How many wicked intentions climb aboard a pure and innocent phrase." The conundrum ultimately undermines his life, "the shipwreck of my entire existence," yet at the beginning produces some graceful and charming episodes. Bento fantasizes seeing his mother throw her arms around his neck and tell him he did not have to become a priest, as if that were her innermost desire that she dared not express. He descends from a bus to remove his hat for the passing of the imperial coach and, returning to his seat, has a "fantastic idea," a theatrical reverie that rivals Brás Cubas's voyage. Bento imagines a full operatic scene, a very comical and surreal vision in which Emperor D. Pedro II's coach pulls up to D. Glória's house, and the emperor enters the front room to convince D. Glória that a career in medicine will be a noble alternative to the priesthood.[7] There is a full libretto, in which the emperor has a solo about Brazil's fine medical education and its societal benefits. He asks Bento if he is willing to study medicine, and the answer is telling: "If Mamma is willing" (29). Extending his hand to be kissed, the emperor departs into a street full of people, faces in every window, envious neighbors, and the family's profound gratitude. Bento claims he actually saw and heard all of this before admitting that it was an impossible vision; but it persisted for some time before he could once again see the faces of his fellow passengers.

Bento repeats three times that he was pure when he entered the seminary, yet he is bothered because he knows that his calling, like the Mass performed by the children, came from Capitu.[8] One day he sees a lady fall in the street, and he blames her for imitating French girls. In his mind, the cassock he wears in the seminary becomes her skirt, and he imagines that all the girls he meets on the street show him their blue garters. All of them return in a dream: "I awoke, I sought to rout them with conjurations and other methods, but no sooner did I go back to sleep than they returned, and taking hands they wheeled about me in a vast circle of skirts or mounting the air they rained down feet and legs upon my head. This went on until dawn. I slept no more. I recited paternosters, Ave Marias and credos" (58). Female visions become the incarnation of vice, and Bento nurtures them so as to fortify himself against female temptation in general. When he returns home from law school with his bachelor's degree and the prospect of marrying and beginning a career, he imagines hearing a fairy's voice pronounce the phrase, "You will be happy, Bentinho, you are going to be happy" (100). José Dias seems to hear it too, to Bento's astonishment, before he retorts dryly that it was Bento himself speaking. Bento nevertheless insists on attributing the phrase to malicious fairies: "It is probably that the fairies, driven out of tales and verses, have taken up their abode in people's hearts and speak out from there inside. This one, for example—I have heard her many times, clearly and distinctly. She must be a cousin of the Scottish witches: 'Thou shalt be king, Macbeth!'—'Thou shalt be happy, Bentinho!'" With the Shakespearean comparison, the voice in Bento's head suggests the foreshadowing of a tortured kingdom entered with a heavy price, with Bento caught between his Brazilian fairies and Shakespearean witches. His horror of the licentiousness and provocation of women established, his account of the stream of women who visit him once he becomes Dom Casmurro functions as a dissimulation and subterfuge to throw the reader off track.

Counselor Ayres's desire to overcome life's imprescriptive laws leads him to fantasize about a possible marriage with the widow Noronha that will restore him to full existence; yet he confesses to his sister Rita that he is in fact "an old, serious, retired diplomat" ending his days, if without the trials of his profession also without any hopes of "promotion," by which he means ascension to another, more promising state, namely, remarriage. He comments that the passion and drama of love, were they to occur, would be enough to reverse his old age and return him to real originality. Ayres may dream of repeating Brás Cubas's kiss behind the parasol with his young fiancée, Nhã-loló, when "the years fell away from me on the way downhill." Thus there is a marked finality to his trip to the docks to bid adieu to Fidélia and Tristão, who are leaving to take up their married life in Lisbon, a finality that goes beyond Ayres's reservations about the husband's motives. Ayres keenly feels the separation on the wharf and returns home to write in his diary. There, he has a vision of the figure of Fidélia on his sofa, looking sincerely and directly into his eyes, until the figure dissolves into poetry. Realizing that Fidélia has just contradicted the verse he has always quoted from Shelley, "I cannot give what men call love," he comes to realize fully what could have been, now made impossible by the sea, but what he did not have the fate or the strength to make real. Ayres is destined to remain with the dead and dying and, summing up his Faustian nature, can only mutter, "Ah! Enough!"

ELEVEN

Humanitas *and Satire:*
Machado's Mad Philosopher

Partamos para os campos do Sonho, vaguear por essas azuladas colinas
românticas onde se ergue a torre abandonada do Sobrenatural.
[Let us depart for the fields of Dream, to wander over those romantic blue
hills where arises the abandoned tower of the Supernatural.]

—Eça de Queirós, *O Mandarim*

Agora direi de uma doutrina não menos curiosa que saudável ao espírito.
[I shall now speak of a doctrine no less curious than beneficial to the soul.]

—Machado de Assis, "O segredo do Bonzo"

MACHADO'S FICTION RESPONDS satirically and metaphorically
to the leading scientific, social, philosophical, and political debates of his
time. His stories subtly criticize prejudice, parasitism, class conflict, weak
mechanisms of social mobility, and other flaws of social psychology and
organization. He satirizes politics as a never-ending carnival and advises
his readers to observe from afar before spending the remainder of their eve-
nings reading *The Praise of Folly* (March 2, 1862). Quincas Borba's philosophical system called Humanitism, introduced in the *Posthumous Memoirs
of Brás Cubas* and continued in *Quincas Borba*, is the epicenter of Mach-
adian satire, his *Candide,* directed against the Spencerian social Darwinism of the survival of the fittest and the philosophy of the generic versus
the individual. Humanitism, the mad philosopher Quincas Borba's supreme
system, will solve the profound struggles, the psychological and ethical sufferings of societies in a discourse that joins an easy Panglossian optimism
to a generic national regeneration. Humanitism shares the primitivist germ
active in currents of sociopolitical and allegedly scientific post-Darwinism
that circulated toward the end of the nineteenth century. Machado's works

answer theories of Auguste Compte and Herbert Spencer, so influential in Brazil, that extended the reach of evolution into social and moral worlds. For Machado, the new so-called scientific concepts—vitalism, instinct, natural selection—would have to be evaluated in the light of the destructive impact they were having on culture, which the author registered in notorious effects of cruelty and eroticism in social constructions and deconstructions in his novels. He viewed the concepts with strong reserve and sharp skepticism, making them the target of his biting irony in a chronicle from 1886 written in verse in his "Gazeta de Holanda" "on Darwinism, scientific and social, applied to the outrage over a crime at the Public Slaughterhouse":

> Darwin's law is correct
> Even in facts. . . .
> Don't leave your mouth open
> You'll soon see why.
>
> They have the same struggle
> for life and such art
> The crude law is carried out
> which is everywhere the same.
>
> There is selection, persistence
> Of the most capable or strongest
> who stays alive
> while the others give in to death.
>
> But for only one who resists
> How many stayed silent
> in the vague and sad shadow
> or uncomfortable beings! . . .
>
> Because in the very events
> the Darwinian law is correct
> I proved it in a moment
> Don't leave your mouths open.—Malvólio.[1]

For Machado, egoism fulfills a negative role comparable to that of the struggle for survival: "Some strange philosopher will say that an egoism that infects men makes them open their pockets only in exchange for some pleasure, and that money that buys bread for the poor had before bought entertainment for the well off. . . . Many speak about egoism, without properly defining what it is. In my opinion, which I don't consider infallible, it is worth as much as the instinct of conservation found in animal groups; it is so to speak the moral instinct that tries to provide for the spirit what animal instinct provides for the senses" (November 10, 1861). *Humanitas* reflects a general preoccupation with the implications and consequences of the supposed natural laws: in this case, the struggle for survival and the mentality of primitive man in a state of nature. Machado also intended it as a satire of metaphysics and of systemic religious philosophies. His short story "The Mirror" opens with a comparable understated parody: "One night, four or five gentlemen were debating several questions of a transcendental nature. . . . Between where the stars twinkle through the limpid, calm atmosphere, were our four or five enquirers into metaphysical matters, amicably resolving the most arduous problems of the universe."

The inventor of this superhuman philosophy is first introduced as Brás's schoolmate, who always played the part of the emperor during the festival of the Holy Spirit, and in games always chose the side of the titled and powerful, done with "poise and gravity, a certain magnificence in his stance" (13). The pendulum swings, and Quincas Borba next appears as a miserable beggar with a white beard but retaining a certain spark in his eyes and a mocking air in his smile. He sets the stage for his philosophical system that similarly reverses terms, beginning with a description of his current dwelling place: "Do you know where I live? On the third landing of the São Francisco stairs, to the left of a person going up. You don't have to knock on the door. A cool house, extremely cool" (59). Brás calls him comical and sad because Borba disdains work, asking only to teach him his "philosophy of misery." Before departing, Borba asks if he can give Brás an embrace, which turns out to be just an excuse for filching his pocket watch. The chapter "An Extraordinary Letter" brings a new watch to substitute for the original, as Borba has come into an inheritance and is now wealthy. Brás looks for signs of lunacy but finds only lucidity, serenity, and conviction in Borba's insistence on putting before him the new philosophical system, which he outlines with a tone of boastful under-statement:

> I ask your permission to come by one of these days to place a piece of work before you, the fruit of long study, a new philo-sophical system that not only explains and describes the ori-gin and consummation of all things, but takes a great step beyond Zeno and Seneca, whose stoicism was really child's play along-side my moral recipe. This system of mine is singularly aston-ishing. It rectifies the human spirit, suppresses pain, assures happiness, and will fill our country with great glory. I call it Hu-manitism, from *Humanitas,* the guiding principle of things. My first inclination showed great presumption. It was to call it Bor-bism, from Borba, a vain title as well as being crude and both-ersome. And it was certainly less expressive. You will see, my dear Brás Cubas, you will see that it truly is a monument. And if there is anything that can make me forget the bitterness of life it is the pleasure of finally having grasped truth and happiness. There they are in my hand, those two slippery things. After so many centuries of struggle, research, discovery, systems, and failures, there they are in the hands of man. (91)

Humanitism is not an ascetic religion, Borba explains to Brás on their next meeting, quite the contrary, a finding in accord with his new status, and although it is related to Brahmanism, his system easily accommodates the pleasures of table, theater, and love. His explanation of *Humanitas* com-pletes a parody of Compte's "Religion of Humanity" and its positivist slo-gan incorporated in part on the Brazilian flag: "L'amour pour principe et l'ordre pour base; le progrès pour but" (Love as a principle and order as the basis; progress as the goal). Brás, in the role of a Sancho Panza to Bor-ba's Quixote, confesses that he was not born for complex situations and takes pleasure in paying attention only to Borba's elegant mode of dress—"the perfection of the frock coat, the whiteness of his shirt, the shine of his shoes . . . his gold stickpin and the quality of leather in his shoes"—explaining that he would have trouble paying attention to the philosophy.

Borba smiles and leaves him with an appeal: "—Come to Humanitism. It's the great bosom for the spirit, the eternal sea into which I dove to bring out the truth. The Greeks made it come out of a well! What a base conception! A well! But that's precisely why they never hit upon it. Greeks, Sub-Greeks, Anti-Greeks, the whole long series of mankind has leaned over that well to watch truth come out, but it isn't there. They wore out ropes and buckets. Some of the more audacious ones went down to the bottom and brought up a toad. I went directly to the sea. Come to Humanitism" (*Posthumous Memoirs*, 109). Borba at last lays out his philosophical system to Brás, for whom the explanation needs more explanations: "'Humanitas,' Quincas said, 'the principle of things, is nothing but man himself divided up into all men. *Humanitas* has three phases: the *static*, previous to all creation; the *expansive*, the beginning of things; the *dispersive*, the appearance of man; and it will have one more, the *contractive*, the absorption of man and things.[2] The *expansion*, starting the universe, suggested to *Humanitas* the desire to enjoy it, and from there the *dispersion*, which is nothing but the personified multiplication of the original substance'" (*Posthumous Memoirs*, 116). He sets about inventing a dogma and liturgy to turn *Humanitas* into the only true religion: "Christianity is good for women and beggars, and the other religions aren't worth much more. They're all equal with the same vulgarity or weakness. The Christian paradise is a worthy emulation of the Muslim one. And as for Buddha's Nirvana, it's nothing more than a concept for paralytics. You'll see what the humanistic religion is. The final absorption, the contractive phase, is the reconstitution of substance, not its annihilation, etc." (157).

The *Humanitas* cry, "To the victor, the potatoes!" is the primordial call to a fight to the finish between two starving tribes, clarified by a parable in which only the most fit of the two will harvest a field of potatoes that is sufficient only for the survival of one of them; thereby the strongest tribe will gain the strength necessary to cross over the mountain, where there are potatoes in abundance. "Fight! Conquer! Dominate!" is Borba's philosophical advice to the novice Rubião. *Humanitas*, the great universal principle of things, the motor of a general and inherent will to live, is a transposition of Schopenhauer's *The World as Will and Representation* (*Die Welt als Wille und Vorstellung*, 1818), in which human action is subject to a collective, generic unconscious. Humans' inner being is said to contain the basic energies of the universe, a microcosm that participates in and is determined by the totality. Every man is a reduction of *Humanitas*, Borba will explain, sharing in the movements of the universal and original substance of existence. Every single body mirrors the universal body, and all changes and events are but the internal adjustments of a single universal substance. The contradiction between individual and species that appears forcefully in Machado's satire has a possible origin in Swift. In Gulliver's fourth voyage—*Travels into Several Remote Nations of the World, in Four Parts. By Lemuel Gulliver, First a Surgeon, and then a Captain of Several Ships* (1726)—impressed by the information about the existence of a race of immortals, the Struldbruggs, Gulliver begins to envision humanity as a garden of tulips in which the importance of any single flower is lost in the constant renovation of the species with each new spring. At the same time, Borba's exposition of his sublime philosophy to the two "ignoramuses," Brás Cubas and the unschooled teacher Rubião, recapitulates the reversible roles of wisdom and foolishness seen in Don Quixote and Sancho Panza, painting Borba as both lofty and mad. The imbalance of the wise fool is repeated in Quincas Borbas's comparison of his idea with Pascal's: "What does he say? He says that man has 'a great advantage over the rest of the universe; he knows that he is going to die, while the universe is completely ignorant of the fact.' Do you see? The man who fights over a bone with a dog has the great advantage over him of knowing that he's hungry. . . . 'He knows that he is going to die' is a profound statement, but I think my statement is more profound: 'He knows that he's hungry'" (162). Universal devouring is thus posited as the root of human consciousness, and the noble Quincas is soon devoured. He returns from four months in Minas Gerais, where with a demented gaze he burned his magnum opus in order to perfect it in a new manuscript; even Rubião sees that he had passed to the inverse side of his own reason, since Quincas was not only mad but knew he was mad, possessing only a remnant of his previous awareness. To Rubião's horror, he invented and performed a macabre dance as a lugubrious rite of Humanitism, and his eyes alternated between a blank stare and small rays of reason.

Humanitism, the philosophical system invented by the "shipwreck of existence," unforeseen beggar, philosopher, and heir Quincas Borba is an original formulation of cannibal theory as a philosophical constant throughout Western literature and culture.[3] After a meal, between the cheese and the coffee, philosophically sucking on a chicken wing, Quincas reveals the principles of Humanitism, an idea so radically reductionist that everything is explained by the "consummation of things," a kind of endocannibalism on a universal scale. Each man being only a component of a universal principle, Humanitism continually consumes its own viscera. The sacrifice of one part means not death, but only an equilibrium that assures the survival of others. Availing himself of the techniques of distancing, Machado creates playful and comic contexts in which to present Borba's "contrary" theories; a space is opened where local otherness, exaggeration, and the inversion of values are incorporated into "imported" philosophical currents from Europe—whether in the grain of madness that Brás Cubas notices in Quincas Borba or in the universal force of hunger. Although more discreet, Humanitism anticipates the veiled, elegant style found in Fernando Pessoa's cannibal story "A Very Original Dinner," written in English in 1907 while Machado was still alive, as well as the impertinent tone and some concepts of Oswald de Andrade's modernist "Cannibal Manifesto" (1928), such that the three authors' cannibals are essentially eating off the same plate. Machado had compared life to a game of chess, in which he also perceived a process of universal cannibalism "in which the queen devours the pawn; the pawn devours the bishop; the bishop, the knight; the knight, the queen; and everybody devours everybody" (February 25, 1894).

If one finds delightful satires of determinism and post-Darwinian social stoicism both in Humanitism and in the vanguardist theme of anthropophagy, constructed rhetorically by their authors with fine irony, there is at the same time an implicit recognition of the new presence and even of the utility of the savage condition, accepted as one of the constants of our mental composition and our social and philosophical evolution. In the cannibal madness of Borba's potatoes there is, through Machado's satire, a serious meditation on Western values. *Humanitas* is based on the application of the cannibal metaphor to psychology and to social philosophy, at the service of imagined Utopian goals meant to rejuvenate, preserve, and diversify civilization. Besides reacting against post-Darwinian scientism,

Machado formulates a new staging of the devouring god, in reference not only to indigenous primitive gods but also to those of Orientalist religious tradition. In the face of those devouring gods, Machado reclassifies the Christian god: "God is a vegetarian. . . . A great philosopher said that it was necessary to redefine human understanding. I would say the stomach too, because there cannot be rational thinking without good digestion, and good digestion is impossible with the evil of meat" (March 5, 1893).

In the mythical context, Borba's theory echoes Chronos, devourer of his own children, whose image is registered in the grotesque, frightening painting by Francisco de Goya of Saturn-Chronos (1819–23). In this over-arching satire of grand, providential scientific theories, such as Darwinian natural selection and positivist order, Machado further anticipates certain key themes of the literary vanguards, above all futurism—primitivism, hunger, war—everything that represents an appeal to aggression through transcendence. Primitive and unrepressed, hunger forms part of the evolutionary struggle, now promoted to the principal function of human existence, causing wars that cleanse society of the weakest and assuring the survival of the victors.[4] By holding survival as the greatest value, Quincas inverts morals, declaring that only war preserves life. Supported by another cannibalistic metaphor, that of the organic decomposition of nature, he alleges that war is also hygienic, eliminating rot, corruption, and social infection. Quincas concludes that the most propitious path to the happiness of the human species lies in warlike paganism. The *Humanitas* cry, "To the victor, the potatoes!" is its primordial call.

The cannibalism of Humanitism, although it does not use the term, appears in its primitivism and in the concepts of hunger, struggle, and body associated with a state of nature. As an illustration, Quincas turns to mythical primitivism, inventing the fable of two hungry tribes that fight over a field of potatoes; there are enough to feed only one of the tribes and permit it to cross over the mountain and save itself. Humans are thus reduced to the most base primitivism: observing the fight between two dogs over a simple bone, Quincas thinks about another, more beautiful spectacle, a fight between men and dogs over the little miserable food left in the world. The primary strain of his philosophy is hunger, the simple physical condition that for Quincas is the only law of life and the principle of survival. Since everything makes up part of the universal body of *Humanitas,* an absolute substance, hunger always ends in an act of unification instead of ingestion: in the pithy phrase of the manifesto of 1928: "Only cannibalism unites us." Humanitism is a cannibal with Kosmic appetites: through hunger, he consumes himself, makes himself manifest, and unites his primitive body, which is the origin and genesis of everything. Remembering his grandmother who was run over by a carriage, Quincas cogitates: "Humanity was hungry. If, instead of my grandmother, it had been a rat or a dog, it is true that my grandmother would not have died, but it would still have been true that Humanity needed to eat" (6). In *Iaiá Garcia,* Machado equates the act of eating with devotion, in an amorous cannibalism in which the believer devours his most beloved saint. Helen Caldwell calls attention to Raimundo, a freed slave who continues to serve, in whom she sees selfless devotion and the gentleness of Brazilian nature, contrary to the civilized barbarity imposed by Europe; his solitary songs were vivid, if faint, memories of the Africa where he was born. His relationship to the saints was innocently culinary: " 'Raimundo,' the girl would say, 'do you like saints that are meant to be eaten?' Raimundo would straighten out his body, begin to smile, and, giving his hips and torso the movement of his African dances he would answer, crooning: 'Pretty saint! Delicious saint!' " (1).

Machado takes advantage of the anthropomorphism of these jumps in logic, which extrapolate the terms of a new universal philosophy of culture from a primitive attribute. The satire is redoubled in the passage from an individual to a generic context: the abstract hunger of Humanitism ultimately devoured the concrete grandmother of the philosopher. There is no death, explains Quincas, denying any significance to the individual and considering the absorption of his grandmother as necessary to the survival of the larger body of Humanitism. In the imperative *"Humanitas* needs to eat," one may read another vector of the formulation of the vanguard manifesto: "Only law of the world" (Única lei do mundo). Cannibalism is thus established satirically at the root of existential philosophy. The cannibal theme has an antecedent in the *Sermon of St. Anthony to the Fish*

(Maranhão, 1654) by Antônio Vieira, SJ, in which Vieira turns from praising to criticizing the "fish" who are listening to him: "The first thing that
distresses me about you, fish, is that you eat each other. This is a great
scandal, but the circumstances make it even greater. Not only do you eat
each other, but the large eat the small. If it were the other way around it
would not be so bad. If the small ones ate the large, one large one would be
sufficient for many small ones; but since the large eat the small, not even a
hundred, not even a thousand are sufficient for one large one. Note how
Saint Augustine was surprised at this: '*Homines pravis, praeversisque
cupiditatibus facti sunt, sicut pisces invicem se devorantes,*' 'Men with
their greater and perverse greed are becoming like fish, who eat each
other.'"[5] Machado, who was an assiduous reader of Saint Augustine, would
have known that he preached to men about eating each other, while Vieira
swung the pendulum and preached to the fish. Men are going about, Vieira
preaches, to eat and be eaten, more avidly than the cannibal Tapuias (indigenous groups in the interior who speak a Jê language considered barbarous by the Tupi). When one dies, he is eaten by his heirs, executors,
legatees, creditors, and even by his wife. And men are so cruel that they eat
each other while they are still alive; Vieira quotes Job, who asked, "Quare
persequimini me, et carnibus meis saturamini?" (Why do you persecute
me so inhumanly, you who are eating me alive and glutting yourselves with
my flesh?). To drive home his point, Vieira asks his fish the rhetorical question implicit in Humanitism, "Do you think this is right, fish?"

The struggle for supremacy affects philosophic systems: Quincas affirms that Humanitism is "destined to bring down the other systems" (117).
The competition between philosophies is the target of another broad satire, in this case about being close to madness, in the imaginary dialogue
Quincas holds with Pascal. The question of the primacy of hunger carries Quincas to begin a debate with the French thinker in which he will
prove the philosophical superiority of Humanitism. Basing his argument
on the existence of cannibalism, he affirms that hunger is more meaningful than death because the consciousness of death lasts a short time and
ends once and for all, while hunger prolongs consciousness of the human
condition and promotes understanding of the universe: "[Pascal] says,

'Were the Universe to crush him, man would still be more noble than that which has slain him, because he knows that he dies. . . . The Universe knows nothing of this.' . . . With all due modesty, I believe that Pascal's thought is inferior to mine, but I do not deny that it deserves to be called great or that he himself was a great man" (142).

Some of the subtle implications of this diastolic theory are that man may worship himself, as a reduced form of *Humanitas,* and since all men are fundamentally the same, there is no need for differential moral systems. Satirizing the social Darwinism of his day, Machado posits that fighting becomes the supreme function: "Life is a fight. A life without fight is a dead sea in the center of the universal organism" (141). Man must raise his thought to the original substance he contains over thousands of years, at which point all human feelings and desires become pure illusions. Death is also an illusion, as Borba explains in the story of his grandmother, since it is merely the reabsorption into *Humanitas* of its own substance. All phenomena are movements of the same eternal substance, thus "every individual would find the greatest delight in the world in sacrificing himself to the principle from which he descends; second, because even then it wouldn't diminish man's spiritual power over the earth, invented solely for his recreation, like the stars, breezes, dates, and rhubarb. Pangloss . . . wasn't as dotty as Voltaire painted him" (117). Citing a passage from Desiderius Erasmus's *Praise of Folly* (*Morias Encomium,* 1511), Borba adds that an idea of superiority, just like one of remorse, reflects the persistency of the conscience of self over philanthropic morality. Borba reads from his magnum opus, four handwritten volumes of a hundred pages each full of Latin quotations. Under Borba's main idea, everything stays the same yet appears and is understood in a different light, certainly a parody of Schopenhauer's concept of the primacy of the mind as a basis for the understanding of all phenomena.[6] Machado's parody extends to all systems, communicated through Brás's praise of formality: "Yes, pleasant Formality, you are the staff of life, the balm of hearts, the mediator among men, the link between heaven and earth. You wipe away the tears of a father, you capture the indulgence of a Prophet. If grief falls asleep and conscience is accommodated, to whom, except you, is that huge benefit owed?" (127).

The grain of madness that Brás senses in Borba is both the glory and the downfall of the great philosophy. Machado's own irony goes further. Rubião, after the death of Quincas Borba, suddenly remembered the deceased philosopher's most famous phrase: "To the victor, the potatoes!" He had completely forgotten both the formula and the allegory. Now, suddenly, as if the syllables had lingered in the air, untouched, waiting for someone who could understand them and put them together, he combined them into the old formula, and uttered it as emphatically as on the day he had accepted it as the true law of life. He did not recall the anecdote fully, but the phrase conveyed a nebulous sense of struggle and victory" (195). The concision and sonority of the old high-sounding phrase, now repeated vacantly out of context, is more lasting than its philosophy. His high comedy combines a human search for wisdom with satire of the aberrations of authoritarianism and egoism, producing a state of transcendent madness comparable to the true humanism of the Cervantine hero, the wise madman Don Quixote, whose novel is quoted by Quincas Borba. In a review, Machado proposes that plays like José de Alencar's *Mãe* are necessary to distract the public from a theatrical politics of the day marked by inverted ideas, warped opinions, and transitory, materialistic interests: "They don't make you laugh like Don Quixote, because Dulcinea's beau, when aiming at the windmills, didn't think of a reward nor did he measure his love by lance thrusts. He had the good faith of his mania, the sincerity of his ridicule. The others didn't" (February 22, 1862). *Humanitas,* in the style of a libretto of opera buffa, dignifies through comedy. Even Quincas ultimately believes in human nobility: "That delicate and noble sentiment, the pride of servitude— absolute proof that man, even when he shines shoes, can be sublime" (156).

Mad Comedy and "The Alienist"

Comedy of many forms pervades Machado's prose writings, whether fiction or journalism, from the braggadocio of opera buffa, the dry satire of Menippean tradition, the wit of psychological perception, the absurd humor of contrasts and tensions, the dark humor of illness and death, to the philosophical humor of experience encapsulated in aphorisms and truisms.

The picaresque Brás Cubas promotes the story of his own delirium, for example, as if he had invented oneiric memory, and he classifies his description as an original contribution to scientific knowledge: "As far as I know, no one has yet described his own delirium; I am doing it, and science will thank me" (7). Brás exploits a strange humor of contrasts when he juxtaposes two chapters of comic fatality, the first one seriocomic in present tense ("This Book's Flaw") and the other historical and reflective ("The Bibliophile") in counterpoint. In the first, Brás tires of his memoirs, even if they do distract him from eternity, and attributes his exasperation to a flaw in his readers: they want a fluent, direct book, whereas Brás's memoirs wander, delay, pause, delay, slip, and fall. In the paired chapter he describes a bibliophile many years in the future. The bibliophile also represents a defect in the old book he tries to read, Brás's memoirs, even using his best lenses in an attempt to perceive its meaning lost in time by reading, rereading, unreading. He is the critic who strains to capture what has become the incommensurate character of an original. His best attempts go nowhere, however, and, unable to determine the text's meaning, the collector-critic takes recourse in the pride of pure possession: he promises to write a memoir describing his discovery of the book, and he would reject all the prizes and accolades of his age—the crown of the Indies, the papacy, all the museums of Italy and Holland—for the prize of simply possessing the first edition that has fallen into his hands.

The chapter titled "A Grain of Folly" introduces a character whom the narrator considers to be insane because he is ruled by the fixed idea that he is Tamerlane (Timur), a ruler of the Great Tartary, because he confuses cream of tartar with identity: "I am the illustrious Tamerlane. . . . Earlier I was Romualdo, but I fell ill, and I ate so much tartar, so much tartar, so much tartar, that I became a Tartar, even king of the Tartars. Tartar has the virtue of making Tartars" (69). Everyone laughed at crazy Romualdo, but Brás is chastened by his mad association and finds no humor in it at all, once written down.

Machado satirizes political elections by revealing their disguised violence through a culinary metaphor, giving his "opinion" that a good election always involves bloodshed: "An election without spilling a few drops of red liquid is like a dinner without a few drops of that other red liquid. It's no good, pale, and tasteless. . . . When it comes to someone dying, my opinion is that it makes the election perfect—an opinion that may not correspond to the dead person's" (March 1878).

Machado's most extensive story satirizing the rigid scientific method of his day, the belief that "science has the ineffable gift of curing all ills," and ridiculing the dynamic of revolutionary politics, is "O alienista" ("The Alienist," 1881, also translated as "The Psychiatrist"). Set in the late 1700s during the reign of D. Maria I, the story was the subject of the film director Nélson Pereira dos Santos's popular comedy *Um azyllo muito louco* (A very mad asylum, 1970). The narrator pretends to have learned of the story from colonial chronicles, to which he alludes from time to time. Dr. Simão Bacamarte, who studied in Coimbra and Pádua, embodies the pendulum of the empire, having refused the Portuguese regent's request to remain in Lisbon because Itaguaí, a municipality seventy-five kilometers west of Rio de Janeiro, is his "universe." In spite of her nutritious diet, his practical wife, D. Evarista, is barren and brings about the complete extinction of his clan, at which time Dr. Bacamarte dedicates himself to cerebral pathology, certain he will become Brazil's sole authority and thinking to cover himself and his nation with laurels. He convinces the city council of Itaguaí to finance the construction of a building to house all the insane of the town, which until that time had ignored them. Thus Dr. Bacamarte becomes director of the "Casa Verde," with fifty windows on one side, and begins to dedicate himself obsessively to a profound study of madness, as a service to humanity. At the opening of the Casa Verde, D. Evarista is dressed ostentatiously in jewels and silks, the very obsession that will eventually lead to her internment. Machado parodies the city council in a column of the same period: "The reason I love our illustrious Municipal Council, above everything in this world, is that there we can say what's in our hearts. Here outside, it's all restrictions and courtesies. One believes that the other guy is a scam and gives him an embrace, and rarely does a poor fool die persuaded that he is. That's how conveniences work, customs of civilization that corrupt everything. In the Illustrious Council it's the contrary."

Within a short time the asylum fills up, and an annex is required to house the many insane. "Who would have believed," said Padre Lopes, "that so many madmen could exist in the world?" The many types of madness exemplified lead Dr. Bacamarte to work so intensely on his scheme of classification that he forgets to eat or to speak to D. Evarista, who falls into a deep depression. His remedy is to send her, in spite of her reluctance and resistance, to Rio de Janeiro in the company of a large retinue. Alone and free to carry on his research, Dr. Bacamarte soon develops grandiose ideas that are bound to "change the face of the Earth." In a parallel to Quincas's charge to Rubião in "Humanitism," Dr. Bacamarte proclaims his theory to the sycophant Sr. Soares: "The human spirit is a large sea shell from which I will try to extract a pearl, which is reason. . . . Madness and reason are perfectly defined. One knows where one begins and the other ends. Why try to change the boundary?" Itaguaí's period of revolutionary "Terror" begins as Dr. Bacamarte starts to divide and classify all the forms of insanity: the violent and the calm; then the manias, deliriums, hallucinations; followed by the antecedents in family and circumstances. His time was totally and excessively occupied; madness, which before had been "lost in an ocean of reason," he now had found in a new continent. Machado's satire stems from their contradiction: the citizens' unbounded respect for the independence of the scientific method is counterindicated by Bacamarte's strict adherence to rigid hypotheses; concomitantly, the citizens' passionate revolt against the Casa Verde is quelled by Dr. Bacamarte's stoic refusal to lower science to an argument with the uninformed.

One by one, the good citizens of Itaguaí found themselves confined to the Casa Verde. The case of Costa predicts the fate of Rubião in *Quincas Borba*: he inherits a vast sum that should last all his days, yet loses it by loaning his vast fortune to the needy and greedy townspeople. Costa is such a gentleman that he forgives most of the loans and even makes a final loan of his last coins, purposefully reacting with generosity to the intentional insults of those who owe him the most. Mateus, a simple saddler who built the most elegant house in the city, is led to the Casa Verde after Dr. Bacamarte suspects that his wide smile disguises an abnormal pride of ownership.

Soon the citizens regard the Casa Verde as a private jail, with no recourse to internment in that "Bastille of human reason." In one of his last series of chronicles, "A + B," composed in the form of a dialogue, Machado discusses human failures with João das Regras, failures which include denunciation of diversion of funds and counterfeit banknotes (September 12, 1886); theatrical metaphors in politics (September 28); closed voting, parliamentary reforms, and hats (October 14); "he cleared up this matter of hats in the senate, declaring that our hats all come from France, in pieces, here what we do is give them form, expose them, buy them and use them. That's what should be done with the tribunal. Then, extending his hand, he said good-bye." These hats continue the satire begun in Brás Cubas with his inaugural speech to the deputies concerning the size of the military caps worn by the National Guard.

In a parody of the French Revolution, the barber Porfírio leads a revolutionary group against the "Bastille," while harboring his own ideas of taking over the city council as he foments cries for the downfall of the asylum and the death of its "dictator." When Porfírio confronts Dr. Bacamarte, however, and Bacamarte stoically refuses to abandon his scientific principles, the barber proposes an in-house compromise by which some of the harmlessly insane will be released for political expediency, while the good doctor will continue to commit whomever he judged in need of treatment. Porfírio's practical tactic failed to be sufficiently radical, however, and he was soon deposed by João Pina, who then took up "the demanding reins of government." Whereas Porfírio had denounced the city council for being corrupt, Pina denounced it for being full of French ideas rather than those of the Portuguese crown. The viceroy's troops arrived to restore the original city government, and with it Dr. Bacamarte rose to the height of his powers.

Unexpectedly, the pendulum of Dr. Bacamarte's thought swung to its inverse position. Who could have imagined that all of the inmates of the asylum would be released into the streets, the narrator asks in astonishment, because of the same rational, scientific inquiry that had put them there? It seems that Dr. Bacamarte was relentless in his search for the basis of judgment, and after reexamining his theory he sent his conclusions to the city council:

> Whereas four-fifths of the population had been committed to the Casa Verde; whereas according to his theory he had committed all whose faculties were not perfect and absolute; whereas the statistical examination of the result proved that the true doctrine was not that one but its opposite; whereas mental disequilibrium should be considered normal and exemplary when uninterrupted; now he intended to free all those previously interned and substitute persons in the opposite condition now described. Anyone judged to be in perfect reason should be committed, divided by class: the tolerant, truthful, simple, loyal, magnanimous, wise, sincere, etc.

Even the barber Porfírio, who now refused to rise up against the latest decision of the city council, was, for that logical consistency, condemned to the Casa Verde. In a chronicle Machado would similarly parody the idea of human perfection:

> What most enchants me about humanity is its perfection. There is an immense conflict between loyalties under the sun. The concert of praises among men could be said already to be classical music. The evil tongues, formerly one of the pests of the earth, today is material for ancient comedies and archaic novels. Dedication, generosity, justice, loyalty, goodness all go together, like those golden coins that Voltaire's hero saw boys playing with in the streets of El Dorado. Social organization can be dismissed. Still, it would be prudent to retain it for some time as a useful recreation. The invention of crimes . . . overly long and tiring narratives. Even though it is useless, in the absence of crimes, the jury is still an excellent institution. ("A Semana," February 26, 1893)

But Dr. Bacamarte's investigations did not stop here; while examining books in his vast, ultramarine library, he arrived at his final syllogism: if he had not actually effected any cures, since those interned had always been sane, then he had accomplished nothing except to discover the natural imbalance of the brain. While he was pleased to conclude that his beloved Itaguaí never had any insane people, he was disturbed to see that his new psychological doctrine had been destroyed, and by his own research. The only rational conclusion was devastating: on finding that he was the only citizen to possess perfect mental and moral equilibrium, attested to and confirmed by all—his wisdom, patience, perseverance, veracity, moral vigor, loyalty, without defects—there was only one thing to do. He committed himself as the sole occupant of the Casa Verde, and there he died, in spite of his wife's tears and entreaties, after seventeen months. Machado's praise of folly reaches a conclusion similar to Quincas Borba's affirmation of human dignity through ridicule and comedy in the vein of Cervantes's hero; in this story wisdom and folly are finally shown to be universal, both in the citizens' exemplary disequilibrium and in Dr. Bacamarte's extreme and unwarranted antitheory that led to the comic fate and demise of another wise fool.

Quincas Borba

The second novel of Machado's Carioca quintet, *Quincas Borba*, while the only one narrated in third person by an unnamed author, is the work that most directly destabilizes the conventions of realist fiction through its subtle application of the philosophy of *Humanitas*. In place of a signifying system, it allows gratuitousness, incoherence, and madness to become its method. The theme of insanity leads to the disintegration, dissolution, and fragmentation of its main characters, who sacrifice or lose their identities in the gradual passage from a deceptive sense of autonomy to forms of entrapment and loss of self. The very form of the novel oscillates between chapter divisions that impose a structure and plot, on the one hand, and a game of fragments, witty references, and apparently meaningless details that overflow the borders of narrative. Sena's essay emphasized the paired structure of the quintet in the first two and last two novels, with *Dom Casmurro* occupying a prime position at the center. While *Quincas Borba* is tied to the *Posthumous Memoirs of Brás Cubas* as an extension or even sequel through the homonymous character and his philosophy of Humanitism, I argue that it simultaneously defies any definitive chronology and assumes the position of a telling, paradigmatic text, opening an epistemological path to the final three novels.

While in Rio de Janeiro on a mission from his hometown of Barbacena in the interior, Quincas Borba dies a "second death" at the beginning of the novel while in Brás Cubas's house, a circumstance communicated in Brás's letter read by Quincas's caretaker, Rubião. Therefore, in terms of chronology, the novel *Quincas Borba* must precede the *Posthumous Memoirs* given that Brás writes his own novel from beyond the grave, following the literary conceit, and here he is still alive to witness Quincas's death. The textual boundaries are thus obscured, leading to the logical suggestion that Brás Cubas is the unnamed author of *Quincas Borba,* his signed letter being placed in the novel as a clue and cameo appearance.

Still another question remains, which is why the novel is named after a character who dies after ten pages, leaving his faithful "ignoramus" Rubião to carry on, while bestowing his name and his existence on his dog. The subject of the novel is decentered, leaving Quincas Borba and his *Humanitas* to lurk on the peripheries of the text. Rubião is the disciple of an idea he cannot and could not ever understand, as he actually thinks that his master's existence has been placed in the dog. Rubião is fated from the beginning to be the sacrificial victim of Quincas's mad legacy. While swinging the cords of his bathrobe as he looks out on the bay of Botafogo as a nascent capitalist, Rubião presents the first symbol of his coming degeneration: lines between reality and myth also begin to whirl out of control. Machado provocatively and consistently inverts the moral content of his allusions and invests commonplace and seemingly insignificant events with enhanced energy. Quincas is Rubião's author in a Pirandellian sense, and his madness begins at the same time and place in which his author succumbed to lunacy. Insanity is thus passed on through the inheritance Rubião received from the mad philosopher. He is no longer a bounded, coherent, single entity, but a character in search of his author, one who lives on in his master's dog with his master's voice.

Taking Quincas's place, Rubião substitutes his own grand and sublime universal idea in his grand passion for the unattainable Sofia. From this slippery beginning, the novel further decenters the notion of a subject and the coherence of its characters by developing incidents of incoherence and insanity, while imperceptibly destabilizing the subject and content of the narration in progress. Lines and borders begin to blur, as their messages are mixed, like the strawberries Rubião receives from Sofia that contain the calculating note actually written by her husband, Palha, who has the habit of parading and exploiting his wife as a trophy. The strawberries, like the bathrobe cord, are the early symbols of Rubião's misreading and the harbingers of further division of his self, once a schoolteacher now a capitalist, about to turn into the china doll that Sofia drops and shatters.

On the surface, the novel tells the story of the disintegration into madness of Rubião, a sane and generous man, told through the narrator's witty and sophisticated treatment of the gradual yet irreversible fragmentation of his reason and personality after he inherits a fortune from his mentor Quincas. Somewhat following the inverted logic of "The Alienist," the author's interest is in narrative play and pure fictionality, the construction of a parable through symbol and moral example, rather than scientific or diagnostic inquiry into the workings of the human psyche. Rubião and the dog named after its master set out in the world to enact their sublime folly in the path of Cervantes's knight of the sorrowful countenance in an allegory of misadventures. With his philosopher-dog and ingenuous knight, the narrator satirizes the idea of an all-encompassing, universal, and eternal principle; instead, he searches for a truth that cuts across and neutralizes oppositions, a swinging pendulum that abolishes antinomies. Here, Machado seems to have developed his fictional idea from a verse he cites from Camões: "A truth active in things / That lives in the visible and the invisible." The visible truth of the mundane world is balanced by the invisible truth of myths and legends. The entertaining idea that Quincas Borba lives on after death through transmigration is both intensified by Quincas's refusal to accept that death exists ("Não há morte") and countered by the doctor, who explains to Rubião that philosophy is one thing but actually dying is quite another. What is at stake here is the question of the order and nature of things, the opposition between determination and chance, life and death, structure and disintegration, reason and madness, illusion and reality, the individual and *Humanitas*. From the beginning, one apparently stable, coherent identity is replaced by elements of chaos and chance. With the death of Rubião's sister, for example, Quincas's near-marriage is undone, and the two men are linked. Roles change, and characters who used to be one thing are now another: "He was comparing the past to the present. What was he a year ago? A teacher. What is he now? A capitalist." Image seems to have replaced essential being and become identical to the self, as in the story "The Mirror." There is a high price to be paid for illusions: Rubião and the dog will return to Barbacena to die in madness and starvation.

The opera buffa of Rubião's life in Rio de Janeiro as a nouveau riche capitalist stems from his inability to read or judge either the city or its people, from the unprincipled who exploit his resources, and from his fatal passion for the beautiful Sofia, who is herself entrapped by husband, social position, and truncated, repressed self-knowledge. As the second novel of the quintet, *Quincas Borba* occupies a place between the story of Brás Cubas's consummated adulterous passion and Bento Santiago's jealously imagined obsession; rather than solitude, remorse, and death, the danger of illicit desire here is madness and the loss of self through dispersal and fragmentation. In Rubião's mind, Sofia's changeability renders her multiple, "so different from herself, now one thing, now another" (80). Imagination and hallucination make it possible for subjects to be doubled through fantasy into second selves of desire. Rubião takes on the identity of Emperor Napoleon, who will be the object of a family discussion at the beginning of the next novel. Both Rubião's and Sofia's fantasies allow for the transgressions they both desire in unreal time and space, without consequences: Rubião's/Napoleon's invented memories of their imagined affair recounted to Sofia in the carriage sound so real that Sofia is confused, and even she fantasizes the phantom affair so vividly that she can feel Rubião's kiss on her neck. The eminently sane Sofia speaks to the roses in

her garden, and Rubião invokes their union under the mute gaze of the
Southern Cross: both are in danger of losing their original selves and crossing the boundary separating the sane and the mad. Sofia, however, in the
midst of a fantasy, is jolted back to reality when she breaks a doll, a porce-
lain mandarin, without realizing it: "Sofia found him in her hands, not
knowing how he got there or when" (105). The narrator omits the moment
it breaks, so that the reader will have to imagine and participate in it, creating a difference between the Sofia who broke the doll and the same Sofia
who was caught up in the semiconscious fantasy of an imagined situation
of violation. The reader's reflections are consistently drawn into the fabric
of the text, as when Rubião is getting dressed and hears an insect singing,
after he had swatted a column of innocent ants in anger and frustration:
"Happily, a cicada began to sing, with such possession and meaning that
our friend stopped at the fourth button of his vest. *Sioooo . . . fia, fia, fia,
fia,* . . . Oh! nature's sublime and pious precaution, that puts a live cicada
at the foot of twenty dead ants as compensation. That reflection is the
reader's. It can't be Rubião's" (90). Rubião, already slipping into episodes
of fantasy and insanity, had casually commented to his habitual dinner
guests on the philosopher in their midst, none other than Quincas Borba,
the dog in his care named after his master, who in turn had appointed Rubião his disciple and the animal's caretaker. The guests could not quite believe or absorb what they were hearing and its implications, anxious to
ignore the unmistakable signs of instability and dementia in their wealthy
host and benefactor. Their reaction is a sign that in this novel, as in *Humanitas,* there is neither full subjectivity nor objectivity, only a pattern of
delusions.

PART FOUR

The Actor-Authors

Brás Cubas, Basso Buffo

Sabe que todo relato autobiográfico é um amontoado de mentiras—
o autor mente para o leitor, e mente para si mesmo. [You know
that all autobiographies are a pack of lies—
the author lies to the reader and lies to himself.]

—Rubém Fonseca, *José*

On est quelquefois aussi *différent* de soi-même que des *autres*.
[At times we are as *different* from ourselves as from *others*.]

—La Rochefoucauld, *Maxime* 113

THE IDEA FOR THE CHARACTER-AUTHORS in Machado's literary world is present at the very first words the narrator utters from beyond the tomb in the *Posthumous Memoirs*: "For some time I hesitated if I should open these memoirs from the beginning or the end, that is, if I would put my birth or my death in first place." Machado continues the conceit in *Dom Casmurro*, where an old, grumpy Bento Santiago writes with a vain desire to unite those two points of his life, while the third narrator-character, Counselor Ayres, leaves memoirs penned by the debonair diplomat who returns to Rio de Janeiro after his retirement to await his inevitable demise. Each narrator enjoys a porous, transparent, and reflective reconsideration of his life and times that is confounded with authorial prerogatives. Their narratives form reflexive frameworks alternating between inside and outside, the comedy of contradiction and the universality of irony, local speech, and eternal maxims. Although apparently unrelated personalities, the narrators are interrelated and reflexive through their writings, since they all involve retrospection, the manipulation of memoir, and the variation of repeating themes. Each of these character-narrators has made his Faustian deal with his particular devil and at the end wishes for the bestowal of acquittal, renewal, or consolation by his readers. Readers must participate actively to distinguish levels of narration and to navigate the tricks, puzzles, and sleights of hand constantly being perpetrated by narrators, an editor, the characters, and the hidden omniscient author-director in these three retrospective accounts.

Brás Cubas's Comedy from Beyond the Tomb

Machado's first failed character-narrator is Brás Cubas, whose posthumous memoirs inaugurate the open literary style for which Machado is celebrated. The first installment of his memoirs in the *Revista Brasileira* (March 15, 1880) carried a quotation from *As You Like It* (3.2):

"I WILL CHIDE NO BREATHER in the world but myself, against whom I know most faults." The posture of conscious self-criticism is joined with the travel theme found in the melancholy Jacques, who finds humorous sadness in contemplating his travels, just as Machado refers in the foreword to the fourth edition to travels by Maistre, Almeida Garrett, and Sterne. The controlling comic conceit in these memoirs is that their author is deceased, writing from the other side of the grave, making Brás the consummate outside insider. Through this pretense Machado creates a space outside the text both for his character-narrator as well as for his role as author in the wings. The *Posthumous Memoirs* is constructed from that double perspective, as if there were two authors: Machado, who participates in shaping the text from behind the scenes, and Brás as the character-narrator whose voice is separated from his own memoir by recollections from beyond the grave. Machado's hand can be seen in the preface, the ironic chapter titles, myriad historical and literary references, and philosophical coloring; Brás controls the setting and telling of his life as he remembers and interprets it in his own voice. The reader must address the space between Brás's story and the wider frame built by Machado, the distance between writing and telling, which is an essential first step in approaching the novel's many levels of meaning.

From his unique perspective as a dead author of memoirs, Brás asserts that he can look back over his life more freely than the living from the

opinions and judgments of his peers: "Be aware that frankness is the prime
virtue of a dead man. . . . My dear living ladies and gentlemen, there's nothing as incommensurable as the disdain of the deceased" (24). The reader
might expect that for this reason Brás would be honest, direct, and objective in the portrayal of his life, now at an end, yet in the retrospective and
chronological reconstruction of his adventures Brás is very much himself.
He shows a lively interest in justifying or at the least assessing the plusses
and minuses of his life from the beyond, as if to gain the reader's good opinion: "I hope to entice sympathetic opinion." The events of his life, or perhaps one should say escapades, constitute his main subject, although Brás
devotes equal authorial space to his ingenious theories and philosophies,
as if he were a great inventor and thinker who has been overlooked; through
his quirky theories Brás prepares the parody of universal philosophy exposed in Quincas Borba's *Humanitas*. In terms of genre, Brás's memoir is
the inverse or parody of a bildungsroman given that it documents his faults
and failure to educate himself at every step in life, and now, writing beyond
time, he is filled with regrets. The very success of Machado's novel is posited in its failures.

Brás is a failed character-narrator first of all because he died without
achieving any of the goals he valued in his life—a wife, an heir, fame,
position—and, second, because of the exaggerated, artificial social status
he assumed, beginning with his concoction of the false lineage of the Cubas ancestors: "Since the surname Cubas, meaning kegs, smelled too much
of cooperage, my father, Damião's great-grandson, alleged that the afore-
said surname had been given to a knight, a hero of the African campaigns,
as a reward for a deed he brought off: the capture of three hundred barrels
from the Moors" (3). This aggrandizement was the first sign that his social
position was based on a fabrication and pretense and that his memoirs are
a self-serving defense of his profligate and egoistic adventures. With an identity based on a fabrication—notwithstanding the charm, humor, and ap-
pealing satire of his memoirs—Brás conjugates wealth, egoism, and
marginality throughout his life as an aristocratic adventurer, the "little devil"
(brejeiro) whom his father always admired despite his tricks: he has a law
degree yet lives on inherited wealth, prefers a long affair to marriage, and

lives the life of a rebellious outsider guided only by his own interests of the moment. At the same time, with Machado's pendulum swinging between history and fantasy, the fictitious Brás Cubas had been purposely named after Captain-General Brás Cubas, who arrived in Brazil in 1531 with the fleet of Martin Afonso de Sousa, later becoming governor of São Vicente and founder of the city of Santos. In this light the narrator Brás is a spurious descendant of a founding historical father of the colonial empire. Social issues raised and satirized in the memoir are those of a traditional colonial elite: the legitimacy of Brás's lineage and surname, his rank and status, marriage, the production of an heir to carry on the family name, politics and gossip, and the prerogative to circumvent or supersede accepted social etiquette and the usual restrictions that apply to social life and intercourse.

Brás's ebullient style matches his great expectations, which he assessed from a perspective of privilege, marginalization, ironic self-perspective, and finally as a close companion to madness: even when he finally accepted a seat in the legislature, when his erotic adventures had come to an end, his inaugural speech on the size of the hats worn by the civil guard was thought to be curiously marginal and eccentric. Satirical humor is intensified at the conclusion of the memoir through dense intertextuality, as Brás faces his own "oblivion." Written in English, the word alludes to a passage from the *Christian Morals* of Thomas Browne that Machado found in Charles Lamb's *Essays of Elia* (1823): Browne defined *oblivion* as the time when there is no one who still remembers one's parents, a maxim that leads Brás to meditate on the changes wrought by time and to act out his own oblivion. Illustrating the idea of change as forgetfulness, he writes a useless chapter and then one containing only three lines of spaced dots after its title to explain why he did not become a minister of state; he publishes an ill-advised, self-destructive attack against the government; Quincas Borba sends an alienist to examine him for madness; the psychiatrist explains the illusion of possession by recalling the "Athenian maniac" from the vein of Menni-pean satire; he writes a chapter complaining about obtuse critics who fail to grasp his subtle style; Quincas Borba expounds on universal hunger and the struggle for life in his philosophy of *Humanitas* before slipping further into madness and dementia; and Brás fails to invent a poultice intended to abolish human melancholy, as promised in chapter 2. The condition of *melancholia*, drawn from the maritime baroque, represents the result of suffering and sadness, an awareness of human uncertainty and fragility, pessimism and spiritual unrest, fleeting time, and the anguished vision of an absurd world in disconcert with its own nature and values. Brás cannot apply the nonexistent cure to the condition he now embodies.

Amid pain, death, madness, and negativity, Brás ends his adventures with his usual self-centered bravado ("Fate determined the contrary . . . these lacks of good fortune" [140]), and as his last twist he adds a final, petulant retort that would turn a deficit into a surplus, a failure into an achievement, and a negative into a positive. Brás, who had joyfully dialogued with the embryo of his son-to-be, whose Cubas lineage was his father's proudest asset, now declares out of spite that the positive balance of his life is that he did not pass on to any creature "the legacy of our misery" (160). This statement, which has sometimes been read as a deep philosophical rejection of life, is only a final petulant complaint with a touch of bitter comedy, contrived with Brás's usual pride and evasion of responsibility; it is his way of blaming fate and fortune for the end of his lineage and of his book. It is the last line in an opera buffa that feigns finding an advantage in failure, or in musical terms ends with a false cadence that defies the norms of its own genre. Brás's failed adventures, nonetheless, are framed by and presented in this mock epic as part of life's allegories and cyclical patterns set in a tropical empire, for which his story constitutes a satirical and comic inversion, reversal, or play on classical paradigms and iconic referents.

By adopting the genre of the first-person memoir, transposed to fiction with a deceased character-narrator, Machado parodies the *Mémoires d'Outre-tombe* of Chateaubriand.[1] Machado enlarges his reference to the genre by rewriting memoirs and confessions with special reference to Saint Augustine, who chronicles his long heretical road to religious orthodoxy,[2] and Rousseau, who confesses his faults and ignoble experiences.[3] Brás's memoirs belong to a grand lineage, one in which he is an imitator and impostor who entertains his reader through sleight of hand, bravado, and a bit of retrospective wishful thinking from beyond. Although this vein of ironic humor in Brás has been connected with sources in the English eighteenth-century novel and especially with Sterne, whom Brás cites in his preface, an original local source has also been posited for Machado's dry humor found in a mode of discourse common in the Brazilian capital. The social joke, obloquy, anecdote, and pleasantry, something lighter than farce and less intentioned than irony, were cited by Barreto Filho as a likely source of the comic method in hiding behind Machado's pince-nez.

Brás, the Opera Buffa Basso

Comic opera, opera buffa, performed in the theaters of Rio de Janeiro provides a generic reference for Machado's *Posthumous Memoirs*; here, Rosen's description of the comic as an essential quality of the classical style in music can be fruitfully transferred to Machado's literary opera buffa. Often performed as intermezzi between acts of opera seria, these shorter operas of popular entertainment presented a counterpoint to the serious and high subject matter surrounding them. Sung in rhythms of ordinary speech, the genre is based musically on clarity of articulation emphasizing structure, sharp distinction between tonalities, incongruous settings, double meanings, the shift from nonsense to sense as a modulation, irregularity of phrase rhythm, use of witty conversation as thematic material, and an atmosphere of civilized gaiety. In the *Posthumous Memoirs*, the sequences of Brás's adventurous episodes may be equated with tonalities, his non sequiturs and interruptions with irregularity of rhythm, his social and political marginalization with incongruity, his literary and historical allusions with double meanings, all presented with personal charm through witty conversation and directed to the reader as a means of preserving the continuity and shape of the melodic material. Brás is the *basso buffo*, the comic character in the opera buffa who specializes in tongue-twisting or brain-twisting texts; his 160 chapters are presented in a rapid succession of rhythms and styles for the express purpose of entertainment. The musical goal of the opera-memoir is to arrive at a symmetrical resolution of harmonic tension through an eventual return to the tonic key. Yet at the conclusion, or last *recitativo*, of the *Posthumous Memoirs*, Brás's final retort to life for depriving him of an heir, his fatalist philosophy from beyond the grave supplants the gaiety of a harmonic resolution, leaving the main melodic line without harmonic support, to end in an unstable, morosely reflective minor key. With this finale Machado once again mixes and deforms the genre, since tradition would require modulation to a major key so as to preserve or restore the comic mode; he comments in the prologue on the "touches of pessimism" (rabugens de pessimismo) that led him to alter the expression of genre: "There is in the soul of this book, for all its merry appearance, a harsh and bitter feeling that is a far piece from its models." In buffa style, Brás attributes the contrast to "a playful pen and melancholy ink" (prologue). Opera had been a principal influence in Machado's cultural education in Rio de Janeiro, highlighted by his youthful passion for two sopranos, one of whom, Candiani, he subtly puts into this novel for Brás's chosen, Virgília, to hear: " 'A box at the opera no less.'—'For Candiani?'—'For Candiani.' Virgília clapped her hands, got up, gave her son a kiss with an air of childish joy, which was quite out of tune with her appearance" (63).

In the celebrated chapter of his delirium (chapter 7), Brás is thrown into a great baroque theater of the world, where he rides on the back of a flying hippopotamus to witness the origin of time. Re-creating a scene from the episode known as the "Isle of Love" from Camões's epic *The Lusiads*, Brás is carried up to the top of a mountain by Pandora—in the epic, Vasco da Gama is escorted by Tethys—to observe the panorama of time and humanity across the centuries (Gama observed the areas of the world to be conquered by the Portuguese). Brás witnesses the calamitous spectacle of the catastrophic human drama, marked by fatality and illusion, its hopes reduced to chimera: his reaction is the jolting laugh of an idiot. When he hopes to decipher eternity by examining the present century, it passes in a flash like the others in an opaque mist. Comic opera is linked in this episode to moral allegory on a grand scale: Pandora represents the categories of selfishness and self-preservation of social Darwinism, here dramatized through satire, whereas Brás's observations reconfirm the medieval Christian theme of life as a vale of tears, a constant theme in the Portuguese maritime baroque world. Brás is about to be recycled, consumed by time, and the voluptuousness of his Brazilian life will be returned to the void: "You great lascivious man, the voluptuousness of nothingness awaits you" (7). After the delirium, Brás continues his chapters in the style of comic opera buffa to disguise the serious underlying allegorical and philosophical moral drama in his memoirs.

Brás's Five Readers

From his beginning note to the reader, Brás involves the reader as a companion and an accomplice. He is concerned about how many readers he will have in comparison to the classics: "Whether this book will have Stendhal's hundred readers, or fifty, or twenty, or even ten. Ten? Five, perhaps," implying the unrecognized stature of his text, while beginning a conversation with his readers that intensifies through rhetorical devices, including direct address. The first two chapters end by apparently turning interpretation of his life and the book over to readers: "You can judge for yourself" and "Let the reader decide" (2). He establishes an early rapport by wishing the reader well: "God save you, dear reader," and creates common sympathy with an exhortation, "Let's go" or "Let's put our feet together now" (13). The reader will eventually be considered almost as a coauthor: "No, let's not lengthen the chapter" (22). In describing Virgília as a "splendid ruin" (5), Brás invites readers to fill in the picture by using their imagination: "Let the reader imagine," and soon praises their perceptivity: "The reader has already come to see that . . ." (8). Finally, in the last introductory chapter before Brás launches into his memoirs, he acts like the master of ceremonies in a literary circus, with a comic, self-conscious invitation to the reader-spectator: "And now watch the skill, the art with which I make the greatest transition in this book" (9).

When Brás later tires and comes to regret his book, however, finding it tedious and grave, the pendulum swings as he turns on his former allies, the readers, who face his shocking accusation: "The main defect of this book is you, reader" (71). Brás assumes the readers want smooth and direct communication in a rapid, fluid style, and he confesses that his "method" is quite the opposite; his book moves slowly, staggers, stops, stumbles, and falls. Its pages are the "miserable leaves of my cypress" of death, and he is in no hurry to watch them fall. His is a very different kind of book, a metonymy of his life, from legs that have a will of their own to sovereign ideas that render him their captive, and he gives it the episodic, arrhythmic form of its referent. Then, perhaps thinking this idea a bit obscure and realizing that he has just insulted the very readers on whom he depends, Brás opens the next chapter with the remorseful thought, "Maybe I'll leave out the previous chapter" (72), thus rhetorically intensifying its humorous and shocking effect. After this omission, Brás loses some confidence in his readers, noting that "one of my readers might have skipped the previous chapter" or another might not remember chapter 23. In a parody of fashionable reading of the time, Brás senses that his story will be abandoned for lack of interest when his romantic episodes come to an end: "And now I have the feeling that if some lady has followed along these pages she closes the book and doesn't read the rest" (135). As Brás faces his "oblivion," he maintains the same conversational tone until his demise.

Brás is intentionally a failed character-narrator and his memoirs a failed book because they are self-conscious variations and rewritings of the classic figures and texts that he cites as points of reference and comparison, certain that they have been degraded and corrupted by the modern world to the extent that his life and his book are inevitably reduced to simulations or parodies of their historical and literary archetypes. He is conscious of being derivative. The greater the distance between his memoirs and their referents, the greater disconnection, dissonance, and comedy will ensue by metalepsis: "For there are really two ways of enticing a woman's will: the violent way like Europa's bull and the insinuative way like Leda's swan or Danaë's shower of gold—three inventions of Father Zeus, which, being out of fashion, have been replaced by the horse and the ass" (15). In his comic-epic mode, Brás cites the superiority of the ass, thus comparing himself to Don Quixote's faithful companion: "an ass like Sancho's, a philosopher, really." When he must decide whether to accompany Virgília and Lobo Neves to the northern provinces, he is a tropical Hamlet: "It was Hamlet's case, either to suffer fortune's slings and arrows or fight against them and subdue them. In other words, to sail or not to sail" (83); and when Lobo Neves superstitiously sacrifices the gubernatorial post because the decree was dated the thirteenth instead of the thirty-first, Brás celebrates Virgília's salvation from the voyage through rhetorical substitution by saluting the red mare sacrificed by Pelopidas in place of a red-haired virgin of Thebes the night before Leuctra. He even muses with his usual hyperbole that a Cubas grandmother might have been saved by Pelopidas's act of substitution, thus connecting the survival of his line through this circuitous episode with Virgília. The theme of virgin sacrifice is at the same time a comic homage to the continuation of his affair with Virgília.

The distance between Brás's adventures and their classical archetypes is illustrated by the triviality of his self-concept when he compares his refusal to recognize or listen to humankind surrounding him at the theater to the sufferings of Aeschylus's Prometheus inflicted by his torturers: "Oh, did you try to chain me to the rock of your frivolity, your indifference, or your agitation? Fragile chains, my friends" (99). When Brás is obliged to attend Lobo Neves's speech in Parliament, he thinks he is the reason for "Achilles' dragging the corpse of his adversary around the walls of Troy and Lady Macbeth's walking around the room with her spot of blood" (129). Brás's comic rewriting of archetypes is made contiguous with the present time of his narrative and undercuts the mock serious and tragic dramatization of his predicaments.

Through his versatility and even his volubility Brás shows that he is a hybrid narrator. First, he controls the chronology and memory not only by his choice of what he tells but also by the opinions and inflections he applies to the characters and at times by obligation to himself. While he ostensibly enjoys the complete disdain of life and of its values and opinions that he attributes to the dead, his purpose for writing is as much of this world as the paper and book he plans to leave to posterity. Paradoxically, Brás is on both sides of the line. His is, comically, a "last will and testament," since he left no heirs, and in that vein it is meant as a retribution and revenge for failure more than just as a memoir, even one dedicated to the worm that devours his cold corpse, that is, to the eternal human condition. On this point, Brás, the comic master, coexists with the openly naïve philosopher, such that the marginal existence of the comic mirrors the utter skepticism and nihilism of the philosopher: "I, ready to leave the world, felt a satanic pleasure in making fun of it all, in persuading myself that I wasn't leaving anything worthwhile" (6). Given Brás's ephemeral position as author and his failure while alive, his authorial ego remains strong and full of hyperbole. He compares his book to Moses's Pentateuch, praising his genius in beginning with his death by comparison; and his theory of the rolling balls is a chapter that Aristotle must have mistakenly left out of his writings. Brás is an expert on Molière, quoting *Tartuffe* (1664) and *Le Cid* (1637), the Comte de Buffon, Chateaubriand's *Itinéraire de Paris à Jerusalem* (1811), and a long series of authors from Bocage to Wordsworth and Shakespeare. While the posthumous memoirs are laced with death and dissimulation at every turn, Brás maintains his playful, superior approach to the topic, from "the greatest transition in this book" that introduces his birth, to the "leap" over his education, to the chapter that is not serious, to the blame he places on the reader for the defects of his book. In his comic role as basso buffo, Brás inserts graphic experiments in the memoirs, such as the dialogue of Adam and Eve put together with punctuation alone, the explanation of how he did not become a minister of state written with three lines of spaced dots, the half a dozen maxims included as a "parenthesis," a short letter berating the book's critics, and the wording on Nhã-loló's tombstone by way of announcing her early and sudden death from yellow fever. The fatal wording of the death notice on the stone ironically ties together the peripatetic humor of Brás's book with the temporal fatality of life that consumes it, which can be answered, although not counteracted, only by an impertinent imagination. In life's hybrid structure, Brás is both insider and outsider in his deathly and comic memoirs.

Brás's curious projects, theories and laws, all bound up in extravagant metaphors, present a baroque world of moral allegory disguised in comic scenarios. Brás fails to produce his cure for human melancholy, promised in chapter 2. His double nature—dead and alive, selfless and egotistical—is bound up in the promised invention of the "Brás Cubas Poultice." Potentially creating the sensation of a magical cure, his invention would, in his theories, have allowed Brás to combine the benefit of substantial financial reward and fame with service to humanity. In the absence of the divine poultice, he must turn failure into victory and marginality into heroism, both in his prose and in his memoirs, retouched after death.

THIRTEEN

Bento Santiago's Grand Dissimulation

One frequently meets among intellectuals a sort of Brazilian Hamlet-type,
incapable of serious work or action, who seems to be covering up a deep
anxiety with words, words, words, a pretended madness, a deliberately
fanciful humor that is not frivolity although it resembles it.

—Elizabeth Bishop, *Brazil* (1963)

Aquela hora—triste se viveu se nunca foi—foi a única que eu vivi, e eu hoje sou
apenas a saudade encarnada dela, o seu eco confuso e consciente.
[That hour—sad if it ever happened—was the only one I ever lived; and today
I am no more than its incarnate melancholy, its confused and conscious echo.]

—Fernando Pessoa, "A perversão do longe"

MACHADO'S MOST COMPLEX failed narrator-author, a master of
dissimulation who writes to disguise the depth and damage of his obsessions, is Bento Santiago, in his own words the "subterranean man" who
carried "death on his own retina" (134). His drama is enacted within the
allegory of life as an opera between God and Satan; Faust, Macbeth, and
Othello are literary and operatic role models for Bento's struggle with ghosts
of the past, remorse, guilt, revenge, and the ravaging and destruction of his
life.[1] The time and circumstances of his writing in a narrative present tense,
explained in a few early chapters, provide essential clues for reading the
memoir to follow, which is the retrospective and chronological account of
his life occupying all but a few chapters of the novel. Bento speaks as if he
were a lawyer for his own defense, although with an increasingly uneasy,
confessional volubility.[2] *Dom Casmurro* is a novel that documents Bento
Santiago's psychological degeneration, "the shipwreck of my entire existence" (20), in his own words put down in his defense. Writing as an old
man now in the final phase of his life and living in the suburb of Engenho
Novo in a house he had built as an exact replica of his childhood home in

the city, he occupies himself by constructing a subtle defense of the acts that have led to his present empty condition, under the pretext that he has nothing better to do than write a few inconsequential lines. Bento is first of all a failed character because in his old age he is isolated, morose, reclusive, and lonely; furthermore, he has brought this condition on himself yet avoids admitting so, or else does not wish to remember exactly why, or pretends not to know. He cannot admit either his guilt or his complicity; he pairs victimization with claims of innocence and normalcy. He writes his memoirs at an unspecified present moment of narration after an interval of forty years from the primary events, at a time when he pronounces himself "ancient and, needless to say, in the worse sense: that is—old and done for" (117). While composing the memoir and reliving selected significant moments of his early life, he often comments on events from his position as author, at the same time that he recounts them from the fresh point of view of a young Bentinho.

The first chapter, set in Engenho Novo and describing his experience on a suburban train, is a lesson on the essential nature of his psychology and narrative strategies. It is indicative of Machado's highly synthetic and reflexive method. On the train Bento meets a young poet with whom he had only a passing acquaintance. The poet offers to read some of his verses to pass the time during their trip. Because Bento nods off while listening, the poet cuts off his reading; moreover, as Bento relates, the displeased poet later invents the nickname "Dom Casmurro" for the nodding Bento, a sobriquet taken up in jest by Bento's acquaintances when they hear the story, although it seems to fit him quite well. As Bento himself explains, "Casmurro" fits his reclusive, morose behavior, while the royal appellative "Dom" was added for irony, an allusion to his supposed aristocratic airs. He was given the nickname by the casual acquaintance he offended on the suburban train, yet the story he tells reveals perhaps more than he intended and establishes a pattern for his thinking that is repeated throughout his memoir. Even though the poet's reaction was in response to Bento's affront and not without a clever touch of humor, it is Bento the narrator who finally resolves to hold no grudge against the poet. By the end of chapter 1 Bento has made himself the victim rather than the perpetrator; in the magnanimity he shows by pardoning the poet for giving him the name, Bento has reversed the situation to exonerate himself and blame the other. At the end of his memoir Bento repeats a similar pardon, accusation, and shift of blame: he pardons his deceased wife, Capitu, and his best friend, Escobar, for betraying him, although he knows that his accusation derives from his own misperception, a delusion tied to one of his hallucinations and to his fits of uncontrollable jealousy.

The pardon is, once again, necessary to support an image presented to the reader of his capacity to reach compassionate and just judgments. Yet Bento is relentless in both cases: in the first instance he defuses the irritating name Dom Casmurro by making it a joke among his acquaintances; he turns the poet into the guilty party through his pardon; and he suggests that the poet is a delusional madman who will claim authorship of Bento's memoirs because he unwittingly contributed the title to the book. By saying that the young poet will probably think he is the author of the text, Bento classifies him with the mad appropriators of the Mennipean satirical tradition and goes on to imply that perhaps the poet on the train did not actually write those verses that put him to sleep, since "there are books which owe no more to their authors; some, not so much" (1). Bento's response in both cases is total, devastating, and unrelenting. At the conclusion of the memoir, after granting his pardon, he again accuses Capitu, the coup de grâce: that she had done no more than nurture the seeds of her unfaithful, flawed character present since her earliest youth. His is a prosecuting attorney's summation: "If you remember Capitu the child, you will have to recognize that one was within the other, like the fruit within its rind" (148). Via this syllogism he confirms her treasonous inner nature without admitting additional culpability and without involving himself. He further implies a class distinction, since Capitu's poorer origins may have been responsible for the moral defect.

In the earlier case of the poet on the train, in addition to his sense of victimization, Bento takes advantage of his sardonic humor to raise the theme of his own sexuality and fertility. A close acquaintance in town invites him to stay overnight and offers him "everything except a girl" (1). Having used a pretext to broach a topic of obvious importance to him, Bento lets his readers know there has been a daily parade of women through his mansion for years. Even in the memoir he reminds readers that ladies' eyes sought him out: "I shall say nothing about them, since I confessed at the start that I was to have future adventures—but they were as yet still in the future" (113). Here is a disarming retort to the more than two years during which he and Capitu tried unsuccessfully to conceive, to his obsession with purity and chastity in the seminary, and to the moments in the memoir when he confessed to feeling less than manly. Being an issue raised so casually, it returns frequently in the memoir. On meeting Capitu for the first time, Bento contrasts his education in letters with his lack of education in the world: "I had had orgies of Latin, and was a virgin in women" (14); he describes himself as the son of the seminary and of his mother, a boy whom the girls would not let alone "whether in the streets or at their windows" (97). After entering the seminary, he sees a lady fall in the street, and his reaction is elliptical and diffuse: "The lady's hose and garters gleamed white and spiraled before me, walked and fell, got up and marched off" (58). Bento confuses the cassocks at the seminary with the skirts, and he mixes their erotic dimensions: the female visions become evils to be conquered by reciting paternosters, Ave Marias, and credos. In his dreams female devils attack him: "A multitude of abominable creatures walked about me ticki-ticki. . . . They were fair, some slender, others stout, all agile as the devil" (58). In those days he kept a photograph of Escobar, his friend from the seminary who had "entered his soul" (56), alongside one of his mother and emphasized his purity when studying in the seminary.

It is for the assertion of his manliness at all costs, ironically, that Bento maintains his accusation against Capitu and the then-deceased Escobar concerning the paternity of their son; in his stubbornness he unwittingly substitutes Escobar for himself, yet he gains strength from making the accusation: "Could it be that there was a new man within me, the creation of new and strong pressures?" (140). At the onset of the memoir, then, before taking pen in hand and in the guise of humor, Bento deflects the complex web of guilt and remorse that led him to re-create his childhood home with a list of unjust offenses made against him: his authorship had been usurped, his name had been changed in an undeserved parody of his self-imposed reclusion, he had been unfairly criticized; yet his isolation was not so bad as it might have seemed ("I eat well and I don't sleep poorly"), and he goes on to tell us that his city friends and many women still seek him out. He is about to write a long, carefully crafted memoir of justification, consolation, and self-defense.

On beginning his memoirs, Bento Santiago is an elite, elderly, wealthy lawyer, and his narrative resembles a summation to the jury, his readership. Although he is careful to present his defects, those of which he is aware, in order to make himself seem normal and sane, he makes use of them as a counterweight to deflect attention from much more serious and perverse acts of passion or even of criminal intent that he has committed. While living in Engenho Novo, for example, one night Bento has a bad headache, an excuse he gives for his perverse wish that one of the trains of the Central line would blow up, "far from my hearing, and the line interrupted for many hours, even though someone should die" (68). As narrator, he excuses himself on the grounds that everyone is born with a certain number of vices and virtues, and he was simply born with these. He claims to counterbalance his wish for death in the train explosion by a beneficent counteraction, which was to offer his cane the next morning to a blind man at the station who didn't have one, as if this small gesture were a counterweight to a fatal act of terrorism. His authority is Montaigne, whom he quotes both as a sign of his enlightened and literate culture in support of his defense by alleging that good always accompanies the bad and as proof that he was acting out of an inescapable inner nature: "Ce ne sont *mes gestes* que j'escris, c'est moy, c'est *mon essence*" (I do not write *my own acts*, but myself and *my essence*) ("De l'exercitation," *Essais*).

Bento makes ample use of lawyers' tricks: he collapses time in his retrospective presentation, devoting two-thirds of his narrative to his childhood development while reducing several voyages to Europe and decades of his current lonely existence to a few lines or pages. Inexperience is the excuse Bento gives his readers for the very long exposition of his early life, and it leads to omissions and brevity in the rest: "I arrive almost at the end of my supply of paper, with the best of the story yet to tell. Now there is nothing to do but pull it along with great strides . . . everything cut short"

(97). He skirts the subject of his repressed attraction to Escobar, a strong father figure who dominates him, while warning that phantom horsemen whom he thinks are courting Capitu are sounding the "trumpet of doom" (73). He gives his story a casual, even trivial, air, as if it were a pastime, yet he reveals key details of a much more dramatic and darker content for the reader who is looking for them—and here is a point where Machado has an obvious hand in the narrative. Almost all of the narration is done from the perspective of the adolescent Bentinho, up to the point where he faces a crisis after the death of Escobar, his special friend from the seminary; he uses the terms "catastrophe" and "abyss" to mark the dramatic change, and he warns his readers. From early on in the lawyer's summation, the confessional side of his story has threatened to escape his control: he acknowledges that he himself is missing, and his life and narrative are an attempt to begin anew in the childhood home and recover what is missing: "A man consoles himself more or less for those he has lost, but I myself am missing, and this lack is essential" (2). His is a story, finally, of all that can never be recovered; it is profoundly melancholic rather than tragic.

Bento refuses to say why he is writing this book, and he resorts to more than one dissimulation: it is because he has nothing else to do; it is in place of the "History of the Suburbs" that he first thought of writing and promises to have the same low level of content and drama; or it is simply to relive moments from the past which, he comments neutrally, are neither so painful nor so pleasant as when they first occurred. Bento cannot reveal the terrible reason that motivates his book: he hopes to feel the pleasure and legal satisfaction of convincing readers of his innocence and take solace in their solidarity. It is one path to restoring the past destroyed by his passions, parallel to the rebuilding of his childhood home in the suburbs. He even confesses that he feels a certain pleasure in retelling a story so full of both pain and joy. Yet he knows that for the sake of consistency and credence he must carefully tie the ends of his life together, a task that as a lawyer he carries out with consummate skill. In a narrative he insists is pure, he will attempt to convince readers, who act as his jury, but he cannot unload the burden of his guilt and remorse over the obstinacy, rage, and jealousy that possessed him, turned him into a madman, and led him

to ruin his life. In the memoir he will confess that his memory is not good
and that he remembers only scattered details of his life by virtue of "continuity and repetition" (59).

Bento will also philosophize that "lying is, many a time, as involuntary as transpiring" and "one of the contradictions of this world" (41). The
only procedure likely to convince the jury would be to characterize his behavior as a part of the process of aging, as balanced between good and bad,
and to connect it to familiar literary and biblical antecedents. For these reasons Bento is an author absent from his own story, living with allegories
and parables of prior realities, shaping the history of a past that haunts him
in search of both a self and a consolation; his narrative is the story of absence and loss, as would be his unwritten "History of the Suburbs," since
at that time in Rio de Janeiro suburbs as yet had no history. To explain his
own story he takes advantage of age-old archetypes found in *Macbeth*,
Othello, *Faust*, and Dante's *Commedia* in order to situate the hidden depths
of his own thoughts and actions within certain well-known and acceptable
parameters. Dom Casmurro writes to expiate his dark acts through a pretense of innocence, a history of victimization, and the rehearsal of archetypes familiar to his audience.

The reason he gives for writing his memoirs is that while living in the
model of his childhood home the busts painted on the walls (Nero, Augustus, Caesar, Massinissa) spoke to him: "[They] said that since they had failed
to bring back the days gone by, I should take my pen and tell over those
times" (2). Veiled by this strange vision is the confession that on his return
visit to the actual house, after the death of all the principals in the novel,
"the whole house disowned me. Outside—the great *aroeira* and the *pitanga*
trees, the well pool, the old bucket and the washing place—nothing knew
me"; at the same time, he thought he heard leaves and branches "begin to
hum something" and the grunting of pigs became "a chorus of philosophical scoffing" (144). Feeling the rejection of place in these odd imaginings,
Bento authorized destruction of his childhood house; this is the same pattern he would apply to the rejection and forced exile of his wife and son.

The model of the childhood home at Engenho Novo is the first of the
novel's many substitutions and represents the pervasive destabilizing role

played by the mechanism throughout the novel. The substituted childhood house, meant to restore a lost time, "to link together the two ends of my life" (64), is symbolically a resurrection and restoration of Escobar, whose soul Bento had compared to a house: "Escobar went on opening up his whole soul, from the street door to the back fence. A person's soul, as you know, is arranged like a house. . . . Escobar pushed and came in. I found him here inside, and here he remained until . . ." (56). Here, Bento as narrator both intimates his intimacy with Escobar and foreshadows his death, which is prepared by a reference to Escobar's sister's death in the same chapter; she was a "devoted creature" (boa criatura) whom Bento would have wished to marry had it not been for Capitu. During the years of their respective marriages, the couples were inseparable, and the two lived between each other's houses, literarily and metaphorically: "While he lived, since we were so close, we had, so to speak, a single house. I lived in his and he in mine." Bento confesses that Escobar's house substitutes for Capitu's in his memory of their childhood houses: "It made me think of the two houses of Matacavallos, with their wall between" (117). The different houses and times symbolize a conflict that Bento will not allow into his conscious mind: he refuses to give the reader the house number "since I don't want you to go there and ferret out the story."[3] Bento is a failed character-author whose life roles are unstable because at every turn his will defers to and is determined by the decisions and actions of others, a pattern set by his mother and José Dias. He is Machado's character in search of an author.

In his Engenho Novo house Bento keeps portraits of his father and mother as youths, from before he was born, an ideal of conjugal felicity in this world and the next: "The loving ones, the lucky ones, who went from this to the other world to continue a dream, most likely" (7). They are the substitutes for the missing parents—his father died when he was a child— and he is the ritual victim of his mother's promise to make him a priest: "My mother took her son . . . she brought the wood for the burnt offering, the fire and the knife. And she bound Isaac and laid him upon the bundle of wood, took the knife and raised it high. Just as she was about to strike she heard the voice of the angel call to her. . . . This must have been the secret hope of my mother" (80). Bento is a substitute for his older brother,

who was born dead; hence Dona Glória, his mother, promised that if her
second born lived he would be given to the Church, a substitution that would
deprive Bento of marriage and an heir: he notices that his mother often looks
at him as a lost soul. His childhood toys were always church things. Bento's first objective in adolescence is to nullify his mother's promise, played
out curiously in another act of substitution in a Mass that the youth "performs" with the girl next door, his sweetheart Capitu: she is sacristan, and
they divide the host, which is a sweet, between them. From the beginning
Bento and Capitu plot to bring about their marriage, a substitution for the
priesthood, although authenticated by the false, metonymic Mass: "One
side of her face was the Epistle and the other the Gospel. Her mouth the
chalice, her lips the paten" (14). In the confused copy of a sacred ritual,
Machado inscribes one of the leitmotifs of Bento's exposition: *Dominus non
sum dignus*. Even Bento's emotions are the result of a substitution: he is
unaware of his love for Capitu until he overhears José Dias warn his mother
that the children might "fall in love": "Then I was in love with Capitu, and
Capitu with me?" (12). Dias, a fraudulent traveling salesman who became
attached to the family through Bento's father, an *agregado* common in Brazilian society, now acts as substitute father and mentor for the family. Bento
leaves the seminary when his place is occupied by an approved substitute,
and Escobar, who had the idea of the substitution, becomes his symbolic
second substitute father when he comes to dinner and courts Bento's
mother, D. Glória. Both Capitu and Escobar vie to establish connections
with Bento's deceased father. Capitu demonstrates her artistic talent in a
pencil sketch based on a portrait, which Bento finds imperfect but in
which he sees potential; Escobar, on his visit for dinner, shows a fascination with the portrait, going more directly to the heart of the matter: "It is
obvious that this was a pure heart." Recounting the comment from the distance of forty years, Bento paints a living portrait of Escobar impressive for
its detail: "Escobar's shaven face showed a fair, smooth skin. His forehead
perhaps was a trifle low . . . but it was still high enough not to swallow up
the rest of his features and lessen their grace. Actually it was an interesting
face: a fine mouth with a salty lift to it, a curved, slender nose" (71). After
the dinner with Escobar and D. Glória, Capitu asked Bento who was that

great friend who meant so much to him. She had been waiting in the window and observing their affectionate farewell, to the point that Bento waited for Escobar to look back from a distance as he departed. Contrary to his characterization of Capitu's eyes as being "like the tide" (olhos de ressaca), he described Escobar's as clear and very sweet. Escobar will compare Bento's eyes to his mother's: "You had to take after someone with those eyes God gave you; they are exactly like hers" (93). The reader is given two immediate warnings about Bento's fascination with Escobar: the first is from Cousin Justina, who accepted his visit with the unexplained reservation "in spite of . . ." (71); and Bento himself follows with two chapters warning of "reversals of fortune," "destiny," and "the final catastrophe." He decides to act on his jealousy of the horsemen who rode past Capitu's window, a decision reflecting Machado's subtle reciprocity, as he replaces the window scene in which Capitu observes his great affection for the departing Escobar with another in which she is at her window being courted, in a sublimated substitution.

After the marriages of the two ex-seminarians, Escobar and his wife, Sancha, become crossed with their shadow couple, Bento and Capitu, in a web of substitutions. Escobar had delivered Bento's love notes to Capitu before their marriage, and when Escobar married her friend Sancha he called Capitu "his little sister-in-law" (98). Sancha names her daughter Capituzinha, just as Capitu will name her son Ezequiel, Escobar's middle name. Sancha and Capitu have family resemblances, and Ezequiel as a child plays by imitating Escobar. The two children are said to resemble each other, a fondness that might have led to marriage, although Bento lets readers know bluntly that it did not, a foreshadowing of dark turns of events of which he is already aware as narrator. The four adults are also crossed by psychosexual substitutions: Bento attempts to seduce Sancha and assume the role of Escobar. In his lawyer's office Bento had placed a photograph of Escobar alongside his mother's, and in the moment of crisis with Sancha he heard it speak to him "as if it were he *in propria persona*."[4] When Sancha squeezes Bento's hand, she leaves an indelible impression: "I still felt Sancha's fingers pressing mine, and mine hers" (118). Bento is substituting Sancha, perhaps unconsciously, for a previous encounter with Escobar, when they decide to become even closer friends: "Escobar furtively gripped my hand so hard that my fingers still tingle. This tingling is an illusion, surely" (94). Perhaps to divert suspicion, Bento accuses Capitu, who might have had a motive for beginning an affair with Escobar, if only to share the intimacy he enjoyed with her husband or to produce the son desired by a possibly impotent or chaste Bento. The only rumored affair seems to be Escobar's with an actress, which because it is reported by Bento may be fulfilling ulterior motives: it both absolves Sancha of her overture to Bento and prepares Bento's accusation of Escobar and Capitu. The couples are thoroughly intertwined by a series of substitutions before the dramatic dénouement.

Bento's hallucinations, fantasies, and daydreams began at an early age; he once described their effects as "disconnected and patched, badly patched, like a botched and crooked design, a confusion, a whirlwind which blinded me and made me deaf" (62). He confesses, "I was not quite conscious of all my acts" (37). Dreams of victimization often took over his mind: "I was persecuted by dreams, even when awake" (63). The deep conflict in Bento between his mother and Capitu emerges when he alternately sobs and laughs during a solemn religious procession: "I went out into the hall and I heard someone say to me: 'Don't cry like that!' The image of Capitu went with me. . . . I saw her write on the wall, speak to me, turn with her arms in the air; I distinctly heard my name in a tone so sweet it made me drunk. . . . José Dias came up and whispered in my ear: 'Don't grin like that!'" (30). While in the seminary, Bento, during one of José Dias's visits, inquires after Capitu and pales when he hears she is happily romancing young bucks from the neighborhood, failing to discount Dias's known disapproval of their relationship. Bento loses control in his fantasy: "An impulse to dash headlong through the great gate, race down the steps, run, get to Pádua's house, seize Capitu and command her, force her to confess" (62). Bento admits to his enormous and universal jealousy: the slightest social contact of any dance partner or neighbor with Capitu tormented him to the point of terror and mistrust. Capitu had been his Mass, his religion, and his only purpose. The intensity and imaginative dimension of his jealousy provoke successively perverse and sadistic visions of punishment and cruelty. Thinking what might have happened between Capitu and the young bucks, Bento feels persecuted and weeps in his room, preceding a dream of revenge:

> I saw myself already ordained, standing before her. She wept
> repentantly and begged my forgiveness, but I, cold and serene,
> had nothing but scorn, scorn and contempt. I turned my back
> on her. I called her perverse. Twice I found myself gnashing my
> teeth, as if she were between them.
>
> As I lay on the bed, I heard her voice. She had come to
> spend the rest of the afternoon with my mother, and probably
> with me, as she had other times; but no matter how much her
> coming moved me, it did not make me leave my room. Capitu
> was laughing loudly, talking loudly, as if she let me know she
> was there. I continued deaf, alone with myself and my scorn.
> And I was filled with a desire to drive my nails into her throat,
> bury them deep, and watch the life drain out of her with her
> blood. . . . Capitu was laughing less now and spoke in a lower
> tone; probably she was hurt at my shutting myself away, but not
> even this moved me. I ate no supper and slept badly.[5]

This wish to punish Capitu notwithstanding, when he is suddenly called home to see his sick mother, Bento unconsciously channels his opposition to the seminary into a wish for D. Glória's demise: "With Mama dead, that would be the end of the seminary." When he becomes conscious of his idea, he confesses with deep shock and remorse: "Reader, it was a lightning flash; no sooner had it illuminated the night than it fled away, leaving the dark more intense from the remorse that it left behind with me. It was the prompting of lust and selfishness" (67). This is Bento's unchangeable pattern: "My fits of jealousy were intense, but brief: in an instant I would tear down everything, but in the same instant I would reconstruct the sky, the earth, and the stars" (107).

There is little ambiguity in this novel, contrary to the critical commonplace; rather, *Dom Casmurro* is an open text that demands the reader's participation and close attention. It traces and catalogues Bento's doubts, dependence, psychological instability, and degeneration within the language he chooses to portray himself. A testimonial to Machado's genius in constructing Bento's monologue is that for almost a century he managed to divert readers' attention away from Bento's own psychological deviations toward the irrelevant or substitute question of Capitu's guilt or innocence. The accusation became firmly grounded in the novel's reception as the key problem; later, a variation of this reading proposed Capitu's guilt or innocence to be an intentional ambiguity to be resolved by the juror-reader, an equally unacceptable reading. Machado, through Bento, succeeded in disguising the psychological portrayal of the narrator's instability, fantasy, and perversion in the literary tradition of Dostoevsky, Gogol, and Chekhov.

Machado read Russian authors of his day; in a chronicle about the suicide of the ballerina Labushka, a mistress of the regent, he writes, "Great mystery that only the Slavic world can give. Was it a telegram I read? Was it some page of Dostoevsky?" (December 16, 1894). And in a chronicle addressed to the czarina, he suggests that she have his message translated: "I had it translated into the language of Gogol that they say is so rich and sonorous" (October 11, 1896). In the story "The Secret Cause," Machado rehearses a case of perversion and cruelty dramatized in the heroine's death, including a visit to the opera.

From the earliest pages of *Dom Casmurro* there is a counterpoint to the courtship theme to be found in descriptions of Capitu—mainly her eyes, her curiosity, and her skill at dissimulation—that will add up in Bento's mind to conflict with the nature of his friend Escobar, feed his jealous hallucinations, and corroborate her guilt in Escobar's death by drowning in the tide. From their earliest acquaintance her eyes had the power to draw Bento into them: "Our eyes met, then looked away, and after wandering nearby returned to sink into the depths of each other" (14). Bento had heard José Dias describe them as "gypsy's eyes, oblique and sly." The crucial comparison Bento makes is between Capitu's eyes and the force of the tide: "Eyes like the tide? Yes, like the tide. That's what they were. They had some mysterious and force-giving fluid that drew everything up into them, like a wave that moves back from the shore when the undertow is heavy" (32). Enchanted with the young Capitu and preparing to comb her hair, Bento is over-whelmed at the idea of touching the head of a nymph, and he writes the name of the mythological figure Thetis before crossing out the word. Read-ers of Camões's *Lusiads* will recognize Thetis as a sea nymph, one of the fifty Nereids who was the passion of the giant Adamastor; when he reached out to embrace her, she transformed him forever into the giant rock that stands at the Cape of Africa and further taunted him by lapping at his shores. The foreboding of this name applied to Capitu at this erotic moment is it-self one of the significant undercurrents in her characterization as femme fatale.

She was endlessly curious in ways that Bento found both explainable and unexplainable, and especially so in wanting to know about subjects deemed improper for girls, like Latin. She read novels, she learned music, she was more than special to the point that Bento thought her "more woman than I was man" (31), a confession he was loathe to make. After their first kiss, Bento's inner voices warn his heart against his weakness: "Here is one who will make no great mark in the world, if his slightest emotions rule him." Yet he compares his discovery of Eros to that of Columbus and exclaims three times, "I am a man!" (34). Capitu's self-possession surprises Bento, who is always terrified by his situation; she disguises their deepening rela-tionship by talking and acting with an aplomb that Bento envies, even as he sees it as false. In diverting the family's suspicion from their plans to marry, Bento notes that they were required to dissemble: when Capitu in-sisted in front of the family that only a Padre Bentinho would marry her after his ordination, Bento is almost surprised by her "masterpiece of deceit" (65).

It is only when Capitu looks down at the dead body of Escobar, however, that Bento makes the leap connecting "eyes like the tide," Capi-tu's seemingly excessive expression of affection when giving her last re-spects, and her responsibility for his drowning. Capitu glances "fixedly" and "furtively," just as the widow Sancha does, but her eyes were "great and wide like the swollen wave of the sea beyond, as if she too wished to swallow up the swimmer of that morning" (123). It is the death of Escobar, not the accusation of infidelity against Capitu, that is the catalyst for the "catastrophe," the dramatic turning point and climax of the memoir and novel. The drowning has been carefully prepared in the text ever since the moment Bento, in a fit brought on by his desire that Capitu pay more attention to him, confessed being jealous of the sea. During his dalliance with Sancha, "the sea pounded forcibly along the shore; and there was the suck of the undertow" (118). The couples often looked pensively toward the sea. His accusation of Capitu is a diversion that substitutes a conscious theatrics in the reenactment of Othello for the "secret cause" of Bento's paranoia and hallucinations.

Bento accuses Capitu of infidelity with Escobar, whereas he would like to find her guilty of his death. Capitu's possible infidelity, her guilt or innocence, is a question secondary to the main issues in the memoir, one that does not resolve the loss of Escobar, although the accusation does succeed in polarizing a trial and placing her in the dock; it is the narrator's most brilliant and successful diversion, since the accusation establishes and fixates doubt in the mind of the reader-jurors over an extraneous issue. Helen Caldwell observed that the title of the novel is *Dom Casmurro*, not *Capitu*, and that the psychological drama lies entirely within Bento. That Capitu's inconclusive guilt or innocence of infidelity is irrelevant to the situation lies in the fact that either verdict would fail to justify Bento's extreme and irrevocable acts. The genius of his accusation against his wife and son is that for the readers, his jury, it changes the terms of discourse by occupying their deliberations with a problem introduced in the final pages, after the dénouement, a problem reviving the age-old dilemma of Othello. In an earlier chapter Bento himself explains the abstract advantage to be gained by any accusation: "A person can be guilty, half guilty, a third, a fifth, a tenth guilty, since in the matter of guilt the gradation is infinite. The simple recollection of a pair of eyes is enough to fix other eyes that remember them and delight in imagining them. There is no need of an actual, mortal sin, or exchange of letter, simple word, nod, sigh or signal still more light and trifling. An anonymous man or anonymous woman who passes by at the corner of the street can make us put Sirius inside Mars" (107). Bento's accusation is a peripheral consideration that will deflect attention from his fragile emotional and psychological state after the drowning of his best friend; it has no definitive solution, yet it is not in the least ambiguous. The accusation involves the jurors in a wider question between the sexes, one which could be aimed at almost any elite male in the capital. That there is not enough evidence presented to prove guilt or innocence simply assures that the question will continue to occupy and divert readers' attention. For more than a century, as I noted, readers of the novel have reduced it to a question of Capitu's guilt or innocence, having been distracted from seeing its great abyss. The evidence that this is a secondary question lies in the fact that no verdict could justify Bento's unrelenting revenge, whose ultimate and intentional effect destroys what he had spent all his years constructing.

Would Capitu's possible infidelity have constituted an acceptable moral justification for Bento's abandoning her to die in Europe, for pretending to visit her on two voyages, for trying to poison his innocent son, for wishing that he would contract leprosy, or for having a feeling of satisfaction on receiving the news of his son's death at a young age? His resolve to exile Capitu in Europe is yet another illustration of the reciprocity and tenacity of his revenge, as it is the inverse of Capitu's childish wish to send him to Europe on a steamship as a means of avoiding the seminary, and the adverse of the European voyage planned by Escobar for the two couples. Furthermore, Bento himself is aware that the resemblance between Ezequiel and Escobar is hallucinatory. When Ezequiel returns from Europe a young man, Bento admits that the deceased José Dias "would have found him the spit and image of me." Cousin Justina asks to see him, but Bento intercepts the threat to his illusion and delays the visit until she dies a few days later: "I believe her desire to see Ezekiel was with a view to verifying in the young man the sketch she had found, perhaps, in the child" (145).

Bento's emotional accusation of Capitu covers and is preceded by the major trauma he suffers after the drowning of Escobar, the friend who "inhabited his soul." The great issue at hand has everything to do with the story of Escobar's death. The reader has ample evidence of Bento's hallucinations and his fantasies of victimization and revenge; it is this accumulated evidence that Bento is able to disguise through his denunciation, even though it is tinged with the usual victimization and self-pity, although now reinforced by a declaration of manliness. When Escobar drowns in the sea tide, in spite of his perfect physical condition, a dramatic fatal substitution takes place in Bento's mind: he hallucinates that the child Ezequiel takes the place of the dead Escobar, whom the child, as noted, had the habit of imitating playfully and may resemble. Escobar thus returns from the grave in Bento's eyes; however, it is a painful, false, and incomplete return, an impossible substitution that embitters Bento to the point of no return. At Escobar's wake, when he observes Capitu glancing down at the dead man fixedly, he takes her composure and caresses in support of the widow to be signs of a furtive passion. Her eyes are the final proof of his condemnation. From this point on, no redemption is possible for Capitu.

On the day of the drowning Bento is admiring Escobar's photograph in his law office, while feeling the guilt of his "caprice" with Sancha the previous day and "wandering without reason." That night he had hallucinations, and he imagined that the photograph spoke to him: "Only once did I glance at the picture of Escobar. It was a handsome photograph, taken the previous year. He was standing frock coat buttoned, left hand on the back of a chair, right hand on his chest, gaze far away to the left of the spectator. It had elegance and naturalness. The frame I had had made to order did not cover the inscription that was written below, not on the back: 'To my dear Bentinho his devoted Escobar. 20-4-70' " (120). Bento decided to hold a pompous funeral yet describes his speech as being only a couple of words long, written out because he could not admit his emotion. His driver is worried about his spiritual state. At the funeral, when he closes the casket with José Dias, Bento is overcome with revulsion: "I had one of these impulses of mine . . . to throw the box, corpse and all, into the street" (124). He decides to throw his life instead, through a tempestuous and irrevocable act of rage and revenge. He read his speech in a trance, he called it a mad outpouring, and in leaving he tore it up and threw the pieces out the carriage window, damning it as worthless.

The following day he bitterly regretted destroying the speech yet could not reconstruct it. Bento as narrator then writes an apocalyptic note addressed to Sancha, who has left for good to live in Paraná; he promises her his love and suggests that they will meet again at the gates of Heaven

transformed into green plants in spring. He warns her not to read any further in his memoirs, since he is about to inflict pain for which he will not
be responsible, and "what is to come now cannot be erased" (129). It is a note
of desperation and warning by someone about to commit a violent act.
Bento quotes a verse from Dante's *Purgatorio*, "Come piante novella, Ri-
novellate de novella fronde" (New trees renewed with a new foliage) (33), as
a symbol of the rebirth of the deceased husband. Bento's intention had been
to replace Escobar by courting Sancha; he is at this moment completely unprepared to find the rebirth in his son, since he has implicitly already rejected his wife, Capitu. At home Bento determinedly ignores Capitu's
cheerful consolation; when she suggests that they live quietly until they forget and rise to the surface again, he is unresponsive: "The tenderness with
which she said this would have moved a stone. But I was not moved" (130).

     Bento's hallucinations return with a vengeance. After Capitu com-
ments on the similarity between Ezequiel's eyes and those of her father and
of Escobar, Bento begins to draw a sketch that comes to life: little Ezequiel becomes the "picture on the wall in memory of what was and can no
longer be" (132), like the portraits in his childhood home. Bento invents a
theatrical "letter" whose message is one of resurrection, as his quote from
Dante had been: "Escobar emerged from the grave, from the seminary and
from Flamengo to sit at table with me, welcome me on the stairs, kiss me
each morning in my study or ask for the customary blessing at night. All
this repelled me; I endured it so as not to be revealed to myself and to the
world. But what I could conceal from the world I could not conceal from
myself" (32). Bento has been to the theater to attend *Othello*—he says for
the first time—which seals his resolve to murder both mother and child.
Bento envisions their deaths as substitutions for "all the moments of my
dulled, agonized life." He is aware of his deteriorating mental condition:
"I grew steadily worse" (132), and he tries to shake the fixed idea from his
brain, yet he finds himself "with death in my pocket" and feels happy
(134). He leaves a suicide note for Capitu and plans to poison himself with
the morning coffee. He grandly envisions himself imitating Cato and
stretches out with a volume of Plutarch but replaces it in the bookshelf so
his intention would not be discovered. This second theatrical pose con-

firms the confusion in Bento's suicidal and murderous mind: when Ezequiel enters the breakfast room, Bento offers him the poisoned coffee,
recoils, then verbally denies his fatherhood to a child too young to understand him. The following chapter, "Enter Capitu," captures his sense of
staging and theatrics: her indignant, analytical response to his statement
and accusation unmasks his theatrics for a moment. Bento is on the point
of confessing his "grand illusion, a madman's phantasmagoria," when
the stage entrance of Ezequiel alongside a photograph of Escobar restores
the hallucination, which Bento confuses with reality. He oscillates between reason and fantasy, just as Rubião had when overcome by his passion for Sofia in *Quincas Borba*; Rubião's fantasy was an extension of
Napoleon, however, whereas Bento's was taken naïvely and impressionably
from *Othello*. From here to the end, Bento substitutes his suicidal solution
with the theatrical revenge he has learned from Othello, and he asks himself, "And why did I not strangle them that day?" (140).

In his final statements in the novel, which are meant to absolve his
guilt for ruining his life in his rage over the death of Escobar, throwing the
corpse onto the street, Bento repeats the pattern of Félix in *Resurrection*,
who has been duped to believe that Lívia was unfaithful or would be unfaithful at some future time. Although Félix at first recognizes that the note
to that effect was a ruse by his rival and enemy, with time and the solitary
life he leads, heading into infinity, he returns to the doubting that was his
nature and once again affirms the validity of the false note. In Bento's case,
he feigns forgiveness, "May the earth be light on them" (A terra lhes seja
leve!) in the style of the priest he never became, a self-serving comment to
the point of being malicious and perverse, as it hides his posthumous jealousy of Escobar, on the one hand, and his criminal invention of Ezequiel's
illegitimacy and exile of Capitu, on the other.

When Capitu shows her emotion while looking at Escobar's body, one
may imagine that Bento was jealous of her grief: if Sancha was the widow,
he in a way was the widower. When he felt Escobar's strong arms the day
before the drowning, they were the synecdoche for his own transformation
into husband and suitor in substitution. Escobar had entered into his soul
previously, and Bento tried to take on his identity when he attempted to

seduce Sancha. After Escobar's death by drowning, Bento witnessed Capitu's tears when she peered into the casket, and he was jealous not so much
of Capitu but that Escobar might have betrayed their brotherhood. The jealousy intensifies through the connection already well established in the narrative between the sea and Capitu's eyes: eyes like the tide, untrustworthy
gypsy eyes. Her guilt is affirmed because she is identified with the sea and
the tide that carried Escobar away. That in itself might not be sufficient to
provoke Bento's intractable reaction were it not for the funeral speech he
wrote and delivered half-unconsciously in the cemetery. His rage against
his loss led him, as noted, to rip the speech into pieces and toss it out the
window of his carriage, even as others asked to publish it. When he was
unable to reconstruct the speech and realized a double loss, the loss of his
personal grief in words, he flew into a rage against the world and obstinately
resolved never to relent. He likewise tore up and threw into the wind his
marriage and his son.

     Capitu perceived two principal flaws in Bento's character of which
he was unaware. The first is his almost existential fear: "[She] fixed me with
her eyes that were like the tide, and asked me if I was afraid." Bentinho does
not understand her intention; he can only see her eyes grow larger and larger.
When Capitu sees the impasse, she lets it go as a joke or her "craziness";
the old narrator, who is now aware of her deep insight, corrects her leni-
ency: "It was Capitu's mistake not to let them go on growing infinitely instead of diminishing them to their normal dimensions" (43). She asks him
openly about his fear of the conflict between her and his mother or that between his own fate and the promise. Bento has relied on fantasy in projec-
tions of his conversation with his mother in the chapter "The Private
Audience." He is filled with terror at a possible confession: "I will tell
Mamma that I do not feel the call. I will confess our love-making." After
their inconclusive conversation he again fantasizes that "I almost saw her
throw her arms around my neck and tell me that I did not have to become
a padre," although he has already betrayed his inner intentions with the
phrase, "I love only you, Mamma" (41). The conflict between the two women,
when exposed, leads to revenge motifs. When interrogated by Capitu
whether, if she were about to kill herself for love if he didn't return right

away, he would leave the seminary against his mother's order, Bento answers, "Yes," leading the incredulous Capitu to repeat the question. In response to his answer, she writes one word on the ground: "liar" (mentiroso). The confrontation elicits a hallucination of revenge: "The name written by Capitu not only leered up at me from the ground but even seemed to tremble in the air. Then I had an abominable idea: I told her that, after all, the life of a padre was not so bad, and that I could accept it without great sorrow. It was a childish way of lashing back at her; but I nursed a secret hope that she would fling herself into my arms, bathed in tears" (44). Her response, however, started a verbal duel and drawing room theater: Bento, imagining himself to be a priest, asks Capitu for two promises: that she confess only to him and that she allow him to be the priest who marries her. Not to be outdone, Capitu rejects the second request and alters it to allowing him to baptize her first child. While shocking Bento with her clever retort, Capitu also injects into the narrative, and leaves planted in Bento's memory, a foreshadowing of his doubt on the question of the paternity of her son.

Capitu's second perception is Bento's lack of faith, an inability to believe in the religious principles that would normally be part of his upbringing and seminary experience. When Bento declines to recant his accusation of infidelity, Capitu reacts analytically, although she is livid and denies Bento's accusation with outrage. She asks what could have given him such a conviction, since he had never showed even a shadow of distrust before, and she understands that the cause is the chance resemblance. It is a case, for her, of God's will versus natural yet unexplainable events; she accepts chance in the scheme of things on faith and wonders how Bento can act with such certainty: "In spite of the seminary, you do not believe in God" (138). Bento is determined to throw everything over, as he had after Escobar's funeral and as he had already confessed to the reader; he is about to admit his "madman's phantasmagoria" when he is again disturbed by another juxtaposition of Ezequiel and a portrait of Escobar. At this point, however, Bento is approaching madness, seeing the return of Escobar in multiple hallucinations in the person of Ezequiel. The fresh expectation of a romance with Sancha, a symbolic identity with Escobar, has gone far beyond any form of rational discussion or conclusion. Bento lashes out for revenge in his usual manner, under the legal term of reparation ("reparação"), which he claims to be justice, whereas his actions in exiling his wife and son repeat syndromes of the past, inverting even the phantom voyages to Europe that he plotted with José Dias to save him from the seminary.

Machado constructs a consciously open work in which the reader is obliged to participate, one full of omissions, as he both states and illustrates in the text: "I will not tell everything, for it would be too much" (94). He includes truncated and obsolete texts as lost or unfinished possible works that affect the reading of what he describes as a "book with omissions," composed by a sly narrator. The reader must fill in lacunae and can draw on all the possibilities that can be imagined outside the book: "What I do, on arriving at the end, is to shut my eyes and evoke all the things which I did not find in it. How many fine ideas come to me then! What profound reflections! The rivers, mountains, churches, which I did not find on the written page, all now appear to me with their waters, their trees, their altars, and the generals draw swords that never left their scabbards, and the clarion releases notes that slept in the metal, and everything marches with sudden soul" (59).

Via the story of the *Panegyric of Saint Monica*, Bento creates a narrative parallel to the memoir even as he ridicules both its author and text; the *Panegyric* has been written to serve a purpose identical to that of Bento's memoir, in the words of its nameless, proud author: "How it takes me back over the years to my youth! I have never forgotten the seminary, believe me. The years pass, events come crowding one upon the other, new sensations, and there come new friendships, which disappear in their turn: such is the law of life." Bento's similarity to the author who had forgotten everything except a twenty-nine-page pamphlet that was his only claim to an accomplishment in life is disguised and distanced by satire: "People have liked it, this Panegyric of mine!" (54). On a symbolic level the topic of Saint Monica speaks directly to issues faced by Bento, including infidelity, heresy and disbelief, and a mother's vigilance and prayer for her son, Saint Augustine of Hippo, who will become a noted author of confessions.

Bento calls further attention to missing or truncated texts with the story of the sonnet he never wrote. The first line occurs to him spontaneously in the seminar: "O flower of heaven! O flower bright and pure!" (155). His pondering of the metaphorical meaning of the phrase parodies the form and its effect: would the flower be Capitu, justice, or liberty? He finds triumph of both thought and form in the perfection of his verse. After enormous effort, Bento comes up with a final line, "Life is lost, the battle still is won," which he again ponders and finds to be sublime, although he is not sure of its actual meaning. He notes that celebrated sonnets flow so easily that one cannot tell whether the idea had fashioned the verses or the verses had called up the idea: does the author write the work or the work write the author? Bento shows even more vanity and obscurity than the author of the *Panegyric*, as he comes to praise the unfinished sonnet he never wrote as if it were a celebrated work. He contemplates reversing the last line, "Life is won, the battle still is lost!" in another unwitting satire of changing meanings in the reciprocity of events, just as he expresses the belief that an author has only to set the atmosphere and a sonnet will emerge. Authorship is reduced to filling in the missing middle, which in Machado's shorthand becomes a clue for reading his oblique book. For the second time he satirizes the author who claims possession of a work, rather than the open form the reader helps to complete.

The degree of rhetorical understatement can be seen in Bento's casual comment about the death of Capitu, which the reader learns through a simple addendum to Ezequiel's return visit: "His mother—I believe I have not yet mentioned she was dead and buried. She was: she reposes there, in the old country, in Switzerland" (145). Note that Bento does not mention her name, the woman who was his great love and purpose in life. His contrasting reaction to the return of Ezequiel shows the degree of his hyperbole: "I'd rather have given him leprosy" and "I would have paid triple never to have seen him again" (146). At Ezequiel's birth, Bento expressed quite different sentiments: "As for my joy when he was born . . . I do not know how to tell it. I have never felt its equal, nor do I believe there can be any joy comparable to it, nor one that distantly or closely resembles it. It was a dizziness and a madness" (108). Bento, the inauthentic first son, transfers a similar status to Ezequiel and exaggerates his sacrifice of the son, perhaps a reflex of his own sacrifice as a Carioca Isaac, with a deliberateness he himself describes as cruel and perverse. When Ezequiel returns for his last visit, Bento can hardly look at him because he sees only Escobar; thus when Ezequiel speaks enthusiastically about his plans to conduct archaeological research with friends, Bento makes a very telling spontaneous comment: "'Of what sex,' I asked laughing?" (145). Bento's offhand remark to the very image of Escobar all but confesses the strong subconscious forces and desire that led him to substitute Escobar, whose photo sat alongside that of his mother, for Capitu.

From the perspective of old age, Bento tells his story within the parameters of allegory, even if the ancient dreams no longer endure. He asks Night why dreams break and shred, and he invokes two Utopian islands, Lucian's Isle of the Blest, where a group of philosophers unite, and Camões's Isle of Love, where Vasco da Gama and Venus celebrate his voyage to India with erotic encounters. Modern dreams, he writes, try to imitate the classical models but are unable to equal them. Throughout his memoir, references to such lost classical antecedents create a parallel, displaced narrative that both explains and provides an alternative outcome for his banal, empty, modern account.

FOURTEEN

The Love-Death Theme of Counselor Ayres

And even if love comes through the door,
The kind that goes on forevermore,
Forevermore is shorter than before.
Oh, I'm so glad that I'm not young anymore.
Et lorsque l'amour frappe à la porte
Même s'il est de ceux qui vous transportent
On est transporté moins loin que jadis
Mon Dieu, mon Dieu, Mais quel plaisir de vieillir!

—Alan Jay Lerner and Frederick Loewe,
"I'm Glad I'm Not Young Anymore"/Maurice Chevalier

Counselor Ayres's Meditations

Machado's final failed narrator-character-author is José da Costa Marcondes Ayres, Counselor Ayres, a diplomat who spent his entire professional life of thirty years representing Brazil abroad before returning to Rio de Janeiro to live out his remaining days. In the nineteenth century the title of counselor was an honorific bestowed on select intellectuals and members of the liberal professions, such as jurists, writers, and the diplomat Rui Barbosa de Oliveira; it was also the term applied to official members of the Councils of State. Although the emperor awarded the distinction liberally, Machado de Assis declined the title; however, he awarded it to one of his characters. Counselor Ayres, the distinguished diplomat, is Machado's ultimate inside outsider, an analyst of the familiar who, after a long absence, speaks on his final return to Rio in 1887 as if he were a voyeur. He decides to live as a recluse, communicating only with the physical city: "I will not live with anybody. I will live with Catete, the Largo do Machado, Botafogo beach and Flamengo. I speak not of the people who live there but of the streets, the houses, the fountains, and the shops" (*Esau and Jacob*, 32). This impersonal geography is another form of the glass cabinet in which Ayres kept the relics of his former life, a collection contributing to a fateful symbolism running through his life and writings: ribbons, medals, old photos, pieces of classical ruins. He is immune to the city's magical effect in its twilight at the turn of the century as a "magnificent spectacle" and world capital. Even with his title and charm, Ayres is a failed character who is keenly aware that his life has been wasted on the courtesies and falsities of the diplomatic profession: "My nature and my life have given me a taste for and the habit of conversing. Diplomacy taught me to endure with patience an infinity of intolerable individuals which this world nourishes for its secret purposes" (*Memorial*, November 12). Yet to all appearances his learned aplomb and neutrality on all questions have led to a position of wisdom, proof of his education in the ways of the world. To fall asleep he recites Horace, Cervantes, and Erasmus. Ayres is aloof, ironical, skeptical, measured, and diplomatically agreeable to all.

Ayres is the reputed author of Machado's last two works, which represent his most advanced stage of interplay between fiction and reality and between language and meaning. Ayres's novel and memoirs are dramatic allegories that, like Machado's earlier novels, encompass a variety of genres and arts, from the diary and novel to mythology, theater, and opera.[1] The memoirs are published with the subtitle "Vignette." In his last two works Machado expands the possibilities of reading and interpretation through a complex game of authorship that places more distance and space between writer and character, editor and text, narrator and reader, language and meaning. Machado's hand as author is reduced to an "M. de A." in a second note to the reader. In a clever dissimulation, Ayres is introduced in a "Notice" to the novel *Esau and Jacob* (1904), where Machado de Assis revives the conceit of the found manuscript. In the unsigned "Notice" Machado disguises the identity of an editor, possibly himself, who has become involved in the discovery of seven boxes of manuscripts left by the then-deceased counselor in an attic: "When Counselor Ayres died, seven manuscript notebooks were found in his study, bound in cardboard. Each of the first six was numbered in order with roman numerals, I, II, III, IV, V, VI, written in Scarlet ink. The seventh had this title: 'Último' [Last]" (*Esau and Jacob*, "A Note to the Reader"). The first six boxes contained the counselor's diary, from which the editor would select entries to compose the novel *Counselor Ayres' Memorial* (1908). In the unmarked seventh box was a completed novel, which the editor decided to publish first, complete as he found it, although under another title he remembered Ayres to have mentioned once, *Esau and Jacob*, a reference to the biblical twins, different from the suggestive yet mysterious title written on the manuscript. The editor characterizes it as "written from the perspective of a unique interior monologue" divided between Ayres as author, character, and observer. The novel is made up of the same kind of multiple short chapters with ironic titles found in the *Posthumous Memoirs of Brás Cubas* and *Dom Casmurro*, whereas the diary entries are annotated with dates and even times of day. Removed from the time frame of the counselor's life and memoirs, the editor-reviser-publisher looks back over old papers and over the life and reflections of his absent author of interest, who is now on "the other side." Since Ayres is no longer around to aid in editing, his manuscripts take on the quality of urtext or universal text that is opened for selection and interpretation by an editor-researcher practicing a kind of literary archaeology. Through apophasis, the editor expands the text by referring to the material he has left out or paraphrased. The editor-publisher occupies a third level of authorship, between Ayres and Machado, commenting on the materials he presents and quoting from them, unable to hide his fascination with the manuscripts and his affinity with the counselor's witty reflections and observations. Ayres himself is fragmented into the author who constructs a novel by bits and pieces, the author who writes and quotes from his memoirs, and the character who observes life and participates in the action. In addition, he frequently addresses, questions, and converses with the reader in the second person. That reader inside the text involves and extends to all readers outside of it, who become active participants in the literary game.

Machado disguises, fragments, and transfers his overall authorial direction to the diplomat-character-writer and to the editor of unexamined material. The "Notice" is signed "M. de A." as if to reveal Machado's heretofore disguised identity as editor, literary sleuth, and partial author of the found novel and memoirs; even so, work with the boxes and manuscripts is different from that of supreme authorial direction of the complex conundrum. Managing author, editor, and character-writer function on parallel planes. Although the Ayres manuscripts are a radicalization of his established reliance on character-authors, Machado's final two works are equally "posthumous memoirs," continuing the paradigm established by the deceased narrator Brás Cubas and the aged Bento Santiago. They make up an unusual pair, however, with their invented chronology and feigned editorial history, sharing a fictional author, an editor as partial commentator and intermediary, and an occult author as outside observer. They multiply and fragment the possibilities of authorship, of reading, and of meaning. Both works are fictional remembrances and meditations on times past, guided by allegory rather than by events. Helen Caldwell finds a parallel in Xenophon, whom Machado read and quotes, since the Greek was also an adviser, retired from public life, observing the surrounding society with detachment, and speaking of himself in the third person in his *Anabasis*. Thematic keys to reading are to be found in a substantial number of literary quotes, allusions, and references. Ayres, Machado's final failed character-author, is his last narrator from beyond the grave, one whose awareness of the end and final things is communicated in the title chosen for his "last" novel.

Ayres's voice returns from beyond only with the aid of the editor, who retrieves his papers from the insignificance of oblivion: the result is a doubly retrospective, selective memoir by a failed character-author of lost or abandoned writings. Comparable to the framework of earlier character-narrators, Ayres's writings are equally self-conscious and self-referential: in the novel he refers to lines recorded in his diary, and in the memoirs he converses with the paper on which he writes. Although *Esau and Jacob* was ostensibly drafted more than twenty years before the editor located it—in the novel Ayres is said to be forty or forty-two when he returns to visit Rio de Janeiro on diplomatic leave from the Pacific around 1871 and sixty-two in the diary for 1889—it is surrounded by the memoirs and connected by the same author and editor. Ayres as dead author is a character in both and an overarching presence. The editor fulfills the function of triple or tertiary authorship, first, through his rescue of the novel he locates in the seventh, sealed box, second and more significant, through his careful selection of lines by the counselor from the first six boxes, which he edits for their potential, thinking they might have enough intrinsic interest to deserve publication as a memoir, and, third, for his role in disguising Machado's authorship. The invention of the editor who presents and comments on the materials found in *Esau and Jacob* creates an intermediary agency between the occult author-in-chief and the ostensibly deceased writer, and he intensifies the theme of remembrance of things past that characterizes Ayres's return to Brazil through his discovery of old papers. Despite a confessed lack of ability, the editor makes deprecating comments to the effect that even with the dull and obscure passages removed the remaining memoirs could be useful only for whiling away the time on the boat to Petrópolis.

The reader is once again disarmed and misled by the implication of the insignificance and even disorder of the counselor's writings, the mysterious title, as if the editor were questioning whether the contents were worth his time and dedication, much less the reader's attention, begging the question whether naturally disordered life can be successfully forged into art by a novice editor. Mirroring Brás Cubas's comment about having five readers, the editor here suggests that despite his struggles to piece together a connected narrative of minimal interest, the diary may be nothing more than another collection of retrospective and fragmentary memoirs by a dead author, of whom he says, "He did not play an important role in this world." In fact, the editor is highly selective: both the novel and the memoirs are focused only on the short period, 1886–89, of Ayres's symbolic return to await death in Rio, the city of his birth. Yet the editor takes a neutral position, justifying his actions solely on formal grounds; he seems not to grasp a meaning any deeper than curiosity or more than commonplace, and his promise to edit the remainder of the diary carries an ominous tone of "nevermore": "The rest will appear some day, if some day comes." The editor belongs to the same family as Machado's deceased narrators, recovering a narrative of which he is the first reader, a vicarious participant, and a passive outside observer. As in the *Posthumous Memoirs*, the theme of

death and disdain for the dead is projected through the final return in retirement of the sixty-two-year-old man of letters, the always-observant,
supercilious counselor, the dead memorialist who haunts the city as if he
were floating a bit above its streets and personages, the presence of an
absence.

Ayres's comments on writing and the contents of his diary form a counterpoint to the city and its politics and social life: "Time is a knowing rat
that diminishes or alters things by giving them another appearance." His
skeptical opinions underlie his method and reinforce his position as an outside observer who is always "keeping notes on his discoveries, observations,
reflections, criticisms, and anecdotes." He wants his diary to be mimetic
and therefore as truthful as a copy of life observed, although he knows that
writing is tuned to imaginative spheres and hidden realms in constant
change. Machado suggests a form of semiotics:

> If I were writing a novel I would strike the pages of the 12th
> and 22nd of this month. A work of fiction would not permit such
> an equivalence of events. On both those days—which I should
> then call chapters—I met the widow Noronha on the street. . . .
> I would delete the two chapters, or make them quite different
> from each other. In either case I would lessen the exact truth,
> which seems to me more useful for my present purposes than
> it would in a work of imagination. . . . All this is repugnant to
> imaginary compositions, which demand variety, and even con-
> tradictions, in behavior. Life, on the other hand, is like that, a
> repetition of acts and gestures, as in receptions, meals, visits,
> and other amusements. (*Memorial*, September 30)

As a wry observer, in chapter 41 Ayres composed a monologue for a donkey being beaten by the owner of the cart it is harnessed to: the donkey's
eyes expressed "profound irony and patience" belonging to an "invincible
spirit," and through Ayres's imagination, according to the editor, he learned
to photograph the invisible and to hear silence. In the manner of Camões's

Canção X, Ayres converses with his own diary, as if it were a guiding and more perceptive virtual self, meant to correct its original:

> Paper, dear foolscap, do not gather up everything this idle pen writes. Wishing to do me a service, you will end up doing me a disservice, for if it should happen that I leave this life without time to reduce you to ashes, those who read me after the Seventh Day Mass, or before, or even before the funeral, may think I confide my love thoughts to you. No, paper. When you get the feeling that I am insistently sounding that note, steal away from my desk and flee. (*Memorial*, April 8)
>
> This, yes, dear paper, this you may record, because it is the pure inside truth, and no one reads us. If someone did read us, he would think me evil, and nothing is lost by appearing to be evil; one gains almost as much by actually being so. (*Memorial*, April 12)

Repeating Brás Cubas, Ayres at one point becomes exasperated and berates readers who would try to change the way he is writing the story, usurping authorship. To a hypothetical female reader who wants the novel *Esau and Jacob* to go in a certain direction, he says, "What you want, dear madam, is to arrive right away at the chapter about love or loves, which is your particular interest in novels. . . . Frankly, I don't like it when people go about guessing and composing a book that is being written methodically. . . . No, my lady, I did not take pen in hand to satisfy the whims of those who give me suggestions. If you want to write the book, I offer you the pen, paper, and an admiring reader. But if you wish only to read, be still, go line by line. I will allow you a yawn between chapters, but wait for the rest, have faith in the narrator of these adventures" (*Esau and Jacob*, 27). The irony cannot be lost on the complaint of a fictional author, and the two worlds of authorship and creative readership may finally overlap until they can no longer be distinguished. With this dialogue, Machado is pressing the limits of narrative to demonstrate the insufficiency of a single point of view. Ayres warns readers to pay close attention to hidden content:

There are contradictions that can't be explained. A good author, who made up his story or placed importance on the apparent logic of events, would transport the Santos couple by foot
or by public carriage or rented coach; but I, my friend, I know
how things happened, and I relate them exactly as they were.
At most, I explain them, with the condition that such a custom
will not become a habit. (*Esau and Jacob*, 5)

Thus was Ayres's conclusion, as one reads it in the *Memoirs*. It
will be the reader's conclusion, too, if he cares to make conclusions. Note that here I spared him Ayres's work. I did not oblige
him to find out for himself what other times he had to discover.
The attentive reader, truly ruminant, has four stomachs in his
brain, and through them he passes the facts and deeds back and
forth, until he deduces the truth, which was or seemed to be
hidden. (*Esau and Jacob*, 55)

Ayres (or Machado) is not beyond using his own failure as a subtext. Behind his constant agreement with everything and everyone Ayres creates a
deeper, hidden level of reading with which he challenges his readers: "If
I am lying, it is not intentional" (*Esau and Jacob*, 3). The perplexed beggar who receives the generous two-thousand-*réis* note without understanding why represents the case of thoughts without words that Ayres
makes intelligible: "I translated them into spoken language so that they
will be understood by those who read me" (3). As author, he finds explanations to be tedious, explaining that "explanations eat up time and paper, they hold up the action and end up in boredom. It's best to read with
attention" (5).

Ayres occupies two worlds: the first is the exterior world of Rio de
Janeiro, and the second is his personal private territory, limited to his manuscript and memoirs. Perhaps because of his training in diplomacy, Ayres
has emptied his mind of any preconceptions or opinions in his interaction
with society: "Ayres thought nothing" (12). His professional agreeability is
a calculated position taken against life's irresolvable duality and conflict:

it is a dissimulation, a purposeful misreading, a diplomatic posturing, yet in his view his compromise is a wise and beneficial synthesis as well as a modus vivendi. At the same time, readers learn that Ayres held opinions that he reserved for his manuscript: "When he did not manage to have the same opinion, and it was worthwhile to write his down, he wrote it. He was also in the habit of keeping notes on his discoveries, observations, reflections, criticisms, and anecdotes, keeping for this purpose a collection of notebooks which he gave the name *Memoirs*" (12). In all these notations Ayres is polite, sincere, and skeptical. He always confirms his position as discreet diplomat, never contradicting or giving opinions. Ayres is also a widower but cuts the figure of a bachelor who has outlived or overcome his passions; and he has been there, done that: Going anywhere else in the world is not worth the price of a ticket. He can therefore observe and judge the world of the empire with an aged, wise and wry déjà vu. He is aware of his "usual drop of gall" sometimes expressed with "wicked mirth" (*Memorial*, December 5).

What politics contributes to the novel is perhaps a material surface that equals Ayres's thumbnail definition of all of diplomacy as just "covering and uncovering" (98). In these notes he even acquires the habit of adding a few random indiscreet, malicious, even perverse thoughts—he admires the sharp-tongued Cesária—that he intimates to Rita and confesses to the paper on which he writes. Ayres in this way duplicates in his person life's conflicts and dualities that he seeks to dispel diplomatically, suggesting that his solution is simply a diplomatic strategy of fleeting benefit and soporific effect. All is material for a baroque great theater of the world or for comic opera on the human condition, as if Machado were staging the aphorism from *Resurrection*: "Life is an opera buffa with intervals of serious music." Ayres is more than aware, however, of the existence of a great abyss ready to consume all the formal structures of life and of his own life now coming to an end, whether from Dante's *Inferno*, Croesus's misreading of Pythia's prophecy, Camões's Cape of Storms, or Natividade's heart: "The heart is the abyss of abysses" (12). In his final return to Rio he is determined to maintain his equilibrium while waiting out an inexorable fate, whether classical, biblical, or tropical, that is the measure of his world and of his philosophy. Ayres could be the Ricardo Reis whom Saramago brings back to Lisbon in his novel *The Year of the Death of Ricardo Reis* (1984).

Esau and Jacob

Esau and Jacob, Ayres's novel in which he is also a character, probes what can be known about the nature of the world, citing its archetypes and questioning what constitutes knowledge and wisdom in a narrative and drama of thinly veiled allegory. Its dramatic themes are death, judgment, fate, and love. Ayres cites a verse from Dante as the epigraph to *Esau and Jacob*: "Dico che quando l'anima mal nata . . ." (I say that when the spirit evil-born . . .) and summarizes, "Who can foretell anything at all?" The verse is spoken at the moment of judgment when the spirits arrive at the gates of Hell to make their confessions to Minos, connoisseur of sin, who will assign them to a circle of punishment equal to the number of times he wraps his tail around himself. There is no appeal of Minos's judgment because all has been fated: "Non impedir lo suo fatale andare: vuolsi così colà dove si puote ciò che si vuole, e più non dimandare" (Do not impede his journey fate-ordained; it is so willed where there is power to do that which is willed; and ask no further question). The only choice is to obey fate of one's own will, without hope.[2]

The first to arrive represent the sin of lust—Semiramis, Cleopatra, Helen, Dido, Francesca, Achilles, Paris, and Tristan—yet all have succumbed to the overwhelming power of love, which has left them in their pitiable state: "Amor, ch'a nullo amato amar perdona" (Love that exempts no one loved from loving in return). Francesca confesses that the power of love is often recognized and valued through sad memory after its loss, a theme Ayres develops allegorically through the genre of memoirs: "E quella a me: Nessun maggior dolore che ricordarsi del tempo felice ne la miseria; e ciò sa 'l tuo dottore" (And she to me: There is no greater sorrow than to be mindful of the happy time in misery, and that thy teacher knows). The epigram is meant as a key to reading: Ayres refers to it as a "pair of spectacles with which the reader can penetrate what is less clear or totally obscure" (13). The geography of Rio, in Ayres's new solitude, was no different from that of any time or place: "The sea there, here the forest and the view, awoke in him an infinity of echoes which seemed to him to be the very voices of the ancients" (33).

Once again in Machado, the narration is characterized by apparent digressions, interruptions, and intermezzos. The editor warns readers that he does not like explanations; the reader should pay attention. The narrator addresses the apparent lack of substantive plot in what amounts to a radical revision of the novel: "Time is an invisible web on which everything may be embroidered—a flower, a bird, a lady, a castle, a tomb. One may also embroider nothing. Nothing embroidered on the invisible is the most subtle work possible in this world, and perhaps in the other" (22). The novel describes even thoughts that have not yet crossed the threshold into words, being only a "humming in the ears of conscience" (3). The description of Natividade's inner character surprisingly resembles the experimental prose of a Clarice Lispector: "Did I not tell you that Natividade's soul was blue? Well, it was" (19). The import of these and other strange remarks is that memory is not sufficient to stop or recapture time, in spite of one's desire and need to do so; rather, "the eye of man serves to photograph the invisible, just as his ears record the echo of silence" (41). *Esau and Jacob* is Counselor Ayres's remembrance of things past, relived in the youth roused only by old letters, with stories of a world in which Ayres had lived intensely but now savors as a fine perfume or exquisite musical phrase. Ayres is able to see beyond the page and to call to mind things past. The rhythm of the novel-notebook is one of nostalgic longing and the fullness of age, punctuated by Ayres's skeptical, witty, and impassioned observations.

The actors in this dialectical drama set in Rio de Janeiro have mythical counterpoints: the fortune-telling *cabocla* on the Morro do Castelo is cast as Pythia, the oracle of Delphi, and the twins Pedro and Paulo, whom she prophecies will accomplish great things, recapitulate her subtle advice to the ruler Croesus that by attacking the Persians he will destroy a great empire. The twins, named for the Christian apostles, vie like Esau and Jacob for the right to their father's world.[3] They were called Castor and Pollux in the Chamber of Deputies, containing the hidden allusion to the question of paternity. When the maiden Flora cannot choose between the twins, Ayres subtly alludes to an alternative by citing Ulysses's confession to Alcinous (103) of his longing to accept the invitation to cease wandering and begin a fresh life with the young girl ready to serve him. Yet Ayres, in his retirement, cannot bring himself to begin a romance with Flora, although he intimates an attachment more than once. He cannot overcome the shadow of death and his fated solitude; as he said of Santos, "A force greater than himself always silenced him" (21).

Ayres contemplates the theme of fateful coexistence of dialectical opposites in Natividade's twins, Pedro and Paulo, and the duality of sensation through their mutual muse, Flora. In this situation he sees evidence of the reciprocal and contradictory nature of events, the pendulum that sets fate against the futile human desire to predict and control it. Remembering the prophecy of the old *cabocla*, Ayres is reminded of Aeschylus's *Eumenides*, in which the sibyl Pythia states, "My prophecy is only as the god may guide." The eternally opposed twins who fought in the womb symbolize the concept of the continual war of opposites, posited by the pre-Socratic Anaximander. Standing in proxy for Esau and Jacob in the biblical world, a comparison first mentioned by Ayres, Natividade's twins raise legal and moral issues of primogeniture, conflict, and deception, just as their mother's name encompasses all births. A chapter title, "Teste David Cum Sybilla," invokes the "Dies Irae," another day of judgment taken from a Latin hymn incorporated into the Catholic liturgy. Ayres embodies the solution of Anaximenes of Miletus to the concept of limitless conflict by elevating the neutral property of air: Ayres. Ayres, the author-observer, also stands in the novel for Logos, Heraclitus's law of constant change that unites universal difference and sameness. Ayres observes "how nature guides the smallest and biggest things, especially if fortune assists her" (51); as narrator he represents their unity or neutralization by adopting an attitude of permanent ambivalence, his form of Logos, which protects him from the constant flux and succession of opposites. When faced with a choice, "he chose neither of the two opinions" (12), and when caught in the contradiction of agreeing with everything, he agrees, "It could be. Life and the world are nothing else" (87). Of the young woman Flora, enamored of the twins, Ayres confesses, "Note that I like her very much: I find a special flavor in that contrast of her opposing characteristics: at the same time so human and so removed from this world, so ethereal and so ambitious at the same time, with a hidden ambition" (59). He considers it an eternal dialectic without a synthesis. Ayres puzzled and charmed Flora by describing her as "inexplicable" and observed that she herself was divided: "Flora was Orpheus and she was the song." Aided by Flora's music and the allegory of opposing relationships, Ayres is drawn to the high baroque drama of classical fates in perpetual conflict and change: "All contrasts reside within man" (35). He invokes Flora's aid in recalling verses from Goethe's *Faust* (1808), "Zwei Seelen wohnen, ach! in meiner Brust!" (Oh, two souls live in my breast!) as the paradigm of the novel's dialectical impasse and of his own compromises. As narrator-observer, however, Ayres would prefer to place himself beyond dialectics by assuming the role of outside observer of life, as if he were immune from duality. He remains aware that he is a character in an inexorable game, whether the linguistic game of his writings or the fatal chess match between Ayres as author and the pieces in his social world, or even, as he says, "where everything will happen as if you were watching a game between two players, or more clearly, between God and the Devil" (13).

Esau and Jacob is at the same time so synchronized with national events occurring fifteen years before the novel was written as to suggest a ready-made allegorical interpretation of the plot: the twins Pedro and Paulo are the Empire and the Republic, their mother, Natividade, is Brazil, while Flora, the girl they both desire, is the new nation. The novel does tell of the abdication of the emperor, the abolition of slavery, and the fall of the monarchy as well as of an elegant ball on November 9, 1889, only days before the declaration of the republic on the fifteenth. All of this has historical interest, but the reader also accompanies imagined events, such as the fantastic interview between the character Baptista, an ex-governor, and the strongman Marechal Floriano. Would allusion to historical events through fantasy be enough to secure the novel's historical foundation? Machado, after all, shows no respect for governmental or institutional politics. To describe a real curfew decree, Ayres ironizes that "at the end of 72 hours, all the liberties were restored, except that of returning to life. Whoever died, was dead."[4]

Esau and Jacob is primed to deceive the reader in its social and political referents, and, besides, the novel is full of enigmas. There is no real plot, aside from the life story of twins who fight and oppose each other by every means that can be invented—the old theme of the human double, as Luciana Stegagno Piccho observes, projected in pairs of twins. Thus, thematically and formally the novel is a *divertissement*.

An allegorical drama framed on a point of philosophy, Ayres's novel has the open form of an intermezzo or entr'acte in the guise of chapter 46, "Entre um ato e outro" ("Between Acts"), or, figuratively, a space removed from representation of a main act, as in performance practice in Italian baroque opera. Machado uses this interruption in the narrative to consider the dangers of creating believable literary or theatrical productions. Ayres invites the reader, addressed in the second person singular, to pretend to be in the theater between acts, when the actors change costumes, the leading lady laughs in her dressing room about the tragic scene she has just performed, and from backstage the flowery scenery can be seen to be only unpainted canvas. The reader is invited to remain in a lady's box in the theater and discourse on the production with the purpose of drying the tears in her eyes that the play has left; the comments should be full of hyperbole, exaggerating both the beauty and the defects that make both the beautiful and the ugly appear less so. The comments are banal, yet they serve the valuable and rare purpose of substituting reality for fiction, making everything seem truthful and sincere. The spell must be broken in the short time of the entr'acte, and here is Machado's irony, that the spectators are in the theater only for the purpose of believing in the play, and the truth of dried tears lasts only until the next act, when the fated performance resumes the expected illusions. The reader-reviewer, duplicating the role of Ayres-narrator, is yet another actor in the reality play between the play, awaiting another illusion of truth.

Ayres thinks of his diary as an exterior space between acts of life, as if it could occupy a space apart, truthful and free of tears: "I will not set down those tears in this place, or the promises made, the reminders given, the pictures exchanged, between godson and godparents." The elaborate staging has been pared down to resemble unadorned truth: "I will not set

down the separate events or unrelated anecdotes, and I even exclude the
adjectives, which held more interest in his mouth than my pen could give
them—only those needed for understanding things and persons will appear
here" (February 4). He lives in the fashion of a comic entr'acte, interview-
ing the theatergoers and waiting for the inevitable dénouement. He expects
to find pure truth in his diary, whose writings should add up to more than
the sum of their contents, with their concentration of sly observations and
witty truths; yet there are moments when he seems aware of his own diary
as performance: "Ayres dear, confess that when you heard young Tristão's
grief at not being loved, you felt a glow of pleasure, which, however, did
not last long, nor did it come back" (December 3). Like Machado's other
character-narrators, Ayres overestimates the narrative truth of his memoir.
Is it not also part of the theater? Ayres as narrator would dismiss the play
in the world theater to go directly to its underlying theme or message as
described in his banal, prosaic, and agreeable review, as if it were immune
from representation. He is aware of the power of the theater, however, and
in one scene "he confessed that he had killed more than one rival. That if
he remembered correctly he must be carrying seven corpses on his back,
done in with various weapons. The ladies laughed" (92). In his entr'acte
Ayres posits deeper truths in the intervals between action, vulnerable to
human moments of meditation and solitude, yet in the end cannot pass
beyond another form of entertainment in his world theater: "Hyperbole
is the way of this world. . . . Only by force of a lot of rhetoric can one fill
[peoples' ears] with a breath of truth" (31).

    Ayres's novel is an allegorical construct, referring to deeper levels of
meaning and interpretation beyond the senses, whether the description of
a banal outing in chapter 57—"I would not write this chapter if it were really about the shopping trip, but it is not"—or the "pair of spectacles" needed
to decipher obscure meanings, or the fabric made of "nothing on top of the
invisible." The novel works because of the gap between its ellipses, mysteries, and metaphors and the narrator's pretense that he writes only what
has actually happened: "I am speaking in metaphors: you know that everything here is the pure truth and without tears" (46). Time and the attempt
to predict the future on the basis of the past is one of the main themes, a

theme in which there is both mystery and philosophy. Natividade consults an oracle, as if she were in ancient Greece. Pattern, archetype, genetics, and cycles are the unforeseen gods creating havoc in a dualistic world of fate, where things are pulled in two directions, things past and things to be. It is important not that her twins, Pedro and Paulo, are a monarchist and a revolutionary, but that they were already fighting in the womb, feeling no pleasure equal to that of opposition. The need for synthesis, which would be the equivalent of having definite opinions and solutions to life, is risky if not impossible. Flora, the sensitive, mysterious girl whom the twins love, cannot decide between them. In a delirium before her death ("Both, what do you mean, both?"), she melds them into one person.

Like Flora and the prophecy, the diary too is inexplicable; like a looking glass or sibyl, it tells the story of Ayres's failure to be, the abdication of his role in this world. Time, memory and the past, and the desire to hold onto fleeting youth cannot be captured in their full reality: "That desire to capture time is a need of the soul and of the chin. But God gives time a habeas corpus" (23). There is no reprieve for desire, however, and Ayres feels pangs of remorse for his age when Flora turns her eyes from him to the young twins. His ongoing battle with Eros confronts his pact with death, beginning with Natividade and her sister, to whom he was once to be engaged. To Ayres, the world, like the twins, has never changed, even if it is beyond one's grasp except as story, myth, or archetype. What is important is that everyone in the world theater keep reading and believing, since Ayres says that all languages lead to heaven. His flexibility, objectivity, and openness indicate his acceptance of his fated role. Ayres dresses for another day with the same, eternal flower in his lapel.

Counselor Ayres's Memorial

Ayres as author of his memorial represents and conveys the presence of death: "All my days are told: there is no way of recovering a shadow of what is gone" (February 13). He is convinced that his return to Rio de Janeiro is a scenario for the final act of his diplomatic life: "I am a gravedigger," he writes in his diary on September 30. Death has taken away the compan-

ions of his generation ("If I were to total the sum of friends I have lost throughout this world, it would come to a number of dozens," February 26), and
he makes reference to his own mortality: observing the young couple Tristão
and Fidélia, he writes, "I saw them with these eyes that the cold earth will
one day devour" (December 22). His comment is both morbid philosophiz-
ing and a vaguely disguised excuse for suppressing and abandoning the pursuit of Fidélia to his surrogate, Tristão. The clock on his wall strikes the
hours "mournfully" and seems to be speaking to him with the message that
he is a gravedigger. Because of his age Ayres considers himself to be part
"of the dead and dying" and is determined to act out a role he believes to
be assigned by destiny.

The life and death instincts are dramatized in Ayres's memoirs by a
dualism: his unexpected attraction to the "widow Noronha" versus the
theme of their mutual permanent widowhood. The dialectic sets the widow
and widower's eternal fidelity to the dead against the omnipresence and persistence of an underlying life force. When meeting his sister Rita in the cemetery to lay a wreath at their family monument, she points out the young
widow nearby at the tomb of her husband, who had died suddenly during
a visit to Lisbon after only several years of marriage;[5] the widow Noronha's
depth of emotion and devotion is symbolized by her having returned his
body to Rio de Janeiro, contrary to Ayres, who had left his wife buried in
Vienna. Ayres is offered a Faustian bargain by his sister, Mana Rita: the
challenge to marry the young, attractive widow Fidélia in the face of Rita's
determined opinion that she will remain faithful to her deceased husband
and never remarry: "She cited the wager between God and the Devil over
Faust, which I had read to her, here at my house, in Goethe's own words"
(February 25). Ayres makes light of the challenge, even as he is weighed down
by his own imminent preparations for death. He feels attracted by a primitive instinct for freedom and Eros, which is nevertheless outweighed and
denied by what he will call life's imprescriptive laws. The reader would have
learned from *Esau and Jacob* that Ayres did not care for marriage, although
he recognized its advantages for one in his profession. The editor reports
that he had proposed to and been accepted by the first eligible woman, yet
because of their differences it was as if he lived alone, and when she died,

"he did not suffer with the loss" (12). Ayres may thus take up Rita's challenge lightly, although one may have doubts about his commitment to winning it. To emphasize what amounts to an alliance with death, Ayres writes, "Life, especially for the old, is a tiresome burden" ("Saturday"). None of the city's sounds—carriages, mules, people, bells, whistles—can overcome his determined march toward death: "I have a wife under the sod in Vienna, and none of my children ever left the cradle of nothingness. I am alone, completely alone" (September 30). As in other of Machado's narrators, his bleak statement hides a more precise and honest truth.

Ayres floats through Rio de Janeiro as might the deceased Brás Cubas, who feigned to turn the absence of an heir into a painful, though insincere, final advantage.[6] Rita's bet with Ayres implies the possibility, however remote, of calling the absent heir from nothingness. To counterbalance Rita's challenge, Ayres quotes Shelley. As in other novels based on quotations—*Resurrection* on Shakespeare and *Esau and Jacob* on Dante—the *Memorial* constantly returns to Ayres's frequent quote of a line from Shelley's poem to Jane Williams, "One Word Is Too Often Profaned" (1822), which ends with the phrase, "I cannot give what men call love." Ayres misunderstands or purposely misstates the meaning of Shelley's line: the English poet cannot give love because his feelings for Jane are more intense than what can be communicated by a word so commonly profaned; Ayres quotes the line to mean that he has passed beyond the will or ability to love.[7] Ayres is actively involved, whether consciously or unconsciously, in the repression or denial of Eros, whether his own or those of other characters, and his literary justification comes through a false memory. Ayres battles false feelings throughout his encounters with Fidélia. After seeing her off on the ship that will take the young couple to Lisbon, he has a vision of her sitting on his sofa, and they are looking at each other. Now that she has sailed, Ayres still can admit his deep feelings only by returning to Shelley: "I giving the lie to Shelley with all the sexagenarian strength left in me. Ah! Enough!" (July 18). He has condemned his possible heirs to remain in nothingness. His quote from Shelley marks the inherent falsity and fragility of memory by reversing the English poet's pretended denial of love. Throughout the memorial, Ayres assumes the role of conspirator in death's power

over an equally eternal erotic impulse. He marks his return to Rio de Janeiro with an inverted Caesarean adage: "Here I am, here I live, here I shall
die" (January 9). The phrase is Ayres's "Veni, vici, mori."

Ayres embodies the struggle between Eros and Thanatos, the essential forces he seeks to reconcile by pretending to assume an external
point of view of the eternal.[8] The struggle takes place in the memoirs on
multiple planes of action, comparable to an opera libretto, beginning with
the archetypal references to Tristan's love-death theme and to the heroic
Fidelio-Leonore's freeing of her captive husband; these plots are adjusted
to a Brazilian setting, where Fidélia continues to honor her deceased husband and Tristão arrives from Lisbon as a disguised challenger and
"brother." A second plane of action lies within the counselor, motivated
by Rita's challenge and by Tristão's growing interest in Fidélia, as Ayres
struggles to deny his own attraction to the widow. The old Aguiar couple
provide another setting for the love-death motif: the sentimental D. Carmo has
devoted her adult life to raising Tristão as a son and caring for Fidélia as a
daughter, two substitutes for the children she never had. The love motif, supported by the renewed presence of the youths with the Aguiar couple, is
bound up at the same time with its deadly consequence, the end of their world,
which is the permanent departure of the new young couple to Lisbon and the
symbolic death of the parenthood of the Aguiar couple, who are last seen by
Ayres sitting silently, staring into space, overcome by their melancholy. Ayres,
the diplomat, is, as usual, on both sides at once, already dead for the reader
and assuming at the time of writing to have purportedly filled his own personal quota of romance that life allows. Thus he maintains diplomatic propriety, agreeing with everyone on every topic, convinced that the fatality of
destiny and the transmuting of love into death is simply a matter of patience
and observation, a "drama performed every day" (March 13).

The *Memorial* foregrounds its mixed genres: Ayres writes in his diary, "If this were a novel" and "If I were writing a novel." The allusion to
medieval romance and the allegory of love and death is confirmed by the
epigraph from late thirteenth-century *cantigas* by Johan Zorro and Dom
Denis I, king of Portugal. The verses introduce the trope of the maiden who
departs from her mother to see her friend, who desires a tryst with her ("Para

veer meu amigo / Que talhou preyto comigo, Alá vou madre") (To see my friend (lover), / Who promised me a tryst). The *cantiga* introduces preparations for traveling overseas, in this case between Portugal, the point of origin and of return, and Brazil. If left to Ayres and the editor, the *Memorial* would seem to be either a novel pretending to be a travel memoir or a memoir disguised as a novel, but there is another generic substratum.

The *Memorial* is founded as an allegory both of life and death, symbolized for the counselor by the figure of the young widow Fidélia at her husband's grave and is on every level a symbolic narrative rather than a realistic memoir. Its entire contents are described by Ayres as being "all imaginings of mine." The allegory is presented as an operatic performance between Eros and Thanatos: the common identity of Fidélia with *Fidelio*, Beethoven's only opera premiered in 1805, is hypothesized in the *Memorial*: "But Fidélia . . . ? . . . Could it have been given to the baron's daughter as a feminine form of *Fidelio* in homage to Beethoven?" (February 11). In the opera, Fidelio is actually Leonore in disguise, and her purpose is to rescue her husband, Florestan, from the prison of the dictator Pizarro, where he is being starved to death. Fidelio is a "Fidelia," the ever-loyal and ever-courageous wife. The significance of her name is transferred to Fidélia's homage to the tomb of her deceased husband, a devotion that introduces the love-death theme and the struggle between Eros and Thanatos. The second operatic theme introduced by the Carioca Fidélia's "brother" Tristão—both have been adopted by the Aguiar couple under different circumstances—invokes Wagner's opera *Tristan und Isolde* (1865), which re-creates a romance of the Middle Ages, perhaps dating from the twelfth century. Tristan, who has killed Isolde's fiancé, Morold (Fidélia's husband in the novel?), is conveying Isolde to be married to King Marke. Meeting in the king's castle, the couple drinks a potion meant to be a poison with which Isolde will obtain her revenge against Tristan; however, Bragane, Isolde's companion, has changed the potion from poison to a love potion. In the ensuing duet between Tristan and Isolde, Tristan sings that only in the eternity of death can they be fully united. The couple performs the drama of timeless love, an eternally repeated spectacle that, according to Ayres, symbolizes renewal: "There is nothing like the passion of love to make original what is commonplace, and new what is dying of old age. That is the way it is with the engaged couple, whom I never tire of listening to, for they are always interesting. That drama of love, which appears to have been born of the serpent's guile and of man's disobedience, has never yet failed to play to full houses in this world. Now and again some poet lends it his tongue, amid the tears of the spectators, only that. The drama is performed every day, in every form, new as the sun, which is also old" (March 13). Ayres annotates the operatic allegories and romances that recur in the scenario and in characters of his city, in which he is both spectator and confidant, scarcely daring to hope that the drama of love will redeem and renew him as an actor as well as an author.

PART FIVE

Conclusion

FIFTEEN

Machado and the Spectacle of the World

E num recanto pôs um mundo inteiro.
[And she set a whole world in one dark corner.]

—Machado de Assis, "A Carolina"

Ao contrário de que se julga, não são tanto as respostas que me
importam . . . mas as perguntas. . . . Observe como elas costumam ter, ao
mesmo tempo, um objectivo à vista e uma intenção que vai escondida atrás.
[To the contrary of what one might think, the answers are not as of great
importance to me . . . as the questions. . . . Observe how they usually have both
a visible objective and, at the same time, a hidden intention behind them.]

—José Saramago, *As intermitências da morte*

A imortalidade é que é de poucos.
[Immortality belongs to few.]

—"A Semana," August 16, 1896

Sim, considerei a vida, remontei os anos, vim por eles abaixo, remirei o
espetáculo do mundo, o visto e o contado, cotejei tantas coisas diversas, evoquei
tantas imagens complicadas, combinei a memória com a história e disse
comigo:—"certamente, este mundo é um baile de casacas alugadas."
[Yes, I considered life, again I mounted the years, I rode down with them,
I looked again at the spectacle of the world, all that had been seen and told,
I considered so many diverse things together, I evoked so many
complex images, I mixed memory with history and said to myself:—
without a doubt, this world is a dance in rented coats.]

—"A Semana," June 11, 1893

I N 1 9 0 8 , the year of Machado's death, the American composer Charles
Ives's "The Unanswered Question" was one of his "Two Contemplations,"
in which one instrument represents the perennial question of existence,

while other instruments vainly attempt to provide answers, until they become lost in dissonance.[1] The continual background is "The Silence of the
Druids—who Know, See, and Hear Nothing." Groups of instruments are
arranged separately, with the strings playing offstage, and the piece ends
in "Undisturbed Solitude." The fiction of Machado de Assis, filled with
unanswered questions, and perhaps unanswerable ones, is a literary companion to these works of Ives. Each of Machado's mature productions is
an unanswered question developed indirectly by suggesting an atmosphere
through acts or gestures rather than words. The novel in which Machado
wrote that "all is music," *Counselor Ayres' Memorial*, was published in the
same year as Ives's composition. And the questions are still more important than answers, just as they continue to be for Saramago, since they seem
to carry unexplained, unfulfilled portents and intentions.

In 1908 Counselor Ayres first observed Aguiar and D. Carmo, the old
couple who were lost in uncomprehending silence after their adopted children Tristão and Fidélia sailed for Lisbon, characters who end in utter isolation. Ayres backs away from the old couple slowly so as not to disturb their
solitude, wary of the unanswered questions they face. The same fate befell
Bento Santiago, left alone in a copy of his childhood home, after the original house rejected him. Throughout Machado's fiction, characters play their
parts unaware of the greater ultimate purpose or meaning or of the author's
intentions; they are comparable to Ives's instruments, which make sonorous, though futile, attempts to answer perennial questions. Machado's unanswered questions are posed in allegories with pursuant philosophical,
theological, and aesthetic implications.

Addressing the theme of wisdom that is of greatest importance in
Machado's fiction, the story "As academias de Sião" ("The Siamese Academies," 1884) closes with fourteen monks from four Siamese academies,
monks who are said to embody all the wisdom of the universe, sailing down
the river in a magnificent junk adorned with feathers and streamers. When
the king had earlier questioned them individually, each denounced his
fellow monks as the greatest idiots in the kingdom, vulgar and worthless,
nothing less than dunces, although of unquestionable moral character. Now
they are singing in unison an ancient hymn, "Glory to us, who are the rice

of knowledge and the light of the world." Astonished by this song and display of unity, Queen Kinnara questioned how together they could be the light of the world and separately a bunch of dunces. The narrator describes this inherent contradiction that undermines any profession of wisdom and exposes irrepressible egoism and jealousy at the highest level of the social hierarchy as a "mystifying trait of human nature." For comic relief to a question for which there is no answer, the narrator appeals to the public for an explanation to satisfy the queen's curiosity: "If someone discovers [an explanation], he or she can oblige one of the most charming ladies of the Orient by sending it to her in a sealed envelope, and for utmost security, to our Consul in Shanghai, China."

Brás Cubas participates comically in the theme of wisdom in his chapter "The Unsolvable Problem," in which he fails to perceive in his one-sided account that consequences exist in ethics and politics. His brother-in-law Cotrim has published a declaration in the newspaper stating that he has no influence over Dr. Brás Cubas or any involvement in his inflammatory article attacking the present government, of which he disapproves. Brás can remember only the political favors he has done for Cotrim, procuring lucrative naval contracts, and he views the statement as an act of impertinence and ingratitude. Brás plays the basso buffo in pondering: "The reasons behind his act must have been very powerful. . . . I must confess, it was an unsolvable problem" (148).

Machado writes that he often climbed the mountain to preach to men, although he lived with them on the plain (January 27, 1895). He observed the spectacle of the world in a few hours or days spent high on a mountain with a view over all humankind, reminiscent of the mount where Tethys looked into a crystalline globe and revealed the history of the future to Vasco da Gama. There, he composed doctrine and formulated moral and ethical critiques while observing the eternal human theater. Yet that universal perspective, he remarks, is an unpleasing exception to nature, which prefers a straight path and soon returns the author to life among men on the plain below. By means of this authorial self-description in a metaphor contrasting high and low, Machado recapitulates the dynamic that defines his work and imbues it with baroque tension and drama. Characters in his fiction are likewise constantly ascending and descending, perhaps reflecting the topography of Rio de Janeiro as well as the author's metaphor on eternal versus temporal perspectives.

As a result of his almost timeless viewpoints, Machado considered technical innovations to be of negligible importance to human nature, which he thought to be unchangeable. In a chronicle dated October 16, 1892, he viewed the latest imports and inventions with ironic humor: "*Tannhäuser* and electric streetcars. We finally have those two great novelties in the country. The impresario of the Theatro Lyrico does us the favor of presenting the famous opera of Wagner, while the Companhia de Botafogo has the courage to transport us more quickly. Will the burro and Verdi fall at the same time?" The donkeys that are put out of work claim philosophy for their race and leave flying high to the eagles and to humans, for whom philosophy will always be a "perfect chimera."

Furthermore, he continues, too much efficiency and mechanization would limit remunerated work for humans, a situation in which, Machado predicted, a form of aggressive futurism lay: "Ten percent of Humanity will suffice for the business of the world. The remaining ninety percent are useless mouths, and, what is worse, reproductive. Twenty formidable wars will put an end to them."[2] The spectacle of the Paraguayan War for Jorge, in *Iaiá Garcia*, was enough to convince him of the irresolvable conflict of human affairs. In *Helena*, Eustácio proposed to Dr. Camargo that humans who are happy are not those who are seduced by distant, vast spaces or subjugated to the will of others, but those who are content with a few feet of space in which to live, a roof, and the obliviousness of history. Machado contrasts the timeless meaning of literature with the insatiable desire for new information in a journalistic age: "In the comedy *Verso e reverso*, by José de Alencar, a character asks every person who comes on stage:—What's new? . . . I confess that this week I began to dislike that question. . . . While at home in the afternoon, it was the first thing they asked me. I ate poorly at dinner; I had a nightmare; three hundred voices brayed from the depths of infinity:—What's new? The winds, seas, Balaam's ass, locomotives, artillery, the prophets, all the celestial and earthly voices formed this unison cry:—What's new?—The earthquake . . . a century and a half ago" (November 5, 1893).

Machado follows the pendulum swinging between his authorial role as philosopher and analyst in the guise of his own Counselor Ayres and his function as a close participant in the customs and rituals of daily life in his city-universe. His lofty perspectives as artist and analyst are the building blocks of his philosophy: he considers life, reviews the years, takes another look at the spectacle of the world, evaluates things both seen and told, compares its diverse contents, reconciles memory with experience, and composes an independent account. From his position on the mountain, Machado predicts Joyce's stance of the artist in his *A Portrait of the Artist as a Young Man* (1916): "The artist, like the God of the creation, remains within or behind or beyond or above his handiwork, invisible, refined out of existence, indifferent, paring his fingernails" (5); while in the society of men, he observes the metaphoric stage exemplified by Calderón's *La vida es sueño* (1635), "que toda la vida es sueño y los sueños sueños son" (that all life is a dream, and dreams are dreamed), that challenges cognition and meaning. In composing his theater of the world, Machado joins these two perspectives by reconsidering experience from the outside, once again looking onto the spectacle of the world, while from the inside he observes the stage where human affairs are subjected to catharsis, illusion, dissimulation, and deception. On this stage is the superior humor of *Don Quixote*, capable of admiring the nobility of human illusion and failure.

Machado's literary structure, philosophy, and materials can be found in the overlapping of these contrasting scenarios. After observing the world theater from outside and inside, he concludes almost reluctantly that life is "certainly a dance in rented coats" performed by characters who are generally unaware of their changeable, transient, and ephemeral world.[3] Machado regarded the world as theater, defined his art through his superior consciousness, recognized the limits of rationality in a largely irrational world, and perceived the ultimate absurdity and vacuity of human nature and behavior with a calculated, distanced humor.[4]

Deceptive, misleading, and distorting possibilities of human affairs and memory are played out in Machado's fiction. In his first novels Machado began to point out errors and illusions of perception, the implausibility of truth, the bitterness of life, the uniform law of the miserliness of human society, and the insoluble conflict of human affairs: "Goethe once wrote that the vertical line is the law of human intelligence" (*Helena*, 16). And in a late chronicle Machado asserted, "Any one of us could have organized this world better than the way it came out. Death, for example, could well have been just a retirement from life, with a fixed date. . . . It could be either a family or public ceremony; there would be the custom of a farewell dinner, frugal but not sad, at which those who were going to die would speak of their longings, make recommendations, give advice, and if they were happy tell light anecdotes. Many flowers . . . like at weddings. And it would be best not to have anything else besides verbal and friendly good-byes" (September 6, 1896). His fiction systematically undermined illusions, revealing the velleities of intentions and interactions that he exposed by techniques of inference, entrapment, and surprise. He compared life in his writings to a chess game, a comic opera, a carousel, and a dance.

The dance in rented coats is a metaphor in Machado's philosophical world theater, an operatic *ballo in maschera* requiring costumes that do not even belong to the dancers, even for minor parts, since the costumes and situations are reusable in the next spectacle; they are part of the wardrobe borrowed from the author's world library, whose themes and costumes repeat indefinitely in variations throughout the ages.[5] They will reappear at the next dance along with a new generation of dancers for as long as the music and the performances continue. Theatrical and operatic performances, with their roles and actors, continue to function as the controlling metaphor in these works of dramatic comedy which, like chess pieces, pit type and category against individual will and character. The operas Machado attended in his formative years provided him with paradigms for his fiction in which he found literary equivalents for phrase length, voicing, articulation, instrumentation, balance, dynamics, texture, mode, dramatics, scene, and character development. The hidden truths of his characters and their world are constructed so as to be glimpsed through what he called plastic motivation, seen in each gesture, step, and movement of the theater, exemplified by the actress Adelaide Ristori and the soprano Augusta Candiani, whom Machado so greatly admired.

Like the stars of the impassive Southern Cross that Rubião invokes with passion before an uncomprehending, astonished Sofia, Machado takes the stance of neutral observer with an eternal point of view when it comes to a philosophy for his human theater. The critic Augusto Meyer saw in this attitude the indefinable lethargy of a spectator of himself, a writer whose stylistic grace, finely honed inferences, and unexpected jumps could not disguise his overly sharp consciousness and the Pyrrhic nihilism of his thought. When Guiomar gazes out at the moon and onto serene skies in *The Hand and the Glove*, the author thinks of a silent eternity: "Eternal, yes eternal, my dear reader, which is the most saddening lesson God could give us in the midst of our agitations, battles, anxieties, insatiable passions, daily pains, and fleeting pleasures, which follow along and end with us underneath that blue eternity, impassive and mute like death" (9). Estela interrogates the heavens to no avail in *Iaiá Garcia*: "This immense, taciturn being has eyes with which to see, but no ears with which to listen. The evening was clear and serene; millions of glittering stars seemed to be laughing at earth's myriad miseries"; her soul was ready to plunge into "the vague and perfidious darkness of the future" (13, 9).

Counselor Ayres had observed Fidélia and the canvas she was painting "with these eyes that the cold earth will one day devour." Beyond Salvador's backyard, in *Helena*, lay "the infinity of human indifference" (21). Machado admits that his is an arid philosophy, as when one is tired of solid earth and "the vast beachless sea calls us" (*The Hand and the Glove*, 10). Insignificance, emptiness, and nothingness are the materials of his life and fiction: "Nothing on top of the invisible is the most subtle work of this world" (*Esau and Jacob*, 22). With this perception, however, Machado asserts his artistic power to see to the other side of material life through form, a position foreshadowing a statement made by the plastic artist Lygia Clark in a publication: "Man is not alone. He is form and emptiness. He comes from 'emptiness' into form (life) and leaves it for the full emptiness of relative death. There, he achieves an ethical state in the highest sense. While the emptiness remains separated from the other side (life), he must study it like an abyss and experience its nothing, death, and lack of meaning. All men feel this interior state. The artist through the work of art shows him this 'slice of eternity'" (*Bichos*, 1960). Ayres anticipates her thought in other words: "The eye of man serves as a photograph of the invisible" (*Esau and Jacob*, 41).

Counselor Ayres, in the foreword to his edited diary concerning material the editor left out, concludes dryly, "The rest will appear some day, if another day appears." The radical uncertainty of his "if" in an unpredictable world is another baroque inheritance that Machado appends to his reflections as a crucial second thought, expressing profound skepticism and resignation. The counselor's aside is even more stark than Camões's sonnet on change, "Mudam-se os tempos, mudam-se as vontades" ("The times change, along with fashions"), with its destabilizing conclusion that change always counters one's expectations by changing in unexpected ways: "Outra mudança faz de mor espanto, / Que não se muda já como soía" ("One further change is the greater woe / that it changes no longer as was its wont").[6] Machado was aware of Camões's poetry of disconcert of the world in the overseas baroque, living in shifting realities where even change itself changes. Machado's pessimism belies its precocious modernity, however, by its skepticism without the support of faith, by a sense of Pascalean tragedy, and by its ridicule of philosophical systems; Benedito Nunes's analysis here becomes the prologue to a radical modernity. The mad philosopher Quincas Borba simply dismisses difficult philosophical problems that might confound his theories by eliminating them like the Gordian knot: "Not every philosophical problem is worth five minutes' attention" (149). Both Ayres and Quincas challenge and ridicule philosophy, thereby supporting Nunes's assertion that Machado makes fun of philosophical systems in his fiction from the outside, an attitude perhaps supported by his agnosticism and his interest in eternity and in an unexplainable, unpredictable universe.

"Why beautiful if lame? Why lame if beautiful?," Brás Cubas questions when tempted by the love of the sincere and modest Eugênia, who is perhaps the only noble character in his memoirs. The mirrored questions speak to the ethical inequality and asymmetry in Nature. Although Brás has an inkling of Eugênia's honesty and depth of character, he looks for an excuse to break off the incipient relationship because of both his restless ambition and his previous knowledge of her illegitimate birth. In response to his innocent comment about her limp Eugênia replies that she has been lame since birth, mortifying Brás only because of the social faux pas. Because he cannot truly sympathize or reconcile a physical imperfection with his social ideal of refinement and of consonance between beauty, class, position, and physical perfection, Brás callously invents an excuse to leave Eugênia, after gaining her first kiss, to return to his father in the city. With his puzzling matching questions, Brás pithily captures seemingly unjustifiable contradictions that challenge and defy the ethical, social, and aesthetic constructs of hierarchical societies. From his own egotistical, if surprised, reaction, Brás unwittingly coins a phrase that epitomizes contemporary existential doubt. His questions have become part of popular lore in Brazil: when faced with any unexplainable contradiction, readers of Machado look at each other with ironic smiles and repeat, "Why beautiful if lame? Why lame if beautiful?"

Asymmetry and the impasses of destiny are illustrated in the stories "A Celebrity" concerning Pestana, a famous composer of polkas whose sole desire in life was to compose classical music, and "Wedding Song," about the old conductor Romão Pires, who could not complete a composition he had begun after his marriage and before his wife's early death. The theme of the contrariness and asymmetries of life recurs more comically when Custódio, the owner of a pastry shop in *Esau and Jacob*, is concerned that he will lose his customers if the name of the establishment does not reflect the current governing party. He would change it from "Pastry Shop of the Empire" to "Pastry Shop of the Republic" if he could be sure that the republic would last. Ayres suggests adding "founded in 1860" to the original sign or "Empire of Laws," but Custódio thinks the added wording will be too small to have any immediate effect. The solution Ayres leaves him with is to name it after himself, "Custódio's Pastry Shop." Here the unforeseen strikes outside of the text, as Admiral Custódio José de Melo will soon lead a naval uprising that makes the name taboo in republican Brazil. Again, the vicissitudes and reverses of events recur when Ayres reminisces about his dalliance with the fashionable actress Carmen during his assignment in Caracas. As he was entertaining her at home, they heard an alarming commotion in the streets: "What noise is that?" he asked Carmen. "Don't be frightened my friend, it's the government falling," she answered. "But I hear cheers," he replied. "Then it is the government rising. Don't be frightened. Tomorrow is time enough to pay your respects."

Machado's efforts to uncover truth beneath appearances are a function of the large catalogue of aphorisms and maxims from the age of reason that made up his practical, rational philosophy, but they are additionally a beneficiary of the experimental medicine of the mid-nineteenth century. Differences between observed behavior and pathology led such figures as Carl von Rokitansky at the University of Vienna and Claude Bernard at the Sorbonne to conclude that truth lay beneath the surface, just as the Vienna school of psychoanalysis would seek to find thoughts in the unconscious mind, as would the modernist portraits of the painters Gustav Klimt and Egon Schiele and the surrealists in experiments of automatic writing. Mystifying traits of human psychology investigated by Machado include cruelty and perversity, cases in which the human heart is a "well of mysteries." The short story "The Secret Cause" presents the curious case of punishment without crime or cause in Fortunato, who at the story's conclusion stands unseen, quietly observing his close friend and partner Garcia bending over the casket of Maria Luísa, Fortunato's wife, who had died from the shock of witnessing her husband's cruelty and enjoyment of suffering, including her own. Garcia's chaste kiss of repressed love and his desperate sobbing gave the impassive Fortunato one more occasion to taste the pleasure of an explosion of moral pain, made more delicious to him the longer it lasted. Garcia discovered Fortunato's obsession only after he became a victim. In *Helena*, when Salvador returns home after his father's final illness in search of his wife and daughter, he finds an empty house. A neighbor gives him directions to where they went, but both sense approaching disaster. Salvador noted the neighbor's pitying smile and gloating humiliation, even though Salvador had never given him the slightest offense. Why, then, did the neighbor take a secret pleasure in his great misfortune, which he even managed to communicate slyly to the sufferer? Salvador can only ask rhetorically, "Why? I leave it to the philosophers to solve this puzzle of human nature" (25).

The aged Bento Santiago also wonders why he feels pleasure in re-telling and reliving old sufferings. Just before this short chapter, Capitu has threatened that at the first new sign of jealous suspicion on his part, all would be dissolved between them, and Bento swore that it would never happen again. In view of his jealous obsession, this new spiritual pleasure seems a cruel sublimation: "In telling of that crisis in my adolescent love, I feel something I do not know how to explain: somehow the sufferings of that period have become so spiritualized with time that they have melted into pleasure. This is not clear—but not everything is clear in life or in books. The truth is I feel a particular pleasure in retelling this ordeal, while it is certain that it reminds me of others which I would not be reminded of for anything" (77). When Tristão decided not to return to Lisbon when called for elections, the witty Cesária remarked in a melancholy tone to the counselor that Tristão loved Fidélia but preferred politics. The counselor detected that the disguised aim of her sharp perception was the pleasure of seeing Fidélia diminished, an emotion he may have shared for a moment, given the rivalry he felt for Tristão. In making this perception, the counselor felt admiration for her wit, her pointed allusions, and her elegant manner; he even shared her pleasure vicariously in his increased admiration for her talented verbal display (November 30). He had penned his own aphorism on the interaction of good and evil: "There is no evil that does not bring a little good, and for that reason what is bad is useful, often indispensable, sometimes delicious" (*Esau and Jacob*, 59). The basis for his thought is found in Nature, as we read in the short story "Uma senhora" (A lady): "Nature, however, is not only immoral, but also illogical."

Machado applied his observations of the world's illogic to a purpose greater than a refuge from or critique of political and social affairs. He confronted what Counselor Ayres called "life's imprescriptive laws" that determine the eternal human predicament. If Machado wrote as a miniaturist and portraitist, his human consciousness was transcendental and metaphysical. His twists of irony emphasize the impossibility of one's knowing whether freedom of thought and nobility of mind and ethics exist to motivate human action. Ayres comments to Dona Perpétua that the night would be the same whether it were clear and warm or dark and cold and that the bay of Rio de Janeiro never changes; at the same time, men might one day fill in the bay with earth and stones, illustrating comically Ayres's supreme maxim: "Everything is possible under the sun and moon." "Even death," he jokes with Baron Santos, "is an hypothesis . . . perhaps a legend" (*Esau and Jacob*, 1). In this, he recapitulates the arguments and contrasts the world-views of the baroque and Enlightenment eras; he is governed by a search for meaning beyond appearances and by systematic doubt. Through his allegories Machado nevertheless conceives positively, if existentially, of life's unknown dimensions and the role of chance, whether for good or ill. In a world of clocks whose ticking anxiously counts down the duration of life and channels one's perception of time, unseen eternal principles are still present behind the scenes. The unknown remains a positive, if daunting, force against the immutable laws of fate, present in Machado's clock with-out hands and in humanity's dance in rented coats. After all, God and Satan may agree to revise their play or to alter the scenario radically or to change the time of the performance. As long as there is birth and renewal in the world theater, the play and the dance will continue repeating their perfor-mances, whether to good or bad reviews, and wise authors will continue to observe them from afar, until in some unimaginable future time the the-ater closes and all comes to an end.

MACHADO IMPRESSED the men of his time with his youthful, lithe-some spirit. In a letter from London on October 8, 1904, Nabuco, the states-man, gives his opinion of Machado, the man behind the mask of fiction: "But what vivacity, with a light touch, what sweetness, what benevolence of spirit, I was going to say, what beatitude! You may cultivate bile and gall in the social philosophy of your novels, but your letters betray you. You are not only a happy man, you live in beatitude, like a Pope, and a Pope in an age of faith, as exists today in the Academy. Now you're not going to say that I've offended you and accused you of hypocrisy by calling you happy?"[7] On the death of Carolina on October 20, 1904, however, Machado strug-gled to maintain his will and his composure. In an exchange of letters with Nabuco, soon to be Brazil's first ambassador to the United States, Mach-ado despairs of his condition and his future:

So far away, by other means the news of my great disgrace reached you and you right away expressed your sympathy by telegram. The only word I used to thank you is the same one I send you now, not knowing any other that could say everything that I feel and that grieves me. The best part of my life has gone away, and here I am alone in the world. Note that solitude doesn't weary me, rather I'm grateful for it, because it's a way of living with her, of hearing her, noticing the thousand cares that my companion of 35 years of marriage had for me; but there's no imagination that does not wake up, and vigilance increases the absence of the person loved. We were old, and I counted on dying before her, which would be a great favor; first, because I could never find anyone who could better help me to die; secondly, because she has a few relatives who would console her for her loss, and I don't have any. Mine are friends, and truly those are the best; but life scatters them in space, in spiritual concerns and in the careers of each one. Here I remain, for now in the same house, in the same room, with the same ornaments of hers. Everything makes me remember my friend Carolina. As I am on the edge of eternal retirement, I won't spend much time in remembering her. I will go to see her; she will be waiting for me. (November 20, 1904)

In his reply, Nabuco tried to raise the author's spirits by recommending a return to writing and study: "In your case imagination, intellectual interests and work is an environment that will allow your pain in part to evaporate. . . . You will understand that the heart's vacuum must be compensated by movement and by the stirring of your spirit."[8]

Two years earlier, in a letter dated August 19, 1906, Machado had commented on Nabuco's collection of thoughts and remembrances in *Pensées detachées et souvenirs*, published in Paris that year. Praising in Nabuco the coexistence of the statesman and the artist, Machado shares his taste for the succinct expression of philosophical ideas and reflections: "From early on I read Pascal intensely, not to cite other sources, and not because I had nothing else to do. Still today when I return to those readings, to console myself with the disconsolate *Ecclesiastes*, I find the same taste in them as before" (August 19, 1906). In his comments on Nabuco's publication, it seems as if Machado is describing his own method of composition:

> Thoughts come alive and live by exact or new observations, by a sharp or profound reaction, and no less do they demand originality, simplicity, and graceful phrases. . . . In these pages history is subjected to religious and philosophical influences, to moral and aesthetical observations, taken from long personal experience. Your intimate thoughts are open here for all to see in that lapidary form that memory retains best. . . . You inscribe them directly or suggestively, and a spiritual tone is another characteristic of your pages. In all of them a serene and strong optimism shines through. (*Correspondência*, 1932, 66).

In selected examples of Nabuco's reflections Machado sees potentially complete books, and his selections of passages are surprisingly close to well-known aphorisms found in his own novels: " 'Very rarely are beautiful lives happy inside; something always has to be sacrificed for the sake of unity' calls to mind historical memoirs, or direct observations, that in the hands of a narrator or psychologist could result in a book." In other phrases he comments on the efficacy of orthography to teach political lessons: "Many times a life is lost because where there should have been a period someone has put a question mark." Machado even cites a reflection that casts doubt on the accuracy of all our observations: "The butterfly finds them heavy, the pheasant poorly dressed, the nightingale hoarse, and the eagle lowly" (August 19, 1906). Aphorisms, to Machado, express beauty, truth, and mystery, even going beyond philosophy to the point where descriptive words have no effect.

In a letter to Nabuco in Washington, D.C., he commented wryly that *Counselor Ayres' Memorial* would be his last novel: "I say firmly that this is my last book. . . . I've finished. As long as the book doesn't disappoint, it will be a good place to stop" (August 1, 1908). In a reply that arrived after

Machado's death, Nabuco saw in the novel a portrait of everything he associated with its author: "As for your book, I read it letter by letter with true delight as a portrait of you yourself, your tastes, your way of taking up life and considering everything. It's a book that produces longing for you, but also satiates it. What freshness of spirit! Again I recommend the company of young men, more intimately, at home. You seem to feel this with Tristão [Tristão da Cunha] and with Mário de Alencar. But the benefit of being close to youth wouldn't be yours alone. You are a perpetual youth surrounded by all those affectations of old age" (September 3, 1908). Graça Aranha, on reading *Counselor Ayres' Memorial*, also saw in the novel a different Machado de Assis, an author who had qualified the ironic and unrelenting critique of life, the doubt and mistrust of earlier writings: "It's another Machado de Assis. No longer the disdainful writer, impudent, daring, who shattered the moral universe and analyzed it cruelly with a spirit that damns and denies. . . . Here petulance of spirit was converted into gentleness, irony into piety, distrust into neglect, doubt into hope for another life."[9] The reactions of both Nabuco and Graça Aranha are influenced by their personal identification as diplomats with the stature and career of Counselor Ayres as author and narrator, enhanced by his tactful diplomatic manner, whether in social discourse or in disguising his inner thoughts and emotions. Neither reader captured the Faustian predicament, marked by barrenness and approaching death, with which Ayres censors his impudent, lively, and erotic spirit, nor perhaps the ironic distance between Ayres as author and his creator. Nevertheless, Nabuco's critical judgment of the value and place of the last novel by Machado de Assis for his generation continues to be valid after more than a century: "The unconscious admiration that you inspired in the previous generation, and in ours, enjoys a reputation today that will oblige posterity to read your novel and to study it in order to understand the fascination that you exercised over your time."[10] The aura of Machado de Assis was captured by Haroldo Maranhão in his novel *Memorial do fim* (Memorial of the end), which reconstructs his death scene, capturing the drama and the transcendent import of the moment of which all those present were intensely aware. One of the chapters is composed entirely of passages culled from the fiction of Machado de Assis.

Nunes observes that Machado's fictional work cannot be used to document the philosophic ideas of the real author, neither by its conceptual content nor by its rhetorical argumentative intention. Machado as a narrator is not the subject of the ideas of fiction, and neither is fiction the objective vehicle set up exclusively for the transmission of ideas. Distanced from reality, the author recuperates it aesthetically, thereby casting associated philosophical ideas differently than they would have been expressed as pure theory. Nevertheless, his own conception of the world and philosophy is invariably connected to and inseparable from his narratives, even if refracted through other layers of meaning. Throughout Machado's fiction, one encounters ideas and rhetorical forms that filter philosophical attitudes and give voice to values that stand up against the corrosive effects of time and customs. Many of those values are affirmed by narrators and characters as the most fundamental or meaningful in life; while not constituting an authorial philosophy, such ideas in literary form contribute to the collection of maxims and aphorisms from the library and to the wisdom of accumulated experience and observation that constitute the worldview of Machado de Assis as author and person.

Machado brings out a baroque countercurrent that embodies and expresses the difference and tension between the world as we could conceive it or wish it and the prisms of society, language, politics, fate, and time that confine and restrict human actions and imagination. Counselor Ayres wryly advises Flora and all his readers against growing old, "that bad habit of growing old. Do not fall into that habit, reader. There are others, also bad, none worse, this is the worst. Let the philosophers say that old age is a useful state because of the experience and other advantages. Do not grow old, my friend, as much as the years invite you to leave spring behind; as a last resort, accept summer. The summer is good, warm, the nights are short, that is certain, yet the dawns do not always bring fog, and the sky is born blue. Thus you will dance forever" (*Esau and Jacob*, 48). Ayres conceives of the nobility that comes from personal struggles for freedom or independence from limitations and restrictions of whatever kind or origin, even against the nature of the world. When Ayres saw that Flora wanted to flee from bright lights and the duties of office any time she wished to become her own subject, he supported her by murmuring, "Every free soul is an empress" and immediately meditated on the import of his spontaneous maxim: "The phrase was good, sonorous, and seemed to contain the greatest sum of truth that there is on Earth and in the solar system" (*Esau and Jacob*, 48). Ayres is aware of the limitations of performance, that truth is both compromised and enhanced by a good, sonorous phrase, as in opera, tinged with circumstance and the parentheses of context, exaggerated as if the voice reached throughout the solar system; nevertheless, within the irony and self-criticism of his formulation, his belief in the fundamental value of the metaphor persists, even when the freedom of his soul is in doubt.

Machado is under no illusion that the wisdom embodied in his writings will have a transformative effect on his readers or on human nature, but he is well aware of its virtues as art and philosophy, since it is found in the masterpieces of the world library that are Machado's direct sources. Each of his major works develops from a literary citation or allusion, and his writing contains hundreds of references to history, art, literature, drama, and philosophy. His concept of the value of literature is placed ironically and reflexively in the mouth of Counselor Ayres, as he observes the thread of a conversation between Pedro and Flora. He was concentrating on their attitude, since the conversation was in murmurs and the couple was absorbed; it seemed that they had a sixth sense, reminding Ayres of conspirators or lovers in a mysterious dialogue that belongs to the ages. It was an archetypal story of youth, perhaps about them alone, or perhaps a series of stories, or one long story about others. Since Ayres was preoccupied with resolving Flora's indecision about the twins, he exulted in the appearance of another suitor: "This world belongs to lovers. Everything else is dispensable; the day will come when even governments can be done away with, and anarchy will organize itself as in the first days of paradise. As far as food is concerned, from Boston to New York will come a process by which people nourish themselves from simply breathing the air. It is lovers who will be perpetual" (*Esau and Jacob*, 95). Continuing his meditative observations, Ayres concludes that "there are states of the soul in which the subject of the narration is insignificant, and the pleasure of doing it and hearing it is everything. It could be that." Telling and hearing are states and ends in themselves, which is the full justification for the literary world of Machado de Assis. Ayres further observes that in such mysterious, inner dialogues, "nature guides the smallest and biggest things, if fortune assists her" (51). His aphorism could have come from the classical and mythological allegories of any baroque opera.

Remembrance and memory play central if duplicitous roles throughout Machado's fiction. Brás Cubas parodies the bibliomaniac who is fixated with first editions for their own sake, and Ayres makes fun of Custódio's old sign at the teashop and of Dona Perpétua's devotion to Evaristo da Veiga's old inkwell, a simple artifact that had been used by the journalist during the first reign and the regency. In a letter to Nabuco, Machado affirms the value of remembrance of things past, whether the memory of those far away or the affection for days long gone: "Two lines are enough to remember that some heart keeps the memory of someone far away and beats with the rhythm of old affections and days past." His position as a writer who finds prime material in the past is so much like an eternal truth that he decides to make it one: "The past (if I didn't read it somewhere, pretend that my experience is saying it now), the past is still the best part of the present—at my age, one understands" (January 5, 1902).

In another letter to Nabuco, Machado addresses the question of the value and survival of his artistic work. He highlights three qualities most likely to promote the universal value of creative work for future generations. It should be profound, artistically crafted, and well written or spoken. Then, he is convinced that the writer will be aided by time itself, which is capable of selecting and recognizing true value: "Time will help time, and what in it is profound, fine, and well said will conserve its great value" (July 7, 1907). Machado, the great synthesizer, was capable of recasting all he had read and the performances he had attended into creative texts carrying his personal signature. He explored the technique of creative blending so thoroughly and even experimentally that by 1880 he had completed the transition from realism to modernist author par excellence. Questions of influence and reader reception would require redefinition after Machado's displacement of authorship, eternal point of view, breaks in the narrative frame, challenges to the reader, and eclectic selection of authors, texts, and ideas. His profound observations of the society of empire opened unexpected and fear-some psychological depths. Throughout his novels and short stories, classical balance and baroque universality were the two opposite poles of the swinging pendulum that circumscribed and energized his literary world.

Readers of Machado's works today share the spectacle of the world recorded by the literary art of the wizard of Cosme Velho and seen in the large cast of characters and dramas in his fiction. There are Brás Cubas's opera buffa; the Faustian dramas of Rubião, Bento Santiago, and Counselor Ayres; the touch of Iago in Félix and Bento; the less than merry wives Virgília, Sofia, and Capitu; Flora's inferno; Fidélia's lyrical voyage of exile over the seas to Lisbon with a new lover; and the supporting cast from the social world of the Brazilian empire. Readers of Machado de Assis attend these great fictional performances and experience a joy similar to that of the young theatergoers who laughed at the comic operas on the stages of Rio de Janeiro, recalled so fondly by Machado himself: "Today Candiani returned, after such a long silence, to awaken echoes of those days. Old people like me will remember something of their youth: the best thing in life and perhaps the only one" (July 15, 1877).

Notes

1. The Wizard of Cosme Velho

1. The photograph is of the assembled literary society called A Panelinha at a luncheon at the Hotel Rio Branco. Present with Machado are Rodolfo Amoedo, Artur Azevedo, Inglês de Souza, Olavo Bilac, José Veríssimo, Sousa Bandeira, Filinto de Almeida, Guimarães Passos, Valentim Magalhães, Rodolfo Bernardelli, Rodrigo Otávio, Heitor Penteado, João Ribeiro, Lúcio de Mendonça, and Silva Ramos. See *A olhos vistos: uma iconografia de Machado de Assis*, Hélio de Seixas Guimarães and Vladimir Sacchetta, orgs. (São Paulo: Instituto Moreira Salles, 2008), 140.

2. Haroldo de Campos, "The Ex-centric's Viewpoint: Tradition, Transcreation, Transculturation," in *Haroldo de Campos: A Dialogue with the Brazilian Concrete Poet*, ed. K. David Jackson, 7–23 (Oxford: Centre of Brazilian Studies, 2005).

3. In a letter dated June 29, 1870, the Portuguese novelist Eça de Queirós replied to Machado's stinging critique of the novel *O Primo Basílio* in a review published in the *Cruzeiro* on April 16 under the pseudonym d'Eleazar. Eça notes Machado's "almost partisan hostility to the Realist School," although it is so well done that Eça considers it to have increased his own authority. While humbly praising the talented review, Eça defends the Realist School, "which he considers to contribute to moral progress." In *Exposição Machado de Assis; centenário do nascimento de Machado de Assis, 1839–1939* (Rio de Janeiro: Serviço gráfico do Ministério da Educação e Saúde, 1939), 198.

4. See Eloy Pontes, *A vida contradictoria de Machado de Assis* (Rio de Janeiro: José Olympio, 1939). Machado himself was aware of these inverse perspectives. In the short story "The Mirror," his character theorizes that "every human being carries two souls within him: one that looks from inside out, the other from outside in." See "The Looking Glass," in *The Psychiatrist and Other Stories* (Berkeley: University of California Press, 1963).

5. For a discussion of Machado's family tree, see Jean-Michel Massa, *A juventude de Machado de Assis* (São Paulo: Unesp, 2009). In his influential book *The Western Canon* Harold Bloom muddied the waters by introducing Machado as the most important black writer in Latin America rather than simply the continent's most important writer. Bloom's characterization overlooks the history of Brazilian miscegenation, which gives Machado status as both white and black.

301

Indeed, racial composition has little bearing on the literary prowess of Machado de Assis, in view of his education in the company of noted intellectuals and Portuguese writers, an education comparable to that of Alexander Pushkin (1799–1837), who is considered the greatest poet in the Russian language and whose mother was a former slave become aristocrat. In addition, he was closely associated with Brazilian authors, lawyers, diplomats, and politicians, including his colleague in the Academy of Letters José Carlos do Patrocínio (1854–1905), who founded an abolitionist society with the statesman Joaquim Nabuco (1849–1910) in 1880.

6. Benedito Nunes, "Machado de Assis e a Filosofia," *Travessia* 19 (1989), 17.

7. Melinda Alliker Rabb, "Confinement and Entrapment in Fielding's *Journal of a Voyage to Lisbon*," in *Reader Entrapment in Eighteenth-Century Literature*, ed. Carl R. Kropf (New York: AMS Press, 1992), 229–60.

8. I am grateful to Julia H. Powers for these observations on Machado's prefaces.

9. *Machado de Assis: The Brazilian Master and His Novels* (Berkeley: University of California Press, 1970), 157.

10. In Machado's time, travel to the mountain city of Petrópolis required a connection by boat across Guanabara Bay.

11. *A vida contradictoria de Machado de Assis*, 20–23.

12. *Dicionário de Machado de Assis: história e biografia das personagens* (São Paulo: Rêde Latina Editôra, 1958).

13. Alois Riegl, *Historical Grammar of the Visual Arts*, trans. Jaqueline E. Jung (London: Zone Books, 2004); Mike Gubser, *Time's Visible Surface: Alois Riegl and the Discourse on History and Temporality in Fin-de-siècle Vienna* (Detroit: Wayne State University Press, 2006).

14. Leonardo Pereira, "Introdução," *Machado de Assis, História de quinze dias* (Campinas: Editora da Unicamp, 2009), 21.

15. *Adelaide Ristori: folhetins* (Rio de Janeiro: Academia Brasileira de Letras, 1955).

16. Rhian Atkin, *Saramago's Labyrinths: A Journey Through Form and Content in* Blindness *and* All the Names (Manchester: Manchester University Press, 2012).

17. Another notorious precursor of these narrators in Portuguese literature of the period is the likewise fictional character-author Carlos Fradique Mendes, who first appeared in Eça de Queirós's and Ramalho Ortigão's (1836–1915) *O mistério da estrada de Sintra* in the *Diário de Notícias* (Lisbon), from 24 July to 27 September 1870. Fradique Mendes later took on full-fledged existence in Eça's *Correspondência de Fradique Mendes (Correspondence of Fradique*

Mendes, 1900), published the same year as Machado's *Dom Casmurro*. Like Pessoa and Eça, Machado let his authors speak for themselves, while providing readers with clues to deeper meanings.

18. Machado frequently cites Camões, Portugal's most celebrated poet, whose philosophical and literary mannerism dominates his epic and his reflective lyrical poetry.

19. Stefan Zweig, *Brazil: Land of the Future*, trans. Andrew St. James (New York: Viking, 1941); *Brasilien: ein land der Zukunft* (Stockholm: Bermann-Fischer, 1941).

20. Karl Galinsky, *Classical and Modern Interactions* (Austin: University of Texas Press, 1992), 150–51.

21. Marina Grishakova, *The Models of Space, Time and Vision in V. Nabokov's Fiction: Narrative Strategies and Cultural Frames* (Tartu, Estonia: Tartu University Press, 2006), 56.

22. "La réalité du métissage ne peut être comprise que selon la production d'une différence—par rapport aux cultures et aux identités impliquées—dans un contexte historique précis, et selon les effets d'universalisation différenciée qui porte cette différence." Jean Bessière, "Notes sur le métissage et sur ses ambivalences critiques aujourd'hui. Pour une mise en perspective littéraire comparatiste," in *Métissages littéraires*, ed. Yves Clavaron and Bernard Dieterle, 13–20 (Saint-Étienne: l'Université de Saint-Étienne, 2005).

23. Described theoretically by Hans-Jörg Schmid and Réka Benczes in *Windows to the Mind: Metaphor, Metonymy and Conceptual Blending*, ed. Sandra Handl and Hans-Jörg Schmid (Berlin: Walter de Gruyter, 2011).

24. Hans-Jörg Schmid, "Conceptual Blending, Relevance and Novel N+N-Compounds," in ibid., 219–21.

25. Réka Benczes, "Blending and Creativity in Metaphorical Compounds: A Diachronic Investigation," in ibid., 247–48.

26. Wladimir Krysinski, "Sur quelques généalogies et formes de l'hybridité dans la littérature du XXe siècle," in *Le texte hybride*, ed. Dominique Budor and Walter Geerts, 27–39 (Paris: Presses Sorbonne Nouvelle, 2004).

27. The writers cited include Ezra Pound (1885–1972), T. S. Eliot (1888–1965), James Joyce (1882–1941), Alfred Döblin (1878–1957), John Dos Passos (1896–1970), Hermann Broch (1888–1951), João Guimarães Rosa (1908–67), Julio Cortázar (1914–84), Thomas Pynchon (b. 1937), and extending to Augusto Roa Bastos (1917–2005), José María Arguedas (1911–69), Céline (1894–1961), Alejo Carpentier (1904–80), Carlos Fuentes (1928–2012), Günter Grass (b. 1927), Milan Kundera (b. 1929), Robert Musil (1880–1942), and Patrick Chamoiseau (b. 1953), among others. Ibid., 32, 36.

28. "Des beaux examples d'un certain style baroque, où la demarche de l'invention est inseparable de celle de la thésaurisation. De lá ce mélange de fraicheur et de decrepitude que, pour nos modernes, fait le charme hybride de ce livre." Jean Starobinski, "La mélancholie de l'anatomiste," *Tel Quel* 10 (Summer 1962), 21, quoted in *Le texte hybride, 33.*

29. See Fernando Pinto do Amaral, "Melancolia," in *Dicionário de Camões,* ed. Vítor Aguair e Silva, 581–86 (Lisbon: Caminho, 2011).

30. Jean-Claude Laborie, "Le baroque au XVIIe siècle: Un espace esthétique atlantique," in *L'Atlantique Comme Pont* (Clermont-Ferand: Presses Universitaires Blaise Pascal, 2012), 181–92.

31. Leopoldo Castedo, *The Baroque Prevalence in Brazilian Art* (New York: Charles Frank, 1964). See Edward J. Sullivan, *Brazil: Body and Soul* (New York: Guggenheim Museum, 2002), 10, 18. In his preface to the Guggenheim Museum exhibition catalogue "Brazil: Body and Soul," Edward J. Sullivan asks what makes Brazilian baroque art Brazilian? Despite regional differences, Sullivan sees coherence and singularities in its intensity, in the theatricality of faith, in the directness of communication between the object and the beholder, in the power to transcend time, and in the hybridization of the European, indigenous, and African sources that characterized Brazilian culture and demography for centuries. Rather than a consequence or appendage of European expression, the Brazilian baroque presents a distinct vision of a syncretic reality that Sullivan observes to be vibrant in the modernist generation in the work of Victor Brécheret (1894–1955), Vicente do Rego Monteiro (1899–1970), and Tarsila do Amaral (1886–1973) and continued in popular imagery in the painting of Alfredo Volpi (1896–1988) and Adriana Varejão (b. 1964). David K. Underwood sees a continuation of baroque expression in Brazilian modernism and its modern cinema in "Toward a Phenomenology of Brazil's Baroque Modernism," Robert Stam and Ismail Xavier, "The Baroque, the Modern, and Brazilian Cinema," in *Brazil: Body and Soul,* 526–38, 572–83.

32. Robert Stevenson, "A Note on the Music of Colonial Brazil," in *The Cambridge History of Latin America,* ed. Leslie Bethell, 2:799–803 (Cambridge: Cambridge University Press, 1984).

33. Jorge de Sena, *Trinta anos de Camões: 1948–1978 (Estudos camonianos e correlatos)* (Lisbon: Edições 70, 1980), 1:63–92.

34. In a long essay published in 1879 in the *Revista Brasileira* titled "Antônio José e Molière," Machado compares the play *Guerras do Alecrim e Manjerona* to Calderón and cites his self-parody: "Es comedia de Don Pedro / Calderón, d'onde hade haber / Por fuerza, amante Escondido / Y rebozada mujer"

(It is a comedy by Don Pedro / Calderón, where there must always be / without fail a hidden lover / and a woman covered by a shawl).

35. Roberto Calasso, *A folie Baudelaire* (São Paulo: Companhia das Letras, 2012), 14.

36. Mariano José Pereira da Fonseca, the Marquis of Maricá (1773-1848), was a philosopher, politician, and author of aphorisms, collected as *Máximas, pensamentos e reflexões* in 4 vols. published in 1837-41.

37. João Roberto Faria states that to Machado the theater was to the people of Rio de Janeiro what the chorus was to ancient Greek theater. See *Machado de Assis do teatro* (São Paulo: Perspectiva, 2008), 34.

38. See Myriam Louviot, "L'hybridité, un concept pour aborder les littératures post-coloniales," in *Métissages littéraires*, 487-94.

2. The Formative Period

1. Scholars who choose to divide Machado's work into two phases commonly posit an inexplicable division or change in Machado circa 1878-80, when he leaves Rio for the mountains to care for his declining health and returns with the strikingly inventive and enormously influential *Posthumous Memoirs of Brás Cubas*. Such a seemingly magical or mysterious transformation, when offered as an explanation for Machado's altered fictional style, discounts an intensive and continuous literary existence and coming of age during the preceding quarter of a century as well as the twenty years required to produce three subsequent novels. In Luso-Brazilian literature, the concept of formative period was applied to the works of José Saramago by Horácio Costa in his doctoral thesis at Yale, published as *José Saramago: o período formativo* (Lisbon: Caminho, 1997).

2. Helen Caldwell, *Machado de Assis: The Brazilian Master and His Novels* (Berkeley: University of California Press, 1970), 67.

3. Jean-Michel Massa, *A juventude de Machado de Assis, 1839-1870: ensaio de biografia intelectual*, trans. Marco Aurélio de Moura Matos (Rio de Janeiro: Civilização Brasileira, 1971); 2d ed. rev., prologue by Antônio Cândido (São Paulo: Unesp, 2009), 68.

4. His readings and references include the poets Hugo (1802-85), Alphonse de Lamartine (1790-1869), Alfred de Vigny (1797-1863), Alexandre Dumas fils (1824-95), Musset (1810-57), and André Chénier (1762-94); the dramatists Gustave Vattier (1827-1914), Émile de Najac (1828-89), Théodore Barrière (1823-77), Victorien Sardou (1831-1908), and Louis Bouilhet (1822-68); the novelist Octave Feuillet (1821-90); the prose drama "Cléopâtre"(1847) by Delphine de Girardin (1834-1900); the librettist Édouard Plouvier (1821-76); and the songwriter Gustave Nadaud (1820-93).

5. Mauro Rosso, *Contos de Machado de Assis: relicários e raisonnés* (Rio de Janeiro: Edições Loyola, PUC, 2008), 15.

6. The group that met in the law office of Caetano Filgueiras (1830–82) included Francisco Otaviano (1825–89), the director of the *Correio Mercantil;* Augusto Emílio Zaluar (1826–82), a recently arrived Portuguese poet who became editor of the journal *Paraíba;* the poet Casimiro de Abreu (1839–60); José Joaquim Cândido de Macedo Júnior (1844–60); and the Portuguese poet Francisco Gonçalves Braga (1836–60).

7. *Paroles d'un croyant* (1834) by Hugues Felicité Robert de Lamennais (1780–1860), *Histoire des girondins* (1847) by Alphonse de Lamartine (1790–1869), *Le monde marche* (1857) by Eugène Pelletan (1813–84), *Histoire des martyrs de la liberté* (1851) by Alphonse Esquiros (1812–76), and the prose poem *Ahasverus* (1833) by Edgar Quinet (1803–75). In Joaquim Nabuco, *Minha formação* (Rio de Janeiro: H. Garnier, 1900), 12; *My Formative Years*, trans. Christopher Peterson, introduction and notes Leslie Bethell (Oxford: Signal, 2012), 7.

8. Machado's first published play, *Queda que as mulheres têm para os tolos*, 1861, is a translation and adaptation to the stage of a comedy, Victor Hénaux's *De l'amour des femmes pour les sots* (Liege, Paris, 1859), itself a work taken from Louis Champcenetz's (1759–94) *Petit Traité de l'amour des femmes pour les sots* (1788). *A Ópera das janelas* from unknown French authors; *Hoje avental, amanhã luva*, an adaptation of Gustave Vattier's and Émile de Najac's (1828–99) *Chasse au lion* (1852); *Montjoye*, a translation of Octave Feuillet (produced on October 12, 1864); *Suplício de uma mulher* (produced on September 30, 1865), a translation of Delphin de Girardin (1804–55) and Dumas fils; *O anjo da meia-noite* (premier July 6, 1866), a translation of Théodore Barrière and Édouard Plouvier; his translation of *Il barbiere di Siviglia, ossia L'inutile precauzione* (produced September 7, 1866), and a translation of *La Famille Benoiton* by Sardou (produced May 4, 1867).

3. Novels of the 1870s

1. Barreto Filho sees the influence of the theater in self-contained scenes, the entrances and exits of the characters, and short dialogues, yet he also notes the importance of backstage activity and the creation of scenic movement, which contribute to a new genre. *Introdução a Machado de Assis* (Rio de Janeiro: Livraria Agir, 1947), 190.

2. See Sharon Allen, *EccentriCities: Writing in the Margins of Modernism* (Manchester: Manchester University Press, 2013).

3. "À présent, je puis considérer l'existence a peu près comme d'outre-tombe, comme d'au-delà; tout m'est étrange; je puis être en dehors de mon corps et de

mon individu, je suis dépersonnalisé, détaché, évolué. Est-ce là de la folie?" (July 8, 1880), *Fragments d'un journal intime*, 4th ed. (Geneva: H. Georg, 1885), 2:289.

4. The Literary Modernism of Machado de Assis

1. Estela Vieira, *Interiors and Narrative: The Spatial Poetics of Machado de Assis, Eça de Queirós, and Leopoldo Alas* (Lewisburg, Penn.: Bucknell University Press, 2013), 20.

2. "Vinde cá, meu tão certo secretário dos queixumes que sempre ando fazendo, / papel, com que a pena desafogo!" in *The Collected Lyric Poems of Luís de Camões*, trans. Landeg White (Princeton: Princeton University Press, 2008), 297.

3. The French authors Balzac (1799–1850), Baudelaire (1821–67), Maxime du Camp (1822–94), Dumas fils (1824–95), Flaubert (1821–80), Anatole France (1844–1924), Edmond (1822–96) and Jules (1830–79) de Goncourt, Victor Hugo (1802–85), Eugène Labiche (1815–88), Maupassant (1850–93), Prosper Mérimée (1803–70), Stendhal (1783–1842), Eugène Sue (1804–57); the English authors Dickens (1812–70) and Hardy (1840–1928); the Americans Dickinson (1830–86), James (1843–1916), and Melville (1819–91); the Italians Gabriel d'Annunzio (1863–1938), Alessandro Manzoni (1785–1873), Gustavo Strafforello (1820–1903); the Russians Chekhov (1860–1904), Dostoevsky (1821–81), Gogol (1809–52), Ivan Turgenev (1818–83); the Portuguese Almeida Garrett (1799–1854), António Feliciano de Castilho (1800–1875), Eça de Queirós (1845–1900), Antônio Nobre (1867–1900), and Ramalho Ortigão (1836–1915).

4. Many of these comparisons are made or repeated in Earl Fitz, *Machado de Assis* (Boston: Twayne, 1989). See Fitz's comments on Machado in comparative context in *Brazilian Narrative Traditions* (New York: MLA, 2005).

5. Henry James, "Gustave Flaubert," in Gustave Flaubert, *Madame Bovary*, trans. W. Blaydes, with a critical introduction by Henry James (New York: P. F. Collier and Son, 1902), vi.

6. Fernando Pessoa's annotations first appeared as *Livro do desassossego de Bernardo Soares*, introduction and selection Maria Alzira Seixo (Lisbon: Editorial Comunicação, 1986); a current edition is *Livro do desassosssego, composto por Bernardo Soares, ajudante de guarda-livros na cidade de Lisboa*, ed. Richard Zenith (Lisbon: Assírio and Alvim, 1998); among various English translations is Richard Zenith's *The Book of Disquietude* (Manchester: Carcanet, 1991).

7. José Guilherme Merquior, "Género e estilo das 'Memórias Póstumas de Brás Cubas,'" *Colóquio/Letras* 8 (July 1972), 12–20.

5. Machado's Pendulum

1. M. L. Foucault, "Physical demonstration of the rotation of the Earth by means of the pendulum" (Philadelphia: Franklin Institute, 2000).
2. The phrase belongs to Michael Gubser, the author of *Time's Visible Surface: Alois Riegl and the Discourse on History and Temporality in Fin-de-Siècle Vienna* (Detroit: Wayne State University Press, 2006). Riegl, an art historian, had argued that art conveys a culture's consciousness of time.
3. Harry Hurt III, "Is Anybody Necessary? Dr. Ying and the Four Noble Truths," *New York Times*, January 4, 2006.
4. The "Christ the Redeemer" statue, designed by Heitor da Silva Costa and sculpted in France by Paul Landowski, opened on Corcovado on October 12, 1931.
5. Wilson Martins, "Sessão solene de instalação," in *Congresso internacional de escritores e encontros intelectuais* (São Paulo: Anhembi, 1957), 39.
6. Ludwig Wittgenstein, *Notebooks 1914–1916* (New York: Harper, 1961), 83.
7. Kenneth Chang, *New York Times*, June 16, 2012, A21.
8. Maurice Maeterlinck, "The Deeper Life," in *Treasure of the Humble*, trans. Alfred Sutro, introduction A. B. Walkley (New York: Dodd, Mead, 1925), 187.

6. Breaking the Frame

1. Fernão Mendes Pinto (1509–83), a traveler and the author of the *Peregrinação* (1614; *The Travels of Mendez Pinto*, ed. and trans. Rebecca D. Catz (Chicago: University of Chicago Press, 1989), was considered to have been a great liar and exaggerator until Catz's research into his book confirmed his geographical references.
2. A collection of animal fables in Sanskrit dating from 300 to 200 BCE, widely translated in Europe in the 1500s and one of the first printed books.
3. This episode parallels a moral quandary that became a motif in nineteenth-century fiction: in a passage in Balzac's *Le Père Goriot* Rastignac asks his friend Bianchon if he recalls a passage in Rousseau in which the reader could become rich by killing a mandarin in China simply by willing to do so. The challenge comes from François-René Chateaubriand's (1768–1848) *Génie du christianisme* (1802), based on a passage from Diderot's *Entretien d'un père avec ses enfants, ou du danger de se mettre au-dessus des lois* (1773). Eça de Queirós dedicated an entire book to the theme, the fantasy *O Mandarim*, published in Lisbon the same year as Machado's novel with the Dalmatian chapter.

4. By writing only the first and last lines of his sonnet, Brás alludes to a form of recognition similar to recent theories of word recognition, based on the first and last letters of any given word. Brás theorizes that by beginning to write, the rest of the sonnet would just come to him automatically. He anticipates composition based on recognition of the whole, rather than partial lines at the beginning and end: "Aoccdrnig to a rscheearch at Cmabridge Uinervtisy, it deosn't mttaer in waht oredr the ltteers in a wrod are, the olny iprmoetnt tihng is taht the frist and lsat ltteer be at the rghit pclae. The rset can be a toatl mses and you can sitll raed it wouthit porbelm. Tihs is bcuseae the huamn mnid deos not raed ervey lteter by istlef, but the wrod as a wlohe." Richard Shillcock, "Visual Word Recognition" (Edinburgh: University of Edinburgh, School of Informatics).

5. "Deste modo, não havia como escapar: a compreensão literária, só inteiramente efetivada quando preenchida pela variação histórica, haveria de incluir, para melhor incorporação das 'grandes obras,' como fonte de conhecimento cultural as reflexões críticas por elas provocadas no curso do tempo." João Alexandre Barbosa, *A biblioteca imaginária* (São Paulo: Ateliê, 1996), 16.

6. Lionel Trilling's essay "The Sense of the Past," in *The Liberal Imagination: Essays on Literature and Society* (Garden City, N.Y.: Doubleday, 1953), posits that new works change not only the meaning of the old but also their historical relationship, which in itself plays a significant role in the process. See R. V. Young, "Literary Tradition, Lionel Trilling and the Transmission of the Literary Work."

7. António Manuel Hespanha, *Cultura jurídica europeia: síntese de um milénio* (Lisbon: Almedina, 2012), 52.

8. Zulficar Ghose, "Reading Joaquim Maria Machado de Assis," *Context* 12.

9. Carlos Drummond de Andrade (1902–87), "No Meio do Caminho," *Revista de Antropofagia* 1 (1928).

10. José Pereira de Graça Aranha, *Machado de Assis e Joaquim Nabuco, comentários e notas à correspondência entre estes dois escritores*, 2d ed. (Rio de Janeiro: F. Briguiet, 1942), 45–46.

11. See *Dicionário de Camões*, ed. Vítor Aguiar e Silva (Lisbon: Caminho, 2011), 581–86.

12. Xavier de Maistre, *Voyage Around My Room*, trans. Stephen Sartarelli (New York: New Directions, 1994), chapter 4.

13. Laurence Sterne, *The Life and Opinions of Tristram Shandy, Gentleman*, (York: J. Hinxman, 1759), chapter 2.

7. Machado's World Library

1. *Encyclopédie, ou Dictionnaire raisonné des sciences, des arts et des métiers, par une société de gens de lettres, mis en ordre par M. Diderot de l'Académie des Sciences et Belles-Lettres de Prusse, et quant à la partie mathématique, par M. d'Alembert de l'Académie royale des Sciences de Paris, de celle de Prusse et de la Société royale de Londres* (Paris, 1759–72). Charles Joseph Panchoucke continued the work by printing supplementary material and an index (1776–80) and initiated a much-enlarged successor, the *Encyclopédie méthodique par ordre des matières* in more than two hundred volumes (1782–1832).

2. Jean Le Rond d'Alembert, *Discours Préliminaire des Éditeurs* (*The Preliminary Discourse to the Encyclopedia of Diderot*) is considered to be one of the foundational texts of the Enlightenment. Denis Diderot, *Encyclopédie*, Jean le Rond d'Alembert, published 1751–72; 28 volumes, 71,818 articles, 3,129 illustrations.

3. The idea of a world library existed in the ancient and medieval world, in the Royal Library of Alexandria (3d century BC–30 BC), in Diodorus Siculus's (60–30 BC) *Bibliotheca historica*, and in Photios I's (810–93) *Bibliotheca* or *Myriobiblon* of Constantinople (a collection of abstracts and abridgments of 280 volumes of classical authors). Private libraries and public libraries existed in the Roman Empire, while the first classification system came from the Han Dynasty in the second century.

4. James Wood, "Shelf Life: Isn't a Private Library Simply a Universal Legacy Pretending to Be an Individual One?," *New Yorker*, November 7, 2011, 43.

5. Raimundo Magalhães Jr., *Machado de Assis desconhecido* (Rio de Janeiro: Civilização Brasileira, 1955).

6. Maria Kodama and Matteo Pericoli, "The World in the Library," trans. Esther Allen, *New York Times*, January 2, 2011.

7. Haroldo de Campos, "Da razão antropofágica: A Europa sob o signo da devoração," *Colóquio/Letras* 62 (July 1981), 10–25; "The Rule of Anthropophagy: Europe Under the Sign of Devoration," trans. Maria Tai Wolff, *Latin American Literary Review* 14 (1986), 42–60.

8. An Italian company presented *Faust* in 1871 alongside operas by Verdi and Giacomo Meyerbeer; in 1886 the company of Claudio Rossi brought a new production of *Faust*. A young cellist named Arturo Toscanini substituted for the conductor at the last minute. See Cristina Magaldi, *Music in Imperial Rio de Janeiro: European Culture in a Tropical Milieu* (Lanham, Md.: Scarecrow Press, 2004), 43–44.

9. See Augusto Meyer, "Introdução," *Exposição Machado de Assis; centenário do nascimento de Machado de Assis, 1839–1939* (Rio de Janeiro: Serviço gráfico do Ministério da Educação e Saúde, 1939), 14.

8. Time's Invisible Fabric

1. "A Semana," November 11, 1897, in *Obra completa* (Rio de Janeiro: Nova Aguilar, 2004), 3:772.
2. Published in "A Semana," *Gazeta de Notícias*, 1894, and included in *Páginas Recolhidas*, 1899. See "Midnight Mass," in *The Psychiatrist and Other Stories*, trans. William L. Grossman (Berkeley: University of California Press, 1963), 94–100.
3. "Dona Paula," *Várias histórias*. See "Dona Paula," *The Devil's Church*, trans. Jack Schmitt and Lori Ishimatsu (Austin: University of Texas Press, 1977), 59–67.
4. Emília Viotti da Costa, "Town and Country," in *The Brazilian Empire: Myths and Histories* (Chapel Hill: University of North Carolina Press, 2000), 185.
5. "Singular Ocorrência," *Histórias sem data*. See "A Strange Thing," *The Devil's Church*, 36–43.
6. *História verdadeira da Princeza Magalona, filjia d'El Rei de Napoles, e do nobre, e valoroso cavalheiro Pierres, Pedro de Provença, E dos muitos trabalhos, e adversidades, que passaram, sendo sempre constantes na fé, e virtudes, e como depois reinaram, e acabaram a sua vida virtuosamente no serviço de Deus* (Lisbon: Typ. de Antonio Joaquim da Costa, Rua do Quelhas no. 59, 1851).
7. The libretto is based on *Têtes rondes et cavaliers* by Jacques-François Ancelot and Joseph Xavier Saintine, which they took from Walter Scott's *Old Mortality*, the first part of *Tales of My Landlord* (Edinburgh: W. Blackwood, 1817). The two stories are set in seventeenth-century England and Scotland, respectively.

9. Theater and Opera

1. Carlos Wehrs, *Machado de Assis e a magia da música* (Rio de Janeiro: C. Whers, 1977), cites the role of music in 91 short stories and locates multiple references in all of the novels. He finds that Machado cites, above all, the piano (102 times), along with 16 other instruments; that he refers 25 times to the opera as well as to 29 other musical forms from "adagio" to "volata"; that he refers 21 times to song; and that throughout his fiction he cites 19 operas by name, 25 composers, and 16 interpreters, including the famous female artists he heard in his youth.
2. The poem was subtitled "Imitado de Su-Tchon," indicating a poetic version of French prose translations by Judith Gautier (1845–1917) of the Chinese poet Su-Tchon (tenth to eleventh century). Illustrating Machado's technique of

appropriation, his poem was derived from poems from the Chinese poet in a French translation by Gautier that Machado encountered in her *Livre de jade* (Paris: Alphonse Lamerre, 1867). See "As canções de Machado de Assis," *Revista Brasileira* 10 (May 2008). See also Brigitte Kodama-Richard, *Le Japon et la Chine dans les oeuvres de Judith Gautier* (Tokyo: Edition Synapse, 2007). See additionally six songs with musical versions of Machado's work in *Echos do passado, 1° álbum de romances, para canto com acompanhamento de piano por Arthur Napoleão,* published between 1867 and 1869, cited in Galante de Sousa's bibliography and in Wehrs, *Machado de Assis e a magia da música,* 91.

3. The prominent figures present include Counselor Silveira da Mota, Baron of Vila Franca (1815–85); Manuel Marques de Sousa, Count of Porto Alegre (1804–75); Supreme Court Justice Agostinho Marques Perdigão Malheiro (1788–1860); José Maurício Wanderley, Baron of Cotegipe (1815–89); Francisco Otaviano (1825–89); Sizenando Nabuco (1841–92); José Paranhos, Baron of Rio Branco (1845–1912); the jurist Gaspar da Silveira Martins (1835–1901). From Ernesto Matos, *Cousas do meu tempo* (Bordeaux, 1916), 286.

4. Verdi's operas were performed in Rio de Janeiro not long after their premieres in Europe: *Otello* was premiered on February 5, 1887, in Milan and in 1894 in Brazil, and *Falstaff* was produced at La Scala on February 9 and in Brazil on July 29, 1893.

5. Her success can be judged by concerts given in her honor arranged three years later: "On 19 March 1862 the company sponsored a benefit that, despite its link to the past, promised to attract considerable attention: it was a tribute to the well-known and loved singer, Augusta Candiani, with the participation of artists from both the national opera and drama companies. The programme included excerpts from *Columella* and a duet from Bellini's *Norma,* one of Candiani's signature roles sung together with Millie L, in Italian and not in Portuguese." André Heller-Lopes, "Brazil's Ópera Nacional: Music, Society and the Birth of Brazilian Opera in Nineteenth-Century Rio de Janeiro" (Diss., King's College, University of London, 2010), 283, 291.

6. Giuseppe Verdi's "commedia lirica" was an adaptation by Arrigo Boito of two Shakespeare plays, *The Merry Wives of Windsor* and *Henry IV,* first performed on February 9, 1893, in Milan and on July 29, 1893, in Rio de Janeiro. It was Verdi's third opera based on Shakespeare (*Macbeth,* 1847, and *Othello,* 1887, preceded) and only his second comedy in twenty-eight operas. Machado attended theatrical performances of Shakespeare in 1871, based his first novel on a quote from *Measure from Measure* (1.5), and adapted *Othello* in the novel *Dom Casmurro* and other works.

7. Marie Robinson Wright, *The Brazilian National Exposition of 1908* (Philadelphia: George Barrie and Sons, 1908), 164.

8. Wehrs, in *Machado de Assis e a magia da música*, recalls the theaters of Rio de Janeiro in the time of Machado: the Imperial Theatro São Pedro de Alcântara (1826), destroyed by fire in 1851 and reopened in 1857; the Theatro Provisório, built in six weeks to replace the São Pedro, later named Theatro Lyrico Fluminense (1854); the Theatro da Praia de D. Manuel (1834) renamed Theatro São Januário (1838), later called the Atheneu Dramático (1862); the Theatro Polytheama Fluminense (1880); the Imperial Theatro D. Pedro II (1871), renamed the Theatro Lyrico after the proclamation of the republic (1890); for dramatic theater, the São Luís (1871); the Theatro Gymnásio Dramático (1855, previously Theatro São Francisco from 1846); the Alcazar Lyrique, also called Théâtre Lyrique Français (1866-80); the Theatro Apollo (1890); and theaters for dramatic art and music, including the Lucinda (1880); the Theatro des Varietées (1877), later called Brasilian Garden (*sic*) and Recreio Dramático (1877); the Theatro Cassino Franco Brasileiro (1872), renamed the Theatro Sant'Anna (currently Teatro Carlos Gomes); and the Theatro Éden-Lavradio (1895).

9. The opera academies were the Imperial Academia de Música & Ópera Nacional (1857-60), Ópera Lyrica Nacional (1860-62), and Ópera Nacional & Italiana (1862-63). Heller-Lopes explains: "The Brazilian Ópera Nacional is associated with the forging of the country's national identity, and as such is comparable to the many 'national opera schools/movements' that appeared in Europe during the nineteenth century; it enjoyed the collaboration of prominent writers, politicians and intellectuals living in Rio de Janeiro during that period, and produced Latin America's most important opera composer, Carlos Gomes." "Brazil's Ópera Nacional," 8.

10. Carl Schlichthorst, *Rio de Janeiro wie es ist: Beiträge zur tages-und sittengeschichte der hauptstadt von Brasilien mit vorzüglicher rücksicht auf die lage des dortigen deutschen militairs* (Hannover: Hahn, 1929); *O Rio de Janeiro como é, 1824-1826 (huma vez e nunca mais); Contribuições dum diário para a historia atual, os costumes e especialmente a situação da tropa estrangeira na capital do Brasil*, trans. Emmy Dodt and Gustavo Barroso (Rio de Janeiro: Editora Getúlio Costa, 1943).

11. Among the European actors performing in Brazil were Francisco Alves da Silva Taborda (1871), Coquelin Ainé (1888), Ermette Novelli (1890), José Ricardo (1895); and the singers Henrique Tamberlick (1856), Julião Gayarre (1876), Francisco Tamagno (1878), Juliana Dejean (1856), Ana Lagrange (1858), as well as others listed in the text.

12. *O caminho da porta* was produced on September 12, 1862; *Gabriela* on September 20, 1862; *O protocolo* on December 4, 1862; *Quase ministro* on November 22, 1863; and *Os deuses da casaca* on December 28, 1865.

13. She appeared in Jean Racine's (1639-99) *Phèdre* (1677), Friedrich Schiller's (1759-1805) *Maria Stuart* (1800), Carlo Goldoni's (1707-93) *La locandiera*, and Paulo Giacometti's (1816-82) *Isabel, reina de Inglaterra* (1863). See *Adelaide Ristori: folhetins* (Rio de Janeiro: Academia Brasileira de Letras, 1955), which is a collection of nine reviews Machado wrote for the *Diário do Rio de Janeiro* under the name Platão.

14. Charles R. Darwin, *The Formation of Vegetable Mould, Through the Action of Worms* (London: John Murray, 1881).

10. Delirium, Hallucination, and Dream

1. *Golden Bough* (London: Macmillan, 1890); *La mentalité primitive* (Paris: F. Alcan, 1925).

2. See Étienne Esquirol, *Maladies mentales considérées sous les rapports médical, hygiénique et médico-légal* (Paris: J. B. Ballière, 1838).

3. Remorse Too Late

> My dark and lovely thing, when you at length lie dead,
> And sleep beneath a slab of marble black as pitch;
> And have, for perfumed alcove and seductive bed,
> Only a rainy cavern and a hollow ditch;
> When the oppressive stone upon your frightened breast
> Lets settle all its weight, and on your supple thighs;
> Restrains your heart from beating, flattens it to rest;
> Bends down and binds your feet, so roving, so unwise;
> The tomb, that knows me well and reads my dream aright,
> (What poet but confides his secret to the tomb?)
> Will say to you some day during that endless night,
> "They fare but ill, vain courtesan, in this cold room,
> Who bring here no warm memories of true love to keep!"
> —And like remorse the worm will gnaw you in your sleep.
> —Edna St. Vincent Millay, *Flowers of Evil* (New York: Harper and Brothers, 1936).

4. In a review of Caldwell, the scholar Raymond Sayers deepens the question of the relationship between Bento and D. Glória: "It is obvious that in pleading his own case Bento was trying to hide his conscious motives for his rejection of

his wife Capitu and his son Ezequiel. However, he was unaware of his subconscious motives. In this part of her analysis Miss Caldwell might have done some deeper probing into the theme of the silver cord than she actually does. It is probable that Bento's aggression against Capitu represents a flare-up of resentment against Dona Glória, his mother, a resentment which he had always repressed in his dealings with the older woman. The book is almost as much a study of mother-son relations as it is a story of jealous love. Throughout his childhood and youth Bento accepted obediently the domination of his over-protective mother, and on marrying he took a wife who was able to exercise over him the same dominance through her superior intelligence and spirit." Raymond Sayers, "Helen Caldwell: 'The Brazilian Othello of Machado de Assis: A Study of *Dom Casmurro*,'" *Romantic Review* 54:1 (February 1963), 73.

5. Sayers suggests an exploration of the theme of Bento's weakness as a source for his demoniacal jealousy: "It would have been interesting, too, if Miss Caldwell, after demonstrating that Bento's jealousy was unfounded, had analyzed the cause of the jealousy; though complicated in nature, it appears to me to have grown out of Bento's doubts about his own merits as a man and a husband. As one reads between the lines of the narrator's brief, one learns that Bento understood how much more intelligent and aggressive Capitu was than he, and it is easy enough to draw the conclusion that he expected her to have moments of revulsion from him and preference for his supposed rival, Escobar, with his strong biceps, his ability as a swimmer, and his beautiful eyes. Furthermore, he had no test or competition in winning Capitu's hand. The homes of the two families had been adjacent when they were youngsters, and access to Capitu was obtained by slipping through a fence gate without a latch. The reader senses that Bento felt his success in love to be due to their continuity rather than to his personal desirability." Sayers, "Helen Caldwell," 74-75.

6. The phrase is from the New Testament centurion, the source of a prayer in the Tridentine Mass to be pronounced before receiving the host: "Domine, non sum dignus ut intres sub tectum meum, sed tantum dic verbo et sanabitur anima mea" (Lord, I am not worthy that you should come under my roof. Speak but the word and my soul shall be healed). Joyce rewrites the phrase "sub tectum meum" in Bloom's entrance to the Holles Maternity Hospital in *Ulysses* as "infare under my thatch," with the inference of sexual relations.

7. D. Pedro II (1825–91), reigned 1840–89.

8. The fatality of the number three, corresponding to the acts of tragic Greek theater, resonates throughout Machado's fiction: Bento repeats "I am a man" three times; Sofia heard her roses say three times "bem feito"; the hammer strikes three times on Freitas's coffin; D. Tonica's fiancé dies three days before the

wedding; Bento's garden is three steps from Capitu's; the leprous Manduca repeats three times "The Russians will not take Constantinople"; Pedro and Paulo give Flora three months to choose between them; "No, no, no," says the narrator to himself about the content of a chapter; Flora's hallucination has three parts, "Fusão, difusão, confusão"; Ayres hopes to solve Flora's indecision between Pedro and Paulo by telling her to choose "one of the three," etc. I am grateful to Javier Sangrador Martínez for these observations.

11. *Humanitas* and Satire

1. A lei darwínica é certa
    Inda em acontecimentos . . .
    Não fiquem de boca aberta,
    Vão vê-lo em poucos momentos.

    Há nelas a mesma luta
    Pela vida, e de tal arte
    A crua lei se executa,
    Que é a mesma em toda a parte.

    Há seleção, persistência
    Do mais capaz ou mais forte,
    Que continua a existência
    E os outros baixam à morte. . . .

    Mas por um só que resiste,
    Quantos passaram calados
    Na penumbra vaga e triste
    Dos seres mal conformados! . . .

    Porque nos próprios eventos
    A lei darwínica é certa. Provei-o em poucos momentos,
    Não fiquem de boca aberta.
    "Gazeta de Holanda," *Gazeta de Notícias,* December 6, 1886, in
        Mauro Rosso, *Machado de Assis: Crônicas, A + B, Gazeta de
        Holanda* (Rio de Janeiro: Editora PUC, Edições Loyola, 2011),
        81–85.

2. Borba parodies Compte's stages of positivism, "theological, metaphysical, and positive."
3. Cannibalism had been associated with Brazil since the mid-sixteenth century in books by Hans Staden (1525–76) and Jean de Léry (1536–1613), based on their

travels and residence in Brazil and, in the case of Staden, his capture by the Tupinambá. The theme is the subject of Michel de Montaigne's (1533-92) celebrated essay "Des cannibales," in Montaigne, *Oeuvres complètes*, ed. Albert Thibaudet and Maurice Rat (Paris: Gallimard, 1962).

4. A connection between cannibalism and capitalism is posited in the first chapter of *Quincas Borba*, when, recently arrived at his new mansion in Rio, Rubião meditates, "What was he a year ago? A teacher. What is he now? A capitalist," unaware that he is about to become a victim of Cristiano Palha, who has made a fortune from bank failures and will soon appropriate Rubião's fortune and abandon him to madness and death.

5. Antônio Vieira, SJ, "Sermão de Santo Antônio aos Peixes" (Maranhão, 1654), *Sermões* (Lisbon: Centro de Estudos de Filosofia, Imprensa Nacional-Casa da Moeda, 2008); *The Sermon of Saint Anthony to the Fish and Other Texts*, trans. Gregory Rabassa (North Dartmouth, Mass.: Tagus Press, 2009).

6. See Thomas Mann's essay "Schopenhauer," in *Essays of Three Decades* (New York: Knopf, 1947), 375: "For paradoxical it certainly is, to say that knowledge can only refer to the invisible, the thought-about, perceived in the mind; it is paradoxical to explain the visible world as a phenomenon, which, in itself worthless, has a reality and meaning only through that of which it is an expression. The reality of the actual—only a loan from the mind!"

12. Brás Cubas, *Basso Buffo*

1. Published posthumously in forty-two volumes (Brussels: Tarride, 1848-50), although originally intended for publication fifty years after the author's death.

2. *Confessiones*, thirteen books written in 397-98, published in Strasbourg by Jean Mantelin in 1465-70.

3. *Les confessions de J.-J. Rousseau*, 12 vols. (Paris: Cazin, 1782, 1789).

13. Bento Santiago's Grand Dissimulation

1. Machado attended *Faust* (1859) by Charles Gounod (1818-93), *Macbeth* (1847) by Giuseppe Verdi (1813-1901), and *Otello* (1816) by Gioachino Rossini (1792-1868) in theaters of Rio de Janeiro.

2. Helen Caldwell describes Bento's motivation in his memoirs: "With a criminal's urge to talk, he discloses, in carefully guarded metaphor, that his jealousy was rooted in aboriginal evil, that it antedated its object, groped until it found an object, then pursued and clung to it with obdurate blindness," *Machado de Assis: The Brazilian Master and His Novels* (Berkeley: University of California Press, 1970), 145.

3. The reader assumes the role of astute investigator, or member of a jury, from whom the narrator must conceal information to avoid self-incrimination.

4. Sancha may also be a substitute for Bento's mother, D. Glória, earlier courted by Escobar, in a disguised case of the Oedipal complex.

5. Chapters 75, 76. Note that not eating and sleeping poorly is the inverse of what he claims his situation to be while alone in old age.

14. The Love-Death Theme of Counselor Ayres

1. Ayres's diary is open to other genres such as the memoir, short story, allegory, and dramatic monologue and may be considered an example of mixed-genre texts, as defined by Norman Fairclough (in *Media Discourse* [New York: E. Arnold, 1995], 89), or hybrid genres, described by John Hartley (in *Key Concepts in Communication and Cultural Studies*, ed. Tim O'Sullivan [et al.] [London: Routledge, 1994,] 129). Jacques Derrida, in "The Law of Genre" (trans. Avital Ronell, *Glyph* 7 [1980], 202–32), considers the distance between genre and one's perception of it to be open, neither inclusive nor exclusive, such that form is not allowed to identify with itself alone, thus denied its ability to engender exclusive meaning; rather, the form becomes invisible or transparent.

2. Fernando Pessoas's heteronym Ricardo Reis repeats the idea in the ode "Só esta liberdade nos concedem / Os deuses: submetermo-nos / Ao seu domínio por vontade nossa" (Only this liberty is conceded to us / by the gods: to submit ourselves / willingly to their control).

3. In their quest to win Flora, in Machado's literary context, they bring to mind Camões's classic sonnet on a biblical theme, "Sete anos de pastor."

4. Machado imaginatively anticipates José Saramago's novel *As intermitências da morte* (Lisbon: Caminho, 2005), in which no one is allowed to die for one year in a certain country.

5. In a chronicle, Machado comments on visits to the cemetery that color Ayres's view of Fidélia: "Visiting the dead is a good Catholic custom; but there is no wheat without chaff; and the opinion of Sr. Artur de Azevedo is that in this situation everything is chaff without wheat," November 1, 1877.

6. The tension between myth and political history in the novel constitutes a parallel with conflict in German baroque dramas studied by Walter Benjamin in *Ursprung des deutschen Trauerspiels* (Berlin: E. Rowohlt, 1928).

7. Caldwell finds Shelley's prose fragment "On Love" to epitomize the theme of Machado's novels in general: "That love is the true manifestation of life, and that lack-love or self-love must be equated with death." *Machado de Assis: The Brazilian Master and His Novels* (Berkeley: University of California Press, 1970), 189.

8. In "The Grandfather Clock" ("A Pêndula"), chapter 54 of the *Posthumous Memoirs of Brás Cubas*, Eros and Thanatos appear in the guise of "an old devil

sitting between two sacks, that of life and that of death, taking out the coins of life and giving them to death."

15. Machado and the Spectacle of the World

1. The other contemplation was "Central Park in the Dark" (1906). "The Un-answered Question" was not performed until 1948.
2. *Crônicas, crítica, poesia, teatro*, 2d ed., introduction and notes Massaud Moisés (São Paulo: Cultrix, 1964), 53.
3. The theatrical metaphor ties together two ends of Machado's literature and thought over three decades by referencing his play *Os Deuses de casaca* (1865).
4. These qualities in Machado anticipate the esthetic program of Fernando Pessoa, which he largely conceives between 1907 and 1914.
5. In "A Genetic Atlas of Human Admixture History," *Science* 343:6172 (February 14, 2014), researchers in the Globetrotter Project identified only ninety-five distinct populations in human genetic history from their analysis of world DNA samples.
6. Translation by permission of Landeg White.
7. Joaquim Nabuco, *Obras completas de Joaquim Nabuco*, vol. 2, *Cartas a amigos*, collected and annotated by Carolina Nabuco (São Paulo: Instituto Progresso Editorial, 1949), 179–80.
8. *Correspondência de Machado de Assis com Joaquim Nabuco, José Veríssimo, Lúcio de Mendonça, Mário de Alencar e outros, seguida das respostas dos destinatários* (Rio de Janeiro: Oficina Industrial Gráfica, 1932), 50.
9. *Machado de Assis e Joaquim Nabuco, comentários e notas à correspondência entre estes dois escritores*, introduction by Graça Aranha, 2d ed. (Rio de Janeiro: F. Briguiet, 1942), 67.
10. *Cartas a amigos*, 2:308.

A Note on Sources

The literary production of Machado de Assis centers on twenty-five books published in Portuguese during his lifetime, including five theatrical pieces, four poetry collections, seven short story collections, and nine novels. Additionally, he wrote important essays on questions of nationality and aesthetics as well as literary translations. Written over four decades, the chronicles appeared in a series of popular journals, where he commented on the literature, life, and politics of the Empire. In light of Machado's habit of publishing in numerous popular journals and his ample use of pseudonyms, collections of unidentified or lost works—correspondence, short stories, criticism, poetry, and theater—began to appear in the half century following his death and contain some writings not included in the complete works published by W. M. Jackson in thirty-one volumes from 1939 to 1957. Currently a three-volume set of *Obra completa* is available from Editora Nova Fronteira. The complete correspondence is being published in multiple volumes by the Academia Brasileira de Letras.

The nine novels of Machado de Assis have been translated into English, some more than once, although not all are in print. Citations from the four early novels are from *Resurrection*, trans. Karen Sherwood Sotelino (Pittsburgh: Latin American Review Press, 2013); *The Hand and the Glove*, trans. Albert I Bagby (Lexington: University of Kentucky Press, 1970); *Helena*, trans. and introduction by Helen Caldwell (Berkeley: University of California Press, 1984); and *Iaiá Garcia*, trans. Albert I. Bagby (Lexington: University of Kentucky Press, 1977). Passages from the five late novels are from *Posthumous Memoirs of Brás Cubas*, trans. Gregory Rabassa (New York: Oxford University Press, 1997); *Quincas Borba*, trans. Gregory Rabassa (New York: Oxford University Press, 1998); *Dom Casmurro*, trans. Helen Caldwell (New York: Farrar, Straus and Giroux, 1953, 1991); *Esau and Jacob*, trans. Elizabeth Lowe (New York: Oxford University Press, 2000); and *Counselor Ayres' Memorial*, trans. and introduction by Helen Caldwell (Berkeley: University of California Press, 1972).

The Posthumous Memoirs is also available under the title *Epitaph of a Small Winner*, trans. William Grossman, introduction by Susan Sontag (New York: Farrar, Straus and Giroux, 2008); *Quincas Borba* was translated by Clotilde Wilson as *Philosopher or Dog?* (New York: Farrar, Straus and Giroux, 1954), while Helen Caldwell's translation of *Esau and Jacob* was published by the University of California Press in 1965.

About a third of Machado's short stories have been translated to English, many of those more than once; they have appeared in both journals and anthologies, principally *The Psychiatrist and Other Stories* (1963), *The Devil's Church and Other Stories* (1977), *The Oxford Book of the Brazilian Short Story* (2006), *A Chapter of Hats: Selected Stories* (2008), *A Machado de Assis Anthology* (2011), *The Alienist and Other Stories of Nineteenth-Century Brazil* (2013), *Stories: Joaquim Maria Machado de Assis* (2014), and *Ex-Cathedra: Stories by Machado de Assis* (2014). A complete table of stories with their publication history is available in Mauro Rosso, *Contos de Machado de Assis: relicários e raisonnés* (Rio de Janeiro: Edições Loyola; Editora PUC, 2008).

For readers seeking further information on his works, José Galante de Souza compiled a massive bibliography, *Bibliografia de Machado de Assis* (Rio de Janeiro: Ministério da Educação e Cultura, 1955) as well as an exhaustive list of sources of study (1958), although neither has been updated in view of the subsequent surge in publication on Machado. Raimundo Magalhães Jr. published a four-volume biography, *Vida e obra de Machado de Assis* (Rio de Janeiro: Civilização Brasileira, 1981), and Francisco Pati compiled a dictionary of his characters in *Dicionário de Machado de Assis: história e biografia das personagens* (São Paul: Rêde Latina Editôra, 1958). Sources in English are scant; readers may benefit from Earl Fitz's panoramic introduction *Machado de Assis* (1989) and Helen Caldwell's classic interpretations, *Brazilian Othello of Machado de Assis: A Study of* Dom Casmurro (1960) and *Machado de Assis: The Brazilian Master and His Novels* (1970).

The main sources for my interpretation of Machado de Assis and his fiction are Benedito Nunes's essay "Machado de Assis e a Filosofia," *Travessia* 19 (1989), José Barreto Filho's *Introdução de Machado de Assis* (Rio de Janeiro: Agir 1947), and Agrippino Grieco's *Machado de Assis* (1960). For Machado's unusual career as a writer I found particularly useful Haroldo de Campos's late and little-known essay, available only in English, "The Ex-centric's Viewpoint: Tradition, Transcreation, Transculturation," in *Haroldo de Campos: A Dialogue with the Brazilian Concrete Poet* (Oxford: Centre of Brazilian Studies, 2005). His essay substantiates and advances in modern critical language observations made by Eloy Pontes in *A vida contradictoria de Machado de Assis* (Rio de Janeiro: José Olympio, 1939). Augusto Meyer's introduction to the centenary exposition, *Exposição Machado de Assis; centenário do nascimento de Machado de Assis, 1839–1939* (Rio de Janeiro: Serviço Gráfico do Ministério da Educação e Saúde, 1939), is particularly perceptive and suggestive. Among the many dozens of fundamental books, Caldwell's titles continue to be reliable and convincing interpretations.

My theoretical position balancing baroque and neoclassical stylistic and aesthetic features is based on Charles Rosen, *Classical Style: Haydn, Mozart, Beethoven*

(New York: Viking, 1971), on the one hand, and studies of the baroque in Camões by Jorge de Sena, *Trinta anos de Camões: 1948–1978 (Estudos camonianos e correlatos)*, vol. 1 (Lisbon: Edições 70, 1980) and of baroque aesthetics in Vítor Aguiar e Silva, *Dicionário de Camões* (Lisbon: Caminho, 2011), on the other. The concepts of conceptual blending and hybridity applied to Machado and his works are based on Sandra Handl and Hans-Jörg Schmid, eds., *Windows to the Mind: Metaphor, Metonymy and Conceptual Blending* (Berlin: Walter de Gruyter, 2011), and Walter Krysinski's essay, "Sur quelques généalogies et formes de l'hybridité dans la littérature du XXe siècle," in *Le texte hybride,* ed. Dominique Budor and Walter Geerts (Paris: Presses Sorbonne Nouvelle, 2004).

For the role of theater in Machado's early development the main sources are Jean-Michel Massa, *A juventude de Machado de Assis* (São Paulo: Unesp, 2009), João Roberto Faria, *Machado de Assis do teatro* (São Paulo: Perspectiva, 2008), among his other books on nineteenth-century theater in Brazil, and J. Galante de Sousa, *O teatro no Brasil*, vol. 1, *Evolução do teatro no Brasil* (Rio de Janeiro: MEC/INL, 1960). Music and opera in nineteenth-century Rio de Janeiro are the subject of André Heller-Lopes's doctoral thesis, "Brazil's *Ópera Nacional* (1857–1863): Music, Society and the Birth of Brazilian Opera in Nineteenth-Century Rio de Janeiro," at King's College, University of London, 2010; Renato Mainente's dissertation, "Música e civilização: a atividade musical no Rio de Janeiro Oitocentista (1808–1863)" (Unesp, 2011); Camille Bellaigue, *Verdi, biographie critique* (Paris: H. Laurens, 1927); Carlos Wehrs, *Machado de Assis e a magia da música* (Rio de Janeiro: C. Whers, 1997); and Cristina Magaldi, *Music in Imperial Rio de Janeiro: European Culture in a Tropical Milieu* (Lanham, Md.: Scarecrow Press, 2004).

Credits

Index